T0057990

Also by Alan Trachtenberg

Reading American Photographs:
Images as History, Mathew Brady to Walker Evans

The Incorporation of America:
Culture and Society in the Gilded Age

Brooklyn Bridge:
Fact and Symbol

SHADES OF HIAWATHA

SHADES OF HIAWATHA

Staging Indians, Making Americans

1880–1930

———•———

ALAN TRACHTENBERG

HILL AND WANG

A division of Farrar, Straus and Giroux

New York

Hill and Wang
A division of Farrar, Straus and Giroux
18 West 18th Street, New York 10011

Printed in the United States of America
Published in 2004 by Hill and Wang
First paperback edition, 2005

Some material in this book appeared in a different form in
The Yale Review, *Raritan*, and *Judaism*.

The Library of Congress has cataloged the hardcover edition as follows:
Trachtenberg, Alan.
    Shades of Hiawatha : staging Indians, making Americans: 1880–1930 /
Alan Trachtenberg.—1st ed.
        p.   cm.
    Includes bibliographical references and index.
    ISBN-13: 978-0-374-29975-0
    ISBN-10: 0-374-29975-7 (hc : alk. paper)
    1. Indians of North America—Public opinion.   2. Indians in popular culture—
North America.   3. Indians of North America—Ethnic identity.   4. Hiawatha,
15th cent.   5. Longfellow, Henry Wadsworth, 1807–1882. Song of Hiawatha.
6. Indians in literature.   7. Immigrants in literature.   8. United States—
Emigration and immigration.   9. United States—Race relations.   10. United
States—Politics and government.   I. Title.

E98.P99T73 2004
323.173—dc22   2004042438

Paperback ISBN-13: 978-0-8090-1639-6
Paperback ISBN-10: 0-8090-1639-7

Designed by Jonathan D. Lippincott

www.fsgbooks.com

Frontispiece: Lorado Taft, "Black Hawk," 1911. Overlooking the Rock River, Oregon, Illinois. (Photography Collection, Miriam and Ira D. Wallach Division of Art, Prints and Photographs, New York Public Library, Astor, Lenox and Tilden Foundations)

For
Naomi, Ben, Anna, Isaac

Pleasant it looked,
This newly created world.
Along the entire length and breadth
Of the earth, our grandmother,
Extended the green reflection
Of her covering
And the escaping odors
Were pleasant to inhale.
　　　—"This Newly Created World" (Winnebago)

And make no mistake, you are never in a place that is nameless, in a region without a name— you always find yourself in some word invented by others—others never seen, long forgotten—before it was recorded in writing. We are always in words.

And not only in words, also in history—that of the present and that of the past.
　　　—Cees Nooteboom, *The Road to Santiago*

Contents

Preface

My subject in this book is the entwining of two figures that preoccupied public attention at the turn of the twentieth century: the Indian and the immigrant. I look at these entangled figures in the light and the shade cast by Henry Wadsworth Longfellow's *The Song of Hiawatha* (1855), America's best-known long narrative poem, which reached new heights of popularity in these years and was often staged with native performers. I say "figures" because I deal chiefly with ideas and images rather than with social or political history, though historical persons do play more or less nonfigurative roles in the drama. The ideas concern the nation itself in an era of consolidation and overseas expansion (or conquest). The cast of characters includes persons native and nonnative, writers, artists, chiefs, politicians, historians, administrators, philosophers, businessmen, government functionaries, characters associated with a particular set of ideas then being incorporated into the larger idea of the nation, ideas of East and West in a new relation to each other.

The terms "East" and "West" are not conspicuous here, yet they must be kept in mind as significant markers of meaning. Just as blacks have meant South, Indians have meant West (also Hispanics and Asians), and European immigrants belonged to the East, even as many traveled on westward. The Civil War seemed to settle the conflict between North and South, a conflict that most white Americans by 1917 probably agreed marked *The Birth of a Nation,* the title of David Wark Griffith's blockbuster movie (the first in Hollywood's young history) of 1915. Griffith's film made it plain that union had been achieved by Northern abandonment of the cause of freedom for African Americans, that the newly reborn nation was distinctly a white nation, ready to enforce its whiteness by violence. If North had become southernized, the postfrontier West was being easternized; patterns of settlement, ideas of culture and cultivation, a hierarchy of social classes based on property in land, money, and culture all made the older image of the pioneering frontiersman, proud of his free-thinking and independence and rough-and-tumble existence, seem nostalgic.

The postfrontier West was in many ways an Eastern creation, as much in the myths of romance as in the new social realities. Eastern writers and artists like Theodore Roosevelt, Frederic Remington, and Owen Wister—all of them "establishment" figures, as one historian has put it—re-created Western experience in story and image and history in light of their own needs for a heroic national past with Anglo-Saxon dominance.[1] Their vision caught on at once. The western—popularized in the film genre that arose in the early twentieth-century (Owen Wister's novel *The Virginian* and its variants was the template)—according to the historian Elliott West "took its modern shape from the yearnings and stresses of late-nineteenth-century America east of the Missouri, those regions that would provide most of the demand and financial sustenance for the commercialized myth." Born in the East, the genre marched westward "and proceeded to change things."[2]

I am concerned in this book with the many ways that Eastern preemption of the West became a powerful nationalizing force. Longfellow's *Song of Hiawatha*, a product of midcentury Boston, was an early shot in the campaign (which included the Civil War) to imagine a continental nation with origins in the West and among the Indians. High among the binding elements in this developing campaign—the military metaphor is apt—were ideas of race and white supremacy, of the rightness of divisions between rich and poor among the whites themselves, of Anglo-Saxon superiority over recent immigrants, and of America's "manifest destiny." Thus was the national narrative rewritten in terms still in effect today though increasingly under challenge: Wealthy whites rule, poorer whites obey, colored people crawl, and the quest for private wealth predominates. This story about the American nation and nationality began to emerge after the Civil War and is still a potent (though not unopposed) version of our country's history.[3]

One of my aims is to shed light on the revisions that were made during those years in popular understandings of "America." This is a subject infrequently discussed by historians: the way ideas and images of Indians and of immigrants interacted, how they affected the perceived meanings of the other, and how they figured together in the making of the new America and of new Americans.[4] In an essay in 1917 on "The Principle of Nationality," the philosopher John Dewey made a distinction I have found extremely helpful in laying out the terms and borders of my own study of Indians, immigrants, and national identity. "Nationality" is curiously ambiguous, he wrote, in that it seems applicable to two conditions at once. One meaning refers to the national state, the *nationalism* that became the defining political fact of the nineteenth century, especially in Europe—a fact all the more apparent in the conflict of nations known as the Great War (World War I) during which Dewey wrote this essay. The other meaning applies to consciousness rather than political membership: "community of language, community of literature, and a certain unity and community of tradition, of historical retrospect, of common memories," which create "a body of people somehow distinctly united by very strong ties and bonds."[5]

A national people in this second regard—Jews, for example—can maintain itself "without fixed geographical association." Dewey called this "cultural nationality," and he claimed that "in the United States we have a distinct situation, for we are perhaps the only national state wherein the principle of nationality has no political standing." The United States has no distinct cultural nationality, then, though its political nationality makes room for countless nationalities that are distinct in language, beliefs, and memory: in short, in culture.

Dewey makes no mention of Americans of native or African descent; his examples were drawn exclusively from Europe. This blind spot was typical of even the most progressive thinkers of the era. Dewey missed an opportunity to take his argument another crucial step, to distinguish between two terms that have bedeviled Indian-white relations: "nation" and "tribe." The idea of racial as distinct from cultural or ethnic (or tribal) difference had long clouded our thinking about the multicultural origins of modern populations. "Tribe"—a Western word applied since the sixteenth century to "primitive" peoples (also criminals) and adopted by natives as an English word for their own primary social and political form—became an invisible term, often used but very little understood or pondered. Just as "Negro" or "black" seemed an adequate label under which to put all persons with overt or covert (a "drop" of "Negro" blood, for example) signs of black identity regardless of African tribal ancestry, so Native Americans have been called "Indian," as if the term designated a separate race, in disregard of their some five hundred distinct tribal entities, many of which still survive, with differences large and small in language, religion, mythology, and physical appearance. At the time of the massive immigrations starting in the 1880s, foreign nationalities or ethnicities were often described as if they were tribal, each a group with tightly defined and stubborn cultural traits, while in the history of its wider use as a descriptive term for native societies, it became a term of denigration and abuse.[6]

Of all the problems of terminology troubling the ideas of nation and nationality in the United States, of tribe and ethnicity, the term "race" has been the most difficult. In the era examined in this book, a set of ideas known as "scientific racism" claimed to offer empirical support for a hierarchy of "superior" and "inferior" peoples, and by 1900 this had become an article of faith among most Euro-Americans. Skin color became a sign of innate and unchanging capabilities, a sign of "race."

It has been convenient for many white Americans to think of their country as biracial, with all so-called colored peoples falling under the inclusive designation of blackness, "redskin" being a variant way of saying "black." But recent scholarship has shown evidence of a tremendous mixing of skin colors in the population (or repopulation, after the great decline in the sixteenth century, by disease and genocidal massacre) of the American hemisphere and the United States in particular. The heritage of mixed races, we are learning, is far more common than the purity implied by the standard racial terminology.

Yet the racialist terms remain in use, freighted with justifications for continuing inequalities. Two things need to be said about this way of thinking. The first is that in the United States the process whereby obvious differences in skin color and body type were fixed as differences in "race" was tied directly to the defense of slavery and to the expropriation of native territory; these were both defended by their supporters as essential to the growth and prosperity of a nation controlled by people of European or white ancestry. Late-nineteenth-century scientific racism was the capstone of a way of seeing the United States as consisting of a dominant superior race called white, Anglo-Saxon, or Caucasian, and subordinate inferior races called African, Asian, Hispanic, Indian, or, inclusively, "black." *National* identity, which many whites thought to be at risk at the turn of the century from the influx of millions of non-Anglo-Saxon immigrants, was, in their minds, thought to be inseparable from *racial* identity. Race, a relatively weak concept in the eighteenth century, became in the nineteenth century a justification for enslaving Africans and their descendants, and for removing natives forcibly from their homelands or exterminating them altogether.

The second thing to observe about racial thinking at the turn of the century is that its confused categories in fact clarify for us its underlying motive: to maintain the inequalities that followed from black slavery and the suppression of native self-determination (and Hispanic, too, in regions of the West and Far West acquired after the war with Mexico in 1848–49). Negro and Indian marked points on a compass of national identity. As Winthrop Jordan has remarked about the period from 1550 to 1812, "The separate meanings of *Indian* and *Negro* helped define the meaning of living in America."[7] Those meanings helped to give whites a presumably safe purchase on their own American identity. Confusion arose from the blanket application of the terms, which often resulted in a revealing slippage whereby natives were called black, doomed to inferiority, and African Americans likened to Indians, savages fated to vanish become extinct.[8]

While there is evidence of cooperation between free blacks and natives in frontier communities, antagonism seemed the more common relation.[9] It's perhaps ironic that the adoption of racial categories by African Americans and Native Americans themselves helped to fasten racial thinking as a halter around the neck of the nation. As Michael Gomez has shown, when enslaved Africans became African American, they took on the term "black" or "Negro" for their own purposes of resistance, rebellion, and self-identity—for the sake of racial solidarity; instead of separate ethnicities, they came to see themselves as indeed a "race" oppressed by another race, the whites.[10] Natives, too—many of whose societies and cultures survived the violent assaults of white settlers, government policy, and the U.S. Army—nonetheless adopted the racial designation of themselves as "Indian," a name for what they shared in common with other natives.[11]

Sometimes blacks embraced Indian identity: escaped slaves in Florida, for example, who joined with the Seminoles in their war against the Americans in the early nineteenth century, a war that began when U.S. government forces moved against the tribes harboring runaway slaves.[12] And sometimes Indians behaved toward blacks in a racist manner similar to that of whites: slaveholding tribes in the South, for example, which in the 1820s and 1830s had been removed to Indian Territory in Oklahoma and fought on the side of the Confederacy in the Civil War.[13] As racial lines hardened, blacks often preferred to think of themselves as closer to whites and better deserving of equality than Indians, who with their tribes and their blankets fell outside the white nation to which blacks hoped to belong. Sometimes blacks joined with whites in violence against Indians: Buffalo soldiers or regular U.S. Army "colored troops" were used in campaigns in the Southwestern border regions and in the military campaign against Sioux Ghost Dancers that resulted in the massacre at Wounded Knee on December 29, 1890.[14] But "black" and "red" presumed that the people so described were incapable of equality in American society, that their status was permanently fixed by their skin color.

Particular cultural identities (as distinct from race) have remained stronger among natives than among African Americans. The several attempts at pan-Indian unity—the efforts of Tecumseh, for example, to rally a unified resistance in the early nineteenth century, and the formation of pan-Indian organizations in the twentieth century—have had to contend with tribal loyalties that challenge the idea that Indi-

ans were one distinct people and, like blacks, should be recognized as
a single disadvantaged race.[15] On the whole, African Americans and
Native Americans have viewed their situations as widely dissimilar.
Blacks have tended to see themselves as part of the nation, unfairly
kept down but hoping to rise. The historian W.E.B. Du Bois, a
founder of the National Association for the Advancement of Colored
People in 1910, described the identity problem of African Americans
as a "puzzling" dilemma. "What, after all, am I? Am I an American or
am I a Negro? Can I be both?" In his immensely successful *The Souls
of Black Folk* (1903), he argued that Negroes must strive to be both,
that in realizing their own black racial and cultural heritage, Negroes
would contribute to a full American identity, which he viewed, as
Dewey would a few years later, as a composite of many racial and cultural strains.[16] Native American intellectuals argued in a similar vein
in the same years. The Society of American Indians, founded in 1911
(Du Bois was the only African American included as an associate member), included the promotion of "citizenship among Indians" among
its goals and promised that "the honor of the race and the good of the
country will always be paramount." But the nationalist pan-Indianism
of the SAI met greater resistance among natives than did the goals of
integration of the NAACP among African Americans. By the mid-1920s,
the SAI had fallen apart.[17]

Indians have tended to see themselves as outside the nation, their
tribes as separate cultural and political entities in their own right. It
has been said that Indians began with everything—the whole country
was once theirs—and ended with close to nothing, while for blacks
and other minorities the case has been the reverse: starting with nothing, and slowly, painfully, winning some things.[18] The tribe, or "the
people" (as most Indian societies called themselves in their native
tongues), was the focus of allegiance and identity, and this made the Indians' political and cultural situation in the United States unique.[19]

U.S. government policy toward Native Americans from the 1880s
until the 1930s and the "New Deal for Indians" basically aimed to destroy these allegiances and practices, at "smashing the tribal mass" (as
Theodore Roosevelt indelicately put it) in order, it was said, to prepare the Indians for U.S. citizenship, but also, and primarily, to pry

loose for white ownership the lands that natives held collectively. The argument was that the tribal form prevented individual Indians from adopting the outlook (individualism) and skills (private ownership of land and goods) required for the proper civil identity of an American. The Connecticut poet Joel Barlow in the eighteenth century looked forward to a time "when their tribes to happy nations rise." In the early twentieth century it was much easier for white Americans to imagine a Pole or a Serb eventually qualifying as an equal American citizen than a Mohawk or an Arapaho. While Indians had always been symbols of the naturalness and independence of the United States in comparison with European nations, the natives' political identity and American identity seemed, and perhaps were, inherently at odds.

Yet the Native Americans fought to keep not only their social and cultural identities but also their sovereignty, their own forms of governance and loyalty, and their own system for making outsiders and newcomers members of their community. The fight continues. While today's battle site is most often the casino (an issue that distracts from the fundamental dangers of chronic poverty and disease on the reservations), a century ago it was primarily the treaty, a document that evolved out of native ways of treating each other as well as from European practices of putting formal state-to-state understandings in written form. Treaties were "essentially plays," as Constance Rourke was one of the first cultural historians to observe, "chronicle plays—recording what was said in the parleys, including bits of action, the exchanges of gifts, of wampum, the smoking of pipes, the many ceremonials with dances, cries and choral songs." Most of all, at least from the native perspective, they were tribal events, ceremonials "springing from deeply rooted communal experience" that "must be preserved" in treaty making "because human dignity was a force that was widely understood." Once printed, the treaties gained "epic proportions as well as an epic theme." They were "our first American plays," inaugurating American dramatic literature in records of a still-unrecognized formative experience of the nation: its encounter with the customs and law of the natives of North America.[20]

The chief thrust of the very complex history of these treaties was the natives' concession of land in return for pledged U.S. respect for and protection of their limited autonomy and sovereignty over their own people. It is said that there is no treaty with Indians that the United States did not find some way to break or circumvent, but its acknowledgment of the natives' limited sovereignty has never been extinguished. It belongs to American law. The leading struggle of native American peoples today is to win more effective recognition for it. Spelling out and accepting that Indian tribes can coexist with the nation will have lasting implications for the entire United States. At stake is our basic understanding of how cultural and political nationality do and should stand toward each other.

The era 1880–1930 was marked by roiling conflict over the proposition Dewey stated as a given: that the United States is exceptional among nations in not having a nationality test or expectation for citizenship. A powerful reaction to the then "new" immigrants asserted the opposite, that the word "American" did denote a set of behavioral traits and a distinctive culture. Many of those who believed that immigrants posed a threat to nationality looked toward the American Indian for evidence of national distinctiveness and proof of nationality. Both conflation of and confusion between political and cultural nationality, then, and efforts by Dewey and others to keep the distinction clear and clean, mark the period. The conflicts between cultural and political nationality appeared among both Indians and immigrants, separately and together, and these are what I wish to illuminate in this book.

The setting is familiar. Rapid, unsettling change in all realms of culture and society made the turn of the nineteenth century an era of transition, with breaks, and a crux, between two ways of life, two mentalities, two sets of assumptions. In the past lay a predominantly agrarian (though expanding) and entrepreneurial republic ruled by large landholders, slave owners, merchants, lawyers, ministers, and a growing number of self-made proprietors and independent artisans. A system of values placed possessive male individualism at the pinnacle of social beliefs, with subservient roles for women, black slaves, servants, apprentices, and wage workers. Communities, even cities, were small, while families were large, face-to-face transactions defined everyday life, and denominational Protestantism had a secure hold on public and private life. In the future lay a new urban, industrial, and imperial order.

The break was not a revolution, but it had revolutionary effects: Megacorporations in industry and finance replaced family businesses, assembly lines became the rule in factories, a new system of distribution and circulation of commodities arose, with mass-produced commodities dominating the marketplace. "Consumerism" became a new way of life and introduced deep changes in private life, domestic households, values of selfhood, and ideals of gender. Although the country's internal expansion was declared at an end by the 1890 census report that no more free land lay available in the West (the "closing of the frontier"), economic expansion continued and took an aggressive turn toward acquiring markets and sources of cheap labor and natural resources among nonwhite peoples overseas, in Latin America, and in the Pacific. The United States joined the imperial nations of Europe in competition, as Du Bois saw it, "for the labor of yellow, brown, and black folks" in order to reap high profits and ensure high wages for white workers at home.[21] The racism that justified overseas imperialism, as it had the conquest and subjugation of Indians, exacerbated domestic tensions. All these changes were accompanied by major social movements among women, workers, ethnic minorities, and African Americans to secure basic rights and social justice.

The arrival of tens of millions of people mainly from non-Anglo-Saxon lands heightened the sense of rapid, bewildering, and threatening social change. Simultaneously the indigenous population was subjected to coercive pressure to abandon its traditional ways of life and join the American mainstream, or else remain in the state of colonial dependency as "wards"—a euphemism for colonial subject.[22] While many millions of voluntary immigrants in search of a new identity flocked through New York and other ports of entry, Native Americans faced continuing assaults against their own systems of social organization and against the religious ideas and practices inseparable from them. To see both these processes as related to each other in the context of racism and imperial conquest is one of my aims.

The importance of imperialism to the meanings registered by the words "Indian" and "immigrant" cannot be stressed enough. Walter L.

Williams has made the point that relations of Europeans and American natives were conditioned by imperial policies from the beginning, that in the course of the nineteenth century the self-government of Indian tribes was severely abrogated by conquest, that individual natives were steadily brought under control of the government as colonial subjects, and that by the end of the century "the federal government held virtually unlimited power over American Indians."[23] Those like Theodore Roosevelt, advocating direct colonial rule of conquered populations in the Philippines and other "insular" natives, pointed to the "subject" status of Native Americans as a model.[24] After World War I it became clear to W.E.B. Du Bois that the United States had chosen a path abroad patterned on its racial behavior at home. In 1920 he wrote:

> America, Land of Democracy, wanted to believe in the failure of democracy so far as darker peoples were concerned. Absolutely without excuse she established a caste system, rushed into preparation for war, and conquered tropical colonies. She stands today shoulder to shoulder with Europe in Europe's worst sin against civilization. She aspires to sit among the great nations who arbitrate the fate of "lesser breeds without the law" and she is at times heartily ashamed even of the large number of "new" white people whom her democracy has admitted to place and power. Against this surging forward of Irish and German, of Russian Jew, Slav and "dago" her social bars have not availed, but against Negroes she can and does take her unflinching and immovable stand, backed by this new public policy of Europe. She trains her immigrants to this despising of "niggers" from the day of their landing, and they carry and send the news back to the submerged classes in the fatherlands.[25]

The story is not so much about how Indians and immigrants viewed each other as how the dominant culture viewed each, and about their relevance to each other and to the background of racial attitudes that were most dramatically displayed toward African Americans. For most Americans, the larger figure of the nation itself was always at stake, the idea of being "American." Both Indians and immigrants were subjected to a process called "Americanization," a set of institutional devices and regimes that operated with an a priori notion of what and who an American was supposed to be, an essentialist idea of a presumed cultural nationality. While blacks were systematically, and violently, excluded from the precincts of American nationality, in spite of (or because of) the legal forms of citizenship for African American males established by the Thirteenth, Fourteenth, and Fifteenth amendments to the Constitution, Indians, who were excluded from these amendments, were now considered prime candidates for American citizenship. I suggest here that the very devices and means used to reproduce the ideal figure of the "American" and its cognitive appurtenances on the bodies and minds of "alien" Indians and immigrants undercut the premise that there was a definable American nationality, something you were born into or acquired through "naturalization." The staging of Indians and making of Americans was basically self-contradictory. If "the American" can be staged and made, then perhaps the "American" identity is better described as performative than natural, as a matter of contingency and a chosen role (implying it can be unchosen). In these critical years the core ideal of a single coherent nation with a singular identity or nationality or national type was challenged by the very means used to support and impose it.

The fundamental shift in representations of Indians, from "savage" foe to "first American" and ancestor to the nation, was conditioned by the perceived crisis in national identity triggered by the "new" immigrants. I begin, then, with the 1880s and 1890s, and the enactment by Congress of an "allotment" policy that aimed to destroy the tribal system and bring Indians within the domain of American society and of Americanness. Early versions of staging, a theme that is carried both backward and forward in time, appear in the chapter on Longfellow's *The Song of Hiawatha* and its revival as a theater piece at the turn of the century. Chapter 2 brings the "new immigration" into the picture, principally through the eyes of Henry James, as well as the troubled issue of citizenship. A specific immigrant language is the theme of Chapter 3, on a translation of Longfellow's poem into

Yiddish. I turn then to notable revisions of the figure of the Indian as "vanishing American" in the photographs of Edward S. Curtis and "first American" in the "expeditions" launched by the Wanamaker Department Store in Philadelphia. Chapter 6 gives an important native writer, Luther Standing Bear, a final say about performance, the Hiawathan Indian, and the idea of America.

A century ago, when Jim Crow laws in the South and discrimination throughout the country tried to deny blacks their national identity as Americans, Indian and immigrant more or less defined each other in many regions of American culture. It was a time that saw the erection of public monuments to Indian "heroes," Indian themes in paintings and book illustrations, a bull market in Indian antiquities and crafts, and private collecting and ethnographic museum displays on a huge scale. Vast audiences rushed to Indian performances— Wild West shows, dances in the Southwest, and, in the East and Midwest, popular performances by Indians themselves of staged versions of the irresistible cadences of the most famous poem in English written by an American, Longfellow's putative Indian epic *The Song of Hiawatha*. The turn toward the "good" Indian might be called an "age of Hiawatha," over which Longfellow's faux Indian cast a long, deep shade. "Shade" also implies something less comforting: a ghost that will not rest. The turn toward Hiawatha as an alternative to Crazy Horse was surely a function of the apparent defeat of the ultimate "savage." Now that he and his kind were gone, vanished according to the same destiny that pledged dominion of the continent to the ascendant nation, Indians could and should be hailed as forefathers and -mothers of us all.

The remarkable drive to incorporate the Indian in these years was clearly related to the drive to incorporate "colored" peoples everywhere as virtual peons in a global American system. The cultural form of the campaign to remake Indians and Americans might also be considered a figurative form of ingestion of a sacrificial meal: the Indian figure as a symbolic "host" consumed in the act and transformed into the "godhead" of the nation.[26] Annihilated as persons, subsumed as "Indians" in repeated rituals of symbolic sacrifice, the indigenous population seemed in certain eyes to promise national redemption:

absolution of the sins of conquest, legitimation by offering themselves as founders and guardians of nationhood. Nothing of this sort entered the national thinking about African Americans, the nation's most prominent second-class citizens; indeed, the much-praised dignity, independence, and virile manhood of Indians were often cited as a rebuke against the so-called inferiority of African Americans. Much of the effort to refurbish the image of Indians was sponsored and endorsed by the same ruling groups whose policies were responsible for disrupting native societies and attempting to destroy their cultures. Partly this suggests a wish to exonerate guilt, but evidence of confessed guilt was rare, while plunder and murder were seen by many as legitimate means of nation building. Theodore Roosevelt expressed a pervasive view when he wrote, against what he called "sentimentalists," "The rude, fierce settler who drives the savage from the land lays all civilized mankind under a debt to him."[27] As first American, the Indian filled a need that was as much ideological as psychological, a need for class and national legitimacy in the face of challenging social change, not least the changes wrought by masses of strangers flooding through Ellis Island and by imperial conquest overseas that brought "brown" peoples under the domain of the United States.

The revival and revision of the idea of the Indian as original and originating American, the simultaneous arrival of "new immigrants," and the reappearance of the shades of Hiawatha provoke leading questions. What did "America" mean under the new conditions? What did it mean to "Americanize"? That term itself, with its hint of something good for you imposed from above, was first applied to boarding-school Indians in the late 1870s before the "huddled masses" of Southern and Eastern Europe began to arrive in the Promised Land. Liberty stood in a posture of welcome at the gate of Ellis Island, and Emma Lazarus's words gave hope. Then, in 1913, a plan was launched by the Wanamaker Department Store to raise in that same harbor of New York an even taller statue showing an Indian warrior making a sign of welcome. After a festive groundbreaking ceremony on Washington's birthday, the plan dissolved, never (or rarely) heard of again. But the very idea of placing an Indian in bronze at the threshold of the nation reminds us how classical and white, how classically white, is the figure of Liberty.

That the Indian memorial failed to materialize sharpens the irony of having a European Liberty watch over America's port of entry. Among Indians, original inhabitants, and new immigrants (the most recent "aliens") there lay a conceptual crux, an unexpected crossing of paths. Otherwise, a chasm in the national culture separated "whites" or Caucasians from "others," "civilized" from "savage" peoples, those with "property" (or at least able to recognize private ownership and legal title) from those without either the concept or social practice of private ownership (in other words, "savage"). This crux interests me as the locus of ideological conflict over key terms in the lexicon of American nationality and identity: "Indian," "immigrant," and "national identity" became realigned during the early years of the twentieth century. I am interested, too, in the ways that those people who were subject to being staged, to making and remaking, nonetheless contributed by their resistance and creativity to rewriting the roles assigned to them. I hope that this process, in which Indians and immigrants have their own say, will be evident throughout.

SHADES OF HIAWATHA

Dreaming Indian

———•———

Indians and *Whites* do not exist. These words do not mean real people—
flesh and blood, sentient humans like those we meet on the street or in
the countryside. Indian and White represent fabled creatures, born as
one in the minds of seventeenth- and eighteenth-century European
thinkers trying to make sense of the modern experience, particularly the
European "discovery" of new continents and their populations. Ever
since, Indians and Whites have been entangled with one another in the
collective thought of both European and New World peoples, like some
artist's image of a mad duo in a dark embrace. To borrow a thought from
the Iroquois, Indians and Whites are *false faces* peering into a mirror,
each reflecting the other.   —Jean-Jacques Simard, *White Ghosts*

The Indian became for Americans a symbol of their American experience; it was no mere luck of the toss that placed the profile of an American Indian rather an American Negro on the famous old five-cent piece.
Confronting the Indian in America was a testing experience, common to
all the colonies. Conquering the Indian symbolized and personified the
conquest of the American difficulties, the surmounting of wilderness. To
push back the Indian was to prove the worth of one's own mission, to
make straight in the desert a highway for civilization. With the Negro it
was utterly different.   —Winthrop Jordan, *White Over Black*

In "The Vanishing Red," a strange, grim poem by Robert Frost, a village miller pushes a man named John, "the last Red Man / In Acton,"
through a manhole in the floor of a mill. Once the murderous miller
shuts "down the trap door with a ring in it, / That jangled even above
the general noise"—the grimmest, perhaps excessively Gothic note
in the poem—we hear nothing more from John. He has vanished into
the savage waters below the floor in which the millstone grinds away:

"desperate straits like frantic fish, / Salmon and sturgeon, lashing with their tails." Told as a ballad in twenty-nine unrhymed lines, this odd capsule of a narrative with echoes of Poe (it first appeared in *Mountain Interval*, 1916) rarely gets mentioned by Frost's critics but clearly belongs among his tales of dark passions, narrow-minded meanness, and eruptive violence in the New England backcountry.[1] The gruesome physical act at the center of the tale tells, however, only part of the story.

As in the best of Frost's narrative poems, it's not so much the happening itself but the perception of the act that matters. This is a story of apparent hatred of "the last red Man" so fierce that it cannot abide itself and finds release, on the flimsiest of pretexts, in violence.

> Some guttural exclamation of surprise
> The Red Man gave in poking about the mill,
> Over the great big thumping, shuffling millstone,
> Disgusted the Miller physically as coming
> From one who had no right to be heard from.
>
> "Come, John," he said, "you want to see the wheel pit?"

It's John's speech, his "guttural exclamation," that brings on the miller's homicidal disgust, a visceral reaction that begs for an explanation the poem leaves unsaid, a matter of surmise; he kills the Indian to silence him, to vanish him out of sight and sound.

The poem rings with implication. Its title makes the story a mordant commentary on the "vanishing race" theory that dominated all thinking about Native Americans until quite recently, the idea that the indigenes of the continent would disappear as a matter of natural course. "Last Red Man" calls up Ishi, "the last Yahi," found and captured in 1911 near starvation in the corral of a slaughterhouse in a northern California town near Oroville ("gold town"!), the only survivor of the massacre of his people, a genocide commonplace in those fields of gold. Turned over to the care of the Berkeley anthropologist Alfred Kroeber, he became a living museum exhibit, "the last wild Indian in North America." He learned some English, wore a shirt and pants except when asked to pose for the camera half naked in breech-cloth, taught the professors his own language, gave museum demonstrations of the bow and arrow and basket weaving, and, sick with tuberculosis, died in the museum like a Stoic in 1916, the year Frost's poem appeared.[2]

Other implications connect the poem with a history of vanishing reds. The name John, the only proper name in the poem and repeated three times, is another kind of vanishing into a white man's image, an allusion perhaps to Indian John, the name by which James Fenimore Cooper's Chingachook is addressed in his old age.[3] The paraphrase of the miller's self-justification for his murderous "disgust," that John "had no right to be heard from," recalls political questions that persist: What indeed are the "rights" of natives as distinct peoples in the Union? This is a remote issue in the poem, to be sure, but Frost brings it in by subtle conflation of the nation's and the miller's exercise of sovereignty over Indians and denial of their right to speak. And at a yet lower layer lies the unstated term "corn," the food the earliest white immigrants received as a gift from natives, token of their generous hospitality toward strangers that all early travelers noted. Corn is both an indigenous food and a native symbol of the abundance and beneficence of nature, "the mystery of germination, not procreation, but *putting forth*, resurrection, life springing within the seed," in D. H. Lawrence's exultant reenactment in mimetic prose, "Dance of the Sprouting Corn."[4] John's "guttural exclamation of surprise" at the noise of the millstone grinding corn into meal may come from deep within a native memory of what once was their bond with nature, shared willingly, but now subject to another mechanical instrument of transformation and in a system of ownership and control alien to original sacral practices of the land.

Yet it is a bit too easy to rest with these implications, too simple to take the miller as representing the vicious campaigns to extirpate savagery by crushing Indians under the wheels of progress and machinery. The proprietor of the mill is simply an individual nasty case. As Reuben Brower has written, "A moment of 'meanness,' if you will, is grasped fully. And this is the poem's 'moral.'"[5] "Oh, yes, he showed John the wheel pit all right," says the poem's closing line, a paraphrase of the miller's perverse boast in the perfect flat tone of backcountry smirking sarcasm. Frost makes us wonder what lies behind the act and refuses the reader the gratification of a simple explanation such as plain Indian hating or racism.

The poem opens into a world of storytelling where what is said has the force of what is real but remains at the same time what is only said.

> He is said to have been the last Red Man
> In Acton. And the Miller is said to have laughed—
> If you like to call such a sound a laugh.

The opening stanza is retrospective; it follows just after the killing when the miller comes back upstairs. He laughs—an unspeakable sound we hear about before we hear John's guttural exclamation— then turns grave, "as if to say, / 'Whose business . . .'" Speech is the imperfect medium of knowledge; we are led into a realm of surmise; every act of knowing is retrospective to an actual act, to what it is we want to know.

The second stanza, preceding the killing itself (hence a retrospective thought), gives the theme of the poem:

> You can't get back and see it as he saw it.
> It's too long a story to go into now.
> You'd have to have been there and lived it.
> Then you wouldn't have looked on it as just a matter
> Of who began it between the two races.

There's no exoneration of the miller, but there is the idea that you have to go back to look through the eyes of the killer to "see it as he saw it," which would make for a very long story, a tale of how "the two races" came together in the first place and what drove them apart. Countless narratives of just this perverse kind expressed the many conflicted ideas of land, corn, and rights.

I

What follows in this book is an effort to tell other versions of the "too long a story" of Euro-American obsession with skin color as "race." We must begin with the paradox of saying "native" in a nation of immigrants. For the least disputable statement one can make about the United States of America is that it has always been and always will be a nation of immigrants of all hues. All Americans, whether of the United States or of any country in the hemisphere, derive in historical time from elsewhere—all, that is, except for the natives whom Columbus misnamed Indians, the indelible sign he didn't know where he was when he touched land he immediately named San Salvador.[6] That exception makes the name "American" an exceptionally rich, multiple signifier with a diffuse ambiguity that affects all aspects of the story that unfolds in the pages that follow.

Though not the only immigrant nation in the modern world, the United States has seemed the most conscious of itself as such, and often, in periodic outbursts of hostilities against newcomers, the most troubled about being so. The outrage and hatred against "aliens" run along a single narrow-gauged track between two imaginary terminals, one called foreign, the other native. That the two terms are relative, arbitrary, and fictional we easily glean from the doubleness of "native," signifying both Indians and anyone who happens to have been born here regardless of where his or her parents come from. Semantic logic hardly mitigates the demonic conviction that something fundamental to self and nation was at risk in the face of aliens, just as both were at risk (ambiguity turning fiercely to irony) in the face of Indians known as "savages."

The rhetoric of xenophobia traffics in enflamed tropes of danger and pollution. Part of its heritage, as we shall see, has been a distorted view of the actual effects of the "new" immigration from the late 1880s to the early 1920s. Fearful and hostile responses to the sight of people who looked so "foreign" jamming the Great Hall of Ellis Island can be taken as the outer edge of a deeper anxiety: the inherently unsettled basis of national identity or nationality in this exemplary nation of immigrants. Anxiety was fed by the ideas of "scientific racism" current at the time, the view that measurement of skulls and limbs "proved" the intransigent inferiority of all people of color and justified a racial order of hierarchy and exclusion: disenfranchisement and segregation of African Americans, exclusion of Chinese immigrants, discrimination against Latinos, confinement of natives in ghettolike reservations, restriction of immigration (finally achieved in 1924) from non-Anglo-Saxon or Teutonic lands in Europe.[7]

The most widely disseminated version of our national story sets the founding of the nation on written propositions negotiated among the first thirteen British colonies, which in 1776 agreed to declare independence together. The propositions rang with universal principle; they set liberty above dependence; they insisted on rule by the will of "the people" rather than by royal decree from an absentee imperial landlord; and they set forth a process of determining that will by majority vote. Who constituted "we the people," eligible to participate in political decision making, arose at once as a principled issue of contention, and coming generations struggled over universal white male suffrage, abolition of slavery, civil war, woman suffrage, and continuing campaigns for voting rights and protection of civil liberties. But except for the constitutional exclusion of slaves and natives from "the people"—monumental exceptions that helped to undermine the official version of the national narrative—the founding principles were otherwise "universal" and "enlightened" in their absence of ethnic, religious, or nationality requirements for citizenship.

The dominance of English, the language of the imperial landlord, and the typically Northern European roots of most of the white population of the first thirteen colonies, together with the exclusion of dark-skinned peoples (the only mention of "the Indian Tribes" appears in the Constitution in the clause that empowers Congress to regulate trade; the Declaration of Independence speaks of attacks on colonists by "merciless Indian savages" incited by King George II) gave the new polity a look and air of homogeneity that the founding documents repudiated. Tensions between the theory that "all men are created equal" and the practical realities of "we the people" arose then and have remained a defining mark of the American national ethos. Indians were apparently in a class or category of their own and hardly figured in discussions of "rights" in the early republic. Between the ravages of disease and conquest, many native tribes and cultures had disappeared even before the founding of the nation. Even by 1760, the Indian population had already declined precipitously, so that a mingling of natives and Euro-Americans was rare and became rarer. Natives and nation seemed to exist in a contradictory relation, driven by interests that seemed doomed to clash. The earliest experiences of the tribes with the new federal government set a fatal pattern: fierce struggle to protect their lands, their communities, their lives, followed by defeat, removal, and, in many cases, annihilation. The theory of the "vanishing race" became a convenient rationale for the nation's refusal to meet the tribes halfway on common ground. Jefferson had hoped that an "enlightened" policy of education and interbreeding of Indians with whites would bring the tribes around to civilized ways and peaceful integration. But, as Joyce Appleby writes, "the yearning for economic independence among ordinary white Americans sealed the fate of dependency for Native Americans."[8]

Who, then, qualifies as "American"? To be native to a place is to be naturally of that place, a condition shared by people born where they reside. The settlement of European colonies in the western hemisphere and then the founding of a nation there introduced a different concept: the notion of a civil realm of laws, rights, and citizenship. The term "native" embodies an idea of "nature"—that which cannot be helped, like being born—as distinct from political society. Europe brought something else to the new lands, too, the name "America," a name to which Europeans at first attached the image of natives. When "American" came to denote a citizen of the United States, "native" also changed in the sense that your place of birth was now understood as a nation as much as a country, a bounded region of the earth. The paradox emerged that natives of the place called America, if they were Indians and thus excluded from U.S. citizenship, were not considered native to the nation. They were in one sense homeless in their own homeland. Yet the nation that excluded them as legal Americans persisted in calling them "American" inasmuch as they were naturally of the place. The word "American" now had two referents, between which the tension seemed irresolvable until, by an act of Congress in 1924, all Indians born within the legal domain were accorded citizenship as a right of birth, whether the tribes wished it or not. In most white minds blacks remained simply blacks, Negroes, unequal members of the order and a significant part of the workforce (as Indians on the whole were not).

By an ironic semantic twist, by the end of the nineteenth century the same Euro-Americans who had once viewed American Indians as alien savages came to embrace them as the true, the natural, the "first Americans," icons of the nation and its territory. Inventing symbolic Indians, playing Indian, dreaming Indian—all of these phrases describing the way white Americans put themselves in relation to the aboriginal population confirm the validity of Jean-Jacques Simard's remark that "*Indians* and *Whites* do not exist" except as each other's fictions. Philip J. Deloria has shown that playing Indian, donning native costumes, and adopting putative native customs and ceremonies allowed nonnatives to believe that thereby they might overcome European descent and become true Americans. I am indebted to Deloria's book for posing this question: How did "playing Indian" become a way of "playing American"? And I consider as central what Simard describes as the mad dance of the mutually constitutive fictions Indian and immigrant and American. We can think of these three terms as texts that, for the first few decades of the twentieth century, the mainstream culture felt an obsessive need to decipher separately and in relation to each other. "American" served, as it still does, as the great indeterminate middle term whose definition was at once transparent (born of parents born of parents born here, though in every white person's past was an original immigrant) and opaque (was it alluding to the name of nation or continent? reserved for whites only, or aboriginals only?), at once a prize for the compliant and a contest for those outside the mainstream.

Playing or dreaming Indian often came about in opposition to official notions of the nation and of the middle-class utopia of progress and material betterment. While dreams of self-improvement and personal success in the evolving settler capitalist order doubtless drove this nation of immigrants toward a society of cities and an industrial-commercial culture of modernity, alternative dreams erupted and persisted in undercurrents of longing and collective desire: yearnings for solidarity in place of the arrogance of class and of competitive and isolating individualism; dreams of archaic forms of community instead of urban anomie, cash nexus, and degradation of earth and sky. Repressed and shunted aside in public discourse, these visions of other identities, of an antimodernity fostered by modernity itself, have had extraordinary tenacity. They represent an undercurrent of persisting ambivalence toward the values and expectations of the dominant social order.

Among such counterlongings, the wish to "go native," to find freedom and fulfillment by adopting certain versions of indigenous styles and practices, to "Indianize" oneself, has a long and still-active history. As Deloria has shown, it figured dramatically in the undertaking known as the American Revolution, an event that included internalizing Indianness as a way of asserting independence. The nationalizing of the Indian, both the interior and the exterior Indian (in Deloria's important distinction), called upon associations long attached to the indigenes of what Europeans called the New World, such as the ecstasy of initial contact expressed by Columbus, Amerigo Vespucci (all Americans are his namesakes), and other explorers and conquerors. The appeal was visceral, as we see in the works of artists from Jacques Le Moyne and John White in the sixteenth century to George Catlin in the nineteenth—the appeal of native ways of adorning the body and wearing (or not wearing) clothing, of hunting and fishing, and of gathering together in villages, playing games, doing combat, or engaging in communal ceremonies. In the nineteenth century, James Fenimore Cooper's Leatherstocking novels and countless other fictions invited readers to identify vicariously with native ways. A half-buried wish to go native has seemed a certain mark of American or U.S. nationality itself. From the beginning of colonization and settlement, such a wish was part of what tempted Europeans to risk the Atlantic voyage; for the "new" immigration at the cusp of the nineteenth and twentieth centuries, popular pulp and celluloid fantasies about Indians and the Wild West helped to acculturate and assimilate young greenhorns into secret rituals of the nation's name.[9]

Jacques Le Moyne, "How They Till the Soil and Plant." Engraved by Theodor de Bry. From Bry, *Bevis Narratio eaorum quae in Florida Americanae*, 1591. (Beinecke Rare Book and Manuscript Library, Yale University)

John White, "The Conjurer." Engraved by Theodor de Bry. From Thomas Harriot, *A Briefe and True Report of the New Found Land of Virginia*, 1590. "They have sorcerers or jugglers, who use strange gestures and whose enchantments often go against the laws of nature. For they are very familiar with devils, from whom they obtain knowledge about their enemies' movements." (Beinecke Rare Book and Manuscript Library, Yale University)

How did it happen that dreaming Indian—playing Indian in fantasy and imagination—became a way of dreaming American, imagining oneself a member of the nation? The path from Indian to American identity (imagined or false) lay through a tangle of paradox all the more recalcitrant for being invisible. Contradiction and implausibility help to account for the residual power of the dream of an Indian mediation of nationality. From the beginnings of a discernible national consciousness in seventeenth-century New England and throughout the nineteenth century, most ruling groups and most of the non-Indian population thought of Indians as antithetical: savage, pagan, probably Asian, possibly Jewish (the "lost tribes"). They perceived them as nomadic hunters always on the move and misunderstood or willfully ignored their distinctive agricultural pursuits and patterns of habitation and social structure. Blind to native modes of living on and with the land, shaping forests and prairies to suit their purposes, white Americans viewed them as profligates in regions without fences and distinct boundaries, thought of them as sinfully wasteful occupants of "wilderness."

Indians were conceived as defining the outer margins of America, a nation of immigrant settlers expanding westward under one flag, a modern capitalist society converting land into exchangeable wealth as it expanded across the continent. The flag stood for laws of private ownership and wealth, laws devised to establish boundaries between public and private realms. The flag stood for a set of assumptions. Americans were national, and the nation guaranteed and protected private property; Indians were tribal and lived by rules of communal ownership. The differences seemed irreconcilable, and violence, barely mitigated by efforts to "convert" and "civilize" the indigenes, seemed the nation's only course to establish dominion over what it claimed as its national territory. Indians who stood in the path had to be pushed aside or wiped away. Yet it was hoped that they would leave something of themselves behind, not merely their bones but also their spirit and their virtues, "their looks and their modes," in George Catlin's words, as fiber for the nation's morale and iconography for its self-representation.[10]

No American artist in the antebellum years gave so compelling and colorful a body of images of Indian looks and modes in the national iconography as did George Catlin. Trained for the law and self-schooled as a painter, he set out in the 1830s to "rescue from oblivion" as complete a record of surviving Indian life as he could manage during seven years of travels in the West. His "Catlin's Indian Gallery," first exhibited in 1837, presented more than six hundred portraits and genre scenes; his *Letters and Notes on the Manners, Customs, and Condition of the North American Indians* (1841) included black-and-white engravings of most of them, and they became the most widely circulated Indian images available at the time. The photographer Edward S. Curtis in the early twentieth century properly credits Catlin as the great precursor of his own epic project of capturing (in more senses than one) the "North American Indian" (the title of Curtis's twenty volumes) in picture and ethnographic text. Immediately after a period of near-extermination by warfare and disease and relocation, each zealously sought to "preserve" in permanent images a "race" thought to be "doomed" by contact with white "civilization." In regard to his finely printed photographs, Curtis would have subscribed to Catlin's view that "phoenix-like, they may rise from the 'stain on a painter's palette,' and live again upon canvass, and stand forth for centuries yet to come, the living monuments of a noble race."[11] Both looked to leave behind, in Catlin's words, not only "a monument to a dying race" but "a monument to myself."[12] The self-portrait of the artist at work that is a frontispiece in Catlin's book beautifully renders the romance of the self entangled with the romance of the unspoiled Indian—a staged romance—that drove both artists.

Catlin's paintings were warmly admired: How can you help falling under the spell of their native verve, presence, and color? Baudelaire remarked after seeing an exhibit of them in Paris in 1846. But Catlin has also been chided for his conviction that Indians were "doomed" and for his resultant deficient ethnography.[13] What has not been given enough credit, I believe, is Catlin's scorn for the vicious, cruel, murderous behavior of white traders and trappers and merchants of whiskey and guns as agents of doom. True, he is "romantic" in the sense that he viewed natives before their contact with settlers as "pure," "knights of the forest; whose whole lives are lives of chivalry."

(*above*) George Catlin, "The Author Painting a Chief." From *Letters and Notes on the Manners, Customs and Condition of the North American Indians*, 1841. (*below*) "Buffalo Hunt, Chase," Plate 5, *Catlin's North American Indian Portfolio. Hunting Scenes and Amusements*, 1844. (Yale Collection of Western Americana, Beinecke Rare Book and Manuscript Library)

But throughout his *Letters and Notes* we get the sense that "vanishing" was *not* inevitable, that coexistence with Indians was denied not by the nature of things but by "the wholesale and retail system of injustice, which has been, from the first landing of our forefathers (and is equally at the present day, being) visited upon these poor, and naturally unoffending, untrespassing people." It's "the system of trade, and the small-pox" that "have been the great and wholesale destroyers of these poor people . . . And no one but God, knows where the voracity of the one is to stop, short of the acquisition of everything that is desirable to money-making man in the Indian's country."[14]

He was speaking of corrigible behavior, and in his indignation at the theft of Indian land, debasement of their lives, and wanton killing, we hear indignation also at the pretenses of "civilization." Catlin is one of the earliest Euro-Americans to raise a cultural critique of "civilization," "the specious accomplishments of the refined world," based on his experience among "savages," a term he also criticizes as mistaken and misapplied. "For the Nation," he writes, "there is an unrequited account of sin and injustice that sooner or later will call for national retribution." And for "American citizens, who lie, everywhere proud of their growing wealth and their luxuries over the bones of these poor fellows," there is "a lingering terror" that at the day of resurrection they will be made to stand "with guilt's shivering conviction, amidst the myriad ranks of accusing spirits, that are to rise in their own fields."[15] The bones of the unjustly vanished will yet have a chance to speak. This side of Catlin's "rescue from oblivion" also asks to be heard.

Among the better-known writers of the antebellum years, when hardly any white person doubted that Indians were already gone or would shortly disappear naturally, as it were, Cooper and Longfellow reaped the most bountiful harvest of "remains" of "vanished" Indians. They created pictures of the Indian that most nonnative Americans came to believe were true, though the "white man's Indian" was a figment of literary, religious, political, and scientific imagination more often than of firsthand experience of the natives' lives. Less well known and less influential was Lewis Henry Morgan's *League of the Ho-de-no-sau-nee, or Iroquois* (1851), the first serious ethnography, which offers a perspective that helps us see what is missing from *The Song of Hiawatha*—Hiawatha himself, to begin with, the historical founder of the Iroquois Confederacy—and from popular images and stereotypes of natives. Morgan, who made a fortune as a corporation lawyer in Rochester, New York, and a speculator in railroads and mining (he later gave all this up to pursue ethnography), was aided significantly in his studies of the Iroquois by a Seneca friend of his named Ely S. Parker and Parker's family; Morgan dedicated his book to Parker. His book is firsthand in the sense that Morgan worked more closely with native sources than anyone before him, and the Senecas adopted him as "One Lying Across," a living bridge between peoples.[16]

The *League of the Iroquois*, "short on history, but long on social organization and the mechanics of a kinship state," in the anthropologist William Fenton's words, "grasped the concept of a whole culture."[17] Morgan had discovered a complex and intricate system of life based on "ties of consanguinity," particularly the forms and terms of a "confederacy" by which five (later six) tribes joined in a single nation while retaining their independent identities and autonomies. In later works, particularly *Ancient Society* (1877), Morgan produced a grand theoretical model of the evolution of kinship relations in all early human societies ("mankind were one in origin"), a work Karl Marx and Friedrich Engels held to be of the same importance in social science as Darwin's work in biological science, and his evolutionist studies had immeasurable influence on the emerging field of anthropology until somewhat put aside by the cultural relativism introduced by Franz Boas in the early twentieth century.

His first book, in 1851, is especially interesting in its conviction that modern American society had something important to learn about itself from the system of life of its "predecessors." It's "an original peculiarity" of the native, Morgan wrote, that "he has no desire to perpetuate himself in the remembrance of distant generations." Without monuments and written records, without a city, the native way of life is as "fleeting as the deer and the wild fowl, the Indian's co-tenants of the forest." The tropes are conventional, steeped in "vanishing race" imagery and in ethnocentric assumptions about "progress" and "stages of civilization" from low to high, from "savage" to "civilized." But Morgan meant no denigration by these terms; "savage" names a human heritage, and the emphasis falls on continuity. Because Indians "must ever figure upon the opening pages of our territorial history . . . it becomes our duty to search out their government and institutions," to recover the structure, the forms, the details of their intricate way of life. It's a duty to ourselves.

> The Iroquois were our predecessors in the sovereignty. Our country they once called their country, our rivers and lakes were their rivers and lakes, our hills and intervales were also theirs . . . The tie by which we are thus connected carries with it the duty of doing justice to their memory, by preserving their name and deeds, their customs and their institutions, lest they perish from remembrance. We cannot wish to tread ignorantly upon those extinguished council-fires, whose light, in the days of aboriginal dominion, was visible over half the continent.[18]

Morgan's book can be taken, along with Longfellow's poem, as another appropriation of an Indian past, and Philip Deloria is right that Morgan's ethnography emerged from his youthful preoccupation with "playing Indian," complete with native costumes and naming or "Inindianation" ceremonies. But Morgan's *League* takes a significant step in another direction, which would not become fully clear until his later works.

In *The Origin of the Family, Private Property, and the State* (1884) Engels wrote an ultimate tribute, saying that "Morgan rediscovered in America, in his own way, the materialist conception of history that had been discovered by Marx forty years ago." Basing his own book almost entirely on Morgan's later work, Engels stressed the American's discovery among the Iroquois of a society without either private property or a formal state, a culture without coercion. "Everything runs smoothly without soldiers, gendarmes, or police; without nobles, kings, governors, prefects, or judges; without prisons; without trials. All quarrels and disputes are settled by the whole body of those concerned—the gens or tribe or the individual gentes among themselves."[19]

The words recover the romantic utopian impulse in Morgan's work, the desire for a practical critical perspective on the emerging reign of private property in the United States. In *Ancient Society*, the former corporation lawyer and speculator worried (in language that recalls Marx's) that concentration of unequal private property had become "an unmanageable power. The Human mind stands bewildered in the presence of its own creation." He looks ahead to time when "Democracy in government, brotherhood in society, equality in rights and privileges, and universal education" will usher in a "revival, in a higher form, of the liberty, equality and fraternity of the ancient gentes."[20]

In his first book, Morgan studied the Iroquois not primarily for the sake of founding a nationalizing tradition but to uncover and understand lines of connection between primitive and modern, to describe the mentality of the "hunter state" in order to explain its differences in outlook and system of life. He wanted to explain the refusal of native societies to accept European ways as due not to innate perversity but to their fundamental differences in outlook and habit, which he described admiringly rather than with the condescension or worse that was typical of early students of Indian life. Mainly he wanted to reclaim their attractive achievements, such as the political intelligence of the Confederacy and the spirit that animated many of their communal activities, as a functional "remembrance" for Euro-America. For example, their games "show that the American wilderness, which we have been taught to pronounce a savage solitude until the white man entered its borders, had long been vocal in its deepest seclusions, with the gladness of happy human hearts."[21] About contemporary Iroquois, whom Morgan assisted in legal battles against a "company of land speculators" whose "degree of wickedness" can "hardly be paralleled in the history of human avarice," he wrote, "They should not only be regarded as our fellow-men, but as a part of our own people. Born upon the soil, the descendents of its ancient proprietors, there is no principle which should make them aliens in the land of their nativity, or exclude them from any of those advantages which are reserved to ourselves." He did not doubt they were doomed as a culture, but neither were they incapable of adapting to changed conditions, though when they might do so, "they will cease to be Indians, except in name."[22]

Not entirely free of ethnocentrism or of ideas of savagism, Morgan shared with Catlin and Longfellow and his friend Francis Parkman (no particular friend of the Indian) the idea of a "vanishing race," but what he sought in the traces of the Indians' past in their present condition was not a myth of national origin but an understanding of a system of life based on a specific material existence. The Iroquois preceded the American nation not as imaginary ancestors but as prior inhabitants of what became the national territory; their system of life deserved recognition and study as national heritage and resource for national self-knowledge, a conscious remembrance. Like John Dewey in a little-known essay of 1902, "Interpretation of Savage Mind," Morgan broke with the practice of describing the mind or mentality of earlier societies "in terms of 'lack,' 'absence,'"[23] but wrote instead in terms that made the "primitive" available as resource for the "civilized." With the invaluable assistance of Ely S. Parker and other native friends, Morgan was able to get beyond his initial romance of playing Indian, or at least subordinate it to rigorous study of material facts. His work on the Iroquois offered an alternative mode of discourse to the fictions that occupied Cooper and Longfellow and their boundless audiences, seeking clues to the evolution of human societies as a whole in the evidence of the complexity with which American Indians shaped their communal lives to meet their needs within the limits of their material existence. Longfellow constructed fanciful legend in the mode of romance. While sharing romantic ideas of racial difference, Morgan sought social knowledge to dispel our ignorance, our not realizing when we tread on the remains of a vanished people and on a whole way of life.

II

Presumed distinctions between "nation" and "tribe" have conditioned thinking about Indians throughout U.S. history. Yet tribe, and its relation to the larger nation, remains one of the least understood aspects of native societies. Indians were also called nations, as when John Marshall, writing for the Supreme Court in 1831, called their societies "dependent domestic nations." The formula held until Congress in 1871 ceased treaty making with Indians, stopped calling them dependent nations and labeled them simply and irredeemably tribal and thereby "wards of the state." This move was part of the federal government's effort to impose order on the "unprecedented racial disarray," in the historian Elliot West's words, that the victory of Mexico in 1849 had created: incorporation of vast new territories (including California) and their nonwhite peoples—Hispanics, natives, and Chinese. A time of failed (or betrayed) "Reconstruction" in the South was at the same time one that saw efforts to reconstruct the racial order in the West (and, by implication, throughout the country). The change in federal Indian relations occurred as part of what West calls a "Greater Reconstruction" undertaken by the U.S. government: the end of Reconstruction in the South and a green light given to the restoration of the old master-slave relations in the new forms supplied by Jim Crow legislation and Ku Klux Klan violence; the exclusion of Chinese immigrants in 1882; the marginalization and segregation of Mexican Americans; continuing military efforts to exterminate native tribes if they would not accept defeat and confinement in reservations.

Of course, even as "wards," individual Indians might become U.S. citizens by one means or another—marriage, military service, and so forth—and many did. In 1890, the year the frontier "closed" and native resistance ended in a bloody pool at Wounded Knee, Indians were still thought of as members of "alien" nations, potential enemies in the path of progress, culturally foreign, backward—everything that "America" was not. To be sure, there were exceptions in the shadow of what Melville sardonically called the "metaphysics of Indian-hating": "Palefaces" taking the side of "red men," some even joining them, tribalizing themselves in Indian communalism and rebelling against American possessive individualism. And many natives, too, traded their Indian identity for that of the stock American, or tried holding both identities together, or alternated between them. But the dominant picture of Indians as antithetical, alien, mired in immutable patterns held fast in the early twentieth century both as perception and as policy. They were red, sometimes called black or brown or yellow, different from white, the color of real America. The difference was their "race." Few Euro-Americans had any understanding of cultural and political differences, the meaning that "tribe" gave to their identity and their existence.[24]

Eventually signs of change appeared. As the United States grew more aggressive on the world stage with imperialist undertakings in Cuba, in the Philippines, and throughout the Caribbean, a new eagerness emerged to incorporate Indians in a positive way into the national narrative: They were defeated enemies, yes, and still "backward" in a land of progress, but their warriors fought well and were loyal to their own "nations," gifted with virtues that deserved a place in a revised version of the national character. Indians now might prove that the nation had an ancient heritage, was not the mere upstart among nations that the English especially liked to say it was. Were not Indians the original Americans, the "first" to bear the national name, not themselves immigrants but ancient inhabitants whose forebears were here before anyone else? Unlike other minority groups—blacks, Asians, and new immigrants—natives were not actively seeking inclusion within the dominant American society (with important exceptions, such as the "Five Civilized Nations" in Oklahoma, and the short-lived Society of American Indians). They did not actively seek to belong in that society; it was a fate to be imposed. The policy of forced assimilation that the federal government adopted in the 1880s gave rise to efforts to rehabilitate the alien native as a newly acknowledged precursor, a figure from whom authenticity might be derived for the nation itself. Theodore Roosevelt's *Winning of the West* (1889–95) and Frederick Jackson Turner's "frontier thesis" of 1893 both signaled a new idea that the origins of America lay in the settlers' early encounters and struggles with aboriginal Indian societies. American "character" arose at first in the West; the argument went, in agonistic conflicts between whites and Indians over the very right to be there.[25]

Behind the new national claim of its native ancestry lay two centuries of European depictions of Indians as emblems of the "new world." The turn in thinking about the place of Indians in the national story called upon ideas and images that had been in circulation since the beginning of the republic, when the Indian princess Pocahontas had been widely adopted as an icon of the new nation. The earliest images of the continent's indigenous peoples contradictorily depicted them as threateningly fierce but also pacific and hospitable. Male and female warriors brandishing weapons and eating flesh were offset by goddesses seeming to proffer their bodies as promise of the abundance of the lush New World. It's not that such people were portrayed as Americans, but that America was portrayed and identified as being made of such people, people not yet conceived of as belonging to a different "race" but as different in how they lived, in how they made do without proper clothing, money, flags, civil governments, towns, and borders. "In the beginning," wrote John Locke in 1690, "all the world was America."[26]

By the close of the seventeenth century, colonization and the founding of societies based largely on slave labor were well under way in the regions known to Europeans as America. Yet early conceptions of this portion of the earth as something like the beginning of the world, a place prior to history or, in Locke's case, prior to inequality and the private possession of property, held fast. Locke's America represented an idea of beginnings, an origin, a pure firstness: something of a measure to set historical societies against, the better to identify what belonged to human history and what to nature. "To understand Political Power right, and derive it from its Original, we must consider what State all men are naturally in, and that is, a State of perfect Freedom." Locke's America was neither a country nor a nation but a mapless terrain, an imaginary condition of firstness, of naturalness prior to history. By America, Locke meant the world before societies, a place like a tabula rasa, free of ingrained ideas and inherited meanings. It was a place, moreover, without a political economy. "For," he continued, "no such thing as money was anywhere known."[27] Locke's America was an imagined site of purity and transparency; money had not yet appeared to perform its work of introducing worth as something more than use, translating things into abstract exchangeable values, bringing inequality and deception in its wake. When all the world

Ferdinando Gorges, "America." From *American Painted to Life*, 1658. " 'Tis I, in tempting divers, for to try / By sundry meanes, t'obtain me, causde them dye / And, last discover'd, undiscover'd am: / For, men, to treade my Soil, as yet, are lame." (Beinecke Rare Book and Manuscript Library, Yale University)

Currier and Ives, "America," 1870. By this date, the menace has been replaced by the cloying Indian maiden, symbol of the nation. (Library of Congress) was America, neither government, restraint, nor coercion was necessary in human affairs. Locke's golden age, his America—both philosophical concept and visionary ideal—was the vestibule of history, the site of an innocence fated like a bronze mirror to tarnish; it was the European mind's imagined memory of its own state before falsehood, superstition, the rule of arbitrary power had arrived: America as the pristine childhood of mankind.

What the philosopher abstracts as the state of the world before the emergence of property and civil government, other Europeans had already understood for close to two centuries as a more mundane place: a landscape new and strange, seductive in its promise of wealth, and intriguing in its unfamiliar peoples so oddly and enviably at home there. Locke's theoretical "America" evoked sundry accounts of actual initial encounters: These green shores and dark peoples must be what the beginning of the world looked like. In early European allegories of America there were no Americans except the indigenes misnamed Indians. "American" meant native, naked, natural, and, even if savagely so, innocent in the sense of prelapsarian. As Europeans established colonies, settled, birthed children (not infrequently upon native women), and raised families, the idea of the "American" altered in European eyes; persons of European ancestry soon appropriated the very name they had invented for "savages" and claimed for themselves a portion of the nativeness and naturalness of the aboriginals on their continent.

The founding of the new nation, which took to itself the generic name America, added a political meaning: an American now meant a citizen in a particular civil entity. The original Constitution was perfectly clear about who could and who could not claim the status of American citizen. Article I, Section 2 excludes "Indians not taxed" (which seems a tautology) from the category of "free persons" whose numbers determine the apportioning of representatives among the states. "All other persons," that is, enslaved Africans, were to be counted as three-fifths of a person, the consequence of being unfree, not a citizen, not an American, but the personal private property of someone with that status and that title. John Locke's theory of the inviolability of private property and of the "social contract" that protected that right lay behind this cherishing of property in persons over the freedom of persons qua persons. In Locke's conception of the original, pristine "America," there were no slaves, no masters. But in fact Locke helped to justify slavery within the theory of natural rights. He was a shareholder in a slave-trading company, and in 1670 he helped write a constitution for Carolina that said that "every freeman of Carolina shall have absolute power and authority over his Negro slaves."

But how could the philosopher of inalienable human rights and of the social contract designed to protect these rights defend slavery? As David Brion Davis has written, Locke found an escape clause by viewing slavery as "the state of War continued, between a lawful Conqueror and a Captive." Slavery lay, in Davis's words, "entirely outside the social contract." Moreover, the slave bore responsibility for his unfree state; he must have, "by his fault, forfeited his own life, by some act that deserves death." Locke had trapped himself, as Scott Malcomson has put it, "within the psychology of slavery": slavery holds within itself "a suicidal murder," in that by killing himself the slave would also kill the master by taking away his inalienable right to hold property. For both legal and deeper psychological reasons, enslaved African Americans, like Indians (virtually by definition they were "not taxed"), had no claim to the name American.[28]

Unlike blacks, Indians were assigned a key place in the emerging nationalist iconography as tokens of the triumph over savagism. Yet the old tension persisted: obliging maidens and noble savages above; fiendish, merciless demons below. The designation "American" reverberated with alternate and opposite meanings: citizen and indigene, nobleman and demon. In the early years of the republic, the years of popular worship of Daniel Boone and other buck-skinned frontiersmen, patria seemed fraught with paradox. Andrew Jackson's policy of removal of the Indians from the Southeastern states had the extirpation of savages as its commanding justification; in the same years, Currier and Ives depicted dignified and peaceful Indians, a popular image making corresponding to the sentimental heroism of Longfellow's great fiction about the gentle Hiawatha. In the South, where in many regions miscegenation laws were enforced, the claim of bloodline descent from Pocahontas or other Indian princesses was a matter of pride and status, while any sign of African descent could be fatal.[29]

John Vanderlyn (1775–1852), *The Murder of Jane McCrea*, 1804. Oil on canvas, 32½ x 26½ in. (Purchased by the Wadsworth Atheneum, Hartford, Connecticut)

Currier and Ives, "The Indian Family," undated. (Print Collection, Miriam and Ira D. Wallach Division of Art, Prints and Photographs, New York Public Library, Astor, Lenox and Tilden Foundations)

This paradox, an expression of ambivalence, nevertheless confirmed and upheld the basic distinction between red (sometimes taken
for black) and white skins. Indian and American developed as symbiotic but antithetical, each the negative of the other. The relation was
profoundly asymmetrical. Euro-Americans saw themselves as civilized, forward looking, ascendant, Indians as stubbornly backward, unchanging, yet vanishing. In the face of railroads, markets, cities,
military hardware, and Bibles, indigenes were doomed to extinction.
An unspoken reply to the familiar question posed by J. Hector St. John
de Crèvecoeur in 1780, "what, then, is this new man, the American?"
was, everything else aside, "not Indian." Yet "Indianizing," Crèvecoeur
observed, fleeing settlements for unhindered freedom of the woods,
turned the heads of a considerable number of whites; some men and
women (and boys and girls) preferred to remain "unredeemed cap-
tives" and take up an Indian life. Not often did a white's "I am American" mean "I am Indian," but a good many whites either lived or
imagined themselves as living within the paradox of the name. And not
only palefaces: In a speech at the Carlisle Indian School in 1893, Frederick Douglass remarked that "he had, himself, been known as a Negro, but for then and there, he wished to be known as an Indian."[30]

This marked an interesting change in Douglass's public statements
about the relation of Negro to Indian. Heretofore, he had always denied any "cross" with Indians in his own heritage. There is evidence,
though, that he may have been part Indian through his mother, and
he recorded in his writings occasions when he was taken for Indian,
though never, until his Carlisle lecture, did he embrace the term.
Moreover, twenty-four years earlier, in a speech to the mainly white
American Anti-Slavery Society in 1869, he explicitly disassociated
blacks from Indians while opposing the idea of a separate black nation: "If we had set up a separate nationality, gone off on the outer
borders of our civilization, right before your bayonets and swords, we
should have been pushed off, precisely as the Indians have been
pushed off." The fact is, "The negro is more like the white man than
the Indian, in his tastes and tendencies, disposition to accept civilization . . . You do not see him wearing a blanket, but coats cut in the latest European fashion." His comments earned the rebuke of a white

female abolitionist, who warned that he was committing "the same sin that the nation has been committing against his own color."[31]

Why the change in 1893? Douglass's speech on that occasion was one of his standbys, "Self-Made Men." It was a topic that fit nicely with the Carlisle program of training young Indians to give up their tribalism and become "white" in their habits and outlook, their clothing, names, food, and religion—to give up the blanket for European clothing. Appearing in his own conventional attire before native youngsters re-dressed in European-style uniforms, and identifying not only Negro with Indian but also Indian with Negro and thereby with whites, Douglass could well claim the native identity as it was undergoing change (even if coerced) without abandoning his program of full equality with whites for blacks.

The question of "the Indian" in the "making" of "the American" arrived at what seemed a perfect resolution in 1887 with the passage of the General Allotment Act, known as the Dawes Act (after its author, Massachusetts Senator Henry Dawes). When Congress ruled in 1871 that native peoples would no longer be recognized as "nations" eligible to make treaties with the United States but only as "wards" of the federal government, terrible questions arose about their fate. Extermination? Starvation? What about their lands already reserved by treaty and special acts of Congress? Promises had been made reaching back to the early years of the nation that the government would provide schools, goods, protection from encroaching white settlers, in other words, that "wardship" would have its benefits. The beauty of the Dawes Act was that here, finally, seemed a peaceful solution; allotment would accomplish two great goals at once: It would "civilize" the Indians, and it would open more of their lands to legal occupation by white settlers, both migrants and immigrants. The act authorized the president to survey tribal reservations, divide the land into sections, and assign these sections or lots to individual tribal members willing to take them up. Any land left over would be put to sale outside the tribe, part of the earnings to be used for "the education and civilization" of the respective tribes. Communal lands would be no more. Ultimately, supporters of the act believed that Indians themselves, having "adopted the habits of civilized life" and been rewarded with American citizenship, would be no more qua Indians. Allotment would dissolve the tribal base, make communal land and resources private, would put each Indian head of family on his or her own, and thereby, with the help of school and church, make Americans of them: the making of Americans by the unmaking of Indians.

In October of the same year, a fifty-seven-year-old local physician with a literary flair published an article in the *Seattle Sunday Star* that put a different though cognate gloss on the question of Indians and Americans. Thirty-three years earlier, in 1854, a Dwamish chief named Sea'thl (Seattle) had given a speech, Dr. Henry A. Smith informed his readers, welcoming a new commissioner of Indian affairs to the newly established Washington Territory. The speech, Smith recounted—he said he heard it and took notes, though it was not known that he understood the language—was destined to become one of the most celebrated of Indian orations. But a cloud of uncertainty hangs over it. Did the event described by Smith really occur? Was there ever a "Chief Seattle's Speech"? Was it reconstructed from fragments of memory and lore or invented out of whole cloth? Whether imagined or remembered, fiction or fact, Smith's 1887 version has its compelling moments. It concludes with a haunting refrain, as if an antiphonal response to Catlin's dire prophecy, a prophecy of haunting:

> And when the last red Man shall have perished, and the memory of my tribe shall have become a myth among the White Men, these shores will swarm with the invisible dead of my tribe, and when your children's children think themselves alone in the field, the store, the shop, along the highway, or in the silence of the pathless woods, they will not be alone . . . At night when the streets of your cities and villages are silent and you think them deserted, they will throng with the returning hosts that once filled them and still love this beautiful land. The White Man will never be alone. Let him be just and deal kindly with my people, for the dead are not altogether powerless.

What the Dawes Act imagined to extirpate, Smith recuperated: the magical spirit of Indian tribalism. It was as if "the triumphant ghost of the race," as Constance Rourke has written of another event, "imposed itself upon the conquerors in spite of the continued struggle and defeat."[32]

The words evoke Dwamish beliefs that the dead are not really dead but somewhere nearby, still inhabiting their place of abode. Smith's version may ring true, but it also rings as a hope and a wish, a white ventriloquist using the voice of an Indian orator and for particular local reasons. Smith belonged by generation and social class to the "propertied elite," one author has written, "that liked to call itself 'Old Seattle.'" In 1887 this group felt itself in a situation they imagined was similar to that faced by the old and by now legendary Chief Seattle. "They had run the town for decades, but by the mid 1880s they were losing power to a growing working class and to a class of urbane professionals and entrepreneurs who styled themselves as 'New Seattle.'" In 1885–86 there were anti-Chinese riots, and in 1886 radical populists won power and threatened the rule of the "dog-salmon aristocrats." Smith wrote a series of "pioneer reminiscences" for the newspaper, of which the Chief Seattle article was number ten. Was this an effort to create a mythic past and a native version of King Arthur who could lend legitimacy and hope for survival to beleaguered "Old Seattle"?[33]

If ventriloquism, the speech rings even more with paradoxical implication. In light of the Dawes Act's intended annihilation of native culture, these words put in Sea'thl's mouth offer the comfort of a double-sided assurance, that the red man will vanish but not really vanish, will disappear and yet remain as disembodied genius loci, harmless to alter the course of events. Having Indians promise that they will dissolve into ghosts, into shades, fulfills two wishes at once—that they will vanish from the land and yet continue to inhabit it as spirits of place—and expresses the perverse wish for a haunted "virgin land." Indeed, the landscape of the nation already echoed with Indian music of Indian presence. "A prodigality of fine melodious names remains," wrote one historian in 1893, "the best legacy which the unlettered red man could leave us before he vanished forever before the march of civilization."[34] It was and remains a legacy constructed of accumulated acts of will, a deliberate construction of an indigenous substra-

tum of names and memories for the nation. Names on the land make
prophecy come true: "The White Man will never be alone."

The perhaps not entirely coincidental appearance in 1887 of the
visions of Dawes and of Smith/Sea'thl registers the persistent contradiction: "We" (white immigrant "Americans") want "them" (native
"Americans") to go away by becoming us, but not really go away.
Becoming American, they abide with us; we become partly them. If
you stood inside the belief system of the expanding nation, this odd
ambivalence would have seemed perfectly natural. It was a way of
annihilating Indians by fetishizing their difference, denying their independent existence, their own inwardness, and most especially their
tribalism, the profound oneness of their political and cultural nationality. They have been "totemized in legend," Louis Hartz wrote, as the
Mayflower voyage has been "celebrated but forgotten because not in
the nature of things relived." Removed, separated, forgotten, or disembodied as an active force in the shaping of U.S. history, the "Indian
experience" wants recovery, Hartz argued in *The Founding of New
Societies* (1964). Now, after countries in Africa and Asia had freed
themselves from colonial domination, "we find ourselves amid cultures where the aborigine has played roles of a different nature." In
this new circumstance, the "continuous significance" of "the Indian
experience" to the self-image and self-knowledge of the nation should
be identified and "relived" in its "operative significance for the culture
as a whole." Hartz predicted that "the history of the American Indian
will rise markedly in importance" as the changing world situation, the
rise of newly independent nations among former colonies of European imperial powers, encourages a "comparative view of United
States history."[35]

The allotment era, which lasted until Franklin Roosevelt's New
Deal reversed it in 1934, coincided for the most part with the era of
"open door" immigration, which ended with the imposed quotas of
the National Origins Act of 1924. The great wave of "aliens" entering
the nation—twenty-three million between 1890 and 1920—added an
important perspective on the "operative significance" of Indian history to national history. Non-Protestant and non-Anglophone immigrants from Eastern and Southern Europe brought an epochal infusion

of strangeness into the predominantly white Anglo-Saxon (mostly Anglophone) Protestant nation. The new immigrants poured into America's cities, making them seem even larger, more crowded, more "foreign" in a culture whose official rhetoric still cherished memories of small towns and farms and pristine landscapes as the basis of nationality. Sprawling factories mushroomed in these years, and city slums loud with strange tongues gave the big cities an air of alien menace. Soon the internal migration of African Americans from the South into Northern and Midwestern cities added to the demographic upheaval. Fueling the sense of momentous change were the emerging megacorporations, a new scale of business power, and the beginnings of imperial military power first displayed in Cuba and the Philippines in the 1890s and early 1900s.

For Indians this was an "age of attrition," in the words of the native historian and novelist D'Arcy McNickle, rather than expansion.[36] Pressed onto reservations ruled by agents of the federal Bureau of Indian Affairs, demoralized by the assault on their tribal cultures, their defeat constantly brought home to them by poverty, disease, surveillance, and the daily humiliations of reservation life, Indians stood outside the norms of national urban existence. Yet this same age of attrition saw a new spurt of public monuments commemorating Indian heroes, the staging of Wild West shows, and the renaming of Indians as "first Americans." The paradoxical logic of Dawes-Sea'thl remained in play, and efforts to incorporate Indians and Indianness into the national emotion abounded. As early as the Boston Tea Party, putting on feathers and paint had been a way of testing an imaginary middle-ground identity. Indian dress, Indian crafts, Indian rituals were further emblems of both defiance and affirmation. And an obverse mirror image appeared in the games and roles scripted for natives themselves to play in the Wild West shows, traditional native roles now recuperated as performance and spectacle. It was a way of their becoming American by acting out their role as ancestors of the nation. For a new immigrant, Indians decked out as first Americans offered pedagogy in Americanization, a chance to imagine for oneself, as a spectator of popular theater and a consumer of images, the new identity of American. For both performer and spectator, native and newcomer, being American was dramatized as a process of becoming, of shedding one identity for another; this transformation was denied to African Americans, whose dark skin was taken as a permanent stigma, like the spots of the leopard.

The initiatory experience of becoming American by becoming Indian appeared nowhere more sharply etched than in Frederick Jackson Turner's 1893 paper on "The Significance of the Frontier in American History." Turner's essay belongs among other efforts at the time, like the Dawes Act, to reconceive the meaning of "Americanization." New circumstances in the 1890s, the announced "closing" of the frontier, the growing numbers of immigrants, and (though this appears only in sublimated form in Turner's paper) new social tensions arising from the proletarianization of immigrant groups called for a new look at how "the American" came into being. Turner told his story—the romance elements were self-evident—of "perennial rebirth along a continually advancing frontier line" explicitly as that of the making of Americans or, more precisely, Euro-Americans. The "common traits" of "American intellect," he argued, had to be acquired rather than inherited. If America was initially a European idea, a Lockean firstness imagined as Indian, and if the term then became the name for a non-Indian, white European nationality embodied in a political nation (with a significant nonwhite subaltern population excluded), an explanation was needed for how the process of white nationalization worked. How did colonizer and settler come to possess those "common traits"? The list is famous: "that practical, inventive turn of mind . . . masterful grasp of material things . . . dominant individualism . . . buoyancy and exuberance." Turner's thesis assumed that rather than being born into Americanness, one acquired it. American identity was an acquisition. "These are traits," he writes, "of the frontier."

Turner told the story in cadences of mythic romance and as a heroic tale of journey and quest and challenges overcome.

The frontier is the line of most rapid and effective Americanization. The wilderness masters the colonist. It finds him a European in dress, industries, tools, modes of travel, and thought. It takes him from the railroad car and puts him in the birch canoe.

It strips off the garments of civilization and arrays him in the hunting shirt and the moccasin. It puts him in the log cabin of the Cherokee and Iroquois and runs an Indian palisade around him. Before long he has gone to planting Indian corn and plowing with a sharp stick; he shouts the war cry and takes scalp in orthodox Indian fashion. In short, at the frontier the environment is at first too strong for the man. He must accept the conditions which it furnishes, or perish, and so he fits himself into the Indian clearings and follows the Indian trails. Little by little he transforms the wilderness, but the outcome is not the old Europe . . . The fact is, that here is a new product that is American.

It always surprises us to be reminded that the originating act of Turner's imagined American is the act of becoming Indian, which is repressed in the subsequent and more explicitly Americanizing moments: "little by little he transforms the wilderness." The wilderness's initial mastery of the pioneer is overcome and its transformation means dispossession of natives, seizure and plunder of their lands. It means reversing the original order—expropriating natives, becoming their masters. Before long, as the Americanizing narrative proceeds, Indians pose "a common danger, demanding united action." Each successive frontier "was won by a series of Indian wars." With "security" against Indians a major concern, the frontier becomes "a military training school, keeping alive the power of resistance to aggression." Indians have become aggressors, an alien force in their own land. The frontiersman becomes a warrior, a killer, turning his guns against his former brothers and sisters of the birch canoe and log cabin—against his own former self as Indian.[37]

The tortured logic of American identity in Turner's frontier thesis projects a peculiar fatality. Each moment subtends the other: to identify as Indian, to transcend (or "master") that identity in order to achieve another, to become sovereign of a domain, to be American. The logic of identity follows the logic of conquest: 1890 marked simultaneously the closing of the frontier and, at Wounded Knee, a decisive blow against the remnants of Indian resistance on the plains. This is the nationalizing process Turner imagined, what Richard Slotkin has memorably named "regeneration through violence."[38]

Describing "the Indian frontier as a consolidating agent in our history," Turner had surprisingly little to say about Indians themselves. They seemed to matter only in relation to the invading settlers, mediators of nationality in the process of stripping away the "garments of civilization," then as obstacles to "mastery." In the historian Richard White's words, "On Turner's frontier Indians were not so much absent as peripheral to the meaning of his narrative."[39] It's as if Indians belonged more to the terrain than to history, as if they were features of the landscape. In an 1891 lecture on "American Colonization," Turner said as much: "The aborigines were to have a profound effect upon the colonization of America. They as well as the mountains and river valleys would determine the lines of advance."[40] This shoving of natives to the margins, making them part of geography, defined their role in Turner's story of nationality. They represented the Lockean "state of nature" quite literally, the overcoming of which produced the "composite nationality for the American people." This was the crux of the narrative, and in telling his frontier story, Turner had one eye screwed tight on Ellis Island.

Turner imagined settlement as a wave, with the ritual of becoming American reenacted at each successive "line" between civilization and noncivilization, the latter being the realm of nature and the Indian. The new immigrants also seemed to come in successive waves. He worried that settlement would outpace immigration, that with the "closing of the frontier" the nation faced a dangerous predicament. "In the crucible of the frontier," he wrote, "the immigrants were Americanized, liberated, and fused into a mixed race, English in neither nationality nor characteristic."[41] Turner believed in the composite character of American identity, a kind of Enlightenment cosmopolitanism, but the exhaustion of "free land" eliminated the site where this Americanized identity could be formed.

In a series of articles published in 1901 in the Chicago *Herald-Tribune*, he wrote,

Since 1860, a change has been in progress. The south and east of Europe have risen in importance, while England, Ireland and Germany have declined . . . It is obvious that the replacement of the German and British immigration by southern Italians, Poles, Russian Jews and Slovaks is a loss to the social organism of the United States. But the free lands that made the process of absorption easy have gone. The immigration is becoming more difficult of assimilation.[42]

Indians had been "mastered," in a kind of "absorption," during the process of settlement, but Slavs, Jews, and other non-WASPs were another matter. Restriction of immigration, a measure Turner supported, was one solution. Different methods of Americanization offered another, and in educational programs designed for new immigrants, Indians will again appear, as if in compensation for loss of the frontier, key players in the symbolic drama of "forging" a "composite" national identity.

Turner was little concerned with "Americanizing" the Indians themselves. While they served the purpose of inaugurating the process of becoming national in the initial frontier transaction, Indians seemed forever, statuelike, on a rise overlooking the wagon trains and then the railroads pushing ineluctably west with towns and the schoolhouses in their wake. In memories of his childhood in Portage, Wisconsin, Turner recalled Indians on their ponies coming into town; once he stumbled upon an Indian family bathing in the river. In his schema of frontier history, they are frozen in such remembered postures, haunting, ghostlike images of irreversible otherness.[43] The Dawes Act had the same image of Indians as outside the composite nation yet portrayed them as capable of being brought inside. Like Turner, Dawes and other "Friends of the Indians" were troubled by the new immigrants who introduced a menacing heterogeneity and heteroglossia to American cities. In devices such as allotment and boarding schools, these reformers crystallized a picture of the model American that could be transferred to all aliens. Indians would be cajoled or coerced by threat of harm at the hands of Indian haters to assimilate for their own good: Join us or die. Immigrants—Europeans with dark skin and Asians—would be induced by less severe means to accept a similar conformity. Indians were pictured in the reform literature as strangers whose claim to civic identity needed to be earned and proved. The Dawes Act proclaimed "that every Indian born within the territorial limits of the United States who has voluntarily taken up within said limits his residence, separate and apart from any tribe of Indians, and has adopted the habits of civilized life is hereby declared to be a citizen of the United States."[44] The reward, as for naturalized immigrants, was citizenship, a certificate of belonging to American society.[45]

The goal of the Dawes policy was double sided: to raise individual natives from primitivism and at the same time to open unalloted tribal land to white settlement and allotted land to white purchase from individual Indians. The United States stood to gain new productive citizens and many square miles ceded to the public domain or to the free market. Transference of land was no small intention of the "severalty" policy. Two motives worked hand in glove: to wrest lawfully as much rich Indian land as possible for private "white" use, and by opposing communal ownership to make private property seem an essential part of civilized life, a fundamental tenet of "the American." The beauty of the allotment policy, as Davis saw it, was that it would demonstrate the fallacies of both tribal communalism and proletarian socialism or anarchism (which the "undesirable foreigners" were thought to advocate) while "opening" Indian lands for sale, speculation, and exploitation. The allotment policy was enacted at the time of workers' demonstrations and strikes demanding eight-hour workdays in the late 1880s and the Haymarket bombing in Chicago in 1886; fear of radicals ran high, and it took only a small leap to conflate bomb-throwing "Reds" and tomahawk-wielding "redmen" as equal threats to the social order. "Such foreign savages," wrote one New York newspaper in 1886, "with their dynamite bombs and anarchic purposes, are as much apart from the rest of the people in this country as the Apaches of the plains are."[46] At a conference of the Friends of the Indians in 1885, Henry Dawes made the link explicit, if in less hysterical language. "They have got as far as they can go," he announced regarded communal ownership and cooperative existence, "because they hold their land in common. It is [the Socialist writer] Henry George's system, and under that there is no enterprise to make your home any better than that of your neighbors."[47] Allotment proposed an anodyne affirmation of market capitalism and nationalism, converting Indians into model Americans while refuting the proposed alternatives to private property and market capitalism. The lesson was not lost on some agrarian radicals and populists, who joined with natives in a vigorous but futile campaign against the Dawes Act. Between 1887 and 1934, when the policy was reversed, 90 million of 138 million acres of Indian land were alienated from Indian hands and much of it opened for settlement: a not insignificant economic resource for the expanding white nation.

Dawes, then, names more than a particular policy; it is an outlook, an ideology. As freeholders, Indians would learn to think of themselves no longer as tribal Indians but as national Americans, individuals whose goal was to "rise." Horatio Alger was proffered as the model for survival. Native children in off-reservation boarding schools would be taught "character"; like Ragged Dick they would climb or fall by their own efforts. They would learn this new way of thinking, this need to look out for themselves, by the hard knocks of the street and the market. "Kill the Indian to save the man" was the famous slogan of Captain Richard H. Pratt, founder and first director of the Carlisle Indian School in Pennsylvania and a favorite speaker at annual meetings of the Friends of the Indian. Let's not mourn the loss of the picturesque in tribal life, loved so much by sentimentalists, missionaries, anthropologists like Frank Cushing[48] (who lived among the Zunis and urged them to preserve their traditional ways), and proprietors of Wild West shows like Buffalo Bill; the only route to salvation is the American way: individualist, independent, competitive manhood. Justice demands, and liberalism and the constitutional principle of equality insist that Indians have their hair shorn, their names changed, their language abolished, their dances forbidden, their medicine men ridiculed. Coercion is necessary and just.

Indian and immigrant often appeared together in Pratt's arguments for his school. If immigrants are good enough to be made over into Americans, why not Indians? They can be as easily educated and developed industrially. "Men of all nations and every quality invited into the national family and promptly utilized and clothed with its freedom and citizenship until the influx reaches a million a year, more than three times as many in one year as all of our Indians, always here and yet denied these privileges. Did ever 'straining at a gnat and swallowing a camel' have a more perfect illustration of inconsistency?" More than five million immigrants passed through Castle Garden (the New York point of entry before the opening of Ellis Island) between 1880 and 1890, he noted, "twenty-one foreigners for every Indian! The foreigners made Americans and citizens by being invited, urged, and compelled to that consummation by their surroundings. The Indians remain Indians because they are walled in on reservations and compelled by every force we can apply even to the hedging about with guns, pistols and swords to remain Indians." Suppose the foreigners were segregated by nationality on reservations, would they make any progress "in becoming Anglicized and Americanized"? True, foreigners may "give us trouble" but only when allowed to congregate together: "Massed in communities by themselves they, more or less, oppose the principles and the spirit of our government." What we don't allow for foreigners, reservations or ghettos as breeding grounds of hostility, we ought not allow for Indians.[49]

Calling for integration in place of segregation, Pratt looked to the dispersion of foreignness and thus its dissolution as the model for Indians. He recounted the case he made to Secretary of Interior Carl Schurz in 1878 on behalf of an Indian school:

> "You yourself, sir, are one of the very best examples of what we ought to do for the Indian. You immigrated to America as an individual to escape oppression in your own country. You came into fullest freedom in our country. You associated with our people, the best of them, and through these chances you became an American general during the Civil War, then a United States senator, and are now in the President's cabinet, one of the highest offices in the land. It would have been impossible for you to have accomplished your elevation if, when you came to this country, you had been reserved in any of the solid German communities we have permitted to grow up in some sections of America. The Indians need the chances of participation you have had and they will just as easily become useful citizens."[50]

The immigrant experience, as Pratt portrays it, with Schurz as the typical case, mediated the Indian's eligibility as potential recipient of the gifts of Americanness.

It's as if Simard's "mad duo coupled in a dark embrace" fused into a unitary figure: the outsider knocking at the gate. It's also as if race was no barrier; indeed, Pratt's republican outlook was nobly free of overt racism. Not so with some natives prominent in the Society of American Indians (founded in 1911), who worried about the "mingling of the races" and possible "miscegenation" among black and Indian students at the Hampton Institute. Arthur C. Parker wrote in 1916 of the Negro's "natural servility and imitativeness," in contrast to the independence and pride of race of Indians.[51] Pratt's resolute environmentalism—his belief that training trumps biology—freed him from conventional prejudice and from speciously scientific theories about race. Take "the negroes," he wrote, once "savages of a very lower state when brought to this country," now "English speaking and fellow citizens." "The 'curse of slavery,'" he said in a speech in 1912, "taught usefulness, made their lives valuable and gave American citizenship to the negroes."[52] An odd view of slavery as beneficial, but like Booker T. Washington urging vocational training for blacks, Pratt envisioned Indians learning useful crafts and trades as an honorable way into the American social order—at the bottom, to be sure, but with hopes of rising. "The Negro was under great prejudice by his change in the South from slavery to freedom under circumstances destructive to the resources and wealth of the Southern people," he wrote, but "the training he was given during slavery . . . made him individual, English speaking, and capable industrially." Indians instead were "driven away" from "our communities" and held "prisoner on reservations." Yet Indians have the capacity "in every way to meet the issues of civilized life at once."[53]

A "Course of Study for the Indian Schools of the United States," published by the government in 1901, shows what these issues were thought to be. The emphasis fell on teaching the native child to be "a willing worker," which required not only "practical knowledge" but also "good habits, self-control, application, and responsiveness." Traits of "character" surpassed such trivial matters as "definitions and unimportant dates" in the remaking of Indians into laborers and entrepreneurs. Teachers were instructed to teach that "nature study and agriculture are very closely related," that one must "watch the face of nature" to know what the weather is, that seeds need to be planted, and that money earned by selling crops gets put into a bank account. As for "History": "Always seek to create a spirit of love and brotherhood in the minds of the children toward the white people, and in telling them the history of the Indians dwell on those things which have shown nobility of character on the part of either race in dealings with the other." Not too much detail, though; instead, "a general view." The Indians should learn enough history "to be good, patriotic citizens," and "a few important dates, such as that of the discovery of America . . . and the birthdays of great men like Lincoln, Washington and Longfellow." "Pay all debts, and own property": These seem the cardinal goals.[54]

Pratt and other Friends of the Indians thought of themselves as protectors of natives against thieves, assassins, rum dealers, and unscrupulous land speculators. They proposed to "uplift" Indians by extinguishing distinctions that constituted Indianness, the major one being that alone among the nation's marginal groups, native tribes still possessed a land base, albeit terribly eroded, within the borders of the United States. And by virtue of old treaties at least a glimmer of tribal sovereignty survived. In their earnestness, the Friends of the Indians lacked only a sense of irony and were unable to see anything odd about their campaign to "Americanize" the original inhabitants of the place they called America. Nor did they see the irony of the very term "Americanize," first coined in England in the early nineteenth century as a term of derogation for a kind of sensational journalism. Nor did they recognize that, while liberal and enlightened in assuming a universal human capacity for emancipation, they were going against the grain of liberal democracy by basing citizenship on an acculturation test, raising a cultural norm for what the Constitution deemed an ordinary political act. And by requiring a display of "competence" as proof of eligibility for citizenship, by stressing appearance and self-representation, their policy insinuated a potentially subversive note, suggesting that Americanness might be more a performance, a calculated role, than a set of "common traits."

Unidentified photographer, "Dilos Lonewolf, Before and After," c. 1880. (Richard
Henry Pratt Papers, Yale Collection of Western Americana, Beinecke Rare Book and Manuscript Library)

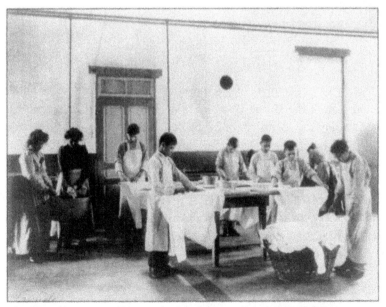

Frances Benjamin Johnson, "Laundry Class, Carlisle Indian School,"
c. 1900–03. (Library of Congress)

In many ways the entire policy made theater out of Americaniza-
tion. To drum up moral and financial support for the Carlisle School,
Pratt often put his charges on the stage to show their newly acquired
American skills. Here's his account of one occasion:

> While rehearsing the girl's industrial scene, a Cheyenne girl
> named Carline, big and stout, who was to manage the wash
> tub, refused to act her part, and I was asked to come and help
> get her in motion. She simply stood by the washing tub in si-
> lence and refused to begin. Realizing her feelings, I said: "Car-
> line, don't you know that cleanliness is next to Godliness?" "You
> have one of the most interesting places in the whole exhibit. A
> woman's duty is to keep her home and family clean." She said
> not a word, but whirled around and cheerfully commenced
> preparations and after that was activity personified.[55]

Turner had the European go native to become American; Pratt
staged the native going American through servility. Unrecognized
paradox took its toll in the death of irony.

III

In July 1919, Secretary of the Interior Franklin K. Lane wrote to the
chairman of the House Committee on Indian Affairs that "granting
citizenship to Indians" should be based entirely and solely "upon the
fact that they are real Americans, and are of right entitled to citizenship."[56] Barely a generation earlier Congress had sanctioned the quite
different view of the General Allotment Act, linking the formal identification of natives as Americans to a fundamental change in the
character of their lives. Take up a piece of land as your own, not your
tribe's, not collectively owned but personally owned, and you are in.
The General Allotment Act notably revised though did not entirely
reverse Chief Justice John Marshall's landmark decision of 1831 that
the Cherokees inhabiting lands designated by the state of Georgia as
part of its sovereign domain "be denominated dependent domestic
nations."[57] Native tribes were not exactly foreign nations, but neither

were they properly speaking American: partly tribes with limited sovereignty over their members and territories, partly "wards" of the United States government, linked to the central government by ties of dependency. By this definition, the federal government endowed the indigenous population with a unique status in the nation: Indians were recognized as a group, an ethnicity, rather than as a collection of autonomous individuals. The recognition of limited sovereignty that continues to this day derives from concessions made by the United States in exchange for land transfers in countless treaties with the native nations that spelled out the limits and rights of tribal sovereignty. Remaining rights of sovereignty fell short of full jurisdictional equality with the federal government, however. As Eric Cheyfitz writes, "Indians [are] the only group of people in the United States who are governed by a distinct body of law," and that law perpetuates their status as colonial dependents in a "trust" relation to the federal government.[58]

Prior to the Citizenship Act of 1924, the conception of citizenship as a right of individuals rather than groups meant that the government had to separate Indians from their tribe before it could recognize even the conceptual possibility of their individual citizenship.[59] The Dawes Act attempted to clarify this equivocal situation—what one scholar describes as "the paradoxical concept of a people within the territory of the new nation and yet outside the processes of its political life"—by defining them as potential Americans;[60] all they needed to do was to separate themselves from the "dependent domestic nations" that gave them their tribal names and take up what Congress called "the habits of civilized life." Citizenship for Indians was conceived as the external form of an internal condition, the achievement of "habits" assumed to represent real Americanness. Not that they would cease to be "Indian" according to what was understood as their "race," but they would cease to be "Indian" in the sense of "savage," "uncivilized," or, in a term that appeared in early-twentieth-century legislation, "incompetent." A "competent" Indian was one who could prove himself to a Bureau of Indian Affairs board of examiners capable of taking care of his property, including selling or leasing it outside the tribe, that is, to whites.[61] Until 1924 citizenship required proof of "competency," evidence that the Indian had expunged enough Indianness to deserve legal recognition as a full civic American (although certificates of competency were often distributed rather freely, to facilitate more speedy sale or leasing of tribal lands). According to law, Indians remained incomplete or perhaps unreal Americans until such proof was properly registered. As the promoters of competency in Americanness, at least in taking care of personal property (i.e., money in the bank), the Bureau of Indian Affairs saw its task as preparing tribal peoples for holistic transformation into Americans.

In 1916 on the Yankton reservation in South Dakota, Secretary Lane presided over a citizenship ceremony designed by the Indian agent James McLaughlin.

The Secretary stands before one of the candidates and says:—

"Joseph T. Cook, what is your Indian name?"

"Tunkansapa," answers the Indian.

"Tunkansapa, I hand you a bow and arrow. Take this bow and shoot the arrow."

The Indian does so.

"Tunkansapa, you have shot your last arrow. That means you are no longer to live the life of an Indian. You are from this day forward to live the life of the white man. But you may keep that arrow. It will be a symbol of your noble race and of the pride you may feel that you come from the first Americans."

Addressing Tunkansapa by his white name: "Joseph T. Cook, take in your hands this plough."

Cook does so. "This act means that you have chosen to live the life of the white man. The white man works by work. From the earth we must all get our living, and the earth will not yield unless man pours upon it the sweat of his brow." Next comes the flag and the recitation: "I now promise this flag that I will give my hands, my head, and my heart to the doing of all that will make me a true American citizen." Finally, a badge showing an American eagle clutching the flag and the words "A Citizen of the United States." It goes a bit different for women, who get purses and workbags and a separate spiel: "This means that you have chosen the life of the white woman—and the white woman loves her home. The family and the home are the foundation of our civilization. Upon the character and industry of the mother and home-maker largely depends the future of our nation. The purse will always say to you that the money that you gain from your labor must be wisely kept. The wise woman saves her money."[62]

In such ceremonies and performances one's political nationality was defined as identical to a cultural nationality, a belief system distilled as a pure essence from a dream of white middle-class life.

In 1893 at the World's Columbian Exposition in Chicago, where Turner read his frontier paper, Simon Pokagon, an elderly Pottawatami chief whose tribe once occupied the lakeshore of what had become Chicago, was invited to help open the fair by ringing a replica of the Liberty Bell and giving an oration. There's something murky about the event. A pamphlet, "The Red Man's Greeting," survives as the text of his speech. This ventriloquized conciliation could have been written by a Friend of the Indians: "We must give up the pursuits of our fathers . . . Our children must learn that they owe no allegiance to any clan or power on earth except the United States. They must learn to love the Stars and Stripes, and, at all times to rejoice that they are American citizens." But, strangely, the address was described at the time by a Chicago professor as "The Red Man's Book of Lamentations." Recently another text has surfaced, written on birch bark and titled "The Red Man's Rebuke." This one, in an angry tone, reads as a rebuttal of the Turner thesis. In the eyes of the native, it says, "the pale-faced race . . . has usurped our lands and homes . . . The cyclone of civilization rolled westward; the forests of untold centuries were swept away; streams dried up; lakes fell back from their ancient bounds; and all our fathers once loved to gaze upon was destroyed, defaced, or marred, except the sun, moon, and starry skies above, which the Great Spirit in his wisdom hung beyond their reach."[63] The Friends of the Indians often evoked a similar vision of catastrophe but with a different purpose in mind. As nature fell under more complete control of civilization, they warned, natives would find their natural sources of sustenance depleted. The need to choose was urgent: Become civilized and American, or die.

Pokagon has been described as a rather questionable figure whose writings, including a novel touted as the earliest native work of fiction in the United States, may have been written by his white editor. One historian calls him "the white man's kind of Indian," another "an archetype celebrity Indian." Apparently self-seeking and ambitious for fame and wealth (he secretly sold off his tribe's claim to shorefront property in Chicago), he was distrusted and shunned by his tribe but taken up and cultivated by patrons among the grandes dames of the Friends of the Indians. He was their favorite Alger-like success story, a model "of Christian smoke-free temperance for the uncouth lower-class immigrant elements of American society." The painted Indian happily embracing his identity as "first American" was dished up as a mediator of Americanness for backward and "uncouth" immigrants. The lesson of this muddled story is that a symbiosis of ideology was needed at the site of the great national celebration in 1893 for which Turner's utterance served as conceptual keynote: the staging of a native rebuke as part of a performance of what it takes to become American, loyal at once to flag and to feathers, to the United States, and to the imagined freedom of life in the woods.[64]

This flimsy charade persisted in pageants and spectacles for several decades: a troupe of native players at the Hampton Institute in Virginia traveled about singing and dancing *The Song of Hiawatha* in concert halls around the country, Ojibway performers of "their" national epic held annual performances in Michigan, and Pottawatami children did the same at the Haskell Indian School in Kansas. In 1909 the John Wanamaker Department Store staged in Montana "the last great tribal council," where revered old chiefs said their farewell, and in another installment of the same show in 1913, Indians were posed before the camera kissing the hem of the American flag in a ragged ceremony put on the road and performed again and again on reservations across the country. Like Buffalo Bill's Wild West Show, the Wanamaker Expeditions dressed their players in buckskin and regalia, symbols of that "wildness" Turner imagined as the catalytic moment of "rebirth." The Wanamakers also set in motion a campaign (it would fail after a grandiose groundbreaking extravaganza in 1913) to raise a monument to "the Vanishing Red" on Staten Island, a gigantic

Unidentified photographer, "Hiawatha #1, Chief," 1909. (Library of Congress)

bronze warrior taller than the Statue of Liberty and closer to the mouth of New York harbor, performing a sign of welcome. These were all phases of the same remaking of alien natives into model Americans, models for those immigrant aliens whose multilingual and multicultural impact on the meaning of American seemed more menacing than the threat once posed by the intractable savage. Lift him up, they said, so all can see what the "first," the "true" (and now truly nationalized) American looks like: the red man before he vanished or got shoved down the manhole. This figure, a construction of the white imagination and filling the need for a contemporary romance of nationality, resembles nothing so much as a shade of the old storybook familiar, Longfellow's ever-recurring Hiawatha.

ONE

Singing Hiawatha

———•———

We wait in the darkness!
Come, all ye who listen,
Help in our night journey:
Now no sun is shining;
Now no star is glowing
Come show us the pathway:
The night is not friendly;
She closes her eyelids;
The moon has forgot us,
We wait in the darkness!
—Darkness Song (Iroquois)

A man who is possessed by his shadow is always standing in his own light
and falling into his own trap.   —Carl Jung, *Four Archetypes*

Whether or not Chief Sea'thl ever said "The White Man will never be alone," the words ring true as someone's wish. A curious, sadly comic history of having "the Indian" nearby is told in a steady antebellum flow of white actors performing Indians on stage and in print: Pocahontas, Metamora, Uncas, and Chingachook, and the crowning figure of the tradition, Longfellow's companionable Hiawatha. Distinctions between real and imagined characters evaporate; the historical Metamora or Metacom, known to his seventeenth-century Puritan adversaries as King Phillip, became on stage as fictive as Longfellow's celebrated hero. Except for a few antebellum memoirs and essays by natives such as Black Hawk, William Apes, and George Copway (Kah-ge-ga-gah'-bowh), white authors and audiences set the terms whereby indigenes returned as shades of memory and myth. The settler culture, creating the Indian in the image of its own needs, haunted itself with ghosts of its own making.

And with no more charming a ghost than Longfellow's misnamed Hiawatha, the most congenial of all the white man's Indians. While his name is that of an actual figure, the legendary Mohawk founder of the Iroquois Confederation, the better-known Hiawatha was born in Longfellow's poem as a transfigured version of a mythical Ojibway culture-hero known by various names including Manabozho, which Longfellow did not find melodious. Almost at once Longfellow's *Hiawatha* leaped from page to stage, from print to performance and worldwide fame. Its popularity and prestige reached a new level in the United States at the turn of the century in pageants, staged spectacles, song and dance, and drama performed by natives of many tribes, a pan-Indian fusion event. By the early twentieth century, the poem had been translated into virtually all the world's languages, including Latin, Hebrew, Ojibway, and Yiddish; it had become a "Universal Hiawatha."[1] The reemergence of Longfellow's living ghost in these unsettled years we can take as keynote of the transformation of "Indian" into "first American."

I

An exuberant reception greeted the appearance of *The Song of Hiawatha* in Boston bookshops in November 1855. In the first six months about fifty thousand copies crossed the counter, matching the record-breaking sales of an American book five years earlier, *Uncle Tom's Cabin*, a work with which it shared certain affinities: liberality of emotion, grandeur of effect, national cogency—and readability. Shortly before the poem's publication, the nation's and soon the world's best-loved poet, Henry Wadsworth Longfellow, had resigned his post as professor of modern languages at Harvard and soon became the first poet in America's history to earn a living from writing alone. He hardly needed the wealth of his wife's family, the mill-owning Appletons, after they made him a wedding gift of his spacious

Cambridge house.[2] Further fame and glory and riches awaited him. "An unprecedented success for a poem," he remarked with obvious delight over initial sales figures.[3]

The success of *The Song of Hiawatha*, interestingly, owed something to a flutter of controversy in the form of parodies, attacks on the poem's moral weight as a mere "Indian" poem and, more pointedly, on its originality and authenticity. "Showers of parodies and shots of ridicule," as one reviewer wrote, only called attention to the poem and gave it a chance to prove itself against detractors. "The book has been fortunate in having excited controversy," another reviewer remarked, "whereby hundreds have been led to examine it from pure curiosity, and then, as a natural consequence, been won by its charming pictures and sustained euphony."[4] Controversy played into the hands of the poem.

A popular theory about poetry, partly as a result of Longfellow's own teaching and writing, underlay the praise of "charming pictures and sustained euphony": an assumption that by pictures and verbal images rendered in harmonious sound and regular meter, great poetry captures the reader with a soothing sense of the real. To the "regret" expressed in the Boston *Daily Evening Traveller* "that our own pet national poet should not have selected as the theme of his muse something higher and better than the silly legends of the savage aborigines," and to the charge of plagiarism in the *National Intelligencer*, which found resemblance to the Finnish Kalewala" [*sic*] ("the poem is only an imitation, not a creation"), another reviewer defended the poem as both "original and aboriginal all over": "Through the whole structure there is the smell of the wild woods, the dash of forest waters and lakes, and the sweetest beauty of bird, and flower, and sky, in their wilderness state." The review hailed "Hiawatha as the greatest contribution yet made to the native literature of our country." "Native" linked to "wild woods" and to "nature" took care of the charges both of savage silliness and imitation of a European poem. These terms of praise in the earliest reviews have clung to the poem throughout its popular history, a defense and celebration of the incorporation of "Indian" into the national narrative.[5]

Hiawatha handily overcame accusations of silliness, imitation, plagiarism only to face a more sophisticated critique starting in the 1890s. In a paper titled "A Lawgiver of the Stone Age," read to a meeting of the American Association for the Advancement of Science, the anthropologist Horatio Hale documented in detail the error perpetrated by Longfellow's chief source, Henry Rowe Schoolcraft, a prolific amateur ethnographer specializing in secondhand information who had identified the Mohawk Hiawatha with Manabozho, "a fantastic divinity of the Ojibways." Without looking into the matter further—he might have learned of the historical Hiawatha from Morgan's *League of the Iroquois*, but there is no evidence he read this work—Longfellow took Schoolcraft's word, and in his "charming poem . . . by an extraordinary fortune, a grave Iroquois lawgiver of the fifteenth century has become, in modern literature, an Ojibway demigod." It was as if a Chinese traveler "had confounded King Alfred with King Arthur, and both with Odin."[6] Soon the story of "the real Hiawatha" began to appear in the press, with no apparent effect on Indian performances of Hiawatha pageants, testimony to the superior power of a charming poem over scientific ethnography. But students of the Iroquois continued to insist on separating the historical from the poetical Hiawatha. Longfellow's "ethnographical boner," wrote an anthropologist in 1948, "had the happiest results for our literature," if not for our history. Folklorists took up the case, charging Longfellow with shrinking the figures of his poem, moralizing away "the primitive awe and scrupulousness with which savage man approaches the great commonwealth of nature upon whose generosity his livelihood depends."[7] He missed the significance of animism in the legends he poeticized and did "violence," in Stith Thompson's words, "both to the original myth [of Manabozho] and to the spirit of the life which he depicts in *The Song of Hiawatha*."[8] The popular performances occurred simultaneously, in short, with damaging criticism of the poem. The poem had sacrificed its real-life sources for the sake of telling a charming tale whose magic—this seemed the point of the sacrifice—enhanced a political vision.

"There is something in the poem," Longfellow mused, "which has taken hold of the popular fancy."[9] Within weeks of publication he referred to "readings, recitations, and the like." Under the title of "The

Hiawatha Mania," a columnist in the Philadelphia *Bulletin* wrote, "Poetical mothers christen their children by the un-christian names of Hiawatha and Minnehaha; ship-builders name their crafts by the same euphonious titles; and last of all, adventurous ladies, disregarding the rights of authorship, recite Hiawatha in Indian costumes, with a background of wigwams and forest scenery, and crowds gather to hear the strange and novel performance."[10] There was something of the spectacle about the poem from the start, including the controversy that furthered its popularity. For the wise and learned Dr. Oliver Wendell Holmes, leading Brahmin of the poet's circle, there was also something of the physical in the poem's appeal. In "The Physiology of Versification," he said of *Hiawatha*'s octosyllabic measure with long-short beats (trochaic tetrameter) that "it follows more exactly than any other measure the natural rhythm of respiration." In remarks at a memorial after the poet's death in 1882, he added, "In this most frequently criticized piece of verse work, the poet has shown a subtle sense of the requirements of his simple story of a primitive race by choosing the most fluid of measures, that lets the thought run through it in an easy sing-song, such as oral tradition would be sure to find on the lips of the story-teller in the wigwam."[11] The reader's confidence that every line will reach its end with satisfying regularity, while drawing pictures of what another reader called "those poor painted children of the western forest," is one reason for the poem's instant and long-lasting popularity.

In the "friendly and flowing savage" stanzas of "Song of Myself," Walt Whitman named the desire both he and Longfellow addressed, the same wish Chief Sea'thl was reported to have prophesized in the same years: always to have "the Indian" nearby.

Wherever he goes men and women accept and desire him,
They desire he should like them, touch them, speak to them, stay with them.

As if in ignorance of the terror that had already been unleashed against natives in the West and Southwest (let alone the decimation of the Eastern tribes long since accomplished), both poets portray the desirable figure as pacific and well intentioned toward those who took their land and ravaged their lives. The difference of address of the two books may obscure their kinship of motive, which was to find a mode in poetry to keep the indigenous alive as an idea and an ideal in the evolving national culture. But the differences in the mode are significant. *Hiawatha* is a story, a magical narrative with elements of conventional romance, and the poet told it in a meter that makes for easy reading.[12] Whitman invented a new form, more lyric than narrative, an unmetered epic of the self that offered unbounded and shameless intimacy with the reader; the "friendly and flowing savage" lines can be taken as a figure for Whitman's own verse and himself as a new savagelike American poet:

> Behavior lawless as snow-flakes, words simple as grass, uncomb'd
>   head, laughter, and naiveté,
> Slow-stepping feet, common features, common modes and
>   emanations,
> They descend in new forms from the tips of his fingers,
> They are wafted with the odor of his body or breath, they fly out
>   of the glance of his eyes.

Ed Folsom reads these lines as Whitman's evocation of an "emerging new white American savage," a figure distilled from the indigene in order to "replace the native savage,"[13] a view that can be extended to include the poet's use of the "friendly and flowing savage" to promulgate a new and anti-Longfellowian American meter, diction, and poetic purpose: "Slow-stepping feet, common features, common modes and emanations . . . new forms from the tips of fingers."

Whitman cajoled his readers to accept the voice of his poem as that of an actual person, a nonliterary effulgence of life on the streets, "one of the roughs," the printed word as alive as flesh and blood. "This is no book," he wrote. "Who touches this touches a man." Such a challenge to the border between art and life doubtless confused and distressed readers in the 1850s who were accustomed to the distance and decorum of Longfellow, whose polished meters and satisfying rhymes stood protectively between the work and the artist. Longfellow drew his readers into a decorous circle to hear a tale they yearned to hear. Like Harriet Beecher Stowe, he had lessons to teach. He made himself present to his readers as a learned but sympathetic voice, heart and head fused in the persona of "the poet." To say that Hiawatha stepped out of the poem onto the stage confirms the essential point: It wasn't Longfellow but Hiawatha, not the poet (as Whitman insisted) but "the Indian" transfigured as national myth, who crossed from print to performance. Whitman's reaction late in life to "Emerson's Books" includes this indirect appraisal of the author of *Hiawatha*:

> It is always a make, never an unconscious growth. It is the porcelain figure or statuette of lion, or stag, or Indian hunter . . . appropriate for the rosewood or marble bracket of parlor or library, never the animal itself, or the hunter himself . . . What would that do amid astral and bric-a-brac and tapestry, and ladies and gentlemen talking in subdued tones of Browning and Longfellow and art? The least suspicion of such actual bull, or Indian, or of Nature carrying out itself, would put all those good people to instant terror and flight.[14]

Whitman's "savage" exchanged the commonplace derogation of that term for a celebration of the uninhibited expression of "such actual bull, or Indian, or of Nature carrying out itself" (including fornication) that Whitman wanted to identify with America.

A pleasing poem that sets out to absorb simple "children of the woods" into the national story was bound to be greeted in the tense year of 1855 with a certain relief by a public whose nerves were on edge: In Boston, there was news of the trial of the captured fugitive slave Andrew Burns and rumors of bloodshed and worse to come from Kansas and Nebraska. Archaism of language, harmonies of sound, and a meter that sounds itself out as both learned and simple, of both the study (head) and the fireside (heart), made for reassurance. The poem affected readers the way the Falls of Minnehaha affected Hiawatha, "Calling to him through the silence": "'Pleasant is the sound!' he murmured, / 'Pleasant is the voice that calls me!'" The poem gave the illusion of a "song" recuperated by the miracle of art from dim regions of the nation's prehistory: battles with monsters, magical flights, encounters with ghosts, the planting of corn and invention of language. The poem's very lack of intellectual complexity or a dialectical argument unfolding by inner dialogue and tension delivers a Hiawatha already prepared for appropriation as theatrical spectacle, easily removed from the poem, an uncomplicated tableau vivant figure, less a character than a picture against the background of a meter itself readily translatable into a score. In many ways the staged Hiawatha fulfills the poem, though there is more to the poem than a simple scenario. Read within the horizon of ideas that Longfellow assumed (and Whitman rejected) about what poetry is and what good it does, *Hiawatha* captivates from opening to closing lines. For William Butler Yeats the secret of Longfellow's great popularity was that "he tells his story or idea so that one needs nothing but his verses to understand it."[15] *Hiawatha* triumphs also for the vision of conquest it sublimates: the white man's arrival, the hero's departure. Unlike Virgil's Turnus, nor like Tecumseh and Black Hawk in real life, he does not stand and fight but quietly slips away.

II

Is it possible to take *The Song of Hiawatha* seriously today? A "white-elephant," writes one disenchanted scholar recently, a mere "cardboard concoction," insipid, shallow, "an ethnocentric armchair fantasy."[16] True, *The Song of Hiawatha is* a concoction (an oblique allusion to melting pot?), but by itself that is no damning indictment. As Newton Arvin wisely wrote, "there are a good many things worse than *The Song of Hiawatha*."[17] The linguist Dell Hymes has proposed a less injurious description than "concoction"; he prefers "multicultural composite," since the meter was taken, via a German translation, from the Finnish *Kalevala* (Longfellow may have encountered the trochaic tetrameter also in Spanish poems by Lope de Vega and perhaps, most intriguingly, from a poem by Heine on a Jewish theme, "Prinzessin Sabbat"); the legends were chiefly Algonquian-Ojibway, the hero

"Hiawatha," studio portrait by Heyn and Matzen, Omaha, Nebraska, c. 1900. (Library of Congress)

"Swift of foot was Hiawatha," postcard published by M. A. Whedon, Minneapolis, Minnesota, c. 1900. (Author's collection)

Ojibway by tribal legend though by name Iroquois, his bride's name, Minnehaha, a Dakota word meaning waterfall. Moved by the idea that nationality in literature called for autochthonous materials, Longfellow dipped into many pots in fashioning a faux indigenous hero who performs his feats not as Ojibway (the recurrence of Ojibway words is the closest the poem comes to cultural specificity) but as "Indian."

Asking in his journal in 1847 whether the words "national literature" can "mean anything," Longfellow noted that the United States already had a "composite" national character, "embracing French, Spanish, Irish, English, Scotch, and German peculiarities. Whoever has within himself most of these is our truly national writer. In other words, whoever is most universal is the most national."[18] An Indian poem promised further to universalize the national "composite," adding a red tint to the cauldron (in the absence from Longfellow's list, we note, of black Africans), and thereby to render the poet more truly national.[19] Aspiring national bards had earlier tried their hands at epic "Indian poems," a sorrowful minor tradition of tortured heroic couplets, doomed warriors, and maidens fading away.[20] The aim was to make the white nation seem an outgrowth of red roots. Only Longfellow in verse and Cooper in prose succeeded in creating credible narratives of this material, winning the credence of large audiences.

The "something" in the poem that bemused Longfellow endowed Hiawatha with the power of return almost two generations later as ghostly presence, a shade fated always to vanish again, always to come again and reperform the act of vanishing. One something was the panoramic mode of the storytelling through an array of "romance" scenes: Hiawatha raised in the woods by his grandmother Nokomis, his wrestling high on a mountain cliff with his father Mudjekeewis, the West Wind, his contriving out of a birch tree a magical canoe that's powered by his wishes, his similarly magical moccasins and mittens, his epic underwater combat with Kenabeek the sea monster and his slaying of the evil magician Pearl-Feather, both recalling underworld episodes in classical epic and medieval romance, the wooing of Minnehaha and the magnificent wedding feast with its dancing and storytelling, Minnehaha dancing nude at night to bless the cornfields, the death scenes of the Orpheus-like Chibiabos, the mischievous shape-shifting trickster Pau-Puk-Keewis slain as a man then changed into an eagle, the strong man Kwasind done in by the Little People, the Puk-Wudjies, and a stricken Minnehaha, victim of famine and disease. Like *Uncle Tom's Cabin*, and a mark of the midcentury culture of sentiment it shares, *The Song of Hiawatha* speaks to the heart with gestures of endearment by loving grandmother, loyal friends, and tender wife, and acts of great physical prowess aided by benign magic. Not only are the scenes prepared, as it were, for stage performance; they are already performances on the stage of the poem's simple meter, mostly end-stopped lines and repeated names and phrases. The poem seems to read itself the way Hiawatha's canoe moves effortlessly on wings of unconscious desire. A "national folk epic," writes a recent commentator, as close to "European Romantic obsession" as America is likely to enjoy.[21]

But "national folk epic" doesn't ring quite true. The legends don't flow from a river of tales already familiar to Longfellow's readers. Nor has the poem functioned as folklore, except insofar as Indian performances at the turn of the century and the modern commercialization of "Hiawatha" and "Minnehaha" qualify as folk expression. Indeed, to portray himself as artificer, Longfellow counted on the exotic character of the legends rather than their familiarity. He spoke of the poem as "This Indian Edda," identifying it with the Old Norse or Icelandic collection of ancient legends, assimilating the poem to a tradition of Northern European culture; the term subliminally implied translation of native texts into a form that not only attached the prestige of Europe to it but also attested to the predominantly Anglo-Saxon literary culture of Longfellow's readers. To make an American epic of Hiawatha one had to stage him in an Nordic epic-romance discourse.

The poem was "founded," Longfellow explained in "Notes," on stories of "a personage of miraculous birth, who was sent among them ["the North American Indians"] to clear their rivers, forests, and fishing-grounds, and to teach them the arts of peace." "Into this old tradition," he continues, "I have woven other curious Indian legends."[22] The weaving brought all the separate elements together into a single narrative, the "song" or myth of Hiawatha. But underlying the explicit myth there is the mythos of the poem itself, its own story of origins and artifice, a mythos centered on the figure "Longfellow," who situated himself between reader and text. The mythos has Longfellow not only as artificer, as skilled engineer of verse, but also as mediator. The artificer whose art is to deny itself, as Virginia Jackson skillfully argues,[23] brings "Indian" home, makes that figure familiar as one who readies the ground (clearing the rivers, teaching arts of peace), then clears the ground of himself, leaving behind a ghostly trace of epic "song."

Mediation began with Longfellow's access to the legends, the mental culture of his Indians. The poem's "Notes" and "Vocabulary" of Ojibway-Algonquian words assures that the poem is seen as derived from sources accessed through Longfellow's reading of some eight authors and editors, including George Catlin, John G. E. Heckewelder, Mrs. Seth Eastman, John Tanner (author of a popular captivity narrative), and most prodigiously, Henry Rowe Schoolcraft. Strangely for a poet-scholar who had mastered many European languages and devoted significant energy to translation, Longfellow apparently made no effort to learn Ojibway, did not consult an Ojibway dictionary, and constructed the "Vocabulary" (including "Ugh, *yes*") from Schoolcraft and perhaps Eastman and Tanner. No native author appears among the sources.

On June 13, 1849, Longfellow noted in his journal: "To tea came Kah-ge-ga-gah'-bowh, the Ojibway Chief, and we went together to hear Agassiz lecture on the 'Races of Men.' He thinks there were several Adams and Eves."[24] Louis Agassiz held that hierarchical differences of "race" among humans resulted from "polygeny" or separate "creations." The idea enlisted "nature" in defense of slavery and other inequalities based on skin color. Kah-ge-ga-gah'-bowh, also known as George Copway, came with a gift of his published autobiography; his reaction, if any, to Agassiz's doctrine of polygeny goes unrecorded. When Copway had lectured in Cambridge the previous year, Longfellow remarked in his journal, "A rambling talk, gracefully delivered, with a fine various voice, and a chief's costume, with little bells jangling upon it, like the bells with pomegranates of the Jewish priests."[25]

Kinship of Indians and Jews evidently seemed to Longfellow a normal association. Copway, the only Ojibway he is known to have met, was conspicuously absent from Longfellow's "Notes." Later, Copway named a daughter Minnehaha after Hiawatha's wife.[26] In 1859, commenting on Kah-ge-ga-gah'-bowh's fall into poverty, indebtedness, and public disgrace, Longfellow linked him derisively with *Hiawatha*: "I fear he is developing the Pau-Puk-Keewis [the trickster destroyed by Hiawatha] element rather strongly."[27] Rather than a liability, the absence of native sources for *Hiawatha* suggests an idea of mediation through reading and study, as if an oral culture as foreign as that of the "North American Indian" could be learned only from the writings of white authorities capable of interpreting what they recorded.

"The stories in *Hiawatha* are all real American Indian stories," wrote the poet's brother Samuel in 1882, "taken down by Schoolcraft & others from Indian story-tellers in the wigwams."[28] The image of wigwam storytelling flowing directly into the ear of Schoolcraft and from there, in Schoolcraft's "plain, spare, prose form," into the "fancy & poetic language" of the poet, is at the core of the poem's own mythos. Although in private Longfellow had complained that Schoolcraft's writings were "a mass of ill-digested material," in "Notes" he praised "his indefatigable zeal in rescuing so much of the legendary lore of the Indians."[29] In his zeal, Schoolcraft had in fact neglected to acknowledge that his own indispensable source was his wife, Jane, daughter of John Johnston, a cultivated Anglo-Irish fur trader, and Neengay, an Ojibway woman (granddaughter of the important chief and ally of the French Mamongazid). When Schoolcraft arrived at Sault Sainte Marie in 1820, he was a geologist in the expeditionary party of General Lewis Cass exploring the sources of the Mississippi River with an eye for deposits of precious metals; he was welcomed into the cultivated Johnston mixed-blood household and fell in love with the poised, talented, and multilingual Jane, who encouraged and guided his growing interest in the Ojibway language and legends. We have these revealing details from Janet Lewis's remarkable documentary novel, *The Invasion*.[30]

The novel shows Schoolcraft fumbling to make sense of his forays into Ojibway oral culture. He was guided and helped by Jane and other family members who indeed had the tales directly from the mouths of winter storytellers. Schoolcraft excised the scatology and polished the prose, and in 1839 he brought out two little volumes of *Algic Researches* as his own gatherings from native mouths. Jane among others appeared in the acknowledgments, though not her mother, who likely contributed tales of her own and whose prestige in the Ojibway community eased Schoolcraft's access. Jane died of a fever in 1842. Longfellow himself makes a cameo appearance in the novel, poring over Schoolcraft's "ill-digested" volumes in his "roomy study in Cambridge." Having settled on an Indian epic and a "simple primitive rhythm, as suitable for a simple primitive tale," nothing remained "but to read and indite." "He went on with his 'fairy tale,'" replacing Manabozho with Hiawatha because of "that awkward *zh*," thereby "descending unaware from the mythic to the merely historical." Because he drew mainly on Schoolcraft's early small volumes, the novel shows us that Longfellow's poem grew from "materials which had, as it were, been selected for him by Jane Schoolcraft," though he did not realize this.[31]

In 1856, capitalizing on the poem's success, Schoolcraft brought out a small volume of recycled tales, *The Myth of Hiawatha and Other Oral Legends*, dedicated to Longfellow for his demonstrating "that the theme of the native lore reveals one of the true sources of our literary independence."[32] Longfellow had long held the same idea. In an essay in 1831 on Sir Philip Sidney's *Defense of Poetry*, he had urged that, to achieve a literature "as original, characteristic, and national as possible," poets should listen to Indian speech such as the "last words" of the aging Choctow chief, Pushmataha: "'I shall die, but you will return to your brethren. As you go along the paths, you will see the flowers and hear the birds, but Pushmataha will see them and hear them no more. When you come to your home, they will ask you, where is Pushmataha? And you will say to them, He is no more. They will hear the tidings like the sound of the fall of a mighty oak in the stillness of the wood.'" If American writers paid attention to words like these, they'd "give a new and delightful expression to the face of our poetry."[33]

In his writings of the 1840s, Schoolcraft had struck a similar note. "No people can bear a true nationality which does not exfoliate, as it were, from its own bosom, something that expresses the peculiarities of its own soil and climate." Echoing the German philosopher Johann Gottfried von Herder, who had argued that the uniqueness of cultures derives from their singular folk traditions, Schoolcraft asked whether any better sources for American literary nationality could be found than "the history and antiquities and institutions and lore, of the free, bold, wild, independent, native hunter race?" In Indian lore lies "the germs of a future mythology."[34]

Longfellow and Schoolcraft agreed that "true nationality" derives from a nation's "singular folk traditions," and that in the absence of a "folk," the United States had its Indians, sadly "vanishing" but gladly rich in accessible lore. But how to process this lore (or ore) as *American* literature? Indians were "a rude and ignorant race," Schoolcraft, Longfellow, and other subscribers to the "romantic racism" of the Herderian *Volkgeist* school believed in the 1840s and 1850s. How could such benighted peoples provide raw material for the "nationality" of a "civilized" people? The logic of Schoolcraft's views on this conundrum was typical. True, natives live mired in fear and superstition, in "necromancy, witchcraft, and demonology." "Everything is mysterious which is not understood; and, unluckily, they understand little or nothing." Because they understand nothing, their language relies on symbols, personifications, metaphors, figures of speech, which prevent self-reflection; they cannot speak on abstract subjects without graphic symbols, the "wild pictography" of their language. Schoolcraft's most telling indictment of native "mentality" was that it cannot give account of itself. "There is no word in the Indian language that means savage. They had no use for such a word." He saw small hope that they would accept "reclamation" offered by Christianity and civilization. They would "pass away from the earth." Still, since their diction was "simple and pure," their sentiments often "exalted," and their legends "tributes to the best feelings of the heart," they offered hope through translation such as Schoolcraft's for the "true nationality" so anxiously desired in the fractured 1850s.[35]

Schoolcraft describes his method of processing the ore in a vivid passage of utmost condescension.

Nothing can exceed the Doric simplicity of an aboriginal tale. It admits of scarcely any adjectives, and no ornaments . . . The closest attention, indeed, is required, in listening to, and taking notes of an original legend, to find language simple and child-like enough to narrate what is said, and to give it, *as said*, word by word, and sentence by sentence. A school boy, who is not yet smitten with the ambition of style, but adheres to the natural method, of putting down no more words than are just neces-sary to express precise ideas, would do it best. And when this has been done, and the original preserved in the words of the Indian story teller, it is often but a tissue of common events which would possess very little interest, were it not for the mys-tery or melodramatic effect, of their singular mythology. To imitate such a tale successfully, is to demand of the writer an accurate knowledge of Indian manners and customs, often his history and traditions, and always his religion and opinions, with some gleams of the language.[36]

All the processor needs by way of literary equipment is "language simple and childlike enough" to convey the native's child-like mental-ity and culture and assure the effect of primitiveness desired in a na-tional mythology of origins.

Out of stories so processed and refined, Longfellow fashioned a fe-licitous romance that made the Indian even more accessible and reli-ably present than did Cooper. Ignoring the paradox that absorption of "low" autochthonous materials into a "higher" discourse necessarily dilutes the forms, most of Longfellow's favored readers believed that the poem was a true expression of the aboriginal. "As a whole it rep-resents wonderfully well that infantile character of Indian life," wrote the historian George Bancroft, "when the inferior animals were half-and-half the equal companions of man, and external nature was his bosom friend."[37] Moncure Conway went farther: "What the greatest poets have done for their lands Longfellow has done for his," "per-haps the only American Epic," comparable to Homer's *Iliad*, Dante's *Inferno*, and Goethe's *Faust*. Longfellow himself called his Indian hero "a kind of American Prometheus."[38]

Longfellow had seemed to solve the problem of transfiguring "in-fantile" natives into ancestral heroes on the order of the great epic he-

roes of Europe. There is no original "song of Hiawatha" and Longfellow made no pretense that there was, though in the Introduction the
master narrator presents the entire poem as the song of "the singer
Nawadaha" who dwelt "Round about the Indian village."[39] Nawadaha,
apparently Schoolcraft's Iroquois name, alludes to Longfellow's major
source. The entire poem is presented as stories repeated by the narrator "as I heard them / From the lips of Nawadaha." Not itself an actual translation, the poem incorporates translation into the reading
experience. Ojibway words pass fluently into English: "Called Way-
wassimo, the lightning, / And the thunder, Annemmekee."[40] Local
parsing of native words recruits the reader as participant in the process of distancing savage phonemes as savagely picturesque. Rather
than an effort to get inside Ojibway mentality through its speech,
the aim is to replace the savage word with an English lexical equivalent while retaining its aura of difference. Presuming that the primitive cannot survive contact with the superior culture of the invaders,
cannot change, cannot even recognize itself and thus must pass
away, the poem incorporates native words for the delight of uttering
them like childish syllables and then supplies civilized meanings for
them.

At how many removes does Longfellow's poem stand from the actual poetics of tribal verse and storytelling? The canto on Hiawatha's
childhood includes a little song, a lullaby, for which we luckily have a
documented origin. Longfellow based it on Schoolcraft's account of
how he came upon "Chant to the Fire-fly," how he "walked out one
evening" to a lawn on the St. Mary's River in northern Michigan to
catch the "shouts and wild dancing" of some Ojibway children. They
were singing to the flitting of fireflies, and Schoolcraft gives first a
transcription of what he heard as "wild" sounds: "Wau wau tay see! /
Wau wau tay see," then a "literal translation": "Flitting-white-fire in-
sect! Waving white-fire-bug! Give me light before I go to bed! Give
me light before I sleep. Come, little dancing white-fire-bug! Come little flitting-white-fire-beast! Light me with your bright white-flame-
instrument—your little candle." "Meter there was none," he remarked,
"at least of a regular character; the words were the wild improvisa-
tions of children in a merry mood."[41] He then provides meter and reg-

ularity, producing an English ballad Longfellow then improved upon in his own meter.

Here are a few lines of Schoolcraft's poem:

> Fire-fly, fire-fly! bright little thing.
> Light me to bed, and my song I will sing.
> Give me your light, as you fly o'er my head,
> That I may merrily go to bed.

And Longfellow, in the voice of Hiawatha:

> Wah-wah-taysee, little firefly,
> Little, flitting, white-fire insect,
> Little, dancing, white-fire creature,
> Light me with your little candle,
> Ere upon my bed I lay me,
> Ere in sleep I close my eyelids.[42]

Compare Longfellow's sweet melody with this recent version by Dell Hymes.

> Flitting white fire, flash light for me
>   Before I sleep, *ey way*!
>   Come, come, *ey way*!
> Flitting with white fire,
> Flitting with white fire,
> Bright white instrument of flame!
> Bright white instrument of flame!

The anthropologist and poet Edward Sapir remarked that the Algonquian verb was itself an Imagist poem. An ear conditioned to identify Indianness in poetry with the spare diction and lightly inflected speech of Imagist verse will most likely prefer Hymes's version. The difference from Longfellow's line is literally measurable, in the sense that Hymes takes actual measure of the syllabic form of the original, counting stresses rather than metrical feet. As charming and tender

and even precise an effect as Longfellow achieves—Gordon Brotherston speaks of his "loving attention to native text" and his inclusion of
Indian words (Brotherston goes on to say that Longfellow celebrates
his hero "only on condition that he disappear")—still, he pressed the
firefly into a four-stress meter foreign to the original recorded spoken
lines. Hymes writes that *Hiawatha* does "not disclose a poetic form
native to Native Americans," not surprising, he adds, considering that
"the poetic form of their oral narratives indeed had not yet been recognized."[43]

III

Angus Fletcher has said that "*Hiawatha* can be read as an implicit
treatise on the nature of language."[44] Rather than an explicit theory,
the poem gives demonstrations, events of reading.

> Ye, who sometimes, in your rambles
> Through the green lanes of the country, . . .
> Over stone walls gray with mosses,
> Pause by some neglected graveyard,
> For a while to muse, and ponder
> On a half-effaced inscription,
> Written with little skill of song-craft,
> Homely phrases, but each letter
> Full of hope and yet of heart-break,
> Full of all the tender pathos
> Of the Here and the Hereafter;—
> Stay and read this rude inscription,
> Read this Song of Hiawatha!

Who is the "ye," the role assigned to the reader? A rambler drawn to
country graveyards, most likely a reader familiar with Thomas Gray's
"Elegy Written in a Country Churchyard," given to elegiac musings
and appreciation of the "homely," which implies a social position
more high than low. "Half-effaced inscription" gives one figure for the

work of the reader; so does the implied act of listening while reading: "Read this Song of Hiawatha!"

It's assumed as a given that the song comes from a distant place and time, an aboriginal antiquity, and that it comes in the tangible form of a ruin, again conflating reading silently and hearing. Ruins, hieroglyphs, various inscrutable ciphers held a particular fascination for antebellum American culture, as we see in Thomas Cole's paintings, in Poe's tales, and throughout Melville's fiction. The idea of the vanishing Indian implied that the "red man" was already a ruin. In his sonnet "Eliot's Oak," Longfellow wrote of "sounds of unintelligible speech . . . Of a lost race, long vanished like a cloud." His posture in the Introduction to *Hiawatha* joins the conventional trope with this difference: To compare the reading of the song of Hiawatha with the reading of an old New England gravestone places Hiawatha within a space sacred to national memory, claiming him as kin in a kinship that remains to be worked out, invented through the reader's acts of translation, cognate with the poet's act of weaving disparate strands into a single narrative. To "read the song" is to recognize that recovery of Hiawatha requires that speech be transposed into writing, oral replaced with written culture, literate and literary at once. The very act (versification) by which the written "rescues [the oral] from oblivion" terminates the oral as living culture. Rescue or preservation destroys what it saves. Reading the "rude inscription" of "the song of Hiawatha" embodies the entire logic of displacement enacted in and by the poem, oral giving way to literate, low to high, savage to civilized, "Indian" to Euro-American.

Displacement and transcendence occur throughout the poem. In the process of his being translated from "song" to written poem, Hiawatha goes about his own world translating and interpreting, functioning as intermediary between savagery and civilization, between "Indian" and "American." He talks with animals and birds and to trees, as in the lilting account of making his canoe: "'Give me of your bark, O Birch-Tree! . . . Give me of your roots, O Tamarack!'"[45] It's by his language skills that Hiawatha proves his kinship, his eligibility to be ancestor to the nation, one of its founders. The proof appears most vividly in what can be taken as the heart of the poem, the canto called "Picture-Writing." Longfellow described it as an "intermediate Canto . . . rather curious than poetical."[46] It follows "Blessing the Cornfields," in which the ineffable Minnehaha dances naked (and decorously unseen) at midnight amid the sprouting corn to a lovely music—"No one but the Midnight only / Saw her beauty in the darkness"—and is followed by "Hiawatha's Lamentation" at the death of his friend, the singer Chibiabos. The poem takes a downward course thereafter through battle with sly deceiver Pau-Puk-Keewis, the death of Kwasind, the appearance of ghosts, famine, Minnehaha's death, until "The White-Man's Foot" appears, requiring in the final canto "Hiawatha's Departure." "Picture-Writing" is intermediate, then, marking a major transition from peace and happiness to grief and sorrow, from triumphs over dragons and giant underwater creatures, a wedding feast, the sprouting of the corn, to grief, violence, death, and departure. By "curious" Longfellow may mean that the picture-writing canto offers not an epic action but a meta-action, a reflection on the reading of the poem itself; it places the heart of the poem, the implicit treatise on language, in the reader's hands.

The canto has Hiawatha "walking / In the solitary forest,/ Pondering, musing in the forest, / On the welfare of his people." His musing represents Longfellow's vision of the sources of human language, origins that recall the "half-effaced inscription" of the Introduction by centering on the effects of time and death: "'Lo! how all things fade and perish!" Men die and are forgotten, words of wisdom "Perish in the ears that hear them, / Do not reach the generations / That, as yet unborn, are waiting / In the great, mysterious darkness / Of the speechless days that shall be!" Sequoyah (also known as George Guess) gave similar reasons for inventing a Cherokee alphabet.[47] How can humans redeem the speech that dies on the air as soon as uttered? How can one overcome time and space, all distances that separate?

> "Face to face we speak together,
> But we cannot speak when absent,
> Cannot send our voices from us
> To the friends that dwell afar off;
> Cannot send a secret message,

> But the bearer learns our secret,
> May pervert it, may betray it,
> May reveal it unto others."

Human treachery joins space and time as enemies of the communion among people that Hiawatha (and Longfellow) cherishes as the highest value, embodied in friendships such as Hiawatha's with his mate Kwasind, of whom he says earlier in the poem, we "spake with naked hearts together." Hiawatha then takes "his colors" from his pouch and begins to paint "many shapes and figures, / Wonderful and mystic figures, / And each figure had a meaning, / Each some word or thought suggested."[48]

By providing mnemonic figures, Hiawatha's invention of picture writing overcomes the absence of tangible forms of tradition. "'On the grave-posts of our fathers / Are no signs, no figures painted; / Who are in those graves we know not, / Only know they are our fathers.'" Hiawatha's "we" shares with the poem's readers the posture of bending over a grave marker, squinting to read and to know. Indian and American seem to meld in this "we," giving the white reader to understand that ignorance of Indian "fathers" can be overcome by reading Longfellow's poem, its ventriloquism of Nawadaha's singing, a song that would otherwise remain wordless without "translation" of what the savage (however gentle) Hiawatha can only draw as picture.

Hiawatha draws and interprets iconic figures for his people, teaching the possibility of defeating death through writing: "Footprints pointing towards a wigwam / Were a sign of invitation, / Were a sign of guests assembling; / Bloody hands with palms uplifted / Were a symbol of destruction, / Were a hostile sign and symbol." Many of the details here—the making and reading of pictographs, as well as the general theory of the origins of writing in graphic mnemonic devices, the effort to preserve oral language by means of a pictorial system— were drawn from an essay on pictographs by Schoolcraft. Arguing that "these figures represent ideas—whole ideas, and their juxtaposition or relations on a roll of bark, a tree, or a rock," Schoolcraft concluded that "picture writing is indeed the literature of the Indians," which was a singularly obtuse remark from a collector of oral tales and

Frederic Remington, "Indian Picture Writing," 1890. (Library of Congress)

songs.[49] "Indian languages," he wrote in 1856, "are peculiarly the languages of symbols, metaphors, and figures."[50] Longfellow had already gathered a similar notion of the primitiveness of metaphor from his reading of the eighteenth-century philosopher and historian Giambattista Vico, who taught that in the figurative speech of poetry lay the rudimentary origins of civilization; the first culture heroes and lawgivers, Vico famously asserted, were poets.[51] Longfellow's poem delivers a Hiawatha who, while confined to the Indian or "savage" stage, becomes an imagined link, a point of transition and continuity with the next and higher stage, the new world that arrives in the penultimate canto of the poem as "The White-Man's Foot."

Language, interpretation, poetry itself occupy the foreground of the entire poem. Translation is fundamental to the kind of knowledge the poem proposes, knowledge of origins, of sources, of the firstness upon which the American nation is founded. The "Vocabulary" or glossary lists 140 Ojibway words in English characters. The poet mediates languages, literatures, and cultures. *The Song of Hiawatha* performs its work as a pretended translation that obliterates in order to preserve (in an antithetical form) the imagined spirit of Indian aboriginality. The illusion of the translation, the illusion that Longfellow's verse is as transparent as pictures, is the poem's ultimate act against the native and for the nation; in Virginia Jackson's words, "translation of 'them' into 'us.'"[52] The poem grounds itself in paradox: It makes Hiawatha or "the Indian" disappear in the act of seeming to give him voice; its own metrical and figurative system disarticulates aboriginal culture from its own systems of thought and speech by subsuming the aboriginal into the Anglo-Saxon nationality of the narrative verse form. The poem thus constructs a "white man's Indian" by suggesting that we can hear the picture speech of natives only by means of the mediating voice of the poet.

The poet-narrator's own metaphors sustain this illusion of translation of picture into word. Here is Mondamin, the youth "Dressed in garments green and yellow," the tassle-headed ear of corn, who has come as a person in answer to Hiawatha's prayers for a source of food more dependable than beasts of the waters and woods. He has "Come to warn you and instruct you, / How by struggle and by labour / You shall gain what you have prayed for." They wrestle for three days, then Mondamin instructs:

> "Make a bed for me to lie in,
>   Where the rain may fall upon me,
>   Where the sun may come and warm me;
> Strip these garments, green and yellow,
> Strip this nodding plumage from me,
> Lay me in the earth, and make it
> Soft and loose and light above me."

Vico wrote about the earliest peoples, "Their poetry was at first divine, because they imagined the cause of things they felt and wondered at to be gods. This is now confirmed by the American Indians, who call gods all the things that surpass their small understanding."[53] And Schoolcraft: "the Indian's necessities of language at all times require personifications and linguistic creations."[54] In the following passage Longfellow's repetitions strung along the four-beat trochaic meter induce a dreamlike spell, a mood of submission and consent to the gentlest stirrings of air and light as animistic signs.

> Can it be the sun descending?
> O'er the level plain of water?
> Or the Red Swan floating, flying,
> Wounded by the magic arrow,
> Staining all the leaves with crimson,
> With the crimson of its life-blood,
> Filling all the air with splendor,
> With the splendor of its plumage?[55]

The question "Can it be the sun descending?" brings the reader into the verse as both sophisticated observer and willing believer (by suspense of disbelief) in the literal (or pictorial) truth of metaphor. Metaphor gives access to the mind imagined as capable of seeing the dying sun as a dying swan—not "like" or "as if," but "as." This exquisite passage is typical of the guileless subtlety by which Longfellow throughout encourages a double awareness on the part of his reader. The interrogative mode allows the reader a space for self-recognition as witness to an alien world, a world accessible only by acts of translation, aided by upwelling of forgotten beliefs and fears.

Fly backward with me, the poem cajoles, backward through translation to an original magical world, a primary field of being and consciousness. The magical nature of the poem's restored universe is segmented into higher (human) and lower (plant and animal) realms and inhabited by figures in the guise of "characters" who are really energies or forces of nature or personifications of primal tribal functions: hunter, warrior, storyteller, magician, lawgiver, planter of corn. Translation reveals its subtext of utopian aspiration toward an imagined "primitive" for sustenance of the imagined nation.

Recall how much of the poem is cast as conversation between speaker and listener. Here are the opening lines:

> Should you ask me, whence these stories?
> Whence these legends and traditions,
> With the odors of the forest,
> With the dew and damp of meadows,
> With the curling smoke of wigwams,
> With the rushing of great rivers,
> With their frequent repetitions,
> And their wild reverberations,
> As of thunder in the mountains?
> I should answer, I should tell you,
> ". . . I repeat them as I heard them
> From the lips of Nawadaha,
> The musician, the sweet singer."

Ask, answer, tell, lips, singer—against the background of the natural sounds of reverberating rushing water and thunder, primordial sounds as if of the first days—recall the arts of repetition, of the passing of story from mouth to mouth: "I repeat them as I heard them." Here is Longfellow up to his own civilized magic, as if the reading of the poem were an encounter with first, primordial, aboriginal things.

Metaphoric language enriches the soil of Longfellow's epic, the ground on which myth arises as if naturally in the modes of action, episode, and story: myth that begins with the Great Spirit's bright promise to "send a Prophet to you, / A Deliverer of the nations, / Who shall guide you and shall teach you." And its dark side: "If his warnings pass unheeded, / You will fade away and perish!"[56] The story follows from the miraculous birth of Hiawatha, the death of his mother Wenonah (who had been raped by the West Wind, an allusion to sexual violence otherwise repressed), his nurturing by grandmother Nokomis (who, in passing, entertains a bear as a lover), his honing the skills of hunting and gathering and healing and talking with animals. He clears streams, builds ships, slays monsters, marries, plants corn, and invents writing. Then follows decline and fall, a new culture arrives, a new stage prefigured by the Black Robes of the White-Man's Foot. Again we detect the presence of Vico and his cyclic theory of history as a succession from an age of gods (Gitche Manito) to an age of heroes which is also the age of poetry (Hiawatha), to an age of men, of "Humanity" (the Black Robes, Christianity).

As early as his 1832 essay on Sidney's *Defense of Poetry* and throughout his career, Longfellow worried that the displacement of poetry by "utility" and intellectualism threatened to install what Vico had called a "barbarism of reflection."[57] The pedagogical aim of *The Song of Hiawatha* was not only to make "Indian" the national ancestral figure but also to reinstall a love of poetry, of the magic of meter and figurative language, in a nation that in the ominous year of 1855 was about to commit civil self-destruction. The figure of Hiawatha carried a full weight of moral and political meaning for his author who, while he composed his romance in 1854, fretted in his journals over the tumultuous state of the Union and, in particular, the justice of returning Anthony Burns to his aggrieved "master."[58] A mythical poem, Longfellow's "fairy tale" descended still further, in its deepening darkness and melancholy, into the "merely historical," especially the impending conflict over the domination of one race by another.

IV

Janet Lewis's *The Invasion* provides insight into the political and historical unconscious of Longfellow's effort to write a myth of America, into the secret, forbidden knowledge the poem represses: not slavery as such but the dispossession of another dark-skinned people. Though he does not include among his sources any works on the history of U.S.-Ojibway relations, or any historical accounts of transactions and treaties with the natives, Longfellow in the end floundered more deeply into history than he apparently realized. Lewis's novel juxtaposes the poem with the fact that just months before it appeared in 1855, the Ojibways had signed under duress a treaty with the United States abandoning certain territorial claims in exchange for certain payments to tribal members along with U.S. citizenship. Lewis writes with fine irony about *Hiawatha*: "Many a child had pages of it by heart before, in accordance with the Treaty of 1855, the bands were dissolved and the Ojibway nation ceased to be a reality."[59]

Longfellow's friend Ferdinand Freiligrath remarked, in the preface to his German translation in 1856, that the ending left something to be desired. Longfellow too felt the "contact of Saga and History too sudden. But how could I prevent it unless I made the poem very much longer? I felt the clash and concussion, but could not prevent it nor escape it."[60] The concussion appears in the penultimate canto when, after the arrival of the white Christians clad in black, Longfellow gave his hero a final prophetic vision that might have been written by a nationalist historian like Bancroft:

> I beheld the westward marches
> Of the unknown, crowded nations,
> All the land was full of people,
> Restless, struggling, toiling, striving,
> Speaking many tongues, yet feeling
> But one heart-beat in their bosoms.
> In the woodlands rang their axes,
> Smoked their towns in all the valleys,

Over all the lakes and rivers
Rushed their great canoes of thunder.[61]

Hiawatha appears now in a new guise as retrospective historian, historian not of aboriginal America (as Schoolcraft's "primitive," he would not have been capable of this) but of the white nation to be. And because his vision of what will be takes form as a narrative about what has already been, Hiawatha impresses his seal of approval on postaboriginal America, the new industrial nation of immigrant masses, smoke-filled cities, and thundering engines. It's the demise of the magical aboriginal world that makes the nation possible, just as surely as the very possibility of Hiawatha as a figure of white imagination rests on the certainty of his eventual departure, a feat accomplished symptomatically by the poem itself. The prospect is not bright.

"Then a darker, drearier vision
Passed before me, vague and cloud-like;
I beheld our nation scattered,
All forgetful of my counsels,
Weakened, warring with each other:
Saw the remnants of our people
Sweeping westward, wild and woful,
Like the cloud-rack of a tempest,
Like the withered leaves of Autumn!"

"All forgetful of my counsels": Hiawatha lays blame on his own people, their inability to transcend their "savage" character, though the smoke of factories and railroads and engines of destruction inject a not-so-covert anxiety on Longfellow's part about the full meaning of "the white-man's foot." Does his lamentation for the loss of the unified aboriginal world include a note of the poet's fear of losing an older white American world for whom "Edda" had immediate meaning? The poem suppresses these hints of a jeremiad. Overtly, Hiawatha brings his people to a certain point; the necessary history of culture determines the people's forgetfulness, that the white foot appear and the hero depart, leaving his legacy to be sung to the white-footed nation as an inheritance mediated by the new singer, the national poet and culture bearer, Longfellow.

We can watch in his journal as Longfellow arrived at a hero who knew enough to step aside in the path of the white men. Hiawatha's farewell vision legitimated the Christian nation of immigrants. That it is Christian in the full sense of the word seems confirmed by two jarring lines in the "message" of the "Black-Robe chief" about Jesus: "How the Jews, the tribe accursed, / Mocked him, scourged him, crucified him." A few years later Longfellow published "The Jewish Cemetery at Newport," which ends with the words "dead nations never rise again." The covert equation of the Jews with Indian nations suggests at the least that Longfellow did not imagine that ghetto Jews from "narrow streets and lanes obscure" would come in masses among the "unknown, crowded nations" that several decades later filled America's smoking towns.

Deviating from previous (white) authors of Indian epics, Longfellow chose to write in the mode of epic-romance rather than of history, to found the poem on traditional lore rather than on unhappy chronicles of warriors, tomahawks, and bloody scalps. His most significant step was the naming of his hero. At first he was called Manobozho, after the Ojibway-Algonquian character in oral culture whose paradoxical behavior—playful and serious, rowdy and civil, devious and loyal, lover of chaos and maker of order—makes him both trickster and culture-hero, a well-known paradox. "A combination or antagonism of culture hero and trickster is a characteristic of North American mythology," writes Géza Roheim. Paul Radin adds, "Trickster is at one and the same time creator and destroyer, giver and negator, he who dupes others and who is always duped himself. . . . He possesses no values, moral or social, is at the mercy of his passions and appetites, yet through his actions all values come into being."[62] This is exactly the wrong sort for a poet who wanted an Indian hero who was both acceptable in polite society and capable of founding an aboriginal tradition for a white Christian nation.

Of Manabozho, Schoolcraft wrote that he represented "the idea of an incarnation . . . the great spirit-man of northern mythology." But he was also "rather a monstrosity than a deity, displaying in strong colors far more of the dark and incoherent acts of a spirit of carnality than the benevolent deeds of a god." His bravery, strength, wisdom, "high exploits," clashed with his "low tricks." Uncomprehending of and uncomfortable with this simultaneous love of order and love of chaos, Schoolcraft put the contradictions down to something inscrutable and "carnal" in Indian character. That Longfellow's Hiawatha derives from this baffled and offended understanding of Manabozho cannot be stressed enough. In an early passage, which he later deleted, Longfellow's hero showed as a shape-shifting trickster; as a squirrel he chats away with other squirrels, even addresses an Indian boy in squirrel talk. But the poet changed course and the poem stripped its hero of all "low" trickster traits, transferring them to the character of Pau-Puk-Keewis.[63]

The change of name was the decisive act in Longfellow's refurbishing of his hero. "Hiawatha is Iroquois," Longfellow explained to a friend; "I chose it instead of Manabozho (Ojibway) for sake of euphony. It means 'the Wise Seer, or Prophet'—Hiawatha the Wise."[64] This name change and transfer of meaning from one culture language to another salvaged his hero as acceptable mediator between stages of civilization, as Promethean culture-hero and prophet of the nation. By euphony, Longfellow intended more than sound alone. Both names fit the meter, but Hiawatha came with better credentials.

How and where did Longfellow find the name Hiawatha? The common wisdom is that he repeated a mistake made by Schoolcraft, who in several passages of his books conflated Hiawatha, the Iroquois sachem, with the archetype to which he assigned the name Manabozho.[65] In 1901, after ethnographers began picking away at the poem, Longfellow's daughter Alice wrote that her father, "feeling the need for some expression of the finer and nobler side of the Indian nature . . . blended the supernatural deeds of the crafty sprite [Manabozho] with the wise, noble spirit of the Iroquois national hero, and formed the character of Hiawatha." Her Introductory Notes to a later edition of the poem include a lengthy passage from Hale's 1881 paper, an apparent sign that this volume was meant to incorporate the historical Iroquois Hiawatha into an official version (sponsored by the poet's family and publisher) of the hero's name, no longer a choice based on euphony alone but also on meaning.[66] Whatever the truth about Longfellow's motives, he seemed to have been moved by a quality or essence rather than an actual character or person. He chose a euphonious name for a euphonious character.

Hiawatha was portrayed in Iroquois history and lore as "the equable man," writes William Fenton, "the ideal chief who put public concern over self and family . . . Hiawatha grieved over corruption in government, blood feud, and repeated acts of reprisal by sorcery . . . He conceived a scheme of a vast confederation to ensure universal peace." In short, he was the epitome of a "founding father."[67] He confronted the Onondaga tyrant and sorcerer Thadodaho and combed the serpents out of his hair, setting his mind straight and converting him to the cause of unity and peace. His name means "He Who Combs," "that is, who straightens out the kinks in men's mind."[68] Longfellow divested him of Iroquois associations, and especially the conflict within him between a "low" body of unruly appetite and a "high" visionary spirit. Here is John Bierhorst's summary of the legend in his introduction to "The Ritual of Condolence," the central Iroquois ritual:

> According to legend the great league was conceived by the hero Hiawatha, who had himself been afflicted by a morbid state of mind. One day, so the story goes, he noticed the reflection of a new face in the surface of the water. Not recognizing it as his own, he looked up and saw peering over his shoulder the beautiful figure of his second self, a seemingly real personage to whom mythmakers have given the name of Deganawidah ("the Thinker"). It was Deganawidah who persuaded Hiawatha to give up the practice of cannibalism and to become, moreover, the advocate of a Great Peace. Having reformed himself, Hiawatha proceeded to reform his people.

It's the Deganawidah face that entranced Longfellow, and he repressed the cannibal for the sake of the saint, redeeming the ambiguous trickster as "an American Prometheus."[69]

Grace Chandler, "Hiawatha in Early Manhood, Indian Play at Wayagamug, near Petoskey, Michigan," postcard, c. 1904. (Author's collection)

At what price in fidelity to sources, historical resonance, and emotional power? "I have always one foremost satisfaction in reading your books," Emerson wrote in thanks for the gift of the book in November 1855, "—that I am safe." It's a "wholesome" poem, he added, "sweet and wholesome as maize; very proper and pertinent for us to read, and showing a kind of manly duty in the poet to write." Four months earlier Emerson had written to another poet in appreciation for his book. *Leaves of Grass*, he wrote in a famous letter to Walt Whitman, is "the most extraordinary piece of wit and wisdom that America has yet contributed . . . I give you joy of your free and brave thought . . . I find the courage of treatment which so delights us, and which large perception only can inspire." Courage, bravery, largeness of perception, power are conspicuously absent from Emerson's praise of Longfellow's "Indian poem." Emerson continued to Longfellow, "The dangers of the Indians are, they are really savage, have poor, small, sterile heads,—no thoughts; and you must deal roundly with them, and find them in brains. And I blamed your tenderness now and then, as I read, in accepting a legend or song, when they have so little to give."[70] To be generous toward Emerson, who elsewhere found much to admire in native cultures, we can take his strong words to mean that he did not think that native speech and culture readily converted into the familiar. The safety of Longfellow's wholesome poem, he seems to mean, is purchased by making the aboriginal warrior compliant in his own undoing. At the core of the poem, Emerson helps us see, lies a "civilized" though ambivalent desire to subdue the primordial and at the same time to appropriate it, to ingest it as a sacrificial meal, to win access by means of translation (or the illusion of such) to secret sources of the aboriginal world. The poem is an amulet against a forbidding future, the poem as a bit of civilized magic of its own.

Eponym not only of the poem but also of a whole way of unalienated being, Hiawatha emerged from Longfellow's imagination as the generic "white man's Indian," the hidden name of every staged Indian who comes to us with melancholic eyes and sorrow in his speech, teaching ancient wisdom while lamenting the inevitable loss of ancient ways and native land, promising always to leave and always to return. Singing the song of Hiawatha in the midst of a national crisis that threatened to undo the civil order of the republic, and at the peak of the first great rush toward an industrial-capitalist order, Longfellow sensed the perils of a rapidly changing world, of an old order crumbling and the new prospect dimmed by smoky mills and noisy engines. In the final canto Hiawatha departs "With a smile of joy and triumph, / With a look of exultation, / As of one who in a vision/ Sees what is to be, but is not."[71] The vision of an American future under "the white-man's foot" has wiped from his brow "every trace of sorrow."

Traces of sorrow are not so blithely erased from the reader's brow. Treachery, violence, ringing axes, and murky towns, a future "restless, struggling, toiling, striving," with peril piled upon peril at the poem's climax—these invite us to read through and behind and beneath the exultation and triumph to a less confident vision and see the clash of Longfellow's myth of American origins with the clouded future already visible to him. Hiawatha promises to return, to "come again to see you." But the people know better; they say "Farewell forever." "And the forests, dark and lonely, / Moved through all their depths of darkness." The poem itself moves through darkness, leaving the reader in the end stranded on a beach squinting after Hiawatha fading into the blackness of night, a finality where vision fails. "And the waves upon the margin / Rising, rippling on the pebbles, / Sobbed: 'Farewell, O Hiawatha!'"[72] "Terminally epic," in Gordon Brotherston's apt words, "the hero follows the solar walk not through its circuit but just westward to annihilation in the 'fiery sunset.'"[73]

In 1873, *Hiawatha: The Story of the Iroquois Sage, in Prose and Verse*, by an otherwise unknown author named Benjamin F. DeCosta, was published. It is, as far as I know, the first notice of the fact that Longfellow's hero was a misconstrual of his historical namesake. "The Red Man in North America has alternately been the victim of the poet and the politician," DeCosta wrote, but "a new 'Hiawatha' is among the possibilities of the future," a poem that would give credit to the political form of the confederacy: "essential republicanism in this country began with the League of the Five Nations, who were taught the advantages of the system by Hiawatha; all of which is worthy of finding expression in a peculiarly American poem." Sad to report, DeCosta's own effort at such a poem was wretched.[74] But the idea of a new Hiawatha, true to his name and to his dual nature, trickster and culture hero, cannibal and civilizer, Indian teacher to the nation, plants a teasing thought. Might the old progenitor yet return in another guise?

V

Early in 1900, a Boston newspaper reported "A Hiawatha Revival" in progress. Anyone who recalled "the persistent and almost savage criticism" of Longfellow's poem, the article explained, "cannot help being surprised at the changed position it occupies in men's minds today." The use of "savage" to characterize the still reverberating charges against the poem catches our eye, especially as a counterpoint to the "love, affection and tradition" attributed to a group of "native denizens of Indian blood" who made a visit to the poet's home in Cambridge to pay their respects. Things had turned around. The reference to "men's minds" also rings as significant in light of the article's discovery that "there is a virile tone" to the poem after all, which will "associate the personality of the poet with primal American life more than anything else he wrote." The visiting Ojibways were disappointed to learn that "the chronicler of their joys and sorrows was no more." But Longfellow's daughter Alice received them cordially and accepted an invitation for her and her party to "come and see us and stay in our royal wigwam on an island in Hiawatha's playground . . . We want you to see us live over again the life of Hiawatha in his own country."[75]

Hiawatha redux: living "over again" as performance, as spectacle, as sacrificial host: a meal set for the nation. This was not exactly the new Hiawatha DeCosta imagined, but the spectacle form of his reappearance did revive the Longfellow construction as modern ritual. Just as "savage criticism" implied that he himself had suffered some degree of sacrifice for the sake of upholding a norm of literary propriety, so Longfellow had contrived a "departure" scene, an Indian "assumption" of a dead or dying god figure redeeming a nation that had in real life spilled oceans of blood and inflicted immeasurable bodily

A scene from an outdoor production of *Hiawatha* in 1902, possibly at the Philadelphia zoo, showing Indians in four canoes and Hiawatha and Minnehaha in front of their tepee. (Library of Congress)

"Hiawatha Legends," postcard, 1905. (Author's collection)

pain to achieve its dominance. Slaughter subsumed as destiny—
"unproductive expenditure," in Georges Bataille's words, for the sake
of disguised symbolic reenactment of the past—seemed a necessity at
a time swollen with an excess of goods, guilt, and national angst. Repeated performance of gentle Hiawatha's farewell passion displaced
and substituted for a history of actual blood sacrifice—the murder
and beheading of King Phillip, the massacre of his people, the assas-
sinations of Crazy Horse and Sitting Bull, killing of Big Foot and his
band at Wounded Knee—and it gave the nation an aestheticized version of its own unspoken historical memory. With blood no longer
running and the tribes apparently "pacified," the expanding and di-
versifying United States could now enjoy a solacing national memory,
a perennial ritual of violence sublimated as art. This was a neat turn
on the "regeneration through violence" of the lost frontier experience.[76]

Already a popular theme for illustrators of numerous editions of
the poem and for prominent painters including Albert Bierstadt, Hiawatha took his place among national folk heroes of song and legend,
something like an Indian Paul Bunyan. In drawings, paintings, sculp-
tures, illustrations, photographs, and cinema, he reappeared at the
turn of the century newly pictorialized. Profusely illustrated editions
of *Hiawatha* like Frederic Remington's in 1890 gathered schoolchildren around an imaginary fireplace to hear and see and recite the familiar cadences; picture postcards displaying scenes from the poem
flooded the nation; statues by Daniel Chester French and African
American sculptress Edmonia Lewis further ennobled the poem's in-
gratiating hero. In pageant and image he was given speech, song, and
dance to enhance his presence as living over again the story of his
good works and his departure. The Hiawatha revival included coloring books for children, photographs of performances, popular ephemera, revisions of the poem into a multimedia cultural event. The poem
became important to a movement among composers who wanted to
revitalize and nationalize American music in the Western tradition
with Indian themes, resulting in further Westernization of the Hiawatha figure; Dvořák based two movements of his *New World* sym-
phony in the 1890s on episodes from the poem, and the Anglo-African
composer Samuel Coleridge-Taylor was dubbed the "Hiawatha man"

for his Brahmsian cantatas, often performed by black church choirs. And the spectacle form for presenting Indianness, already established as "historical" in Wild West shows, reached a kind of apex in 1909 with the staging of "The Romance of the Vanishing Race" at the Wanamaker Department Store in Philadelphia and New York, an elaborate confection of images, lantern slides, moving pictures, and music whose centerpiece was a filmed version of *The Song of Hiawatha*.

A new element in all this was the participation of natives in reviving the fiction that Longfellow's Hiawatha was an actual Indian figure. A 1891 photograph by Frances Benjamin Johnson shows a class of Indian students at the Carlisle School; a blackboard surmounted by a portrait of George Washington lists topics under discussion: "Hiawatha's Childhood; Nokomis, Who was she? Why was she called daughter of the moon?" As Lonna Malmsheimer writes aptly, this photograph shows native students "in the very act of disappearing" into a view of themselves and their tribal past as transfigured into Euro-American poetry, just as they themselves undergo transformation, sitting at their desks, their noses in the book (except for the young man on his feet reciting the poem for the white teacher on her feet at the right), into what Luther Standing Bear would call "imitation white men." In the photograph, Indians perform their abandonment of their Indian selves by accepting Longfellow's Hiawatha as their own.[77]

Starting in 1881 and running for about thirty years, Indian students performed a staged reading of "Scenes from Hiawatha" at Carnegie Hall in New York and in other theaters and summer resorts in New England. In a letter to Longfellow's grandson in which she enclosed a copy of the script, Cora Folsom, a sympathetic teacher of Indian students at the Hampton Institute, explained that the performances began as an attempt to raise money for a stained-glass memorial to Pocahontas in an Episcopal church in Hampton. It was included as late as 1919 on a program at the school for "Indian Citizenship Day," perhaps in celebration of Indian veterans of World War I who were made citizens in reward for military service.[78]

But the event to which Alice Longfellow was ceremoniously invited in 1900 represented a striking new turn in Hiawatha perfor-

Frances Benjamin Johnson, "Classroom at the Indian School, Carlisle, Pennsylvania," 1903. (Library of Congress)

Soule Art Company, "Give your children, O Father!" The Kempton Pictures, 1904. (Author's collection)

mances. From her narrative and from newspaper sources, we learn that the visiting Indians were in Boston "to illustrate Indian life" at a Sportsman's Show. They were to be accompanied by the old chief Buk-wij-ji-ni-ni, son of the famous chief Shing-wauk, from whom some believed Schoolcraft first heard the legends of Hiawatha by word of mouth, though "it is said" (according to an article in *Everybody's Magazine* reprinted in a Cambridge newspaper) that Buk-wij-ji-ni-ni himself believed "to his dying day," which happened to occur just before the trip to Boston, "that he told the legends personally to the author of Hiawatha." He charged his successors Kabaooa and Wabunosa to make the invitation, which was graciously accepted by the Longfellow daughters.

It happened, wrote Alice Longfellow, that the expedition to Boston had been arranged by a "Canadian gentleman" who "had been cherishing the idea of training the Indians to perform scenes from 'Hiawatha' in the forest on the shores of the 'big sea water'" (which was actually Lake Huron, not Superior, the "Gitche Gumee" of the poem). L. O. Armstrong of Montreal, apparently in the employ of the Canadian Pacific Railway, had translated sections of the poem into Ojibway. In 1901 a pamphlet with Armstrong's Ojibway version printed opposite lines from Longfellow's poem appeared under the imprint of the Canadian Pacific Railway Company along with information about how to reach the location, near Desbarats, Ontario, and Petoskey, Michigan. Coincidentally, Ernest Hemingway's parents had a cabin nearby. At age two or three, about the time the Hiawatha pageants got under way, the Hemingway child amused his parents by performing passages from *Hiawatha*. Spending his summers there while growing up, Hemingway became intimate with local Indians; he used the region as the site of several stories of initiation in the 1920s such as "Indian Camp" and "The Three-Day Blow." Come visit "the land of the Ojibways," the railway pamphlet suggested, and see the "Ojibway Indian Play." A further inducement was that "Canoe trips with Fishing and Shooting can be enjoyed there in their perfection."[79]

The Longfellow party loved the performance on a rugged offshore island, the daughters were initiated into the tribe ("the redmen expressed a deep and sincere national feeling," said one newspaper account, "in electing the poet's daughters as daughters of their tribe"), and an expanded annual event was launched; it was performed more than fifty times in 1902, sixty-two the following year, and its three hundredth performance occurred in 1903 when the production went on the road. By then an elaborate musical score had been added. A pamphlet published in 1914 by the Grand Rapids & Indiana Railway Company (entrepreneurs on the American side were hardly lax) described added amenities in Petoskey for tourists: a bathing beach, a dining hall with "genuine 'HOMECOOKING,'" and an Indian handicraft shop where one could purchase hundreds of pictures in "platinum etching and oil . . . from the Studio of Grace Chandler Horn." Her photographs of the site and performers adorn the pamphlet as they do a handsome publication of the poem, called "The Players' Edition," brought out by Rand McNally in 1911. The Ojibway performers, we are assured in the preface (repeated in the 1914 pamphlet) "are intensely proud of the legends connected with their early life, are proud of the grandeur, of the wealth of their traditions that Longfellow's poem had made immortal." Many of the performers claimed descent from "hereditary chiefs" like Shing-wauk and Buk-wij-ji-ni-ni.[80]

Longfellow himself "had no idea," remarked a writer in *Everybody's Magazine*, "that the time would come when men would be able to see in the flesh the romantic characters created by him from the ancient legends of the Ojibways." Press coverage of the 1900 event added an important dimension, stressing how the theatrical performance realized the poem by visualization. But "in the flesh" barely states the extent of Hiawatha's new visibility. With smaller cameras and faster film, and refinement of halftone reproduction of photographs in newspapers, in magazines, in brochures, and on cards, the imprint of flesh on film could be reproduced and circulated with ease. The persons, events, and settings of the poem appeared live on stage and again in mass-produced images. In 1904 in Boston a series of thirty consecutive photographs by the Soule Art Company appeared, apparently for use in school, a protocinematic telling of the familiar narrative that foreshadowed the filmed versions soon to come. Photographic visibility lent a sense of closeness to Hiawatha and his staged gestures, a new intimacy with the figment of Longfellow's imagination materialized first as performance and then as image. Employed to extend the visibility of performance into a universally available experience, photography became a key resource of spectacle.

"It may not be generally known," wrote *Everybody's Magazine*, "that the legends embodied in the 'Song of Hiawatha' are genuine; that the Indian names and words employed are identical with those used among the Ojibways, and that the geographical locations are correct." By time of the 1911 "Players' Edition," the location had a new, Indian-sounding name: "Way-ya-ga-mug, near Petoskey, Michigan." "As is shown by the photographs," the preface continues, "no artificial stage or painted scenery is used. The forest itself, through the trees of which gleam the white tepees of the Indian village, forms a fitting background." As for the performers, "they are living out what, to them, is life, real life."[81]

"Real life," we learn, was in large part reconstructed with ethnological assistance. "Unfortunately for romance," a Boston newspaper explained, "the Ojibway learned the arts of the white man at the expense of many of his own." Examples of "good" Indians, "the best types of aboriginal American in existence," were few, and the Ojibway "contact with the white man has cost him his nationality and dominion." Presenting their "real life" in theatrical form would have the happy result of "reviving" among them "knowledge of their own ancient customs, ceremonials, arts and styles of dress"; it would make better performers of them.

Armstrong found drawings and photographs in the ethnological collections of the Smithsonian Institution to teach local Ojibways "forgotten skills in the art of porcupine quill and bead embroidery." Longfellow's Hiawatha gave an occasion, as the press presented the event, for a Canadian-English artistic entrepreneur to "restore" their forgotten culture to the Ojibways, including a chance for Christian Indians to perform rites of their ancient religion that Longfellow had sympathetically preserved. The performance invited comparisons with the "mystery" play, a "religious observance" like the famous German passion play at Oberammergau. Longfellow's "fairy tale" became flesh at Way-ya-ga-mug as a lost ritual recovered, and the Indian performers had a chance to perform their loss in someone else's version for the pleasure of white audiences and perhaps their own fun: Sacrifice was sublimated as entertainment.

The conviction that this was real life was a paradoxical effect of theatricality, the spectacle mode of the performance. Here are excerpts from the description in *Everybody's Magazine*:

> After the audience had assembled in front of the stage, on the green slope, . . . signal-fires were lighted here and there at the back of the wigwam. The dense smoke caused by burning birch-bark soared aloft through the trees, and in response to this primitive summons a number of Indian braves attired in the war panoply of their tribes came hurrying through the wood from various directions. As they approached the stage they reduced their pace to a walk and finally to a stealthy, crouching tread . . .
>
> When all were gathered on the stage, facing one another with glowering looks, a loud voice, that of Gitche Manito, the Mighty, suddenly called them in the Ojibway tongue to cease their warring . . . the braves cast off their deerskin garments, dropped their weapons and dashed into the lake, where they speedily cleansed themselves from their hideous war-paint . . . the Indians sat down in a large circle, and, one after another, took a puff from the peace-pipe . . . This was the end of the first act.

The cleansing is the key. The spectacle gives us an Indian assuredly "genuine" in his speech, setting, costume, and accoutrements. Within a few years, music by Frederick R. Burton was added, making for "a musical-dramatic-spectacular work," in the words of the Boston *Evening Transcript*. Expanded with a full orchestra and "white singers disguised as Indians . . . to sing the more complex passages," the troupe held regular performances at the Lake Huron site and also brought the elaborated spectacle to New York, Philadelphia, Boston, and Chicago as "adjunct" to local Sportsman's Shows. "Great crowds" watched the shows with eagerness and awed attention, "striking evidence of the strong hold the poem has taken upon English-speaking people"—proof again that Longellow had caught and preserved "whatever is high and good and human in the redman."[82]

Newspaper accounts suggest how audiences understood what they witnessed. There are good Indians, the ones portrayed by Cooper and Longfellow, "noble tribes of warriors" not to be confused, one article instructed its readers, with "poor degenerate Indians," the "hapless creatures as creep about the stations and reserves in the west." Hiawatha and his wife "were of a different and far nobler model, and we may all regret that they have practically vanished from the earth." Proof of Hiawatha's nobility is his "knowing and foretelling the fading out of his race." Do we need remind ourselves it is Longfellow's ventriloquism of which the writer speaks? "Hiawatha had to depart, and the new times had to arrive for America's sake and humanity's, as no one could better have sung than the gentle and gifted poet." That Longfellow's vision was honored by the reliving of faded nobility in spectacle of song and action was taken as "singular proof of the power of true poetry to influence history . . . and shows how deeply the American bard must have entered into the spirit of the ancient races whose disappearance was proceeding under his eyes." By performance the good Indians were being reclaimed simultaneously as modern Christian Americans (though still Ojibway, still native, still "colored") and noble tribal people. To be sure, the performers understood that they were playing roles, but their mimesis was all the more effective because white audiences believed they were performing their own genuine "mystery play," the "fairy tale" composed by Longfellow in his Cambridge study not so long ago.[83]

Newspaper commentary constructed the performance as that of Indians putting on their ancient fading selves in both historical and mythical pageantry, enacting the return of Hiawatha in his perpetual act of departing "for America's sake." This Indian minstrelsy reached a peak during what the historian David Glassberg calls a "pageantry craze," when casts of hundreds and thousands mobilized by "pageant masters" acted out episodes from the histories of towns and cities all over America. A scarcity of living Indians in the East led to recruitment of Boy Scouts and the Improved Order of Red Men to perform

Albert Bierstadt, "Departure of Hiawatha," 1868. (Courtesy of National Park Service, Longfellow National Historic Site)

N. H. Losey, "Hiawatha's Farewell," 1911. Apparently somewhere in Indiana. (Library of Congress)

the Indian roles; one pageant writer proposed using Italian immigrants, swarthy and dark, as Indians. In other cases organizers declined to use available and willing natives; the St. Louis *Pageant and Masque* disguised white performers as Indians with copper paint. The "masque" part of the St. Louis event was created by Percy MacKaye, a leading originator of pageants on timely civic themes, many having to do with immigration and citizenship. In St. Louis he deployed Indian symbols but no Indian performers. A giant puppet represented Cahokia, spirit of the Mound Builders and "pinnacle of the social aspirations of the Indian race, regarded ethnologically."[84]

MacKaye was a Progressive who believed that pageants served civic reform. The Mound Builders had represented a cooperative community; it fell to "Powers of Chaos," but Cahokia cries out, "dreams are born and rise from ruined worlds." A new civilization, carried by white settlers, will emerge in their place: "ruined worlds," a polite euphemism for "the cyclone of civilization." Historical pageants typically included Indian scenes, not all so rife with overblown symbolism as MacKaye's, but few actual natives appeared in them.

Not so with the Way-ya-ga-mug Hiawatha, which brought large audiences from far and wide, make-believe witnesses of tribal history as national memory, prehistory passing over into the blessings of actual American history. Hiawatha returned in a time of need with a message on his prophetic lips, if only the vacationers, tourists, and seekers of Indian treasures could decipher it.

TWO

Conceivable Aliens

———

From no one ethnic source is America sprung: the electric reciprocations of many stocks conspired and conspire. This opulence of race-elements is in the theory of America.
—William Swinton, *Rambles Among Words* (1859)

And when a man dies on your great wide soil, America,
It is as if he died in many countries at once!
—Berysh Vaynshteyn, "On Your Soil, America" (1936)

Is it merely coincidental that Hiawatha revived exactly in the years of great immigration from "the unknown, crowded nations"? His prophecy, "Speaking many tongues, yet feeling / One heart-beat in their bosoms," had lent a comforting rhythm to Crèvecoeur's vision of unity out of diversity. But by the late 1890s, a diversity of "alien" tongues, religions, cuisine, and dress and personal habits had multiplied with seemingly ferocious suddenness. The earlier predominantly Anglo-Saxon and Protestant immigration from Western and Northern Europe was giving way to a flood of newcomers from Eastern and Southern Europe. The casual harmonies of old white settler Americans seemed about to collapse into a cacophony of inharmonious difference. "Hordes" of Italian Catholics, Orthodox Slavs, and Jews of all degrees of religiosity (including none) were inundating cities, factories and mines, schools and public spaces all over America. In the 1840s, the arrival of hundreds of thousands of Irish Catholics had stirred the first outbreak of nativist reaction; fears of displacement and pollution flashed up again at the turn of the century. Social turbulence—the national railroad strike of 1877, the Haymarket bombing of 1886, armed clashes of workers and troops in the 1890s—made the words "Italian," "Slav," "Serb," "Jew," and their slur versions connote "dangerous classes," anarchy, socialism, disorder of all kinds.

When it became apparent that the scales were tipping away from the old stock, talk of "foreign peril" inflamed the air. In 1896, immigration from Italy, Poland, Russia, and Hungary for the first time exceeded that from England, France, Germany, and Scandinavia; by 1907, as if on a cresting wave, the flood rose to more than 80 percent of the total. How could the United States absorb all these people and continue to feel "one heart-beat"? Yankee blue bloods and others watched with alarm the increase of "undesirable" groups—"races," wrote the patrician Massachusetts Senator Henry Cabot Lodge in 1891, "most alien to the body of the American people."[1]

One body, one heartbeat: This traditional metaphor for corporate nationality construed the nation as an organic entity of assimilated difference; the body absorbs and converts heterogeneity into homogeneity. A biological figure of the unitary body underlay the popular chemical metaphor of conversion, the melting pot that blends difference into sameness and produces an amalgam, a composite, an organic aggregate. The nutrient parts lose their distinctiveness when they merge with the whole, coloring its character but not altering its wholeness and its one heartbeat. Anything irreducibly "alien," indigestible and unassimilable, threatened the health of the body with pollution, contamination or, worse, "mongrelization."

Biological and chemical figures filtered into public-discourse imagery of disease, degradation, and corruption. The commissioner of immigration, Frank P. Sargent, in an interview with *The New York Times* in 1905, predicted an "immigration peril": "Today there is an enormous alien population in our larger cities which is breeding crime and disease at a rate all the more dangerous because it is more or less hidden and insidious."[2] The peril extended through invisible germs and visible crime, endangering the fiber and spirit (the breath itself) of the national body. Arguing for restriction of immigration in *The Atlantic Monthly* in 1896, Francis A. Walker, a prominent political economist, commissioner of Indian affairs in 1871–72, president of the Massachusetts Institute of Technology, and supervisor of the 1890 census that had declared the "closing" of the frontier, worried about the dampening effect on "the vitality and reproductive capability of the American people" of "vast throngs of ignorant and brutalized peasantry from the countries of eastern and southern Europe." He cited a falling birthrate among "native" Americans, "increasingly unwilling to bring forth sons and daughters who should be obliged to compete in the market for labor." It was bad enough that the influx of immigrants reached 5.25 million between 1880 and 1890, but the problem was "aggravated by the addition of some millions of Hungarians, Bohemians, Poles, south Italians, and Russian Jews." "No intelligent patriot" can avoid feeling "the gravest apprehension and alarm." This new cohort lacked the "inherited instincts and tendencies" of the immigrants of "the olden time"; these were "beaten men from beaten races," without the traditions of "self-care and self-government" that descendants of those who "met under the oak-trees of old Germany to make laws and choose chieftains" had brought to American citizenship.[3]

In 1911, the congressional Dillingham Commission recommended restriction of immigration because of what it claimed to be "the unassimilable character of recent immigrants." This anxiety, according to a recent commentator, "rested on a model of the United States's dominant ethnic identity as an Anglo-Saxon one, traceable to English settlers and subsequent northern European immigrants. It was not a melting-pot assimilationist model—despite rhetoric to the contrary."[4]

Talk of "national origins" and "race" introduced differentiating terms for American identity. Crèvecoeur's unequivocal image of "that strange mixture of blood" coursing the veins of "the American, this new man" had been adopted in the early republic—Jefferson, Emerson, Melville, Whitman, Lincoln, Longfellow all gave ringing voice to this core principle of a "nation of nations"—and diversity and homogeneity "intertwine," as John Higham writes, throughout the national experience.[5] Turn-of-the-century reactions to "aliens," which allied blue bloods, political scientists, and labor leaders in a campaign for restrictions on immigration, brought to the surface tension between "consent" and "descent," in Werner Sollors's terms, between a political definition of identity based on compact and a cultural definition based on vaguer attributes of group membership or putative "nationality." At the figural core of Crèvecoeur's cultural "mixture" was the melting pot, a site of biological as well as chemical conversion: "The migrant, imagined as a *man*, becomes American by 'being received' in the 'broad lap of our great *Alma Mater.*'"[6] Here individuals of all nations are melted down into a new race of men. As Sollors observes, the frontispiece of the 1787 edition of Crèvecoeur's *Letters* depicts Alma Mater as an Indian woman suckling infants—Pocahontas, mythic "mother of us all," in whose lap the European figuratively undergoes rebirth into the American.[7] Crèvecoeur was describing at once the literal place of the American land and the figurative place of the Indian woman's womb. "Indian" becomes the buried mediating term between "European" and "American."

This turn-of-the-century rhetoric produced what Henry James in 1907 called "the inconceivable alien," inconceivable in the sense both of unthinkable and unregenerative, unable to be conceived or bred as "rebirth," as if "aliens" were a different breed of humankind. Anxious over the integrity of the "one body," restrictionists like Lodge and Walker made a person's "origins" (what came to be known in the 1950s as "ethnicity") seem indelible features of his identity, something as unerasable as it was unassimilable. National origin or ethnicity was thought of by nativists as analogous to the "leopard's spots" that, racists held, condemned all African Americans to bestiality, or the one drop of "black" blood that doomed all mixed-race persons to the social and legal fate of blacks. In the land of the "self-made man," national and familial affiliations were regarded, ironically, as irrevocable stamps of personal identity. Individuals disappeared into ancestral (and racial) groups. The immigration law of 1924, which set quotas based on "national origins," in name of saving oneness, installed ethnic differentiation (another irony) as an ingrained feature of national identity, making citizens, even of the "old" sort, think of themselves as implicitly hyphenated. To be an "American" came to mean, more self-consciously than earlier, that you had come from elsewhere or you descended from someone who wasn't American. Hierarchical discriminations were taken for granted, and some origins, especially

"Nordic" ones, were said to be more naturally "American" than others, and African the least, in spite of the presence of enslaved blacks virtually from the beginning of settlement.

Among the "old" Americans dismayed by the "new" immigration, Henry James holds a unique place. His responses appear in *The American Scene* (1907), a book of "impressions" of his native land written after a twenty-five-year absence. For Lodge and others, the new "aliens" had created a crisis of major proportions, and James's language echoed Lodge's discomfort, but in the course of his wanderings and observations in New York City, he veered significantly to more complex and challenging positions. How, James asked his fellow citizens, might the inconceivable become conceivable? James's speculations—not of a social scientist but of a novelist and critic or, as he described himself, a "restless analyst"—address core issues in public discourse of the time: the melting-pot trope, the changing culture of the city, the place and plight of "the Indian," and American identity as such. His book alerts us with remarkable perceptivity to nuances of meaning and countermeaning attached to key words—"immigrant," "alien," "American," and "race"—in the lexicon of national identity.

I

The American Scene consists of "impressions" James gathered during ten months of travel in 1905 and 1906 from New England to Florida; a second volume on travels in the West never materialized. But the book is about not *what* James saw but how he elicited something from what he saw, "the whole of the latent vividness of things." In the Preface, where he sets out "the Author's point of view and his relation to his subject," James explains that he was after not "information," "matters already the theme of prodigious reports and statistics," but "features of the human scene . . . properties of the social air, that the newspapers, reports, surveys and blue-books would seem to confess themselves powerless to 'handle.'" Information is exactly the obverse of his quarry. "Incapable of information, incapable alike of receiving it and of imparting it," he planned to go after "the human subject . . .

the appreciation of life itself." The numerous subjectivities of the scene, "much too numerous," as Ross Posnock writes, were his subject.[8] To this he brought a "cultivated sense of aspects and prospects," a vibrating "curiosity," and "a state of desire." He aspired to "intimate intelligence" with those aspects and prospects not reducible to "information."[9]

Casting himself as both an "inquiring stranger" after his quarter century abroad and an "initiated native," James acknowledged a paradoxical relation to his subject. He would be author, concerned with "the consequent question of representation," and a central character, too, experiencing and reflecting upon his experience in the same breath. "I" appears freely, but so do third-person epithets for himself: "the story-seeker," "the picture-seeker," "the repatriated native," "the lone visionary," and most pointedly, "the restless analyst." The narrative gives not only experience but also extended reflections on how experience might be represented: "if representative values and the traceable or the imaginable connection of things happen to have, on occasion, for your eyes and your intelligence, an existence of any intensity, your case, as a traveler, an observer, a reporter, is 'bound' from the first, under the stirred impressions, to loom for you in some distressful shape." "I shall not find such matters scant or simple," he warns the reader. "I would take my stand on my gathered impressions, since it was all for them, for them only, that I returned."[10]

The book bristles with self-questioning commentary. The analyst cannot rest until he has made sense of what he sees. To admit that "the cluster of appearances can *have* no sense" means "to go to pieces; it being the prime business and the high honour of the painter of life always to *make* a sense—and to make it most in proportion as the immediate aspects are loose or confused."[11] What met James's probing eyes as he roamed every scene with a street photographer's passion for revealing gesture and detail often seems disjointed and incoherent; the strain of listening for voices of buildings and places, of the air itself, makes the book seem an ordeal of consciousness. W. H. Auden called it "a prose poem of the first order."[12] The New York sections on skyscrapers, hotels, streetcars and streets, parks and cafés have a gymnastic play of language both lucid and lurid that deposits you breathless at the foot of extraordinary insights. "The last thing decently permitted him [the "painter of life"] is to recognize incoherence—to recognize it, that is, as baffling; though of course he may present and portray it, in all richness, *for* incoherence. That, I think, was what I had been mainly occupied with in New York."[13]

James describes how he stood one winter day by the rail of the visitors' balcony at Ellis Island, absorbed in the scene below. The authorities had built a gallery for visitors curious to see for themselves what the "new" immigration looked like. What they saw was hardly the stuff of high drama: the drudging process of long, snaking lines of travel-weary people hunched under their bundles of belongings, filing before the bored eyes of medical examiners and immigration officials. It was neither a pretty picture nor one that easily disclosed what it meant and why the authorities had made an exhibition of it by opening the viewing gallery. The gallery gave perspective, distance, a way of connecting with the scene by removing yourself from it. From your place above, individuals blurred into a mass. You could generalize the scene into a picture of "huddled masses," hear a babel of tongues instead of unique voices intoning their uniqueness against the official language of the inspectors. Distance defined a relation, a way of taking in and processing the scene as something apart, something alien and yet impinging.

From his position at the gallery rail, James saw Ellis Island as the stage of a "drama poignant and unforgettable," the newly arrived "knocking at our official door." "With a hundred forms and ceremonies, grindings and grumblings of the key, they stand appealing and waiting, marshalled, herded, divided, subdivided, sorted, sifted, searched, fumigated"—a "prodigious process," as James put it. Fumigation tells the distressful part of the story: persons treated chemically were possible bearers of contamination. The transactions in this zone, indeed what defined the zone as a national border, were part of a process whereby each newcomer was inscribed as an alien, in the official sense that he did not yet belong to the system of rights that constitute America's political society of the inside, or to the system of competencies that signaled the inside as a culture as much as a body politic. To enter this zone, to cross this border, was to undergo an ini-

"Immigrants Just Arrived, Ellis Island." Note the viewing balcony above.
Underwood and Underwood, c. 1904. (Library of Congress)

tiatory process of estrangement from your previous place of belonging. To be herded, sorted, and sifted was to learn the meaning of nonbeing; separation from one's old self was the price of admission through the gates. In James's theatrical metaphor, "It is a drama that goes on, without a pause, day by day and year by year, this visible act of ingurgitation on the part of our body politic and social."[14] It resembled the initial process of conversion from "Indian" to "American," the symbolic fumigation of renaming and reclothing undergone by native children at government boarding schools.

The gallery gave Americans the "new" immigration full in the face, a sensory experience of unmitigated difference; it gave or produced something foreign that bisected your field of vision and forced itself, as James went on to say, across the once-sheltered horizon of your national identity, your way of saying who you were. In the face of so many and such strange outsiders clamoring to get in, what was the fate of an American identity that once believed itself (so James assumed) secure in sameness? Obsession is not too strong a word for the concentrated intensity with which James sought the answer.

The gallery viewpoint suggests another complicating perspective, an imaginable reversal. James's posture at the rail watching the arrival of uninvited strangers recalls with unexpected irony a scene occasionally portrayed in nineteenth-century paintings: near-naked, feathered Indians on a bluff overlooking the sea, squinting at the horizon with surprise and dismay as unfamiliar birdlike sailing vessels head their way: a version of Hiawatha's shock at "the white-man's foot." The scene at Ellis Island registers another fateful coming of white-skinned strangers, this time weary seekers of a new homeland. Columbus has devolved into a "wop washerwoman," as Hart Crane would write in *The Bridge* (1930). The role of the startled, fearful native is taken now by America's most sophisticated and Europeanized novelist, whose own already embattled claim to the privilege of "native" is exactly what he felt was being challenged by the new wave of voyagers.

James made his belated return voyage not to repossess a frayed American identity but to see with his own "restless" eyes the present look of his country and to find out how it had changed in a quarter of a century. What can the aspect of things tell of the inner life of the na-

Joshua Shaw, *Coming of the White Man*, 1850. (The Elizabeth Waldo-Denztzel Studios, Northridge, California)

tion, the spirit of the scene? In a peroration concluding the book (omitted in the 1907 American edition), he wrote of being in a railroad car on his way to California and put forth the "last question" posed by his impressions. The railroad and other forms of mechanized motion (including bridges) served as James's prime symbol of the ceaseless expansion and multiplication of sameness by which American commerce and industry colonized American space. He interrogated the railroad: Have you, with your "great monotonous rumble," planted a "germ of anything finely human, of anything agreeably or successfully social"? And he replied, as if in conversation with the massive engine, "If I were one of the painted savages you have dispossessed," "a beautiful redman with a tomahawk," I'd have a ready answer: "Beauty and charm would be for me in the solitude you have ravaged, and I should owe you my grudge for every disfigurement and every violence, for every wound with which you have caused the face of the land to bleed." But while the "if" protected James from the unwarranted simplicity of an "Indian" response, he wouldn't otherwise "have been seated by the great square of plate-glass through which the missionary Pullman appeared to invite me to admire the achievements it proclaimed." His location as spectator betrayed that he "accepts your ravages"; rather than complaining about what the railroad has made, he felt justified in listing "the 'arrears'" of the "undone" it accumulated, "the great symbolic agent" that "stood for all the irresponsibility behind it."[15]

Imagining himself Indian occurs nowhere else in the book, at least not overtly. Poised with his eyes open in the gallery of the Great Hall at Ellis Island, in what Ross Posnock nicely calls a "primal moment,"[16] James reenacted and transposed an original (and originating) American moment of encounter between old and new: wonder and fear on both sides. Not quite brandishing a tomahawk, at the gallery rail he uncannily conflated white Anglo-Saxon Protestant and red responses to the sight of strangers. By occupying (at least as we might imagine) two positions at once, "native" being the doubled sense of red man and white, James brought the weight of an unhappy history to bear on the meaning of the fraught term "alien."

In 1905, at the time of Henry James's visit, awe and mystery hung over the bureaucratic "forms and ceremonies" visible at Ellis Island. Until 1890 these had been rather casual, often administered by volunteers there and at the other ports of entry. Castle Garden at the Battery had served as the New York receiving station; roughly eight million aspiring Americans came to New York through Castle Garden between 1855 and 1890, mainly from Northern and Western Europe. In 1890, the federal government took charge of handling the sharply rising numbers and Ellis Island was designated an official port of entry. With the recently installed (1886) Statue of Liberty close by, the location seemed apt.[17] In 1892, a new receiving station opened in a wooden building; it burned down in 1897. A spacious new fireproof brick building in French Renaissance château style replaced it three years later. Before it shut down in 1954, Ellis Island welcomed about 80 percent of the influx of immigrants to the United States, approximately eighteen million (of which about 30 percent returned "home"), an unprecedented number.[18]

Images of the poor in photographs and drawings, stereographs and moving pictures—the disheveled, those huddled with bundles and frightened young children on benches or in corners of the vast, gloomy Registry Room or Great Hall (it could hold five thousand people)—gave the place its aura of what Henry James called an "infusion of the alien." (Only steerage passengers were required to pass through Ellis Island; those affluent enough to travel first and second class were considered "passengers" and normally cleared customs and entry aboard ship.) In the Great Hall, with a giant American flag hanging from the balcony, the process of inspection could be a nightmarish ordeal. Immigration officers sat on high podiums, as if judging the poor bedraggled petitioners from a place in the sky. Immigrants were directed to drop their luggage in one place and get in a line in another place, women and children separated from the men. The air was filled with voices shouting directions that few immigrants understood, and people feared for their luggage. How could one keep one's bearings in that smoky space, to see where to stand or how to behave, to keep one's parents or children in sight, to find your way back to your luggage and all your worldly possessions? A challenge of perception as well as of language greeted the newcomers. Three thousand deaths (including suicides) at Ellis Island tell yet another story of the ordeal.[19]

A different challenge of perception faced those like James who came to observe the scene from above. Ellis Island attracted a steady flow of curious, sympathetic, and disapproving spectators. The balcony view obscured individual people, personal identities, histories and destinies. In press reports, lurid notes mingled with picturesque details. *The New York Times* described the Great Hall with its lines of railings as "an immense spider web." Among the facilities was a bathing house large enough for two hundred people at a time, or eight thousand a day. "'We expect to wash them once a day, and they will land on American soil clean, if nothing more,'" *The Times* quoted one official as saying.[20] In a 1905 *Times* article on the "immigration peril" the writer gave an inside view: "Crowding the benches outside the railing were specimens of nearly every nationality under the sun. Chinamen elbowed Magyars; Celts and Teutons rubbed shoulders with Gauls and Latins; Russians, resembling so many John the Baptists in their primitive sheep-skin coats, trod the heels of ale-hued Turks; screaming children, scowling men, and patient, resigned women made up the curious ensemble." He described "men, women, and children herded like cattle and hardly more intelligent, until, throwing open a door at the far end of the building, a motley assemblage of vice-ridden, stolid, bovine parodies of manhood was disclosed."[21]

For several years beginning in 1904, the photographer Lewis Hine saw the Great Hall from a different perspective. Perhaps overlapping one day with Henry James, Hine recognized as James did that Ellis Island challenged the eyes to see beyond or beneath surfaces, to perceive nuances of difference. Verbal pictures in the press such as "hatchet-faced, pimply, sallow-cheeked, rat-eyed young men of the Russian-Jew colony" moved Hine to focus on faces and expressions of individuality. He sought to portray the person, not the stereotype. A teacher at the Ethical Culture School who had been inspired by the Progressive reform movement—he would devote the next ten years to documenting the visible facts of child labor across the country— Hine came to Ellis Island with a personal mission quite different from James's but akin to it; his pictures supplement James's intensely self-reflexive prose. Less overtly interested in the "national identity" question, Hine portrayed immigrants as living persons. Like other spectators from above, James saw only a mass without distinguishable persons. But in Hine's pictures persons present themselves with an often disarming frankness, not as "immigrants" but as people whose dress, gestures, belongings, and especially faces told stories, evoked histories, elicited curiosity. Hine's photographs at Ellis Island discovered persons at the threshold of a new world. Strangeness clung to them like another garment. In *Young Russian Jewess*, the curved mass of light and the rectangular piping at the rear frame the girl's aloneness, connecting her with definite social fact: the processing hall of Ellis Island.

Portraying individuals entangled in history and society, Hine's pictures, dense with implication, appeal to our imaginations like fragments from an unwritten realist novel, perhaps in the manner of Henry James himself. They reveal the photographer in his work of eliciting pose, expression, and, at their best, moments of compelling inwardness. Resembling James's self-conscious way of looking inward in the act of looking outward, Hine's pictures make a place and a scene for the photographer himself; they portray his own experience coincident with that of the strangers who paused for a moment before his camera, a cognate even if antithetical supplement to James's meditation on "the alien." Hine behind his camera, James at the rail, share resistance to stereotype and convention, a willingness to enter the scene even while detached, to find in detachment or aesthetic distance a medium of connectedness.[22]

II

At Ellis Island, James resisted the merely picturesque view of the massive event. With his unappeasable appetite for implication, he converted the gallery perspective into vibrant complexity and resonance, an event within his own consciousness. While the immigrants remained fixed in his increasingly alarmed gaze as herded masses undergoing an official process, he turned inward and discovered himself complicit with his gallery perceptions.

Photographs by Lewis Wickes Hine, Ellis Island, 1905

"Young Russian Jewess."
(Private collection)

"Mother and Child, Italian." (Private collection)

"Jew from Russia at Ellis Island."
(Photography Collection, Miriam and Ira D. Wallach Division of Art, Prints and Photographs, New York Public Library, Astor, Lenox and Tilden Foundations)

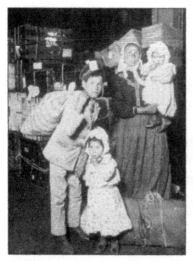

"Climbing into America." "A Slavic group waiting to get through the entrance gate." (Photography Collection, Miriam and Ira D. Wallach Division of Art, Prints and Photographs, New York Public Library, Astor, Lenox and Tilden Foundations)

"Italian Immigrants." "Lost luggage is the cause of their worried expressions," Hine wrote. (Private collection)

"Albanian Woman from Italy." "At times, the Island looked like a costume ball with the multicolored, many-styled national costumes." (Private collection)

I think indeed that the simplest account of the action of Ellis Island on the spirit of any sensitive citizen who may have happened to "look in" is that he comes back from his visit not at all the same person that he went. He has eaten of the tree of knowledge, and the taste will be for ever in his mouth. He had thought he knew before, thought he had the sense of the degree in which it is his American fate to share the sanctity of his American consciousness, the intimacy of his American patriotism, with the inconceivable alien; but the truth had never come home to him with any such force. In the lurid light projected upon it by those courts of dismay it shakes him—or I like at least to imagine it shakes him—to the depths of his being; I like to think of him, I positively *have* to think of him, as going about ever afterwards with a new look, for those who can see it, in his face, the outward sign of the new chill in his heart. So is stamped, for detection, the questionably privileged person who has had an apparition, seen a ghost in his supposedly safe old house. Let not the unwary, therefore, visit Ellis Island.[23]

The immigrant's estrangement translates into a shock of alienation on the part of the "sensitive citizen," an alienation within "one's supreme relation . . . one's relation to one's country." As a result, what he experiences as a relentless assault on the primal conditions of identity comes to mirror the immigrant's ordeal in the border zone. Like the ghost in James's story "The Jolly Corner," contemporary with *The American Scene*, the Ellis Island shade forces self-recognition; Ellis Island gives the visiting citizen a chilling sense of difference in "one's supreme relation," one's nationality, as a result of gazing upon the face of difference among the harried newcomers. The visitor departs with knowledge of violation, violation that calls into question previous assumptions of something inviolable in one's "supreme relation." "The idea of the country itself underwent something of that profane overhauling through which it appears to suffer the indignity of change."[24]

"Haunted" by "this sense of dispossession," James perceived at Ellis Island that the designation "American" could no longer be taken as a "simple and strong and continuous" idea. It was no longer the name

of something "perfectly sound." But did the name *ever* stand for anything simple and uniform? Diversity of population and cultural heteroglossia had been the case, since the first settlements of Europe's
"new world," as John Dewey and other Progressive thinkers argued.
James's ghost of dispossession harbors other ghosts, repressed voices
and images of a less homogeneous America qualifying the image of
loss that haunted the restless analyst.

A shade of the repressed returned for James later on in his book,
during a curious moment in his visit in Washington to the "labyrinthine pile" of the Capitol, "a vast and many-voiced creation." He saw
"the great terraced Capitol hill, with its stages and slopes, staircases
and fountains" as a spectacle of power hinting at "immeasurable
schemes of which it [the Capitol] can consciously remain the centre."
In the "vast spaces" of its terraces, "the great Federal future seems,
under vague bright forms, to hover and to stalk." In this theater of national dominion he met one morning "a trio of Indian braves, braves
dispossessed of forest and prairie, but as free of the builded labyrinth
as they had ever been of these." Their dispossession came in the form
of their "neat pot-hats, shoddy suits and light overcoats," looking like
nothing so much as "Japanese celebrities," or "specimens, on show, of
what the Government can do with people with whom it is supposed to
be able to do nothing." James reflected on the sight in typical fashion
and produced a faceted image of dispossession and domination that
reverberates suggestively with his Ellis Island perceptions:

> They seemed just then and there, for a mind fed betimes on
> the Leatherstocking Tales, to project as in a flash an image in it-
> self immense, but foreshortened and simplified—reducing to a
> single smooth stride the bloody footsteps of time. One rubbed
> one's eyes, but there, at its highest polish, shining in the beau-
> tiful day, was the brazen face of history, and there, all about
> one, immaculate, the printless pavements of the State.[25]

The passage compresses James's insight that domination and re-
pression work hand in glove: the pavements of the state bear no trace
of the bloody footprints of slaughtered braves.

On the streets of New York, the waves of shock expanded from Indians to immigrants as James saw his "inconceivable aliens" assume an air of "settled possession," a "loud primary stage of alienism," as if they had "nobody to thank" for their possession of the streets and streetcars. "So that *un*settled possession is what we, on our side, seem reduced to—the implication of which, in its turn, is that, to recover confidence and regain lost ground, we, not they, must make the surrender and accept the orientation. We must go, in other words, *more* than half-way to meet them; which is all the difference, for us, between possession and dispossession."[26] "*More* than half-way" prefigures a subtle shift, for James's quest for "impressions" opens him to more poignant personal encounters.

What haunted James at Ellis Island may have been fear that by sharing space with aliens, "old" Americans risked becoming alien themselves, ghosts of their former identity. To imagine that your role might be to take the part of the stranger in a new exchange was to raise an apparition of yourself in a state of absolute difference. So the ghost frightened the sensitive citizen into imagining something like an Indian raid on the homestead of the American ego. James allowed full play to the tremors of this imagined condition in passages that followed, in which sensation and speculation commingled in an elaborate fusion of self-consciousness and civic awareness.

He intended *The American Scene*, he explained in the Preface, to be a very personal book. Recovery of his own past recalled from far back was among the desires James carried with him in his explorations of the American scene. He opened the book in New England, where, on a river excursion to Albany, an ancestral home in that it was where grandfather William James of Curkish, County Cavan, Ireland, had settled and become rich, James re-encounters a whole swarm of small forgotten things. Excursions of personal memory are counterpoints to hotels and railroads, and the counterpoint established a theme, a syncopated opposition between personal and impersonal, between acts of memory and the many acts of forgetting and excision of the past (destruction of old buildings, for example) that confront James throughout his American journey.

Preoccupied with the human history of places, the seasoned traveler and novelist noted an American refusal to consent to history. In its lust for money and power, in its constant tearing down and building anew, American society seemed engaged in a perpetual repudiation of the past. Moments of recovered personal memory and association served James as a measure of civilization and civility, a measure by which the American scene fell short, poignantly so when he stood at the site of his birthplace in Washington Square and found "a high, square, impersonal structure, proclaiming its lack of interest with a crudity all its own." The effect was that of "having been amputated of half my history." Similarly, in Boston, the razing of a house he had inhabited for two years in his youth left him feeling "as if the bottom had fallen out of one's own biography."[27]

How did Ellis Island and "inconceivable aliens" figure in this design? To note that they represented another assault on stable identity and self-possession, that they fit a pattern of merciless modernity, only begins to explain the connection. James yoked together the moments of Ellis Island and Washington Square—the haunted house and the amputated history—by means of dramatic juxtaposition. It was just after his visit to Ellis Island that he turned to "that ancient end of Fifth Avenue" in search of memory, a move that he called "an artful evasion of the actual. There was no escape from the ubiquitous alien into the future, or even into the present; there was escape but into the past"[28]—an escape that amputates, to a past whose bottom falls out.

Was it only the insistent presence of the alien that disturbed James's "supreme relation," his sense of *possessing* an American identity? And was it America as cultural scene or America as state to which the "sensitive citizen" enjoys a "supreme relation"? James doesn't engage this question directly, but it insinuates itself at certain junctures. Immigration seems both a cause and an effect, especially the effect of victimization. James's aliens mirrored his own condition, the homelessness and world seeking he brought to his belated American venture. And Ellis Island may have reopened buried memories of a more intimate sort, memories of his own family's immigrant past only two generations back. Was the ghost he raised a reminder of his grandfather's birth in Ireland and immigration into a land dominated by Anglo-Saxon culture, a personal ghost of ethnic difference?

The primary ethnicity James treats in his novels is that of "the American" against the sundry nationalities of "the European." His

American heroes and heroines seem perfect physiognomic examples of the stereotypical Anglo-Saxon. "Long, lean, and muscular," with "a very well-formed head, with a shapely, symmetrical balance of the frontal and the occipital development, and good deal of straight, rather dry brown hair," Christopher Newman, the "powerful specimen" of *The American* (1877), defines the type. "His complexion was brown, and his nose had a bold, well-marked arch." It is an account that echoes, perhaps more than incidentally, conventional descriptions of the classical shapeliness of Indian posture and physiognomy. To be sure, physiognomy doesn't count for everything. "The traces of national origin are a matter of expression even more than of feature."[29] But features are the media of expression and Newman's seem significantly composite. As John Higham has shrewdly remarked, by describing Newman's face as consisting of ambiguities and contradictions—"vagueness which is not vacuity," "blankness which is not simplicity"—James was projecting a type compounded of opposites, "frigid and yet friendly, confident yet shy, shrewd yet credulous," a "blend" of "innocence and experience."[30] While there is no mistaking Newman's identity as other than white, Protestant, Anglo-American (especially, writes Higham, in his "simple consciousness of preeminence and rightful possession"), the catalog of opposite character traits brushes oddly against the grain of the physiognomic catalog. This may be a telling discordance, suggesting a desire to leave the case open and unsettled about what and who, in regard to "national origins," James's "American" really is.

III

If the American is something you are, how do you recognize it? When you feel it challenged, what is that part of you that feels the assault? A separate organ? A mode of experience? Is there one way of being American? James raised such questions in the course of his extended encounter with "alienism" on the streets of New York, and his responses share the discourse of crisis at that time regarding nationality.

Public views split along several lines: those who wanted to restrict immigration, those who accepted it but wanted swift "Americaniza-tion" of the newcomers, and others who welcomed the new diversity of peoples. Americanizers like Theodore Roosevelt spoke of "Ameri-canism" as "a matter of the spirit and the soul,"[31] while liberals like John Dewey argued that the nation had always been "interracial and international in its make-up," "composed of a multitude of peoples speaking different tongues, inheriting diverse traditions, cherishing varying ideals."[32] By 1924, restrictionists won the day, for antiforeign and racist hysteria in the war and postwar years—the spread of the KKK in the 1920s, for example—added steam to the efforts in Con-gress to pass the exclusionist National Origins Act, which set quotas for European nationalities and excluded Japanese immigrants alto-gether.

Americanization or Americanism as an ideal was nowhere better and more potently expressed than in speeches and essays by the most conspicuous national political figure at the time, Theodore Roosevelt. Designed to provoke and to unsettle, Roosevelt's views on "true Americanism" are part of the implicit background of James's troubled thoughts about national identity. Roosevelt abhorred any hint of dual loyalties. To a group of newly naturalized citizens in 1915 he pro-claimed, "There is no "hyphenated American who is also a good American. The only man who is a good American is the man who is an American and nothing else." "Our object," he explained, "is not to im-itate one of the older racial types, but to maintain a new American type and then secure loyalty to that type." "It is our duty . . . to secure the complete Americanization of our people." Roosevelt acknowl-edged the contributions of immigrants to the "new American type," but he insisted on rapid Americanization, abandonment of native tongues for English and native ways for the American way. "A man has got to be an American and nothing else."[33]

Americanization went significantly beyond citizenship for Roo-sevelt. The "ideal citizen must be the father of many healthy children [he leaves to inference what this implies for women]. A race must be strong and vigorous; it must be a race of good fighters and good breeders." In an apparent swipe at Henry James, he pitted the ideal American man who performs his work and lives his life "purely as an

American" against "the over-civilized, over-sensitive, over-refined" and "undersized man of letters, who flees his country because he, with his delicate effeminate sensitiveness, finds the conditions of life on this side of the water crude and raw; in other words, because he finds that he cannot play a man's part among men."[34] True Americanism, Roosevelt insisted, denotes behavior as well as legal status, a certain way of experiencing the world, of feeling and thinking.

John Dewey saw things differently, arguing that anxiety about "foreigners" arose from a dangerous misunderstanding about nationality. There is no valid American "type," Dewey insisted, and he rejected the hypermasculine as well as the Nordic model. During an outbreak of antiforeign feeling when the United States was preparing to join the European war, he wrote in 1916, "No matter how loudly any one proclaims his Americanism, if he assumes that any one racial strain, any one component of culture, no matter how early settled it was in our territory, or how effective it has proven in its own land, is to furnish a pattern to which all other strains and cultures are to conform, he is a traitor to an American nationalism."[35] Dewey echoed the French historian Ernst Renan's view that nation-states are conglomerates of disparate nationalities; their unity is fundamentally political rather than ethnic or cultural. In his celebrated essay of 1882, "What is a Nation?" Renan remarked that "the leading nations of Europe are nations of essentially mixed blood." "There is no pure race, and to make politics depend upon ethnographic analysis is to surrender to a chimera." Scratch the surface of any nation-state and you will find "deeds of violence": James's "bloody footsteps" effaced by the "printless pavements of the State." Nations require "forgetting" and a monumentalization of "historical error" in order to support the illusion that they each represent one people. They go about inventing national traditions and calling them immemorial: The French have their Gauls, the English their Britons, the Germans their Teutons, and Americans their Nordic ancestors, and perhaps their Indians.[36]

The motto *e pluribus unum* would seem to have exempted the United States from the European need to invent fictive ancestors. In its abstract universalism, America appeared to Dewey and his followers as a global concept: less a distinct place than a new conception of the world, a state of being more than a state of governance. Whitman was the grand rhapsode of this vision: "One of the Nation of many nations," he announced in "Song of Myself." "Of every hue and caste am I, of every rank and religion . . . I resist any thing better than my own diversity." Even earlier, anticipating Whitman's "Passage to India," Crèvecoeur had written, "Americans are the western pilgrims, who are carrying along with them that great mass of arts, sciences, vigour, and industry which began long since in the east; they will finish the great circle." America would realize and complete itself in Asia. Freed of nationalist particularism ("The Americans were once scattered all over Europe"), Crèvecoeur's "new man" was freed of the fetters of feudal restraint to self-improvement: "Here the rewards of his industry follow with equal steps the progress of his labour; his labour is founded on the basis of nature, *self-interest*: can it want a stronger allurement?"

Crèvecoeur's American is the bearer of the bourgeois revolution, which reconfigured New World "nature" itself into an abstract principle—not a particular terrain that might through being habitated emerge as a "landscape" or "home" or *patria*, but as an economic resource ("We are a people of cultivators") promoting self-interested enterprise. Universalist underpinnings prepare the American to act as a competitor in the marketplace, an entrepreneur guided by self-interest. The relevance to cultural immigration and the logic of identity of this transnational and ahistorical American, rooted in European bourgeois individualism and in the marketplace's redefinition of persons as economic players, has to be noted. Neutrality, anonymity, and universalism conceptually nurtured the capitalist enterprise, with its inequalities of wealth and power and its freedom for self-realization. Abstract political freedom was undercut by unequal material resources.

While in theory citizenship in the United States requires only allegiance to abstract principles, in practice it assumed a cultural norm: English as the de facto official language; Europe (especially England) as the parent culture; Pilgrims, Puritans, founding fathers, pioneers, emancipators—and Columbus the discoverer—as the true story of the past. And whiteness the skin color of true citizens. The collective memory that made Americans was, for Roosevelt and his camp, a cultural term. Still, pluralism was then as now a practical reality, in religious and "foreign"-language schools, community cultural centers, "foreign"-language newspapers, city enclaves of Asian and Hispanic groups. Multiculturalism won its argument at street level, and localities like the Lower East Side of New York were the cauldron in which it brewed. Horace Kallen, a disciple of Dewey and advocate of "cultural pluralism," saw culture as "psycho-physical inheritance," an "inalienable" feature of human life. In 1915 he wrote of the East European Jew, "Behind him in time and tremendously in him in quality, are his ancestors; around him in space are his relatives and kin, carrying in common with him the inherited organic set from a remoter ancestry. In all these he lives and moves and has his being. They constitute his, literally, *natio*, the inwardness of his nativity." The United States, being a country of cultural immigrants, Kallen argued, should think of itself as "a democracy of nationalities, cooperating voluntarily and autonomously through common institutions in the enterprise of self-realization through the perfection of men according to their kind . . . a multiplicity in a unity, an orchestration of mankind."[37]

It's striking that both Dewey and Kallen took a notably ethnocentric view of the diversity they applaud. Not an Indian in sight, and hardly any African Americans. Their copluralist Randolph Bourne spoke derisively of some Euro-Americans as "half-breeds," stripped of their native culture without achieving anything in its place. James's few pregnant allusions to Indians in *The American Scene* at least recognized that the meaning of "native" is entangled with the meaning of "alien," conceivable or inconceivable. Within James's horizon, Indians remain in view as a stark reminder of Renan's "deeds of violence" at the birth of the nation. Moreover, as W.E.B. Du Bois remarked in a paper at the Universal Races Congress in 1911, "Americans of Negro descent . . . one of the most American groups in the land" are also natives.[38]

At the turn of the century, African Americans were begrudgingly recognized as legal citizens, but at the state and local levels throughout the South, they faced a barrage of legislation, the Jim Crow laws, to limit their rights. An epidemic of lynching of black males at the turn of the century showed that at the edge of local law stood the noose and kerosene. Regarding Indians, the cry was: Let the first Americans become real Americans through citizenship. "When dealing with Indians," wrote Roosevelt in his 1902 annual message to Congress, "our aim should be their ultimate absorption into the body of our people." With typical bluntness in his 1901 presidential message Roosevelt had collapsed "deeds of violence" into a striking trope of "forgetting": "the General Allotment Act is a mighty pulverizing engine to break up the tribal mass"; we must "recognize the Indian as an individual and not as a member of a tribe."[39] American and nothing else. Founded at the height of "new" immigration, largely by graduates of Pratt's Americanizing regime at the Carlisle School, the Society of American Indians took a mitigated version of the same position: Citizenship was the first step toward integration of natives into the American body. The notion of "Indian rights," which the SAI and reform-minded white supporters espoused, implied an endorsement of the redefinition of Indians as one ethnic or racial group among many; liberated from their corporate tribal identity, individual "natives" could be recognized as "citizens," at least potentially.

Charles Eastman, born a Sioux, a doctor, author, and prominent member of the SAI, carried the vision of integration even farther. In "The North American Indian," a paper presented at the Universal Races Congress in 1911, he wrote, "Since it is admittedly impossible for the Indian to continue to exist as a separate race, with his proper racial characteristics and customs, within the limits of the United States, race amalgamation is the only final and full solution of the problem, and only in this sense, implying no lack of vitality, but quite the reverse, is the American Indian a 'dying race.'"[40]

We might wonder: Given the abundant "vitality" Eastman attributes to Indians, did his "final" solution imply an Indianizing of the American population and add a shade of Hiawatha to the defining skin color of the nation? Pratt had ridiculed the theory of Frederick Starr, professor of anthropology at the University of Chicago, that under the influence of "the potent American climate and environment," Americans were "developing marked Indian characteristics."[41] At the same Universal Races Congress, the Columbia University anthropologist Franz Boas delivered a paper on "The Instability of Human Types," in which he claimed to prove through measurements that "the child born in America, even if born only a few months after the arrival of the parents, has the head-form of the American-born." "Social and geographical environment" make a difference, he announced, proving "a decided plasticity of human types."[42]

Just months after the restrictive National Origins Act shut the "open door" on immigration, Congress in 1924 passed the Indian Citizenship Act. The proximity in time of the two acts signals Hegel's "cunning of history." With its aim of preserving an American national "type," the National Origins Act injected a heightened awareness of "origins" into the debate and made it an indelible feature of American identity.[43] The Indian Citizenship Act conferred birthright citizenship on all natives (about two-thirds of whom were already citizens), thus removing their "alien" identity in what amounted to group "naturalization"—a paradoxical ironic twist to the meaning of their original condition. The question that bedeviled the issue of citizenship for Indians was whether, as tribal members, Indians fell fully under U.S. jurisdiction. As The Washington Post noted a few years later, in words that echoed the descriptions of the "new" immigration, "Taken as a whole, they are probably the least homogenous people in America. Each tribe has its own tongue, its own history and each its own traditions, a condition, it must be admitted, which makes it very hard for the politicians." In their debate, some senators wanted to "put them on a plane with white people" and make them "part of this country," in effect eliminating "Indian" as a legal category, while others worried that "making them citizens would make insecure their title to their reservations."

The result was an inconclusive compromise that reflected unresolved tensions in law and in the culture at large between the concepts of "tribe" and "nation."[44] As a concession to continuing tribal self-government, and to existing treaties with the United States, the act added the significant qualification that federal citizenship would not infringe on the rights and privileges of tribal membership, such as access to tribal property—in effect, granting dual citizenship. But not quite. "While all Indians are now citizens, not all are voters."

There were state qualifications—"writing or reading or ownership of property"—that still had to be met. "The law is a most peculiar one," wrote *The Survey*: "As the law stands the Indians will become citizens and at the same time remain wards. Such a status is so anomalous that it may take years to clear up . . . Moreover, certain rights, immunities and exceptions which Indians have heretofore enjoyed must now legally come to an end."[45]

Rather than clarifying the relation between citizenship and "national identity," the two acts of 1924 clouded the picture. The first set a discouraging condition on the universalist premise that had undergirded the "open door" policy of free immigration, the premise, in the historian Philip Gleason's words, that, "To be or become an American, a person did not have to be of any particular national, linguistic, religious, or ethnic background. All he had to do was to commit himself to the political ideology centered on the abstract ideals of liberty, equality, and republicanism. Thus the univeralist ideological character of American nationality meant that it was open to anyone who willed to become an American."[46] Now one had to be allowed in before one could make active choice. The second act, a belated acknowledgment of Indians as indeed "native" in the full sense of U.S. law, was a halfway measure, keeping them both as citizens and as members of nonfederal sovereign peoples—sovereign yet dependent. What did it mean to be a native and an American? The question remained, and remains, undecided.

IV

Wondering whether an "amalgam"—which evoked "amalgamation," a word used widely for racial mixing as a solution to the "race problem"—would ever emerge in "the cauldron of the 'American character,'" James writes, "What meaning . . . can continue to attach to such a term as the 'American' character?—what type, as a result of such a prodigious amalgam, such a hotch-potch of racial ingredients is to be conceived as shaping itself?" Taking the stance of an old American confronting the new, James used language that seemed to shudder before "the inconceivable alien": "the terrible little Ellis Island," "the Hebrew conquest of New York," "the swarming . . . of a Jewry that had burst all bounds."[47] Such epithets flow too easily from his pen and make James out to be another high-toned prejudiced WASP, only more elegant. But surprises lie in store for the attentive reader.

James, realized that he, too, was a migrant. He had returned temporarily from a European expatriation whose effects upon his sensibility, powers of recognition, and memory are constantly tested against new impressions. Page by page his personal implication in the American scene he observes became more apparent, more demanding, more revealing.

James portrayed his "alien" as a figure in a great cultural drama, an agon in which the opponents shifted and elided. There was, to begin with, the drama of change in James's own awareness, which can be charted by his move from the viewpoint of the Ellis Island gallery to that of the street. At first he sounds the familiar alarm and warns that America must remain culturally unitary in order to preserve itself as an integral nation.

James's alchemical tropes of amalgam, cauldron, and conversion evoke the melting pot theory of assimilation only to move beyond it. For James, assimilation goes more properly by the name of mitigation, a softening of differences, a trying-out of the more conspicuous marks of difference. But his quest for signs of mitigation turns upon itself, as his perception of gross difference undergoes a mitigation of its own. It's this inward process that makes James's encounter with "inconceivable" aliens so remarkable in the history of thinking about American identity. As he roams the city and rides the streetcars and wanders the Lower East Side, James keeps his eye out for clues to mitigation, signs of "the conversion of the alien." "Conversion" recalls the medieval idea that winning the Jews over to Christ would trumpet Judgment Day. And indeed there is no more seemingly immitigable figure in this anxious drama than that of the Eastern European Jew, virtual synonym for "alien" in James's text as in the wider culture. Can there be any hope of "brotherhood with aliens in the first grossness of their alienism," the grossness especially of the strange, discomfiting sound of their language? The "machinery" of conversion is to be found "in the form of the political and social habit, the common school and the newspaper," but will speakers of Yiddish and other outlandish tongues submit to "swift convertibility"? "What becomes, as it were, of the obstinate, the unconverted residuum?"[48]

By the time James poses the question, his tone has already altered. The process launched at Ellis Island and flowing into the streets now inspires a sense of mystery rather than insecurity. "The operation of the immense machine, identical after all with the total of American life, trembles away into mysteries that are beyond present notation." What follows seems an emanation from regions of self-consciousness left undisclosed and unsaid. "Who and what is an alien, when it comes to that, in a country peopled from the first under the jealous eye of history?—peopled, that is, by migrations at once extremely recent, perfectly traceable and urgently required . . . Which is the American, by these scant measures?—which is *not* the alien, over a large part of the country at least, and where does one put a finger on the dividing line, or, for that matter, 'spot' and identify any particular phase of the conversion, any one of its successive moments?" Brushing one thought against another, James asks whether it is possible to calibrate degrees of Americanness. If not, if there is nothing measurable to convert to, is Americanness destined to remain a trembling mystery, a passage rather than an arrival, a journey without fixed destination?

Under a new ensign of empathy and tolerance, James journeys deeper into the quarters of mystery. A Broadway streetcar makes him "gasp" with "a sense of isolation," but immediately he recovers and names his polyglot fellow passengers as "companions." They seem so very much "*at home*" after only weeks or months in the new land, and "*he* was at home too, quite with the same intensity." He finds a new sensation of sharing the promiscuous space of a crowded Manhattan vehicle "strange." "There is fascination," he notes about himself, "in the study of the innumerable ways in which this sense of being at home, on the part of all the types [including himself, "the restored absentee"], may show forth."[49] Fascination and strangeness, like his apparitions and ghosts, wind a thread of the uncanny through James's narrative; his encounters fade imperceptibly into self-encounters. Gazing closely into individual faces of Jews and Italians and Slavs, he observes their already having achieved a sense of being different, in whatever degree, from what they had been in their *old* homes—a sense of "consciously not being what they *had* been." And that perception marks a difference in himself.

Seeking knowledge of "the aliens at home," James goes in search of the Jews. One summer evening, a Jewish literary friend, a "brilliant personality" (it was the dramatist Jacob Gordin) escorted James to Yiddish theaters and cafés on the Lower East Side. James's account of this experience compresses all of his complex sense of crisis into a single passage that is dense with as many unpleasant epithets as illuminating insights. In some ten pages he speaks of "Israel" as "swarming," of "Jewry" as "immitigable," marked by an "over-developed proboscis," resembling "small strange animals, known to natural history, snakes or worms, I believe, who, when cut into pieces, wriggle away contentedly." He speaks of "lurid meaning," of "the 'ethnic' apparition . . . like a skeleton at the feast," of "the Hebrew conquest of New York," and of his evening in the neighborhood as "phantasmagoric." Yet he also writes of the Jews' "reverence for intellect" and finds "the individual Jew more of a concentrated person, savingly possessed of everything that is in him, than any other human, noted at random." He calls his evening a "rare experience," having "seen with one's own eyes the New Jerusalem on earth," the population so very much at home and secure in their self-display.[50]

While "the blaze of the shops" express "the grand side of the city of redemption," the look of the tenements and the fact of poverty bespoke a new condition of oppression, "under the icy breath of Trusts and the weight of the new remorseless monopolies that operate as no madnesses of ancient personal power thrilling us on the historic page ever operated." In the Jewish quarter of the Lower East Side, James made a chilling prophecy: "There is such a thing, in the United States, it is hence to be inferred, as freedom to grow up to be blighted, and it may be the only freedom in store for the smaller fry of future generations."[51]

"Truly the Yiddish world was a vast world." James's narrative of his brief but intense expedition concluded with his making the rounds of "beer-houses and cafés" with his "fellow-pilgrims." In the company of his hosts, among the "fostered decencies" and "present urbanities" of

Lewis Wicke Hine, "Market Day in the Jewish Quarter of the East Side, New York City," 1912. (Photography Collection, Miriam and Ira D. Wallach Division of Art, Prints and Photographs, New York Public Library, Astor, Lenox and Tilden Foundations)

their evening of conversation and enjoyment, James caught the "faint groan of his ghost" inwardly objecting to the "unprecedented accents" of English spoken by Yiddish tongues. "The incurable man of letters," James cannot help filtering his experience in "the light of letters": "it was in the light of letters, that is in the light of our language as litera- ture has hitherto known it, that one stared at this all-unconscious im- pudence of the agency of future ravage." In this light the cafés became "torture-rooms of the living idiom" and James himself a St. George roused by the dragon of Yiddish to defend the "honour that sits astride of the consecrated English tradition." The entire East Side experience comes down to this, a matter of the "Accent of the Fu- ture": "The accent of the very ultimate future, in the States, may be destined to become the most beautiful on the globe and the very mu- sic of humanity (here the 'ethnic' synthesis shrouds itself thicker than ever); but whatever we shall know it for, certainly, we shall not know it for English—in any sense for which there is an existing literary mea- sure."[52] The qualifications keep the passage from sinking into a simple surly thought. His evening of pleasure returned James to himself as defender of the old faith on which his old Americanness was founded.

Yet it was not a *national* identity at stake but an idea of the literary language. Still, is not the prospect of "the very music of humanity" it- self a mitigation, however slight? It suggests the decencies and ur- banities of the café tables where James played his part in making the music, as he participated in fractured conversation across the tables, even while cringing. And it resonates with Whitman's remark, first published in 1904, that with their "renovated English speech," "en- riched with contributions from all other languages," "the Americans are going to be the most fluent and melodious voiced people in the world."[53]

The many figures James used in this passage catch us by surprise. Was he being merely droll in describing himself as St. George, or the café as the torture chamber of the Tower of London, or the pleasures of his café hopping as "a pious rosary of which I should like to tell each bead"? There is a hint of self-mockery in the excessiveness of the tropes. This is not to underplay the seriousness with which James took "the question of our speech," the title of one of the lectures he gave during his American tour in 1905. A relaxation of stiff-necked refusal to meet the immigrant on the immigrant's own ground is suggested in the subtleties of tone and extravagance of metaphor. He opened his eyes and ears not just to taunting difference but also to possible dialogue.

One sign is found in his surprisingly empathetic surmise about the immigrant's own self-awareness: "Whatever he might see himself becoming, he was never to see himself that again, any more than you were to see him." The Jewish immigrant is conscious of being now, in however small degree, different from what he knew himself to be in "the other world"; James imagines "luminous" self-discoveries as "weighted communications" in letters to the old homeland, imagined documents of the immigrant's inwardness. Naming the "various positive properties" of native culture that in New York seem so swiftly to go into "eclipse" (particularly among Italians, he noted), James remarked that "it has taken long ages of history, in the other world, to produce them," and wondered "into what pathless tracts [another echo of Cooper's Indians] of the native atmosphere do they virtually, do they provisionally, and so all undiscoverably, melt?" Then he wondered further whether this "extinction of qualities ingrained in generations is to be taken for quite complete." "Do they burrow underground, to await their day again?—or in what strange secret places are they held in deposit and trust?" Might they not "rise again to the surface, affirming their vitality and value and playing their part?" This "speculation," he concluded, "is a sign of the interest, in the American world, of . . . the 'ethnic' outlook."[54]

James's speculation typifies the large drama of his encounter with the American scene, his discovery of meaning in the scenic surface of appearances and in his surrender to its sensations. Speculation about the "ethnic outlook" developed when he took the point of view of the "alien," by mimicry of him, becoming that figure by imagining what it felt like to have the bewildering sense of having won a home in the course of losing one. Posing cultural survival as a question, James gave voice to the "alien" in the act of wondering what this "America" was that had happened to me. Where or what has the former me melted into? Where in the "pathless tracts" of this new land, in what regions of the city's soul or mind might I find my older self mirrored back to me?

James found in his own speculations a pattern that mirrored the immigrant's self-awareness and his own doubleness. An unlikely Natty Bumppo, dispossessed of the secure sense of home that the implacable nativist enjoyed, James found himself uncannily "at home" among his alien "companions" on Broadway; free of the isolating possessiveness of the racial snob and unencumbered except by consciousness and curiosity, he is free to venture into those pathless tracts where cultural residues intermix with the "native atmosphere." Immigration, he saw, was a cultural process undergone by "aliens" and "natives" alike, a dialogic exchange and reciprocation he joined by imagining and giving voice to the other. He discovered or invented his own Americanness exactly in this: his cosmopolitan capacity to enter into the lives of others, to take their view of things. James met the ghost on its own grounds, that figure of loss that defines all Americans as "alien" and alienness as the defining condition of Americanness.

Rooseveltian "true Americanism," which also included a paternalistic stance toward the "darker" peoples of the world, derided this cosmopolitan capacity to put oneself in place of the other and to adopt provisional identities as "effeminate" deficiency of patriotism. In 1898, James reviewed Roosevelt's *American Ideals and Other Essays Social and Political*, in which "true Americanism" appears, and remarked that the author proposed "to tighten the screws of the national consciousness as they have never been tightened before."[55] He detected something "violent" in "the puerility of his simplifications" in "an age when so much of the ingenuity of the world goes to multiplying contact and communication, to reducing separation and distance, to promoting, in short, an inter-penetration that would have been the wonder of our fathers." Tightly patrolled borders of national identity, and the notion that one should live and breathe "purely as an American," seem out of place at a time when new means of transportation and communication open up vastly wider perspectives for the enhancement of individual consciousness. What does it mean to think "as an American"? "To describe the way an American thought shall be expressed is surely a formidable feat," James writes, and it was one for which Roosevelt had no resources. James takes Roosevelt to task for making "very free with the 'American' name," as if it were "a symbol revealed once for all in some book of Mormon dug up under a tree."

In James's reflections on his gathered impressions, aliens shed

their cloak of inconceivableness through a process of exchange, negotiations of loss and gain within diverse horizons. He recounts street
dramas of glances and the touching of elbows in crowded spaces, the
rub of bodies against bodies, toleration of unaccustomed smells: a
drama in which physiognomy and odors perform ideas and insights.
Plasticity becomes the rule. Roles shift, identities change, and alien
and native alike are dispossessed and achieve shared at-homeness.
Worldliness, the ability to feel at home among differences—what
James's brother William admired so much in Whitman's city poems—
was James's enacted idea of American possibility.

James offers a method of "luminous discovery," a cosmopolitan
lens upon unmitigated yet mitigable difference. Anticipating the "trans-
national America" proposed in a famous essay by that title in 1916 by
Randolph Bourne, James deplores the prospect of immigrants deprived of their vigorous, boisterous alienness by the "great assimila-
tive organism," the "huge white-washing brush" of Anglo-Saxonism.
The racial allusion cannot be incidental. Like James, Bourne worried
about "our cities . . . filled with these half-breeds who retain their foreign names but have lost the foreign flavor" and proposed a view of
America as a "cosmopolitan enterprise." Echoing Dewey's notion
of the American as a composite figure, Bourne wrote, "Only the
American—and in this category I include the migratory alien who has
lived with us and caught the pioneer spirit and a sense of new social
vistas—has the chance to become that citizen of the world. American
is coming to be, not a nationality but a trans-nationality, a weaving
back and forth, with the other lands, of many threads of all sizes and
colors. Any movement which attempts to thwart this weaving, or to
dye the fabric one color, or disentangle the threads of the strands, is
false to this cosmopolitan vision." In a companion essay the same year
on "The Jew and Trans-National America," Bourne wrote of a "cooperative Americanism, that is, an ideal of a freely mingling society of
peoples of very different racial and cultural antecedents, with a common political allegiance and common social ends but with free and
distinctive cultural allegiances which may be placed anywhere in the
world that they like."[56]

James joined Dewey and Bourne in having us see that from the
perspective of the street, "American" means more than heterogeneity,

more than coexistence among cultures. It also allows for the possibility of interplay, and it lays to rest Roosevelt's anxious wish for a homogeneous nationality. Enclaves exist and old traditions persist, but reciprocal experiment invites thoughts of a "music of humanity" in some "very ultimate future." Immigrants move with relative ease into the Anglo-American mainstream and back to their native languages and beliefs, in the process acculturating the mainstream itself. And while this mobility has been denied to African Americans for most of the nation's history, the white assimilation of black cultural forms has shaped mainstream culture, speech and music and thought. "Some day on American soil two world-races may give each to each those characteristics both so sadly lack," wrote Du Bois, a student at Harvard of Henry's brother William, in his book *The Souls of Black Folk*, which James mentioned (but did not discuss) in *The American Scene* as "the only 'Southern' book of any distinction published for many a year."[57] Some cultures have faded into norms initially associated with white Anglo-Saxons, but many more have persisted. Being American emerges from James's difficult pages not as a condition one is born into or ever confidently arrives at but a continual process of invention, reinvention, and revision. It is Boas's plasticity applied to "national types."

V

What he called "the process of mitigation and, still more, of the conversion of the alien" kept Henry James's attention and kept his eyes and ears on the alert. The question was "the 'American' character," not just what America would make of the alien but also what the alien would make of America. Speculation about ultimate futures and the attainment of "the very music of humanity," he conceded, offered a too-comforting "escape from the formidable foreground" of "the vast foreign quarters," the "pathless tracts" and the "babel of tongues." But realities insist upon themselves. At one point he pictured the melting pot or "cauldron" as a "tub of hot water" washing away the "color" and particulars of immigrant cultures, brightening the water and tinting "fellow-soakers in the terrible tank." Nothing is lost, then;

"the property washed out of the new subject" is "rubbed off on any number of surrounding persons," producing a new collective hue. It would be nice to think so, but that gives only "short-sighted comfort." In fact, the "positive properties" of a culture, its manners, cuisine, costume, and especially speech, are too easily shed and eclipsed by the workings of the "colossal" machinery of assimilation. James saw the loss of particularity, indeed of "alienness" itself, as a "sacrifice" to the "profit" of an "'American' identity" which "has meanwhile acquired (in the happiest cases) all apparent confidence and consistency."[58] It was "conceivable" that in the long run, through "slow comminglings and makings-over," lost cultures might "rise again to the surface, affirming their vitality and value and playing their part." But in the short run the foreground was "formidable."

The dual perspective of "ultimate future" and "formidable foreground" complicated James's perceptions. He saw signs of an evolving composite nationality yet worried over immediate effects: immigrants on one hand, shedding their inherited cultures and hence their "historic consciousness" of their native identities; on the other, corrupting or mongrelizing American English by their "unprecedented accents." In the distance one might imagine an eventual American tongue as "the very music of humanity," but the foreground was all noise, a "babel of tongues" and worse.[59] Something he called "fluent East-side New Yorkese"—he meant most likely colloquial English inflected with accents and words from Yiddish and other "exotic" tongues—was mistaken for English itself. Whitman celebrated the absorptive powers of American English and took joy in the accretion of new words and sounds and accents; James, even while detecting however faintly in American speech an ultimate harmony, deplored much of what he heard in colloquial English as a falling-off from standards that were essential to civility. And the blurring of linguistic boundaries suggested a worrisome blurring of culture itself.

One experience in his wanderings of Bowery night spots stood out as an exemplary exception. While "everywhere else" in the Bowery reigned "everything vulgar," in a German place serving only soft drinks—"a beerhouse innocent of beer"—he found charm, "saliency and consistency," "decency and dignity." The host's secret was that he had "succeeded, as by an inspiration of genius, in omitting, for all his years, to learn the current American. He spoke but a dozen words of it, and that was doubtless how he kept the key of the old Germanic peace."[60] There was hope for English (or "American"), then, if immigrants stayed within their own language; only when they assayed English did their incompetence (or worse, lack of respect) torture and transgress the host speech in the form of "accent."

Spoken English underlay James's reflections on the fate of Americanness itself, and it proved to be the sore point, the occasion of ambivalence, in his views on "the ubiquity of the alien." His anxieties focused especially on Yiddish, largely because of the vast numbers of Jewish immigrants "swarming" lower Manhattan (recalling Carlyle's contemptuous epithet for democracy, "swarmerai")—"a Jewry that had burst all bounds"—but also because Yiddish, while both a literary and vernacular language, was known by non-Jews only as a spoken tongue, a distinct style of vocalization and gesture. Yiddish literature, written in Hebrew characters, was a closed book to most nonspeakers. Perceived as a jargon, an eclectic and syncretic speech of a people always alien where they resided, Yiddish was often targeted for disdain and ridicule, even by some Jews themselves. James's discomfiting view of the language was typical of a wide range of responses to Jewish immigration.[61] Fascinated by the "vast Yiddish world" of the Lower East Side, he saw the easy amalgamation of Yiddish with English as a threat, the exemplary threat of the entire immigrant assault on the sound of English.

In "The Question of Our Speech," an address he delivered to the graduating class of Bryn Mawr College in June 1905, James explained to the young women embraced under the "Our" of his title that they ought not be complacent about the state of speech in the United States. Without good speech "the very imparting of a coherent culture would never get under way." "The vocal form, the vocal tone, the personal, social accent and sound of its intercourse" is a gauge of whether a society "has achieved civilization." By this standard, "it must be frankly said, our civilization remains strikingly *un*achieved." Civilization required a shared "tone-standard," recognition of "certain vocal sounds as tone," and renunciation of their negation, "negations all the more offensive in proportion as they have most enjoyed impunity."

The greatest challenge to civilized speech in the United States was the pervasive view that "no form of speech is provably better than any other," a heresy James blamed on public schools, newspapers, and "a convergence of inscrutable forces (climatic, social, political, theological, moral, 'psychic')." The common schools could not be counted on to cultivate the fineness of discrimination in matters of speech required for a national (and nationalizing) "tone-standard." Newspapers were a distinctly negative influence, "their ubiquitous page, bristling with rude effigies and images" and "black eruptions of print" reminding him "of some myriad-face monster" with "the grimaces, the shouts, shrieks and yells . . . of a mighty maniac who has broken loose and who is running amuck through the spheres alike of sense and of sound."[62]

Foremost among inscrutable forces deranging "our" speech was that in a few years "a hundred million people . . . will be unanimously, loudly—above all loudly, I think—speaking it, and that, moreover, many of these millions will have been artfully wooed and weaned from the Dutch, from the Spanish, from the German, from the Italian, from the Norse, from the Finnish, from the Yiddish even, strange to say."[63] The note of hospitality James would strike in *The American Scene* two years later was here conspicuously absent. America more than other nations needed to be resolutely jealous of and vigilant about its most precious possession, the English language. The "vast contingent of aliens" behave

as if they have as much property in our speech as we have, and just as good a right to do what they choose with it—the grand right of the American being to do just what he chooses "over here" with anything and everything: all the while we sleep the innumerable aliens are sitting up (*they* don't sleep!) to work their will on their new inheritance and prove to us that they are without any finer feeling or more conservative instinct of consideration for it, more hovering, caressing curiosity about it, than they may have on the subject of so many yards of freely figured oilcloth, from the shop, that they are preparing to lay down, for convenience, on kitchen floor or kitchen staircase. Oilcloth is highly convenient, and our loud collective medium of intercourse doubtless strikes these new householders as

wonderfully resisting "wear"—with such wear as it gets!—
strikes them as an excellent bargain: durable, tough, cheap.[64]

The implication can hardly be mistaken: loud voices, cheap oilcloth, the street trades of the Lower East Side, Yiddish speakers and
others plotting sleeplessly to "lay down" English on the cheap. Addressing the freshly commenced young women of Bryn Mawr—well-
spoken, well-scrubbed daughters of the American white upper
crust—James took a strikingly, even stridently, alarmist stance toward
the imagined threat of linguistic pollution from aliens within. Rehears-
ing themes he would treat with nuance and complexity in *The American Scene*, James defended a simple "high" standard of speech values
on behalf of a "coherent culture."

The fear of incoherence arising from bad speech in a nation so little endowed with traditional "national" markers went back to Noah
Webster's obsession with a "national language" to provide a "national
tie." Webster's *American Spelling Book* (1788) and *American Dictionary* (1828) were efforts to establish and inculcate uniform spelling,
pronunciation, and usage explicitly to provide the glue for a shared nationality, responses to a diversity Webster imagined as menacing to the
idea of a unitary nation. Webster cringed at "provincial dialects" (New
England, mid-Atlantic, Southern) with their Irish, Scotch, and German intonations. "Our political harmony" needed uniformity of linguistic sound and sense, which would "render the people of this
country *national*."[65] Uniform language standards corresponded to
Webster's federalist view that "nation" presupposed a distinct central
power and authority. Like the role of a central government in a federal
system, uniform speech would bring the disparate parts and peoples of
the country under one national roof—the tongue of the original colonial rulers now as a means to dominate aliens and natives alike.[66]

Not "political harmony" as such but the question of "a coherent
culture" troubled James's "American" identity: nationality not as a
civic matter but as shared values that can be taken for granted in social intercourse, that can be assumed, supposed, and expected from
any one American person to another. "American" may in fact have
limited James's horizon in "The Question of Our Speech." His per-

spective was more transatlantic than strictly American. English, he wrote, is our "mother tongue"; our relation to it is familial; we are sibling to all its other offspring speakers. He was not concerned with the question that absorbed Webster in his way and Whitman in a much different way: how English became "American." It was the proprieties of English as such he wanted to honor and protect, the sound of English, its vowels, syllables, parts of words, and sentences, the integrity of consonants in particular. The importance of "the way we say a thing" could not be overestimated; "it is very largely by saying, all the while, that we live and play our parts," and if saying gets slovenly, the entire fabric of social relations suffers. James's tone hinted at a coming struggle between fineness and coarseness, between those who respected the mother and those who desired to besmirch her good name. He wanted to recruit the young ladies of Bryn Mawr as crusaders pledged to a do-or-die defense. "I am asking you to take that truth well home and hold it close to your hearts, setting your backs to the wall to defend it, heroically, when need may be."[67]

Whatever pedagogic interest may lie in James's honest concern that "rotten diction" leads to "the corruption of man," as Emerson remarked, the zeal of his rhetoric and his obvious distaste for the accented English of immigrants suggest that his worry over the pronounced sounds of English overlies a deeper worry about "the coherence of culture." Whitman took pleasure where James fretted, pleasure at "that great thing, the renovated English speech in America," and relished rude speech and the dialect of African Americans, for example, in which he caught "hints of the future theory of the modification of all the words of the English language, for musical purposes, for a grand native opera in America." What James disdained as immigrant speech rude toward proprieties of English might alternatively be seen as a language in the process of renovation that Whitman heard in everyday speech. There were diction and rules that do not get into dictionaries: "The Real Dictionary will give us all words that exist in use, the bad words as well as any,"[68] and in this book of the "real," nothing human can be "alien," no utterance outside the circle of the conceivable.

THREE

Yiddish Hiawatha

—Those were the Yiddish poets (*ubi sunt*
Leyvick and Halpern, Leyeles, Mani Leib,
Glatshteyn and Teller, Yehoash—who, by dint
Of innocence wove a Hiawatha, babe
In the Yiddish woods, into another tongue?).
                —John Hollander, "On a Stanza of H. Leyvick"

In his excursions into immigrant New York, Henry James seemed especially haunted and fixated by Yiddish, at once horrified and fascinated by what seemed its importunate assault on the citadel of proper spoken English. Exclaiming how difficult it was for him in the face of "the scale" of alien "infusion" to make a legible word out of the "too numerous" syllables of his impressions, he wrote, "The *il*legible word, accordingly, the great inscrutable answer to questions, hangs in the vast American sky, to his imagination, as something fantastic and *abracadabrant*, belonging to no known language."[1] A "cabalistic word," according to the OED, not itself a Yiddish word but used in medieval Jewish mysticism and magic, "abracadabra" conveys an old belief and fear that ancient tongues, Hebrew and Yiddish, evoke arcane, magical, possibly demonic forces: It could be the secret language of the Jews in their "strange secret places." Is it a dangerous Yiddish word, perhaps Yiddish itself, that hangs in the "vast American sky"?

Did James's response to "the vast Yiddish world" include an unspoken fear that the fate of English in America was not only to become Yiddishized but also to go the route of Yiddish itself, an amalgam language fashioned by Ashkenazi (Middle and Eastern European)

Jews who experienced simultaneous separateness and doubleness? They were Jews living by themselves among gentiles, sharing lingual and bilingual competence with the dominant culture. The experience of the Pale shaped and marked Yiddish with the accretive mosaic character that Emerson identified with language as such, which consisted of the "spoils" of all human activity: "The poorest speaker is like the Indian dressed in a robe furnished by a half a dozen animals. It is like our marble footslab made up of countless shells & exuviae of a foregone World."[2] A "pure" language or speech, seen in this Indian light, was a contradiction in terms.

Yiddish was an exemplary case. Benjamin Harshav has described Yiddish as "a language, almost by definition, used by multilingual speakers," hence a "fusion" language. The historical work of Yiddish was the work of mediation; it served "as a bridge to and from the external, Christian world and . . . the Gentile milieu," "a junction, a noisy marketplace where 'internal' and 'external' languages and cultures met and interacted. It was the coherent floor of a schizophrenic existence."[3] Put another way, Yiddish has always served as an instrument and medium of informal on-the-street translation. In their exile and diaspora, Jews have inhabited at least two worlds of culture and language. Yiddish enabled them to invent social identities by a precarious balancing of separate yet mingled linguistic systems. Translation, Harshav suggests, is of the very nature of Yiddish, a continuous process of making the alien familiar; it has an ingrained suppleness and agility reflecting seasoned skills of survival through accommodation and experiment in Ashkenazi life. Informal oral translation of bits and pieces of surrounding or "host" languages enlarged and renovated the semantic horizons of Yiddish speakers. Both a product and a symptom of diaspora, Yiddish represents the experience of dispersion, the scattering of Jews among the nations: a kind of universal cosmopolitan tongue capable of making itself seem at home (however precariously) anywhere.

In the United States there evolved a distinctively Jewish way (or ways) of being American, of living as an aspiring and then equal member of the gentile-dominated world yet doing so in a manner recognized and accepted by Jew and non-Jew alike as Jewish Americanness. Yiddish served this process in a major way, most often as Yiddishism, scraps and shreds of it appearing in English or in mergings of English and Yiddish, two exemplary fusion languages. Linguistic "impurity" through language contact and interchange marks the entire history of English in the Americas—the incalculable enrichment of American English with Indian terminology is a major case in point—especially within the milieu of cultural infusion at the turn of the twentieth century. On city streets, in markets, and at places of popular entertainment, speech patterns changed, dozens of Old World languages were diluted and lost their hold on youngsters growing up in American public schools, then virtually disappeared in the course of a generation. And this is not to speak of the continuing erosion and loss of Indian languages. In defense of a law "prohibiting the use of *the Indian vernacular* in instruction" (my emphasis: as if there were but one Indian language), an editorial in the Carlisle School newspaper, *The Red Man* (probably written by Pratt), argued, "If the Indians are to be Americans, *in our sense of the word* [my emphasis], they must not only speak our language, but it must be a second nature to them." Hence coercion was justified: "Forcing the language of the conquerors upon the conquered is not so new a thing," and "when, as with the Indians, the conquest sought is over savagery," force is all the more justified. It's for their own good: "the language to be taught holds that brotherly kindness which we have come to feel is the foundation of our right to existence as a nation." Unacknowledged paradox again, and the death of irony.[4]

Along with the natural osmotic process that modified immigrant tongues in porous exchanges with American English, which itself underwent renovation of the kind that James deplores ("New Yorkese"), the pressures to learn English and to add English (or "American") words to the native tongue proved irresistible. It was a means toward assimilation, secularization, and modernity. Yiddish was not exceptional in facing a troubled future on the American scene, though both its cultural and linguistic features made it a special case. Italian, Russian, German, Finnish, Greek, and Hungarian each signified a territory, a cultural place. These languages were ties to a specific homeland, links with a shared past recently left behind; to speak one was a mark of a member in an identifiable nationality, now transforming into a hyphenated American identity. Jewish immigrants arrived from many of these same countries, particularly Russia, Poland, Austria-Hungary, and the Slavic countries, but centuries of dwelling apart—by option or compulsion, separateness and exclusion, persecution and periodic pogroms—made a shared national identity very dubious even after gradual "emancipation" in the nineteenth century had granted Jews a modicum of civil rights (granted by the U.S.S.R. after the Soviet revolution in 1917) and religious freedom. On the whole, forming the majority of the population in certain regions of the Pale, Jews held themselves as a distinct transterritorial people by religion and language, by a highly ritualized and linguistically distinctive culture system, a transnational phenomenon that knew no borders (except for regional differences).[5]

I

In the era of the great immigration, Yiddish became the focus of intense controversy about language and nationality. During the eighteenth-century enlightenment, or Haskalah, especially in Germany under the influence of Moses Mendelssohn, a Jewish intelligentsia sought integration with the coterritorial national culture by dropping Yiddish in favor of the national tongue. Hebrew was revered as the language of holiness, *loshen kodesh*, and Yiddish had aroused scorn as a medieval dialect of German, a low and corrupt language of the ghetto, incapable of expressing high concepts or fine discriminations, thus a barrier to Jewish emancipation and full cultural development. It was expected to fade way, to vanish. But, mother tongue or *mama loshen*, Yiddish persisted as the home and folk language, and by the close of the nineteenth century had become the language of choice of many serious writers and thinkers in Eastern Europe and the Americas. Nationalist stirrings in the same years cast a new light on Yiddish, and an ideology emerged, "Yiddishism," which claimed both that Jews constituted a multinational nationality unto themselves, which deserved and required recognition and protection by modern nation-states as a legitimate "minority," and that Yiddish was the national language. The emerging Zionist movement countered that national identity required territorial integrity, that Palestine was the only valid national home of the Jewish people, and that Hebrew, which it proposed to revive as both a spoken and literary language, was the national tongue. The burden on the Yiddishists was twofold: to buttress the claim to "minority" nationhood with a theory of multinational nationality, and to defend Yiddish as a language capable like any other of answering to the full need for communication, science, and expressive tools in modern life. The challenge was to prove Yiddish viable as a means to propagate and preserve Jewish national self-consciousness, and to help Jews survive as citizens in the swift currents of modern societies.

The "national rights" dimension of the Yiddishist program failed to arouse significant support in the United States, where Jewish immigrants were swept into the experience, unique for them, of membership in a national polity that promised equal civil rights and absolute religious freedom. Could Yiddish survive and flourish when the pressures on immigrants to assimilate was all but irresistible? The linguistic aspects of James's "colossal" machinery of assimilation included the formidable array of public schools, daily newspapers, advertising, large department stores, popular entertainment (soon cinema and radio), classes in English for "foreigners" and would-be citizens.[6] And from the other side, even while holding on to native tongues in "foreign-language" newspapers in immigrant languages, accommodation to English was an inescapable if burdensome (even loathsome) necessity.

In 1902 Alexander Harkavy, an immigrant from Novogrudok, Russia, published a handbook that, in its practical advice about getting along in English by means of Yiddish, shows perfectly the linguistic process of exchange. *Amerikanisher Briefen-Shteler*, or *Harkavy's American Letter Writer*, offers some three hundred pages of "useful information" about spelling English names and terms in Yiddish (you can *see* the transfer of English into Yiddish before your eyes), translations of Yiddish names into English sounds and spelling, with aids to pronunciation and model letters and telegrams in both English and Yiddish on facing pages.[7] The crux of the matter is found on some forty pages devoted to transpositions of English words into Yiddish spelling, with an emphasis on correct English pronunciation of the vowels and consonants. A typical entry appears in four columns: an English word in type on the far left, such as "clean," followed to its right by the same word in script, followed by the same word spelled in Yiddish characters, and on the far right, "*rein*," the Yiddish word in English characters. Less an exercise in translation than in mimicry, we go from Yiddish to English and back, with Yinglish as the switch in the middle.

The distinguished Yiddish journalist, editor, and novelist (in both English and Yiddish) Abraham Cahan described Harkavy in 1899 as "the philologist of the ghetto, an indefatigable disseminator of English in its tenements and sweatshops," whose book immediately "met with signal success."[8] Harkavy went on to write more than twenty books, including English-Yiddish and Yiddish-English dictionaries, helping those who knew only Yiddish "to learn English words of everyday use and the rudiments of English grammar without a teacher," as Cahan put it. He imagined himself "the invisible teacher of hundreds and perhaps thousands of scholars scattered over the ghettoes of America, and the picture thrilled him."

The simplicity of the Harkavy method and the pragmatic uses to which the dictionary could be put appealed to Cahan. The bilingual dictionary functions as a fulcrum between languages, giving immediate and convenient access to meanings and, as a condition of its use, facilitating the passage from oral to literate culture, initiating speakers in the necessity of reading to improve their speech. As editor of the major Yiddish newspaper in New York, the *Jewish Daily Forward*, Cahan understood the need to make writing as simple and as immediately communicable as possible. Yiddish is already a rich and legitimate national language, Cahan wrote in an essay in the radical intellectual journal *Di Tsukunft* (The Future) in 1907, but it made no sense to ignore the fact that Yiddish in America remained primarily the spoken language of uneducated immigrants. Hence, "whoever wants to write Yiddish today must make it one of his most important duties to learn to popularize, to learn how to explain thoughts in an easy, common vernacular."[9] In 1909, the *Forward* offered the latest Yiddish-English dictionary as a gift to new subscribers.[10] With illiteracy widespread among immigrant Jews, with spoken Yiddish fragmented into many dialects, and with access to English a daily urgency, the bilingual dictionary became a key immigrant text, as we see in

Cahan's first work of fiction in English, the novella *Yekl: A Tale of the New York Ghetto* (1896).

The opening scene sets the tale in a revealing linguistic context of New York ghetto life. It shows a group of workers in a small cloak shop during a break; one reads "a socialist magazine in Yiddish," swaying "to and fro droning in the Talmudical intonation," and others chat with each other in a Yiddish that is presented to the reader's eye as perfect English as if already translated (giving it dignity), sprinkled with heavily accented English words, as if spoken by speakers primarily of Yiddish, drawn mainly from popular American sports and entertainment (which appear in italics to call attention to their linguistic function as a kind of "interlingual interference" in the primary language); another sits reading an English newspaper with a "cumbrous dictionary on his knees." The initial tableau puts the story in motion within a panorama of different modes of translation as linguistic accommodations by speakers of Yiddish, "the omnivorous Jewish jargon" that remakes bits and pieces of English in the color and sound of its own voice. On one side stands the tale's protagonist, the man called Jake who once was Yekl, an illiterate immigrant eager to assimilate into the America of dance halls and sports arenas and whose speech rings with Yiddishized Americanisms. Opposite stands or sits Bernstein, the man with the dictionary; in a later scene he appears "bent over a book, with a ponderous dictionary at its side," resembling the stereotype of the old-world Talmudic scholar, "a dyspeptic face ringed with a thin growth of dark beard," the dictionary significantly preempting the function of the sacred book as reference text not for holy truths but the meanings of strange words.[11] In the end, Bernstein and the dictionary win out; he marries the old-world wife whom Jake divorces for the sake of a dance hall sweetie and can look ahead to solid middle-class family life as proprietor of a grocery store. Cahan the author not only practices translation in his dialogue of broken English admixed with Yiddish that looks and reads like perfect English but also makes it a potent subliminal theme. The dictionary is the key that unlocks the story.

As the dictionary elevates, it also assimilates and helps its readers climb up the American ladder of success. Practical devices of translation like Harkavy's brought English into the realm of Yiddish, proving the latter's powers of amalgamation while helping its speakers negotiate the space between their bedraggled lives and the cloying visions of American happiness advertised all around them. Instrumental linguistic assimilation of this sort was precisely what worried Yiddishists. They envisioned a flowering of Jewish culture in *Yiddish*, the coexistence of Yiddish and American English as coequal languages. Rather than Hebrew, the "sacred" tongue of Judaism, the resolutely secular Yiddishist movement held that Yiddish represented the immanence of an international Jewish nation, "the Jewish people." In the absence of a territory, the Jewish nation, they argued, possessed something more enduring, more relevant to their diasporic survival as a "people": a universal language. And for about a generation on the Lower East Side in early-twentieth-century New York and in enclaves of Jewish immigrant settlements in cities throughout North and South America, a flourishing Yiddishkeit seemed permanent: newspapers, literary journals, talented poets, novelists, dramatists, critics, and journalists, theaters and drama groups, schools, choruses, libraries, trade unions—all these were venues where Yiddish was the coin of the realm. Before long, however, immigrants and their children living their lives primarily in English viewed Yiddish as the most conspicuous sign of a burden of difference that hampered their desire for integration and acceptance through assimilation. "The mystique of Yiddishism," in the words of one historian of the movement, began to wither.[12] When Judaism and the synagogue came to seem sufficient in the multiethnic currents of American life, Yiddish became an embarrassment, a voice reserved for comedy, nostalgia, and the self-hatred peculiar to the harassed condition of Jews, as Sander Gilman argues.[13]

Still, Yiddishists tried to resist the drift of Yiddish into irrelevance, into mere Yinglish. Interwoven with the story of decline is a story of extraordinary achievement, of promise prematurely aborted. The two stories of declension and of resurgence belong together, the former proving an essential condition for the latter in that an encroaching sense of defeat in the linguistic struggle with English prompted Yiddishists to strive all the harder to keep alive not just the language but also the cultural life founded on it. Americanization seemed to doom the mother tongue to fragmented dispersion into the host language (and vice versa), bits of speech, sayings, whimsies, code words typically dipped in the acid of a bitter, stoical humor that even turned against its own cloying nostalgia.

The same process that stripped the language of a base in living speech and vulgarized it also gave rise to remarkable achievements in theater, song, and especially poetry, an astonishing if short-lived renaissance of Yiddish verse, exuberant with experiment, riddled with despair. The flowering in Europe and the United States of Yiddish writing in the early years of the twentieth century was all the more remarkable in the face of the scorn heaped on the *mama loshen* by learned Jews who treated it as mere dialect compared to Hebrew, good for the kitchen but not for poetry. In a newspaper story written in English in the 1890s, Cahan has a rabbi say: "'Yiddish is not much of a language. It does not come up to the holy tongue, the tongue of the law and prophets. You see, in Yiddish you can write no poetry, no lofty thoughts.'"[14]

Between traditionalist prejudices like this and the pressure to succumb to English, Yiddish writers confronted obstacles on all sides. "Yiddish literature here in America," said an editorial in the short-lived journal *Di Yugend*, "has been boarding out with the Yiddish press that treats it as a stranger, a stepchild." "Yiddish belles-lettres [are] in exile here, being treated with cynical abandon." Linked to a group of poets known as *Die Junge* (the Young Generation), the journal expressed the Yiddishist program by aiming "to create for Yiddish literature its own, independent home to free it from its bruising, battering exile."[15] But the premonition of a vanishing tongue even before the eradication of the great European centers of Yiddish culture in World War II was unrelieved. A gnomic verse from Leyvick's 1930s lament, "Yiddish Poets," captures a tone of mingled resignation and defiance, a shrug of the shoulders and a stubborn will to carry on:

> Sometimes, like frazzled cats, dragging
> Their kittens around, distraught,
> We drag our poems between our teeth
> By the neck through the streets of New York.[16]

The grotesquerie of the trope lays bare the bitter predicament of Yiddish poets obliged by history to compose in a language already, in John Hollander's words, "sentenced to an early death."

II

While the two-way street of translation between Yiddish and English eased everyday assimilation and successful advancement into business, the professions, literature, politics, and commercial entertainment, Yiddishists had loftier ends in view: formal literary translation as a means of entry into the literary culture of the United States. Literary translation would satisfy the double desire for intimacy with gentile culture and for refinement and the preservation of Yiddish as a legitimate literary language. Preeminently an act of Haskalah, literary translation would establish a place for Yiddish within the horizon of cosmopolitan culture. In early-twentieth-century New York, a remarkably talented group of Yiddish poets worked to achieve a Yiddish speech in poetry, an *American* Yiddish speech expressing Jewish-American experience.[17] Translations of writers—Poe, Longfellow, Whitman, Dickinson, Howells, Edward Bellamy, Jack London, and from other literatures, Ruskin, Nietzsche, Rilke, Baudelaire, Rimbaud, Chinese and Japanese poets—contributed to the swelling chorus of Yiddish literary voices striving for recognition.[18]

In 1910, two years after an international conference in Czernowitz, a largely Jewish town in Austria, laid out a program (with strong encouragement for translation) for furthering Yiddish as a legitimate national language of the Jewish people, *Dos Lied fun Hayavatha*—Longfellow's poem rendered in Yiddish—appeared in New York, the work of Russian-born poet Solomon Bloomgarten, who wrote under the name of Yehoash. The volume included a lengthy introduction, "On the Value of Translation" by Dr. Chaim Zhitlovsky, which put Yehoash's *Hayavatha* in the context of the Yiddishist program for a national Jewish culture based entirely on the common language.

Yehoash could not have found a sponsor more auspicious in New York Jewish circles than Chaim Zhitlovsky, "the outstanding thinker," one historian writes, "of the Jewish cultural renaissance in the Yiddish language in the twentieth century."[19] One of the conveners and leading voices of the Czernowitz conference, learned, fluent in several languages, charismatic as lecturer and essayist and as advocate of both socialism and Yiddish, the Russian-born Zhitlovsky (1865–1943) earned a Ph.D. in philosophy from the University of Berne in 1892 and settled in New York in 1908. The power of his voice lay in the lucid coherence and consistency of his thought and his seamless vision of Yiddish as the ground of a genuine nation. Placing Yehoash's translation centrally within the Yiddishist program, his introduction adds a significant conceptual dimension to the poem. Here, Zhitlovsky says, is exactly what Yiddishism wants for its realization: a raising of Yiddish to the level of a serious literary work through a feat of creative translation. After centuries of oppression, he writes, the Jewish people are awakening from their "historical sleep," awakening as a "people," not to be defined as anything else but Jews. "We are not 4% of anyone else, but 100% of ourselves." Wishing to create a national culture in diaspora, without a state or territory and with an increasingly tenuous relation to Judaism (as it seemed to Zhitlovsky and the predominantly secular Jewish intelligentsia), Jews had only the mother tongue as their resource. Jews were Jews by virtue of speaking, reading, and writing Yiddish, a language that in translation opened the entire world and its cultural treasures to the Jewish masses. "If we hold on to our language," Zhitlovksy wrote elsewhere, "it becomes a raft which can save us from drowning."[20]

About the importance of land or territory to peoplehood, he wrote,

> As important as its own land may be for the life of a nation, it is no more than a condition, a qualification, an aid to life, but not a part of its being in the world. A nation does not consist of weather, earth, hills, valleys, forests and fields. The forests and fields cannot be even the smallest part of the nation which consists rather of living people, with a unique body and soul, with different levels of attainment, with attributes and defects; in whom with the best microscope there cannot be found even one grain of sand, even one atom of land.[21]

So much for the Zionist argument that only settlement in Palestine could make Jews a nation. So much too, implicitly, for the commonly held idea that geography and landscape were essential ingredients of nationality. For Jews in the disapora, only Yiddish provided a "spiritual national home."[22]

In his *Hayavatha* introduction, Zhitlovsky elaborated these formulaic principles by addressing the Jews' situation in America and the relevance to it of Longfellow's Indian poem. Echoing speakers at Czernowitz, Zhitlovksy called translation a primary need if Yiddish was to achieve stature as a national language. Critics must cease treating translations as "stepchildren" but accept and encourage them as essential to the health of the language. When an awakening people "takes upon itself to build a culture of its own in a speech which was spoken only by the harried masses," it needs the help and guidance of its "young national progressive intelligentsia" to show "with the power of a miraculous word that they have a right to 'make shabbes [Sabbath] for themselves'"—that is, to have their own separate table, to make their own culture. Translation gives power, overcomes the hindering notion of "Yiddish language poverty," and proves the maturity of a people and its language. Fluent in European philosophy as well as Jewish tradition—he wrote essays on Kant, on Job, and on Hasidism, and in 1919 translated into Yiddish Nietzsche's *Thus Spake Zarathustra*—Zhitlovsky proposed "life-energy" and "form" as inner principles of national existence and encouraged translation as an opening of oneself to the "general human culture." While "a people is an end in itself, just as is a unique person," it achieves itself by harmonizing its "yearning for its own unique culture with a connection to the general human progress"; "everything mankind has created is created for mankind, and we are a part of it . . . Goethe's *Faust* is our *Faust* . . . What does mankind gain when Goethe's *Faust* exists yet again in a Yiddish version?"[23] The general enriches the particular, and vice versa.

Zhitlovsky thought of translation as a dialectical process, a reaching outward for the sake of reaching inward, othering oneself for the sake of selfing the other, so to speak. The soul of the people, in Zhitlovsky's Herderian terminology, demands this exercise, rising to the challenge of bringing the alien within the domain of the home place without surrendering what is *eggns*, unique and particular to the folk. Hence, as between nationalism and cosmopolitanism (tantamount to surrender of particularity for the sake of an abstract humanness), Zhitlovsky offered the mediation of translation, *ibersetzung* (elsewhere he advocated writing Yiddish in Roman characters), by which outside or foreign (*fremde*) treasures, "the richest products of humanity," live again in Yiddish. Zhitlovsky in 1910 thus made a conceptual setting for Yehoash's *Hayavata* with concerns about language and nationality that worried Henry James in the same years and that anticipated the pluralist, transnational views of John Dewey, Randolph Bourne, and especially Horace Kallen. Like Bourne and Kallen, he made the transnational character of Jewish identity a basis for a critique of the unipolar or melting-pot ideal of a singular American national identity and proposed socialism as an alternative national form, a reconfiguration of the idea of nation into a complex of coexisting nationalities.[24]

It's striking that America as such had no particular significance in Zhitlovsky's screed. In spirit, he wrote, America *is* Europe. The cultural treasures he yearned to bring within the domain of Yiddish belonged to America only insofar as America belonged to Europe. Only in permanent contact with Europe, which was humanity at its "highest rung of development" (an idea espoused by Hegel in the early nineteenth century), and not with those "hundreds of millions left outside or behind it," might Jewish culture achieve its true national identity. "The European spirit works powerfully on us. We are European, and that is us." "A people that wants to live with and in mankind must, therefore, bring into itself all of Europe's treasures, from Homer to the present." "Europeanism must become the basis for new original endeavors and for the further development of those elements of the traditional Jewish culture that are not contrary to it." Europeanism will discipline Jewish self-realization, and translation will be its instrument. And a telling remark: "a new combination with Asiatic culture is not worth darkening the light of the sun." Jewishness needed to be redeemed from association with those unspecified millions—Zhitlovsky seemed to conflate Asia with all that is not Europe—who still lived in darkness and backwardness. "Our pedigree which reaches back to the pyramids has only disreputable worth." He added that Jews were a "piece of Europe [*shtick europa*] thrown into Asia," as Heine had put it.[25]

Why was *Hiawatha* chosen, a faux Indian poem that Longfellow

presented as a faux translation of songs from a nonexistent original—
"I repeat them as I heard them / From the lips of Nawadaha"? "Why
did Yehoash fall on this work?" Zhitlovsky asks. "About this the poet
need not answer. It's Longfellow's luck! Any other great work would
have no less earned the honor. But properly, the Jewish people earned
the honor to have this over other great works in its literature."[26] He
assumed that the question answered itself.

Born in Lithuania in 1872 as Solomon Bloomgarten, Yehoash had
begun his writing career in Hebrew. He immigrated to New York in
1890, found work as tailor, bookkeeper, peddler, and Hebrew teacher,
a miscellany of jobs typical of the hand-to-mouth existence of many
literary immigrants at the time. Suffering from tuberculosis, he spent
ten years in a sanitarium in Colorado, where he turned from Hebrew
to Yiddish. He was an inspiring influence on the younger "introspec-
tivist" poets who emerged after World War I; their "Manifesto" of
1919 praised him as "the most important figure in all of Yiddish poetry
today," "one who is close to us."[27] A volume of his *Gezamelte Lieder*
(Collected Poems) appeared in 1907, earning him recognition as one
of the leading poets of his generation, known for the refinement and
purity of his Yiddish. Yiddish as a medium of translation emerged as
one of his primary interests; in the same years as the *Hiawatha* translation he also put into Yiddish Aesop's *Fables* and the Persian poem of
wisdom and meditation, "The Rubaiyat of Omar Khayyam." In the
early 1920s he began an epic project of translating sacred Hebrew
into the vernacular Yiddish; daily installments of the Pentateuch (the
first five books of the Bible) were published in the newspaper *Der Tog*
(The Day); they would appear posthumously in two volumes in 1941,
fourteen years after his death at age fifty-five in 1927.

The Russian-born Yehoash's choice of Longfellow's poem reflects
the high standing of this American poet in Russia, where *Hiawatha*
had been translated in 1896 by the distinguished novelist Ivan Bunin.
Bunin said that he had ardently loved the poem since childhood and
offered his translation as "a small homage for my gratitude to a great
poet who gave me much pure and lofty joy." Another Russian-born
poet, Saul Tschernichowsky, who translated *Hiawatha* into Hebrew in
1913, also recalled his childhood love of the poem in Bunin's transla-

tion.[28] But still we might wonder why Longfellow rather than Whitman or Poe, whose poems were more likely to appeal to immigrants in the clamoring streets and fetid slums of lower New York. Young Yiddish poets living the mysteries of the city and struggling with linguistic and spiritual alienation often evoked Whitman's inclusive chants and Poe's dark isolation and feverishness rather than Longfellow's courtesy and deference.[29] Yehoash's choice may also have reflected his temperament. His own lyric poetry tended toward a neo-Wordsworthian and Symbolist naturism of "mountain storms" and "evening sounds." One of his poems was titled "The Maid of the Mist," a reverie on a seductive maiden dancing in the spray above Niagara Falls.[30] Against the "sweatshop poets" David Edelstadt, Morris Winchevsky, and Morris Rosenfeld, Yeohash stands out as an elegant lyricist, "caught," as Irving Howe writes, "between the clashing impulses of traditional folklike song and modern idiosyncratic speech.[31] His "Woolworth Building," a fine example of the latter, anticipated Hart Crane: "Evening falls / like a deaf fly on the knot of blent/ wire and mortar and cement."[32] But in "The Strongest" he writes, "I'll be the word that heals, the hand / That unseen and still, as from above, / Gives love."[33] Although the unseen hand may echo Whitman, the sentiment is closer to Longfellow: the poet as healer and comforter to his people. In his introduction to the *Hiawatha* translation, Zhitlovksy wrote, "What we city-dwellers lack is nature and the love of nature. Among our spiritual treasures we lack . . . just what woods and fields, mountains and water call out, and it is exactly with the air of field and woods, with the spirit of mountain and water that Longfellow's writings are so richly suffused."[34]

The *Hiawatha* translation was partly an exercise in poetics. See with what ease and confidence Yiddish could make Longfellow's unrhymed eight-syllable trochaic lines seem natural in accented Yiddish vocables:

> Fregt ir mikh, vu kh'nem di mayse,
> Di sipurim un di skazkes,
> Mit di reykhes fun di velder
> Mit dem duft un toy fun lonkes
> Mit dem roykh-krayzn fun vigvams,

Mit dem rash fun shtarke shtromen,
Mit di ofte viderklangen,
Un meshugundika ekhos,
Vi in berg di duner-klangen?

Should you ask me, whence these stories?
Whence these legends and traditions,
With the odors of the forest,
With the dew and damp of meadows,
With the curling smoke of wigwams,
With the rushing of great rivers,
With their frequent repetitions,
And their wild reverberations,
As of thunder in the mountains?

In this opening stanza of the Introduction, the translation seems exact
and accurate. But the inversion in line one ("Fregt ir mikh": "Asked
you me," in place of "Should you ask me") and minor substitutions in
lines two and eight make for a difference in tone and "atmosphere" (a
key word in Zhitlovsky's introduction), a transformation (something
more than literal translation) of Longfellow's English in Yehoash's Yiddish. The difference lies in what Harshav has called the "'semiotics' of
Yiddish," a second level of meaning in which "fregt ir mikh" subverts
or cancels the poeticism "whence" in a Yiddish speech-act with a certain colloquial intonation familiar only to speakers of the language.[35]
The process of question and response that Longfellow put into motion in stanza one completes itself in stanza two: "I should answer, I
should tell you; / From the forests and the prairies . . . I repeat them
as I heard them / From the lips of Nawadaha, / The musician, the
sweet singer." In Yiddish: "Aykh an entfer vel ikh geben . . . Ikh dert-
seye vi kh/hob gehert zey, / Fun di lipn nevadaha's . . ." This inversion
back-translates as literally: "You an answer will I give . . . tell them as
I heard them, from Nawadaha's lips." The effect of these subtle varia-
tions is to make the transaction between imagined question and reply
sound more like a Talmudic conversation than a rhetorical pattern of
English poetry.

Not slavish imitation, then, but repossession, what Walter Benjamin in "The Task of the Translator" called an "afterlife" of the original. The ease of translation conveyed by Yehoash's able versification implied a "kinship" that enriched and refined the translator's own language by requiring that he "expand and deepen his language by means of the foreign language." Benjamin writes: "A translation, instead of imitating the sense of the original, must lovingly and in detail incorporate the original's way of meaning, thus making both the original and the translation recognizable as fragments of a greater language, just as fragments are part of a vessel."[36] Yiddish reclaims itself in the act of realizing an American-English source as an appropriate text for its own idioms and vernacular accents.

Later in the Introduction, Longfellow's "Tones so plain and childlike" reappear in a distinctly Yiddish sound as "azoy zis, naiv un kindersh." The patronizing sentiment may be Longfellow's, but the voice is Yiddish, which gives the language its particularity as a scene of interaction and communication. The words translate not only the sense of the original poem but also Yiddish's own assumed conventions of linguistic behavior. Thus Yehoash does more than "translate" in the literal sense; adopting the conversational mode characteristic of Yiddish, whose origins in speech cling to its sound and sense in writing, he rewrites Longfellow's poem as a Yiddish speech act, repossessing the original as a fully *Yiddish* poem.

The process of remaking the poem begins with the list of "Indianisha Namen un Werter" (Indian Names and Words) that Yehoash placed before the poem proper, a version of the "Vocabulary" that followed Longfellow's original. Longfellow's list of Indian names and words, supererogatory to the reading of the poem and without a pronunciation guide, acknowledged the presence of Algonquian terms written out as English sounds, as if to say that Indian terminology need not be translated within the text because it had been incorporated into English. Yehoash explained that he was following Longfellow in giving Indian words in Yiddish, in both cases for the sake of "genuine Indian color." Yehoash Yiddishized his list, however, and adapted it to the needs of his Yiddish audience, by adding terms absent in Longfellow's list ("wigwam," for example), by explaining the pronunciation of the vowel sound "ay" according to Lithuanian speech ("*litvisha oysshprakh*"), and by defining Indian terms in idiomatic Yiddish (for example, Longfellow's "*Ka'go*, do not" becomes "loz es zein" or "let it be"). The translator respects both ends of the transaction, the English and the Yiddish, and the implicit third party, the Algonquian language as the mythic source of the presumed urpoem. As Zhitkovsky put it, it was Longfellow's luck to have Yehoash as translator and the luck of Yiddish that Yehoash chose this particular already acculturated monument of Euro-American literature for his own complex act of further acculturation.

Zhitlovsky reserved discussion of Longfellow's *Hiawatha* itself for the concluding section of his introduction, where the ambiguities latent in his Europeanized conception of America and of Yiddish appear as internal contradictions. After praising Yehoash for his recent accomplishments in "Yiddish translation-literature," Zhitlovsky explains that bringing *Hiawatha* into Yiddish answered two Jewish needs: for "nature and the love of nature," and for a feeling knowledge of a strange or alien people ("*a fremd folk*"). As city people, Jews missed the "scent of ghosts" in which Longfellow's poem is "so richly steeped."[37] The implicit point was that Jews had no land of their own, no territorial gods and spirits; instead, as he had earlier argued, they have Yiddish, part of their bone marrow and nervous system. Translation of Longfellow's nature myths could remedy the Jewish lack and supplant the absence of "nature" in their cultural self-knowledge. But Zhitlovksy buried the allusion to territorial nationalism implied by this formula, buried everything implied by the encounter (by means of translation) between diasporic Jewish yearnings for a homeland (transmuted into love of Yiddish) and the dispossession of Indians, which also lies buried and unmentioned by Longfellow except obliquely in the final cantos.

If Yiddish was a surrogate for national territory, translation into Yiddish of Indian lore and nature love was the emotional equivalent for possession of land. For Longfellow the capture of Indian legend and nature myth gave the poem a nationalizing effect: This land now "ours" comes with a hauntedness of human story, also now "ours" by means of Longfellow's putative translation, now "American," now the validation of "our" possession. For Zhitlovsky the issue was not America but nature, territory in the abstract. The aim was to naturalize Jewish immigrants into a European conception of "Indian," a premodern and antiurban romantic fantasy of a lost world rich in emotional gratification. It took a Yiddish translation of an American poem to achieve what Zhitlovsky viewed as a goal of Yiddishism: the Europeanization of the Jews.

The second need filled by the translation came from what Zhitlovsky saw as the conceit of Jews that they were "the most cosmopolitan people in the world." In truth, their emotional lives were so narrowed as a result of the troubles in exile ("*tsores in goles*") and they had "long forgotten" the commandment to "love the stranger," to understand "the soul of the non-Jew"; our "whole atmosphere [is] filled with so much chauvinism, small hatreds of others, that we will soon lack air to breathe." Hence all the more need for translation. "The poetry of a strange people teaches us empathy with them, with their joys and sorrows." Because Longfellow's poem gave "the psychology of the whole Indian people," translation into Yiddish broke down "national separation," overcoming "the hostile antagonism between the national 'I' and the national 'you.'" Taking Longfellow at his word, that the poem presented authentic indigenous voices, Zhitlovsky repeated this comforting illusion in Longfellowian accents: "The poetry of another people teaches us empathy with the other, to feel, enjoy, or suffer with him. In this sense Longfellow's 'Hiawatha' is one of the most valuable works in European literature." Its value lay in the feeling of "solidarity" it inspired, its unifying vision of a family of nations in which "every nation undisturbed can unfold what grows in its own soul and help other people in the mutual progress of all humanity."[38] Zhitlovsky's name for this condition was not "America" but "socialism," the alternative to both the melting pot and abstract cosmopolitanism.

Reckoning "America spiritually as Europe" was true to the spirit of the time, at once shrewdly correct and terribly wrong; it failed to reckon with that very presence of a defeated aboriginal people that Longfellow's poem disguised, failed to notice that the Indian presence helped to explain how "American" deviated from "European" in the realm of spirit and culture. A flock of questions arise. Was it claimed that Longfellow's *Hiawatha* was a genuine Indian poem?

Were Indians truly one "people"? How did empathy with Indians satisfy the goal of connection with the great tradition of Europe? Empathy with the culture of non-European people whom Zhitlovsky called "wild" and "primitive" seems squarely at odds with "Europeanism." And besides, empathy aroused by the translation was not with Indian peoples in their own voice but with an already Europeanized version of "the primitive." Did Zhitlovsky tacitly recognize this gap in his argument, or did the aura of Longfellow's poem blind him to certain imperatives of his own multinationalist argument, that native peoples also deserve the opportunity to unfold their "soul" in their own way? The argument ascends to a certain ideological rapture in a blur of historical reality.

In 1910, the same year as Yehoash's translation, Abraham Cahan announced a multivolume *History of the United States* in Yiddish, of which two volumes soon appeared. The aim, he wrote in the "Foreword to the Series," was to make Jewish immigrants "familiar with their new home, the fatherland of their children." And the foreword to the first volume promised several chapters on "the social organization of the Indians" and "a short overview of the primordial American people, the noteworthy 'Mound Builders.'" The first European explorers and settlers "did not understand . . . these red-skinned people," a failing, Cahan implies, that could be corrected in a Yiddish history for immigrant readers.[39] But a motive of this sort is not evident in Zhitlovsky's account of the value of Yehoash's translation of *Hiawatha*, a work of literature rather than history but with an implicit claim to historical truth.

In choosing Longfellow's text for remaking as a Yiddish poem, Yehoash chose an American epic that represented itself as a translation from a seeming indigenous American text of aboriginal myth and legend. What better choice for entry into the America immigrants experienced on the streets of New York, a fast-stepping modern world that still dreamed itself innocent by imagining origins in an imaginary Indian past? What better opportunity for a bridge into America than a Yiddish Hiawatha: the return of Hiawatha speaking Yiddish? At stake was the credibility of Yiddish as a medium of access to the inner life of the American imagination: Yiddish, the immigrant tongue perhaps most alien, apart from Indian tongues, to older Americans like Henry James and many less sympathetic than he. Yet Zhitlovsky, under the spell of "Euro-peanism" and of utopia, a multinational socialism, ignored the social and historical dimensions of "the value of translation" almost entirely. About Yiddish in America, about the relation of Jews to the particularity of the mainstream American culture, and especially about the similarity of predicament faced by Jews and Indians as perceived "aliens," outsiders, even "Asiatic" in their culture, he remains silent.[40]

III

In Yehoash's "high" poetic translation, Yiddish-speaking Indians cause no linguistic disruption, for it's understood that Yiddish is the normative language of the translation. Zhitlovsky gave no sign of see-ing anything incongruous about Hiawatha, the "beau ideal" of his people, speaking Yiddish. But Yiddish in the mouths of Indians and of Jews performing as Indians, assuming Indian names, appurtenances, and linguistic markers, emerged in the same years as a popular comic convention in the "low" forms of immigrant theater that so amused Henry James. One surviving script of a vaudeville performance in 1895 carries the teasing title *Tsvishn Indianer* (Among the Indians), which points ahead to the goofy Yiddishizing of Indians and Indianiz-ing of Jews in Mel Brooks's *Blazing Saddles* (1974) and Gene Wilder's *Frisco Kid* (1979), as well as to the more serious magical comedy of Bernard Malamud's unfinished and posthumously published novel, *The People* (1989).[41] The vaudeville skit has two Jewish clothing ped-dlers showing up in "a small place in Kansas," plying their trade among the Indians. Unaccountably, a "farmer's daughter" makes an appearance with black field hands. The atmosphere is carnivalesque: Indians looking for bargains in a "few dozen suits," including an outfit for their god Hoptis, the "farmer's daughter" a flirtatious "old maid" in "elegant clothes"; the black field hand Dixon listening, then joining the singing when one of the peddlers does "a Jewish liturgical num-ber." It's all in Yiddish but with fine distinctions making for verbal comedy: Indians speaking broken Yiddish meant to represent broken English, the Kansas lady meant to be speaking German, parody of an uptown German Jew, and the two peddlers. In the editor Mark

Slobin's words, "both speak East Side (i.e. Americanized) Yiddish."
There's a send-up of genteel "high" culture: one peddler lists the
"classics" he has read: "Shelley's 'Night before Passover,' Shakespeare's 'Jalopy,' Byron's '1001 Nights,' Milton's 'Saturday Night,' and
more and more"; the names Rockefeller and Gould bounce around as
names of lucky or crooked wealth. Burlesque with a point, the little
drama ridicules virtually everything on the immigrant's horizon,
makes comedy out of stereotypes of blacks, the West, farmers' daughters, Indian chiefs, robber barons, and classic British poets. The
ridicule purges threats, contains anxieties, and clears the field for wily
Jewish peddlers making their way in the new American world with
only wit and the "buy cheap, sell dear" market philosophy in their bag
of tricks. Certainly this music hall shtick seems "low" proto–Borscht
Belt humor, but with more sophistication than meets the eye.

Two examples from the 1920s of linguistic impersonations in Yiddishized English of Jews as Indians are particularly striking. In 1921,
Fanny Brice recorded "I'm an Indian," in which the singer explains
how she came to be a "yidishe squaw." It started with her meeting
with Big Chief Chicamahooga," who "right away" grabbed her "for his
squaw." The song opens with an already stale *Hiawatha* allusion:

> I'm Minnehaha
> Minnie-who?
> Minnehaha
> Ah ha . . .
>
> And now oi oi my people
> How can I tell them how
> Their little Rosie Rosenstein
> Is a terrible Indian now.[42]

The humor comes from both linguistic and sartorial incongruity
("down on the feet is the moccasins for the shoes") and recognition of
a certain aptness in that an immigrant Jewish young woman might already seem wildly foreign in American eyes. When Cahan's Yekl at
Ellis Island first lays eyes on his wife, Gitl, after a few years of separation, he takes her for a "squaw" with her dark complexion, face

bronzed from ten days at sea, "prominent cheek bones, inky little eyes," and "smooth black wig." Even as it plays out the comedy of the identification, Brice's song in part recuperates what may have been an anxiety among immigrant women that being foreign, at least on arrival, was as bad as being Indian. Yet to be Indian was also to be American in a way wholly unavailable to Jews: "native" by birth rather than "alien" by immigration. A "yidishe squaw" can then comically seem the perfectly assimilated Jew. The fact that the song is an impersonation, the performance of a Jewish woman (the persona of the song) performing herself as Minnehaha, adds another twist. To be "yidishe" is already to be "squaw" and at the same time never to be "squaw," to be "American" in one sense of the word (native-born) all immigrants faced as the abiding threat to their American identity.

A more elaborate example of verbal comedy drawing on *Hiawatha* appears in the humorist Milt Gross's *Hiawatta: wit no odder poems*. The jacket blurb prepares us: "Hiawatta becomes an epic of Indian Nize Babyhood, in a steam-heated 'appotament' tepee on the shore of Geetchy Gooy (pronounced Bronx)." The gag here is the East Side Jewish immigrant rising from tenement house to apartment house with a view of water: "Frontage feefty fit it measured / Hopen fireplaze—izzy payments." The immigrant rises in the American world but his telltale accent sticks to him, made more comic (though lovingly) by the Hiawathan meter and allusion. Jewish readers on the Lower East Side eyeing a move across the river to the Bronx would understand the scene at once:

> Fiftin meenits from de station
> From de station jost a ston's trow
> Fiftin meenits like de bull flies
> In de beck a two car gerredge
> Gave a leff "Ha ha,"
> De wodder—

The plot has it that in the apartment "liss" there's "a cluzz No cheeldren, / Stoot a warnin 'Hedults honly.'" Along comes baby Hiawatta, "de squaw Nokomis" makes a motion that she be allowed to "adapt de baby," and everything ends agreeably. Gross's parodic adaptation of

Hiawatha into heavily accented Yinglish makes of Longfellow's "Indian Edda" an urban tale of Jews moving uptown, higher into America: a bathetic underside to the Yehoash/Zhitlovksy vision of Jews discovering their Europe (which is also their America) through translation into high, literary Yiddish.

In 1920 the Yiddish journal *Shriftn* (Writings) published an issue devoted largely to translations of Indian verse. As Rachel Rubinstein explains, the issue was a response to a special number of Harriet Monroe's *Poetry* in 1917 devoted to renderings in "modern" American English—"not translations, but interpretations," the editors noted—of songs of "our aboriginal tribes" and their "fast-disappearing folklore."[43] But the aim of the *Poetry* issue was not to salvage ethnography, which had already in the 1880s begun to record and transcribe examples of native languages and expressive verbal culture, not, like the photographer Edward S. Curtis's in the same years, to catch what is already fading before it vanishes altogether. Poetry of contributors like Mary Austin and Alice Corbin sought something grander: revitalization of American letters and culture by an infusion of the spirit of the aboriginal. Ethnologists had "overlooked the literary significance of the Indian songs," wrote Corbin in a note. Striving to avoid having Indians sound like Elizabethan singers, she explained that she sought to "keep within the spirit" of the originals. Like most of the contributions to the issue, Corbin's "interpretations" have the look and feeling of a style of poetry that had already established itself in the young modernist movement.

Listening

> The noise of passing feet
> On the prairie—
> Is it men or gods
> Who come out of the silence?

Whatever role Indian song may have played in the emergence of Imagism, which by understatement, indirection, and concreteness strove to break free of Victorian sentiment and effusiveness, it's clear that Imagism gave modern poets an idea of what to recognize as Indian verse. It's not clear that any of the translators in the *Poetry* Indian number knew any Indian languages firsthand. Their renderings are of verse already translated by anthropological linguists or other poets— not in itself a fault, but something to remember when we consider whether translations or interpretations are true or false to the spirit of the original. In the end, the renderings in English asked to be read as poems in themselves for better or worse rather than as true "aboriginal" expressions.

Imagist verse, as Rubinstein shows, had great appeal for Yiddish poets in the 1920s as a mode or style by which they could display credentials as both modern and, especially in light of Whitman's contribution to the Imagist movement, American. The translations in the 1920 *Shriftn*, many by the editor David Ignatow, clung to the Imagist imperatives: spare, uncluttered, direct. On the whole they were reworkings in Yiddish of versions of tribal songs that had appeared in the 1918 anthology edited by George W. Cronyn, *The Path of the Rainbow*. None of the Yiddish translations were directly from native originals, but they were, as Rubinstein observes, presented without apparatus, which Cronyn's volume had, such as anthropological information framing each translation, and are taken out of Cronyn's order, as if to say that the Yiddish poets were confronting the original with as little mediation as possible. In many instances the Yiddish version is pure idiomatic Yiddish: "Weeping, awake I start," a rendering of a Sioux song by Mary Austin, becomes "veynendik khap ikh sikh oyf."[44] Speaking Indian in Yiddish meant being Indian for the duration of the poem, fusing two voices in a new syncretic construction of native and stranger, a new construction. The investment of the Yiddish translators inevitably differed from that of the contributors to the *Poetry* issue: It was made not to preserve the "aboriginal" as either revitalization or precursor of the modern but to achieve an American voice in an "alien" tongue, not by "putting on" the native but inhabiting it from within two cultures at once, remaking it as Yiddish-Indian.

There is yet another issue at stake in Yiddish Indian translations. Zhitlovsky spoke of "nature and the love of nature" as virtues missing from the Jews' national existence without a territory. He did not speak of "rootless cosmopolitans," but the idea that Jews without land represented an absolute and even a menacing antinational trait arose in writings by non-Jewish advocates of the revitalization offered by "Amerindian" art. In the midst of her work on Indian art and culture, Mary Austin took several occasions to express the view that Jews disqualified themselves by cultural inheritance to join or even speak of American nationality.

After the success of her first book, *The Land of Little Rain* (1903)—a masterpiece of description and narrative of the land and the peoples, native and Mexican American, of a California desert— Austin (1868–1934) wrote many novels, stories, poems, plays, and essays on the West, the plight of women, and native cultures. Identified with California and the Southwest—she lived often in Santa Fe—her writings were known for their lyricism and for a mystical sense of land and culture that colored her view of big cities, foreigners, and Jews. "There's nothing un-American in being a Jew," she conceded in a tirade against New York critics in *The Nation* in 1920, but considering "his profound complex of election, his need for sensuous satisfaction . . . and his short pendulum-swing between mystical orthodoxy and a sterile ethical culture—can he become the arbiter of American art and American thinking?"[45]

In an exchange of letters in 1921 with the novelist Ludwig Lewisohn, who had apparently asked for some changes in an article she had submitted to *The Nation* (of which he was then an editor), she took offense that her "learning" had been challenged and blamed Lewisohn's "race," according to the editor's reply. The words are Lewisohn's, apparently quoting Austin back to herself. She had said that with "no spiritual traffic with God," unable to understand "love as the Anglo-Saxon knows it at its best," he had no "access to the American mind" and therefore was ineligible to judge her work.[46] In a review of Lewisohn's 1922 memoir *Up Stream: An American Chronicle*, she took a friendlier approach but again spoke of race: "The race of Jews in Europe was cut off from some of the most formative experiences of the European mind, from the best of feudalism, from Christian mysticism, from chivalry, from the Renaissance."[47]

While deploring the discrimination Lewisohn described experiencing at college, Austin asked implicitly how "a Jew of pure descent" could be "one of us." There was also the suggestion that Lewisohn was a bit too touchy in his reaction to exclusions, that if he were less a "book-made man" and less "German" and "radical" in his outlook, less of a believer in "deliberate rationalization of the social organization," he would have less of a sense that all good things in America were coming to him. The non-Yiddish-speaking Lewisohn—he was born in Berlin, came to the United States as a child, and was raised in the South—nevertheless represents the Jew as deracinated outsider. Austin charges that Lewisohn avoids the deeper waters of his own racial identity and thus his book gained importance for its "subconscious" expression of the Jew's "experience of his racial inheritance."

The intellectual ground of these views can be pieced together from Austin's writings on Indian poetry and nationality. In her introduction to the *Poetry* issue, she spoke of "the poetic faculty" as the human mode "most responsive to the natural environment," that this responsiveness to the land's "skyey influences, its floods, forests, morning colors" was the basis for "new national ideals," that there was a "whole instinctive movement of the American people . . . for a deeper footing in their national soil," that therefore the American poet needed to "put himself in touch with the resident genius of his own land."[48] It's not exactly clear what the signs of this "instinctive movement" were, apart from a growing artistic interest in native themes, or whether by "American people" she meant immigrants or even Indians themselves, whose creative work was presumably finished once their "resident genius" had been available to non-Indian artists for "interpretation" or "reexpression."[49] Austin elaborated these thoughts in *The American Rhythm* (1923), where, in an aestheticized version of Turner's frontier thesis, she gave credit to the land for making Americans out of European colonizers and colonists: "Streams of rhythmic sights and sounds flowed in upon the becoming race of Americans from every natural feature."[50] Escaping the "overhumanized" landscape of Northern and Central Europe, they found "free flung mountain ridges, untrimmed forests." Whitman and other nineteenth-century writers sought to express such new experience, but all the while "there was an American race singing in tune with the beloved environment." In a review in *The New Republic* in 1926, she made the interesting observation that though Longellow "garbled the story of Hiawatha out of all resemblance to its Ojibway original," nevertheless "he preserved a saving primitiveness, largely by his selection of an authentic aboriginal rhythm." He could not have known that "there existed Amerind verse forms entirely adequate to the poet's needs, and must be thanked rather than blamed for selecting, in the Finnish Kalevala, a form of nearly identical cultural level as the Hiawatha hero cycle."[51] In Amerindian songs, Euro-Americans could find their way back from their "over-humanized" world to the sources of all national poetry itself in the rhythms of human perception of the land and adaptation to it. New immigrants groups, "Russ and Pole and Serb," brought with them "subconscious" memories of folk expression that awaited reactivation by contact with the American rhythms of the Amerindian, a source for personal and national renewal.

More than occasionally an image of "blood" surfaced in Austin's work, suggesting a deeper level of racial thinking. There are times in her studies of Indian arts, she wrote, when she herself "succeeded in being an Indian."[52] In her autobiography in 1932 she wrote of "a special grace which has been mine from the beginning," perhaps the "persistence" of "an uncorrupted strain of ancestral primitivism" from some "far-off and slightly mythical Indian ancestor."[53] And among her notes on Indians: "The time is rapidly approaching when we will think of this aboriginal strain as more to be treasured than any later addition to our blood from the slums of Europe, just as we are now learning that their art is more of a contribution than what comes to us from Armenia or the Balkans."[54]

The absence in Zhitlovsky's essay of any speculation about Jews in relation to Indians, about the history of relations between Indians and Jews (peddlers, merchants, photographers, tribal members[55]), the way their separate predicaments in relation to the dominant society mirror and illuminate each other, seems a missed opportunity to take the problem of translation in regard to nationality one step further. Austin, too, was blind to a certain resemblance. Unless we consider slavery as an Americanization, of a sort, of Africans, Indians were the first ethnicity subjected to that process, in boarding schools where they faced punishment for using their native speech, lost their names, their dress, their food, and everything that signified their nativeness. Ridiculed, defamed, ghettoized, stereotyped as racially "other," as the permanent stranger and outsider, Indians epitomized the oppression of peoples denied selfhood and individuality along with loss of homeland. Dispersed in enclaves "reserved" for them across the national territory, as well as scattered in cities and towns, Indians, too, lived in a kind of diaspora both like and unlike that of Jews and African Americans.

But the resemblance of predicament was not lost on many of the great Yiddish poets. Sympathetic figures of Indians (also of African Americans) and Indian poems in Yiddish flow throughout the body of American Yiddish poetry, perhaps an afterlife of Yehoash's translation, perhaps in recognition of a shared marginality and ironic similarities in the fated relation of each group to a dominant America. Mani Leib, for example, made Indian dispossession an explicit motif in the sonnet "The Bit of Land," which concludes that wherever blue-eyed Christian Europeans claim a piece of the American land, the "breath of the Indian" can be felt and heard.[56] In another sonnet, "To the Gentile Poet," Leib spoke of Yiddish poets as "dust-bearded nomads," "desert wanderers," biblical figures who as "nomads" and "wanderers" might be said also to breathe the air of displaced Indians.[57] At least one Yiddish poet, Reuben Ludvig (1895–1926), attempted to speak in an Indian voice not in translation but in original poetry. An immigrant from Lipovets, near Kiev, and afflicted with tuberculosis in the 1920s, Ludvig wandered with his wife through Arizona and Colorado and California in search of health; he took the Southwest as the landscape for many poems, and in "Indian Motifs" spoke directly as a Pima Indian in lament of a passing way of life. In a section of this suite of songs in the manner of Imagism titled "In the Dusk," he wrote:

> Stanchions of telegraph
> Stretch themselves along the way
> Like shadowy crosses . . .
>
> With them
> Longings for home
> Awake in our children.
> Under them
> Lies buried our joy—
> The tranquility
> Of our people.[58]

An Indian cry in Yiddish, a *benkshaft* (longing, nostalgia, homesickness) against a symbol of conquest and control, Ludvig's poem conjoined Indian and Jew in lament for a lost home, a shattered identity. The fusion of perspectives made for a poignant rejoinder to those like Mary Austin who implicitly placed Indian and Jew at opposite poles, one a nationality rooted in rhythms of blood and land, the other a perpetual wanderer, out of touch with where he is, "colour blind," as she writes in her review of Lewisohn, "to the particular shade of green that is coming up" between the "desiccating leaf stalks of last year's culture."[59]

In "On a Stanza of H. Leyvick," John Hollander meditates on the heroic entrance and sad demise of Yiddish on the stage of poetry in America. In accents recalling Aeneas in the underworld, the speaker in the poem encounters forebears, ghosts lingering in corners and alleys; he calls out their names, an honor roll of warrior poets: Leyvick, Halpern, Leyeles, Mani Leib, Glatshteyn, Teller, Yehoash. In their hard-won lyricism these and other Yiddish poets in America occasionally tested the possibility of joining the perspectives of dispossessed Indian and estranged Yid, a "babe in the Yiddish woods," a motif or theme or argument that deserves more investigation by scholars of the Yiddish word in the United States. Yehoash's *Lid fun Hayavata* broke the ground in serious verse, made the first and most heroic effort to reach out from the ghetto vernacular of an immigrant tongue to remake a central poem of alien gentile (but perhaps secretly Jewish?) American literature into something familiar, something Yiddish. Since its appearance, the number of Yiddish readers in the United States has declined precipitately. As Hollander writes, "The native speakers of our dialect, / Are few and dying," perhaps alluding in a whisper to another ground of Indian-Jew kinship. Yehoash's *Lid fun Hayavata*, much like Longfellow's original itself, survives as a relic of a moment of exalted belief in the power of translation to overcome differences of identity. It recalls a fleeting radiant moment when becoming American in Yiddish, by creating an Indian mediation for a Yiddish-American identity, seemed a plausible prospect.

FOUR

Ghostlier Demarcations

I shall vanish and be no more,
But the land over which I now roam
Shall remain
And change not.
— Warrior Song of the Hethúshka Society (Omaha)

For most in the United States a century ago, the word "Indian" brought to mind mental images rather than actual persons sharing a neighborhood, a school, a church, or a community. Except in certain regions of the West and Southwest, living natives were visible to non-Indians mainly as performers: feathered and painted "savages" in the immensely popular Wild West shows, picturesque figures in the landscape presented to tourists by enterprising companies in the Southwest and in the Great Lakes region, "primitives" on display at world's fairs such as those in Chicago, Omaha, and St. Louis. Early western movies, picture postcards, growing numbers of art and ethnological photographs all trafficked in images of primitiveness and exoticism. Ethnology and entertainment kept Indians at a distance defined by "otherness," "their" way of life moribund, their demise taken as proof of the triumph of "our" civilization. Testimony of need for such proof lay in the incalculable number of photographic images of natives produced at the turn of the century, as if once the guns went silent after Wounded Knee, out came the camera, instrument (or weapon) of choice to confirm conquest and proclaim victory. The rise in the sheer quantity of such images, in painting and statuary along with photographs, was related to the spreading popular taste for the "regional," fascination with places and ways of life left behind with the burgeoning of cities and urban populations. Indians, who in fact contributed to the growth of population in cities like Chicago, Minneapolis, and Los Angeles, were portrayed as the most unequivocal markers of the backward, the lost, the residue of American progress. The more "vanished," the more visible as image.[1]

It was the genius of Edward Sheriff Curtis to understand the timely need for a portrayal of this "vanishing race" that would dissolve the threat of "savagery" into something beautiful and reassuring. Some years before embarking on his major Indian project, as a prominent studio photographer in Seattle in the 1890s he had already made occasional pictures of local Indians; he recalled that his first native portrait was of an aged, wrinkled clam digger known as Princess Angelina, daughter of Chief Sea'thl, already a favorite with local camera bugs. Curtis paid her a dollar for the privilege of fulfilling her father's prophecy that "the White Man will never be alone."[2] At a time of major changes in America's ethnic and demographic composition, a time when melting pot reigned as the most persuasive figure for neutralizing differences and achieving national oneness, Curtis set about to assimilate "the North American Indian" not by acculturation—the method of the allotment policy and the boarding school—but just the opposite: by preserving difference as a beauty lost forever, the spectral beauty of national origins.

"Vanishing race" gave Curtis the conceptual cover for his Indian work, but the most significant focus of his enterprise was nationality, the ethnogenesis of the nation, as Mick Gidley has argued in his richly documented and indispensable book on Curtis. More effectively than anyone else in his generation he made a place for and gave a role to "the Indian" in the American drama, a place as iconic image and a role as national memory. Curtis was known at first as a "photo-historian," but his mode is more properly understood as myth making. Gidley shows indisputably that the shadows this great "shadow catcher" caught were of his own culture's constructions of itself; he gave back the myth of America embodied in images of the otherness through which his America perceived its own uniqueness among nations. He labored obsessively, possessed of a vision he could not lay to rest until

Cyrus E. Dallin, "Appeal to the Great Spirit." Cast in bronze in 1909, Dallin's statue now stands in front of the Museum of Fine Arts, Boston. A painting of the sculpture, 1921. (Library of Congress)

"He-Nu-Kaw (The First Born)." Undated poster for the Buffalo Bill Wild West Show. "The Handsomest Indian Maiden in the World." (Beinecke Rare Book and Manuscript Library. Yale University)

Edward S. Curtis, "Princess Angelina," 1899. v. 9, *NAI*, 1913. (McCormick Library of Special Collections, Northwestern University Library)

the final of the twenty volumes he promised to his patron, J. P. Morgan, in 1906 appeared in 1930.[3] He was himself the arch romancer, the central figure of his myth of adventure, of challenges overcome, sacrifices undergone, descent into an imaginary underworld, and transcendence.

I

At the height of his celebrity, Curtis himself walked in an aura of legend and myth. He was the man who lived with the Indians, who saw through Indian eyes, and who, with the help of J. P. Morgan (known to his intimates as "Chief"), proposed to preserve the "vanishing race" in magnificent photographs and informative texts. Curtis's plan, with Morgan's backing, called for sumptuous volumes of pictures and texts, each accompanied by a portfolio of large sepia-toned gravures printed in india ink. These large gravures, along with the deluxe printing of the books, sealed the entire project as "art," while the illustrated volumes with texts—part narrative, part accounts of daily life and labor, part mythology—represented the "science" of ethnography. It would be, wrote the *New York Herald* in 1907 (a year after the project was announced), "the most gigantic undertaking since the King James edition of the Bible."[4] Audubon's *Birds of America* (1827–38) was often mentioned as a national work in whose path Curtis followed: the product of firsthand experience in the wild, a marriage of science and art, something epic in scale and epochal in significance. Like birds, were not Indians part of the natural domain, the fauna, of the land? Another mark of prestige was the terms of publication, only five hundred sets to be printed and sold in advance to subscribers at the princely fee of $3,000 or $4,000 each, as agreed on with Morgan. In the end, about 270 people subscribed, a small but telling portion of America's ruling class. So this was an elite production in the strictest sense of the word: Touching the handsome volumes and seeing the stunning gravures were hardly popular experiences.

Yet Curtis hoped for "popular interest." And he did reach a wider audience not only with his lectures and a musicale but also with numerous illustrated articles in popular periodicals.[5] "I have endeavored," he wrote in his 1911 draft for the introduction to his project, "not to make pictures or text so scientifically dry that there is no red life-blood in them. It should be a work pulsing, throbbing with life and nature, and yet as scientifically founded as the rocks of the mountain." Red-blooded masculine vigor was integral to the Curtis story as it unfolded. "Morgan's Millions to Save Indians from Oblivion," proclaimed one headline. For a few years, until about 1914, news stories, journal articles, lecture tours, the film *The Land of the Head-Hunters,* and his "Indian Picture-Opera" called *The Vanishing Race* kept Curtis in the public eye. Publicity began to fade at the time of World War I, and when the curtain came down on the entire project with the publication of the final volume in 1930, no one seemed to notice or care.

Curtis seemed driven by the belief that the nation knows itself truly only by identity with its virtually obliterated indigenous peoples. In the draft of a report to subscribers, he began by pointedly evoking national self-knowledge: "Long after time has obscured from popular sight the world over practically all traces of the primal rise of the American people, and supplanted in its stead the vision of certain social and political customs only as distinctive features of the Americans, America will stand out boldly as having been the home of a race as different from any other found on the globe as the Caucasian is from the Ethiopian."[6] Addressed to wealthy individuals and powerful institutions, Curtis's words conflated the indigenous and the national, the "American people" as both Indians and the white nation, and "primal rise" the mysterious origins of the indigenous peoples and the nation, shrouded (in good Romantic and Herderian theory) in the obscuring mists of time. What distinguished "the Americans" was not their "social and political customs" (this seemed to refer to the white nation) but the fact of their living in a place that had "been the home" of a "race" that differed from all others as white does from black, Caucasian from Ethiopian—and America from all the nations. The unspoken idea was that the nation partook of a racial character neither white nor black but tinged with red. This conflation seems deliberate, though it may be an unconscious thought, all the more revealing of Curtis's compulsive desire to embed images of the primal, primitive, and indigenous within American nationality.

Image was central to Curtis's version of the national idea. "Words alone" cannot give "anything like an adequate conception" either of the look of "the red man himself" or of his physical domain. The at-oneness of person and domain is the powerful donnée, the pre-assumption, of his entire work, "the story of their life in pictures and words," "the native American in his primitive haunts," "the Indians and their environment."[7] Seeking origins for the sake of the nation, Curtis sought the "primitive," and where he could not find it he invented it in staged tableaux and visual fictions. Curtis's texts, com-posed in the discourse of ethnography and passed before the paid ed-itorial eye of a legitimating ethnologist, Frederick Webb Hodge of the Bureau of American Ethnology, were to attest to the accuracy of the pictures. Elsewhere Curtis remarked, "I resolved at an early period in my work with the Indians that my photographs must show the native without dress or artifact that betokened his contact with white civi-lization if possible."[8]

The report to his subscribers did not mention fabrications made to conform to another donnée: that these were pictures of a vanishing and mostly already vanished people. The camera was Curtis's chief fabrica-tor: "Being photographs from life and nature, they show what exists"—or what was made to exist for the moment of exposure before the camera eye. The work, Curtis explains, "is the result of actual first-hand study by one person." Photography requires that the image maker be an actual witness to what the image shows, that he *had been there*. His medium certifies authority. I was the man, I was there, I gathered the information and stories, I sought the purest expression—often having to scour to find the old people "who know the esoteric rites in their purity"—I set the camera, and I saw everything with my own eyes.[9]

And with a pressing sense of urgency. At least as early as Catlin in the 1830s, artists and early ethnographers like Schoolcraft worried that time was running out, that the natives would soon be either ex-terminated or so assimilated as to be no longer Indian. The only true Indian was a vanishing Indian. "The change in the Indian life is rapid," Curtis wrote, and once "the primitive Indian life" is over—he gave it another twenty years—"the Indian as an Indian will have passed from the face of the earth."[10] Indian equates with primitive, an unchanging aboriginal condition, and Indian does not exist without the look, speech, and customs and beliefs of a traditional culture. Once these go or begin to change, so goes Indian, like *Hiawatha*, into the sunset.

Curtis announced that it was not his purpose "to theorize on the probable origins of the Indian." Neither was he concerned with probable causes of demise or with the Indian's destination. Partly the Indian's fate was "the working out of the inevitable," but the process had been accelerated by deliberate acts on the part of the white nation, and Curtis, so far from flinching from the history of genocidal atrocities against natives, put them in the foreground of his 1911 report. In the same sentence in which he acknowledged that his work will not "be taken up with a continual reiteration" of "wrongs," he wrote of "treatment of the so-called savages" by "civilized and Christian people" (so-called) as "worse than a crime." He directed his work "to all those of us who have crushed out most of his [the Indian's] life and are fast perpetrating extinction."[11]

Among his subscribers were railroad magnates like James Hill and Edward Harriman, industrialists like Andrew Carnegie, and financiers like Morgan himself, all of whom would have understood their role in perpetrating the Indians' "extinction" and would have justified it in the name of national "progress." By excluding a study of origins and decline, Curtis thereby excluded history itself from his discourse, though his use of phrases like "crushed out" and "are fast perpetrating" conceded an ongoing history of genocide even while dismissing it from the horizon of his work. Yet his select audience's relation to the capitalist-industrial program of national expansion that made destruction of Indian societies a sine qua non was the enabling condition for Curtis's project in the first place.

There was purpose to this equivocation between "inevitable" and "crime," to this dismissal from Curtis's texts and pictures of the "seemingly endless series of damaging political and economic decisions made by human individuals and agencies," in Gidley's words, and his pictorial disguise of the process as inevitable and natural.[12] Numerous remarks scattered throughout the volumes show that Curtis knew well enough that the present condition of natives represented the cumulative effect of policy and purpose and morally indefensible acts by white settlers. In September 1923 he wrote to a friend about the treatment of California Indians:

> The principal outdoor sport of the settlers during the 50's and 60's seemingly was the killing of Indians. There is nothing else in the history of the United States which approaches the inhuman and brutal treatment of the Calif. tribes. Men desiring women merely went to the village or camp, killed the men and took such women as they desired. Seemingly feeling that the Indians might later be given some protection and rights they killed them off as fast as they could.[13]

The account speaks for itself. In his introduction to his third volume, on the Plains Indians, he wrote:

> Strong sympathy for the Indian cannot blind one to the fact that the change that has come is a necessity created by the expansion of the white population. Nor does the fact that civilization demands the abandonment of aboriginal habits lessen one's sympathy or alter one's realization that for once at least Nature's laws have been the indirect cause of a grievous wrong. That the inevitable transformation of the Indian life has been made many-fold harder by the white man's cupidity, there is no question.[14]

Why, then, did he insist that a "reiteration" of savage acts against natives had no place in his work? The present condition of Indians might not have been his overt concern, but his comments ensured that it could not be ignored.

Was yet another donnée, then, that knowledge of white "wrongs" was the hidden condition for whites' acceptance and celebration of the primitive? Curtis offered his images as if his camera were present to witness primal primitiveness before any white people arrived. They showed how Indians could be imagined to have looked before they began to fade away. The alleged disappearance of the Indian as Indian made it possible, even necessary, to think back to the initial rise of the nation itself, to make an imaginary recovery of ancestral origins. Partly Curtis offered an assuaging of guilt. But more important, he effected a radical shift in perspective. Stop thinking of them as savages, he told his subscribers: "if we are to take the general definition of the word, there were no savages in North America at the time Columbus landed, as they all had a religion." Only obstinate blindness perpetuated views to the contrary, he asserted. The natives of North America lived according to elaborate religious rites; they were nothing if not steeped in piety, beginning with morning prayers facing the rising sun. When we recognize this, we are better able to incorporate their heritage as our own.

"You who have followed in the pathway of commerce," Curtis admonished his subscribers, "and do not know the byways and nooks of nature and primitive life, do not tell me that I picture a life that does not exist. To you it may not exist, but to the primitive man there is no Wall Street and no Stock Exchange." Hence "there is much in the study [of Indians] of which we can profit immeasurably." For subscribers accustomed to windfall profits on Wall Street, the sentence read like a homily in the mode of Curtis's friend and supporter Theodore Roosevelt's plea for the "strenuous life." Preserved in the purity of the already vanished, transfigured as image, stripped of all signs of contact with white civilization, "the Indian" offered a tonic and a possible redemption for an America that had grown soft and unheroic, as William James also lamented. "We must get at the Indian's logic," Curtis wrote, we must learn to "see from the Indian's point of view," and thereby revitalize our own bourgeois existence.[15]

Curtis might have been laying it on a bit thick, in a document aimed at winning financial support from the nation's elite, but the rhetoric and imagery of his argument took on a life of their own. The source of Indian logic and the Indian way of seeing lay in tribal "myth stories," especially in legends of the "miracle performer—the person of miraculous birth, or Indian culture hero," none other than Hiawatha, "the character [Longfellow] so beautifully elaborated from Schoolcraft's studies." Is it any surprise to encounter "Longfellow's Hiawatha" at the threshold of Curtis's project as genie of "the Indian's logic"? Although the name Hiawatha appeared nowhere in Curtis's finished volumes, the entire project exuded a Hiawathan aura, a distillation of "legend" collected from natives and rendered in Curtis's own language, just as Longfellow's repossessed material was already processed by Schoolcraft and others.[16] A 1907 letter to Hodge expressed how deeply important the idea of capturing Indian myths—in the flesh, as it were—was to Curtis: "The special effort of my pictorial work the coming season will be to get as many pictures illustrating the incidents of the myth stories as possible. This will give me a splendid chance to make the most of the nude."[17] Seeking "the Indian's logic" in native bodies, Curtis in his own brilliant blindness initiated his search from within the logic of the white nation. It's not the Indian's logic but the logic of the myth of America that we must "get" in order to see Curtis's North American Indian for what it is, a great pedagogical construction with lessons for old and new Americans of his time.

II

Curtis's photographs seem monuments of perfect stillness. All photographs give the illusion of motion in abeyance, as if everything visible was holding its breath. Curtis's went farther. He made stillness palpable, a living presence in a silent landscape, the atmospheric equivalent of the simple epochal idea of "vanishing race" that governs his great quixotic project. His self-imposed task was to record in photographs and ethnographic text every Indian tribe west of the Mississippi and north to Alaska, and to do so in such a way as to make visible the pathos of their demise, their silent descent into darkness and simultaneous ascent into national memory. They appear (were made to appear) in the act of disappearing, leaving traces of themselves preserved in gold-toned stillness of emulsified platinum or in somber tones of india ink. A momentous historical process lay untold but immanent in Curtis's pictures. His pictures transfigured loss as beauty and pain as reverence; they memorialized what once was and never would be again. And they gave additional currency to the Hiawathan myth of an original "American people" at one with an original American "nature." What the Hiawatha pageants staged as the Indians' own story, what Buffalo Bill performed with his showman's hoopla and yelping, Curtis achieved with the unheard click of a shutter: the peopling of national memory with eloquently silent ghosts. In a florid brochure syndicated to newspapers across the country in 1911, Julian Hawthorne, son of Nathaniel and a popular novelist in his own right, captured the effect of the pictured Indians: "They muffle themselves in their blankets and disappear over the edge of the hill into the dark valley. They go in silence, taking their secret with them."[18]

Curtis's Indians were stripped of their speech in two senses: They were portrayed as silence personified, and the sounds of their own tongues were muffled by Curtis's own voice in his books and in the lectures accompanying his "musicale" or "Indian picture-opera" *The Vanishing Race* in 1911. In notes for one lecture on "ceremonials" Curtis wrote:

> The phase of Indian life which I desire to emphasize is the ceremonial, the devotional, the religious, and my greatest desire is that each and every person here enter into the spirit of our hour with the Indian. I want you to see his beautiful poetic, mysterious, yet simple life, as I have grown to see it . . . Toward that end let us close our eyes for an instant, and in that flash of time span the gulf between today's turmoil and the far-away enchanted realm of primitive man. We have entered what is to us a strange land, Man and nature are one, and atune.[19]

The frontispiece to Volume 1, *The Pool—Apache,* is overture to the spectacle of the entire project: The eye opens to a vision emerging from darkness, a near-naked male body standing amid woods and brush, the dark pool in front of him bearing his doubled image as if on the ground glass of a camera. Close your eyes and, like a camera shutter, open them upon "an enchanted realm." The camera conspires with nature to wrench from time and space a stilled image of perfect primitiveness: reflections mirrored on water, tangled shadows, the hyperreality of a dream.

By means of gestures toward an elsewhere beyond the frame, or passage across the plane of the picture, or recession rearward into depths of silence, space in Curtis's photographs is often made to seem boundless. *The Apache* in the portfolio to Volume 1 shows the same figure (so it seems) from the rear. Similarly the famous recessional image that opens the first portfolio and gives the keynote to the entire project, *Vanishing Race—Navaho,* is echoed by the concluding image, *Out of the Darkness,* a shot-reverse-shot giving illusion of continuous space. Cinemalike techniques produced echoing and mirroring effects, a sense of perfect stillness, as if each image were about to fade into another. Many images hover on the edge of self-annihilation, about to be overwhelmed by internal darkness, with Indians disclosed as their own inversely mimetic negative. Curtis's great achievement was to make photography itself seem master trope of the vanishing race and himself as the mythic American adventurer or prospector into the realms of wildness and pastness in quest of the golden primal moment.[20]

In traditional romance, a hero sets out on a quest, travels to strange lands, encounters challenges, threats, temptations, bewildering scenes often in an "underworld," wonders whether he is charmed or damned, and with luck and grace returns home enlightened and enriched with wisdom and insight that are often embodied in a physical object, a grail or amulet of some sort. In the prime of his fame, Curtis was portrayed in such a heroic mold, the artist as adventurer, outdoorsman, man of the West, and romancer. "Hunting Indians with a Camera: The Adventures of Edward S. Curtis" announced the headline for an article in *The World's Work* by Curtis's Seattle friend Edmond S. Meany, professor of history at the University of Washington.[21] The days of warfare having passed, it was fitting that authority to speak of Indians had passed from the man with a gun to the man (decidedly a man) with a camera. Not scalps but pictures were his trophies. In his foreword to Curtis's first volume, Theodore Roosevelt lent his own vigorous red-blooded American manliness in delivering Curtis as a national figure of near-mythic proportions. "Blest," as the nation's bully president put it, with "a singular combination of qualities," Curtis was "able to do what no other man ever has done; what, as far as we can see, no other man could do." Having "lived on intimate terms with many different tribes," Curtis "caught glimpses, such

Edward S. Curtis. (*left*) "The Pool (Apache)," frontispiece, v. 1, *NAI*, 1907. (*below*) "The Apache," v. 1, *NAI*, 1907. Curtis called this "Life Primeval," "the Apache as we would mentally picture him in the time of the Stone Age." (McCormick Library of Special Collections, Northwestern University Library)

Edward S. Curtis. (*above*) "Vanishing Race—Navaho," and (*below*) "Out of the Darkness—Navaho," v. 1, *NAI*, 1907. Curtis wrote: "The thought which picture is meant to convey is that the Indians as a race, already shorn in their tribal strength and stripped of their primitive dress, are passing into the darkness of an unknown future." This thought "inspired the entire work," thus its prominence as "the first of the series." (McCormick Library of Special Collections, Northwestern University Library)

Edward S. Curtis. (*above*) "Scout—Apache," v. 1, *NAI*, 1907. (*below*)
"Watching the Dancers," v. 12, *NAI*, 1922. (McCormick Library of Special Collections,
Northwestern University Library)

as few white men ever catch, into . . . [their] strange spiritual and mental life." A rugged Westerner whose eye penetrated surfaces, Curtis performed "great service" to "our own people" because he had recovered and recorded "conditions through which our own race passed so many ages ago that not a vestige of their memory remains."[22] Today was the "last chance" to do that.

It's intriguing that it was not not until his final volume that Curtis actually thought he "caught glimpses" of something truly original, the "unspoiled" Nunivak Island Eskimos:

> The natives here are perhaps the most primitive on the North American Continent . . . Think of it. At last, and for the first time in my thirty years work . . . I have found a place where no missionary has worked . . . I hesitate to mention it for fear some over-zealous sky pilot will feel called upon to labor the unspoiled people. They are so happy and contented that it would be a crime to bring upsetting discord to them. Should any misguided missionary start for this island, I trust the sea will do its duty.[23]

Their "almost total freedom from Caucasian contact . . . has thus far been their salvation . . . In all the author's experience among Indians and Eskimo, he never knew a happier or more thoroughly honest and self-reliant people."[24] There are more smiling faces among the Nunivak than elsewhere in Curtis's volumes. Here Curtis may have found the amulet he had long sought: the look of happiness.

A man of seemingly preternatural powers, a strapping outdoorsman with drawing-room manners, equally at ease in Eastern parlors and the lodges of native warriors and shamans—a kind of sorcerer himself, capable of winning over all big chiefs, J. P. Morgan as easily as Red Cloud and Geronimo—Curtis seemed to his early admirers an outsized figure, running risks and courting danger, legendary in his feats of endurance on the trail of Indians. "Just before the last crest of eagle feathers disappears over the brow of the rise into the dark arroyo," wrote Julian Hawthorne, "there comes from the northwest a white man, a man of thew and sinew, of endurance and courage."[25]

Edward S. Curtis, "Woman and Child—Nunivak," v. 20, *NAI*, 1930. (McCormick Library of Special Collections, Northwestern University Library)

After the appearance of the first volume of *The North American Indian* in 1907, the critic Sadakichi Hartmann wrote that although Curtis was "just now the most talked-of person in photographic circles . . . it is difficult to tell [his] whereabouts at this moment"—as if it were Odysseus he were writing of, or some other shape-shifting trickster.[26]

Some of the romance imagery originated in Curtis's own self-promoting articles, letters, descriptions of fieldwork and of his larger ambitions for his project, and a famous self-portrait in soft-brimmed Western hat and trim Buffalo Bill beard. "I have myself passed over the trails, climbed the mountains, crossed the river, waded through the mud and snow, and endured cold and hunger," he boasted, like Paul Bunyan, about his early Alaskan goldfield adventures.[27] And actual prospecting for gold, digging for hidden treasures in the earth, occupied some of his time in the 1920s. His "fieldwork," as he referred to his trips to Indian territory, in many ways resembled prospecting, scratching around for something of enduring value.[28] The published accounts of the man must have responded to a desire for such a figure, handsomely endowed with talent, energy, strength, and charm, capable of moving freely in antithetical worlds East and West, among bankers and wild Indians. In many ways he was his own mythographer, and the story line shows signs of a self-making imagination along the lines of Jay Gatsby: a chance meeting with influential Easterners on a slope of Mount Rainier leading to his commission as official photographer of the Harriman Alaska Expedition in 1899 and the beginning of his fame; success in persuading a dubious J. P. Morgan and in overcoming the resistance of skeptical natives, what he called "the deep-rooted superstition, conservatism, and secretiveness so characteristic of primitive people"; enduring hardships of weather and terrain, natives who shot at him and threw dust in the eyes of his horses (as Meany reported); and throughout, single-mindedness of purpose. He carried a gun, his son recalled, and once had to brandish a knife.[29] He traversed countless miles by horse and wagon, canoe and sailboat, in often stormy waters, crossing the continent by rail about 125 times, making some 40,000 negatives—before collapsing at the end in 1930 and disappearing from view for a while. In all this Curtis loomed as the nation's resolute and battered Odysseus, though his wife as it were

Edward S. Curtis, self-portrait, c. 1899. (Collections, University of Washington Libraries, Neg. no. UW1234)

proved no Penelope but an outraged, neglected woman who smashed his glass negatives in revenge. At a low moment when cash was short, he wrote, "We have announced to the world that we are doing this thing and now to give up for the lack of a few dollars would place us in an embarrassing position. We cannot hesitate, but rather must forge ahead to the very utmost. We owe it to ourselves; we owe it to the world. We are committed to the cause, and it is necessary to make good our promise."[30]

Curtis wore a guise fit to the mythopoeic character of his self-imposed tasks. Like Turner's frontiersman who learned the arts and crafts of survival from Indians, Curtis presented himself and was viewed as a traveler back and forth between the primitive and the civilized, between native life and the life of modern industrial society, the latter never represented in his work but everywhere implicit (the camera, the book, the entire production and financial process it presupposed). He presented himself, and was construed in the press, as mediator between "the Indian" and the rest of the country, interpreter of the "Indian race" for posterity. Curtis undertook to "live with the Indians" on behalf of his elite audience, to "play Indian," Turner's primal moment in the making of Americans, as their surrogate (including, according to his own apparently unconfirmed story, participating in a Hopi snake dance and other esoteric ceremonies). As intermediary he is found among figures like George Catlin, the anthropologist Frank Cushing, and the showman Buffalo Bill Cody. His was a sublime obsession and an increasingly lonely one.

III

In an essay on "Pueblo Migration Stories," first published in 1986, Leslie Marmon Silko wrote:

Pueblo potters, the creators of petroglyphs and oral narratives, never conceived of removing themselves from the earth and sky. So long as the human consciousness remains *within* the hills, canyons, cliffs, and the plants, clouds, and sky, the term *landscape*, as it has entered the English language, is misleading. "A portion of territory the eye can comprehend in a single view" does not correctly describe the relationship between the human being and his or her surroundings. This assumes the viewer is somehow *outside* or *separate from* the territory she or he surveys. Viewers are as much a part of the landscape as the boulders they stand on.[31]

The idea of oneness between Indian and "nature" runs throughout Western as well as native thinking about North America's indigenous peoples. In 1896, the writer George Bird Grinnell, who became Curtis's friend in a few years, wrote:

> Like the wild bird and the beast, like the cloud and the forest tree, the primitive savage is a part of nature. He is in it and of it. He studies it all through his life. He can read its language. It is the one thing that he knows. He is an observer. Nothing escapes his eye. The signs of clouds. The blowing of winds, the movements of birds and animals—all tell him some story. It is by observing these signs, reading them, and acting on them that he procures his food, that he saves himself from his enemies, that he lives his life."[32]

Except for the words "primitive savage"—and it is a very big exception—Grinnell's language and Silko's correspond almost exactly. To be sure, the view of Silko and other native writers regarding Indian belongingness within the natural realm is considerably more sophisticated, detailed, nuanced, and politically pointed than Grinnell's. But the idea of the inseparability of Indian and nature persists.

When we take the terms "Indian" and "landscape" and "nature" not as names of real things and persons but of concepts about reality, mutually dependent points on the mental map by which we all take our bearings, is it possible to think of the American "landscape" without at once thinking and saying to oneself "Indian"? And isn't the obverse just as true? Think Indian, and an image comes to mind of a near-naked figure like Curtis's Apache in an unspoiled natural place—

a path in the woods, a cliff in the desert, a rock by a rushing stream—
a setting present to our imaginations in the form of what Western art
calls landscape. This visual identity of Indian terrain corresponds to
the belief that Indians *belong* to nature.

Shared by natives and nonnatives, and perhaps deriving from
"middle ground" exchanges centuries ago, this habit of seeing and
knowing "Indian" as "nature" had a practical ideological effect of providing land-hungry Euro-Americans with a rationale and an apology
for their wholesale transfer of territory. The convolutions of logic in
the system of justification for the vast alienation of title that made the
modern American nation possible are labyrinthine and obscure, but
as the land itself was increasingly made over in the image of European
practices of land tenure and property rights, the Indians themselves
tended to recede from view and were pushed to the margins of awareness. They had little presence in the first significant landscape painting in the United States, the Hudson River and Luminist schools. If
the expansion of the United States equates with the alienation of Indians from their homelands or, in the white imagination, with the redemption of nature by its conversion into a "civilized" value based on
its alienability, then the link between Indian and nature marked a
fateful divide: Only by abandoning their inherent naturalness, their
Indianness, might native peoples share in the new America. The famous Currier and Ives print of 1867, *Westward the Course of Empire,*
drove the point home with diagrammatic clarity: Lost in the smoke of
the railroad pressing forward across the blank sheet of the Western
desert, the horse-bound natives are simply left behind.

Expansion westward was imagined as ineluctable, manifestly destined, and benign. Resistant and antithetical Indians must be vanished in the imagination in readiness for their vanishment in fact. Yet
as the writers Irving, Cooper, Poe, and especially Thoreau and Morgan understood, they were always there, their traces remaining not so
much as palpable monuments or ruins but in stories attaching to
places and configurations of the land, in place names that often held
buried and cryptic fragments of half-remembered narrative, in practices of land care and management, in everyday knowledge of plant
life, and in the mystery of rapport among human, plant, and animal
existences.

By the end of the century, the vanishing of the native often took the paradoxical and perverse form of a heightened visibility in Western landscape painting and photography and in photographic portraits, on canvas and on paper and in stone, as stereotyped representations or misrepresentations. Even when they were present, natives often remained in some important respect invisible, part of the scenery, "natural objects" inviting both "scientific" and "aesthetic scrutiny." Pictured Indians often seem as if they were on a proscenium stage performing themselves as picturesque specimens, *their* individuality, *their* inwardness, *their* view of the scene submerged in a pictorialism that answered to the artist's need rather than to their sense of the place they inhabit.

One sees this construction of a landscaped Indian with special clarity in photography, a medium in which it takes a certain technical effort to efface particulars for the sake of general effects. Curtis mastered the craft of theatrical illusion and of disguising of persons as performers in an allegory of a lost world caught in its final moment of self-expression. Identifying the Indian way of life with the environment was the key principle of the allegory. Curtis portrayed figures draped in hides and adorned with feathers and masks; his scenes of shamans, dancers, and players of games were made to appear timeless, occurring in a vague natural domain called "Indian country." Curtis explicitly connected Indian, landscape, and nature, each expressive of the other, each a synecdoche for the other.

Anticipating Mary Austin's wish similarly to ground poetry, social forms, and culture as such in landscape, Curtis wrote, "to overlook those marvelous touches that Nature has given to the Indian country . . . would be to neglect a most important chapter in the story of an environment that made the Indian much of what he is." He wrote of the "beautiful mountain wild," "the depths of the primeval forest," "the refreshing shade of canyon wall," and "the broiling desert sun, the sand-storm, the flood, the biting blast of winter." "Nature tells the story," he added, alluding to his pictures but also to his words: "in Nature's simple words I can but place it before the reader." "Nature" is both the teller of the story, what the story is about, and the medium through which "Indian" is made present to us. "It is thus near to Nature that much of the life of the Indian still is; hence its story, rather than being replete with statistics of commercial conquests, is a record of the Indian's relation with and his dependence on the phenomena of the universe—the trees and shrubs, the sun and stars, the lightening and rain,—for these to him are animate creatures."

The Indian way was "just as incomprehensible" to the "workaday man of our own race" as "the complexities of civilization [are] to the mind of untutored savage."[33] The unstated assumption was that if the Indian's land, his place, his "environment" was so much the medium of his way of life, then loss of place, of homeland, equated with loss of being, with vanishing. The already accomplished dispossession of "our aborigines," which Curtis brushed aside as mere "statistics of commercial conquest," was precisely the historical condition implied even as it was denied by the allegory of a vanishing race.

The idea of a primitive rapport between Indian and nature that pervades Curtis's writings gives the theory of vanishing its cardinal principle. It also supports another major claim: that his photographs are both scientific and artful at once, scientific because they are a matter of information and data, intended as "illustration of an Indian character or some vital phase of his existence," and artful and aesthetic because they are "directly from Nature" rather than from an artist's studio. Nature is the artist, Curtis implies. "Nature" has shaped "Indian country" with "marvelous touches." "Nature tells the story." Evoking the popular idea of photography as a privileged truth-telling medium, he suggests that photographs made in Indian country cannot fail to be both true and beautiful; the Indian in his natural setting cannot but appear picturesque; it's in the nature of things.

In a remarkable passage in his "General Introduction," Curtis places himself directly within Indian country.

At the moment I am seated by a beautiful brook that bounds through the forests of Apacheland. Numberless birds are singing their songs of life and love. Within my reach lies a tree, felled only last night by a beaver, which even now darts out into the light, scans his surroundings, and scampers back. A covey of mourning doves fly to the water's edge, slake their thirst in their dainty way, and flutter off. By the brookside path now and then wander prattling children; a youth and a maiden hand in hand wend their way along the cool stream's brink. The words of the children and the lovers are unknown to me, but the story of childhood and love need no interpreter.[34]

In the domain of nature, as in a photograph, no interpreter is needed. The songs of the birds and the speech of children and lovers have the same status as natural events, accessible directly through the senses to the understanding. Did Curtis imagine himself Apache? What is transparently evident here is not an Apache view of Apacheland but a recognizable landscape, both sentimental and picturesque, of Curtis's Euro-American imagination. Curtis kept "commercial conquest" out of sight, but he was himself acting out a corollary of conquest, occupying the scene as an aestheticized equivalent to alienating Indian land and the dispossessing Indian nations. This was a story that history, not nature, told about the North American Indian.

IV

Curtis began his Indian work in the late 1890s, when scores of photographers were rushing to Indian territory to take pictures of natives still living more or less traditional lives, performing the old dances and ceremonies, bearing on their bodies signs of their obscure but vivid difference.[35] The desire to see native bodies and faces arose with unembarrassed insistence. A sense of uncertainty was in the air: The frontier was closed, masses of new immigrants were arriving, the prospect was opening for a new making of Americans. It was a setting ripe for consolations and utopian fantasies of romance—which, as Fredric Jameson argues, tends to appear at times of harsh transition.[36] Earlier, in the 1870s and 1880s, a typical photograph of natives was the before-and-after sequence, wild-looking long-haired youngsters transformed by their boarding school experiences into regular-looking Americans. Now, the "before" images reappeared in their own right but drained of the old dread and hatred; in their place was desire, at once erotic and political. With the wars ended, hostile remnants rounded up, the threat extinguished and assimilation trumpeted as on its way, the photographs opened another front of struggle, a surrogate realm of ghostlier demarcations.

How are we to understand this perverse upsurge in "Indianizing" at a time, as D'Arcy McNickle wrote, of "attrition" in native life, with many tribes held as virtual prisoners of war under conditions of poverty, disease, deprivation, exclusion, insult? One reason for the perversity in the imagery was simply the mangling of social truth for exculpatory purposes; another was that in their memorializing function, the images are a self-congratulatory tribute to a fallen people. The Indian as worth, as value, emerged as a common locution in nationalist discourse. "These pictures," wrote Curtis, "were to be transcriptions for future generations that they might behold the Indian as nearly lifelike as possible as he moved about before he ever saw a paleface or knew there was anything human or in nature other than what he himself had seen."[37] "Lifelike" rings ominously of effigies, museum displays, and ghostly emanations. To picture the Indians of "long ago" was to imagine yourself seeing them for the first time, putting yourself in the place of the first European explorers and conquerors. "I wanted to camp where they [Lewis and Clark] camped," Curtis explained one of his motives to be, "and approach the Pacific through the eyes of those intrepid explorers."[38] It was to recover an originating moment: "discovery" of the savage Other, and yourself in their eyes as "white," as ascendant, a Christian American. Looking at Indians as emblems of the nation's beginnings was to learn, especially if you were an immigrant child, the difference between "us" and "them," whites and redskins. It was to reaffirm whiteness as the color of the United States.

Indians, viewed as the nation's first people, their "savage" origin transcended by acts of violence that proved the mettle of the conquerors, were then reabsorbed at a time when the nation's masculine fiber needed revitalization. They symbolized the nation's manifest destiny in a double sense: redeeming the continent and American manhood at the same time. Defeated, the once-vicious foe could be seen as a source of national virtue and strength. Lament for the inevitable defeat of the noble savage served symbolically as an outlet for the sense growing among sections of the ruling elite that change had occurred too rapidly, that the past slipped away too swiftly, the frontier gone, the cities filled with strange new peoples and voices. Commemoration of the vanishing race answered several needs at once—for a historical narrative of legitimacy, for mourning the passing of old ways, and for absolution of guilt for "worse than criminal" acts.

The scope, scale, intensity, and brilliance of Curtis's work, not to say its grandiosity and its obsession, put it in a class of its own, even though it shares premises and pictorial conventions with the work of other photographers. But modern viewers have wondered what he *really* felt toward his native subjects. How much did he know and understand? To plumb his heart for a single coherent motive proves fruitless, however, and distracts us from the pictures themselves. Still, his prose deserves to be read as closely as his pictures, not only for clues to his beliefs and intentions but also for signs of the larger frame of reference. To free the pictures from their illusion of stillness, we need to take measure of the ideology that holds them in place. Rather than worry over Curtis's stated beliefs, as important as they were, a more fruitful approach is to take his project as a symbolic event within a specific frame of ideas, a working-out of answers to unstated questions about "the Indian," about race and nation, and also about photography, about what he called the "value" of his own undertaking to the nation.

Certain terms recur with tantalizing frequency in Curtis's texts, the words "value," "nature," and "gold" among them. When he died at the age of eighty-two in 1952, the walls of Curtis's room were covered with research notes for a work in progress on "The Lure of Gold."[39] A short story found among his papers, "The Lost Mine of Dead Man's Gulch," tells a tale, in the manner of a dime novel melodrama, of "lust for gold" bringing murder and cannibalism along with it. "There is nothing known to humans which can so arouse the emotions as the sight of virgin gold; nothing that so positively engenders greed which passes sanity."[40] Curtis understood both the romantic lure and the sodden realities it leaves behind. Another manuscript fragment, "The Forgotten Map Maker," concerned the sea otter, a "forgotten" creature of the sea whose pelt he compared to the value of gold. "The wearing of the fur placed one among the nobility: garments of it were for kings, queens, potentates, nobles, their wives and consorts." He wrote of a "fever to make fortunes" in the sea otter that spread like a "conflagration" in the late eighteenth century. "Like stories of gold strikes, tales filled the air of great profits made." Men risked everything for the hunt. "Only virgin gold could cause men to endure comparable hardships." And like the lure of gold, this was a story of the high price of unbridled lust and greed. "One is justified in saying that every skin procured was stained with human blood."[41]

Curtis himself had been subject to that lure at least as early as the Klondike gold rush in 1897, when he trekked with his camera to Alaska to cover it "on the most gigantic scale ever attempted," as a Seattle newspaper put it.[42] The previous year his studio in Seattle had announced "a new type of photograph on a gold or silver plaque . . . beautiful beyond description."[43] Precious metals had been linked to photography from the beginning, and gold toning was common practice among professional studio photographers. In the 1920s, he occasionally joined his son Harold, a mining engineer, in the gold fields of Colorado; Curtis himself took a correspondence course in metallurgy; he contrived and patented a device he called "the concentrator" for gathering gold dust left over at abandoned mines. "I mean to do something in gold mining," he wrote to a friend at his lowest point in 1932. "My gold concentrator equipment has proved a complete success in saving fine gold."[44]

When he described his epic project to make a "permanent record of Indian life of all tribes yet in a primitive condition," Curtis often slipped into a language of political economy, speaking of "wealth" and "value." And while he did not always refer to money, though cash flow was often on his mind, the figurative associations implied an unconscious echoing of capitalist enterprise. "The value of this work," he wrote in his 1911 draft, "will be its completeness and breadth, and from the fact that the whole is the result of actual first-hand study by one person."[45] Actually, the "work" was collaborative from the start, with assistants, a darkroom manager, and, not least, the many hundreds of natives who participated as paid performers in his theater of the "vanishing race." The structure of production resembled manufacturing, from a kind of "prospecting" in the field to the refinement of raw material in a distant darkroom, engraving and printing, publishing, and distributing. The financial structure was tied to banks, loans, interest rates, the paper forms of value taken for granted by his patron and subscribers.

J. P. Morgan lent the prestige of his name as well as cash to launch Curtis's project, and the name Morgan was interchangeable with the gold standard. In 1895 and again in the Panic of 1907, Morgan dramatically intervened to prevent a depletion of the country's gold reserve and a collapse of its currency. "You have saved the country when no one else could," Curtis wrote to his patron in November 1907.[46] As much as a material substance, gold served as a symbolic measure of trust. Between Curtis and Morgan there passed sheaves of paper, not just notes bearing cash value but also letters of understanding couched in contractual terms. Safe-deposit boxes and "the Morgan vaults" were regularly alluded to as places to store and protect prints, manuscripts and, most precious, negatives. Through Morgan, Curtis's project counted on gold quite literally; figurative associations add a hermeneutic supplement. Morgan's continuing investment of capital in the project, Curtis wrote in 1909, "proves that he . . . believes in its value." And in 1913 he wrote that "with comparatively small outlay," Morgan has "done humanity a service of inestimable value."[47]

Did he mean by value that which is worthy of esteem for its own sake, or an amount of something measured by its equivalence to something else? Was value intrinsic, derived from its own nature, or extrinsic, dependent on some established measure of equivalence? Curtis seemed to use both senses interchangeably. Working within an economic structure to produce a lavish and exclusive commodity, he spoke of the inherent esteem his work would achieve in the future. "Mr. Curtis selected," noted an admirer, ". . . paper, inks and binding which will last throughout the ages . . . time-defying papers and unfading inks."[48]

This comment, appearing in an interview with Curtis published in 1912 as "The Vanishing Red Man" (a few years before Frost's poem with almost exactly the same title), introduces another cogent facet of the trope. Here Curtis spoke with regret of "a new American race" of which the Indian might have been "a racial ingredient of inestimable value," but "we" failed to recognize what a "fine race" they were, "the most admirable primitive of the world." The metaphoric implications of the term "ingredient" added yet another compelling feature to Curtis's understanding of Indians, his own photographs, and the concept of value. The context made it clear that Curtis had in mind the familiar image of the melting pot, and melting pot evoked alchemy, the old wishful process by which baser elements of earth were transmuted into the finer element of gold; it evoked fire and alembics of transmutation and purification. Is there something here of the logic of the "concentrator," scooping up the particles of gold scattered at abandoned placer mines? The pictures confirmed both how fine a "race" the Indians were and how they had vanished in history, recuperated as gold-toned image.

But Curtis was up to something besides unfolding the logic of Indian entelechy or, in Kenneth Burke's phrase, their "curve of history." The Indian, he tells us, represents a squandered opportunity: "Had we preserved him and accepted from him those fine qualities of blood and brain . . . the American of now and of days to come would inevitably have been a more distinctive race. It is our fate to build ourselves of blended blood, yet we scornfully refused one of the best strains that offered, accepting instead much of what is inferior from European races which have formed a part of our enormous immigration and which we have welcomed with open arms." "Fine qualities," "one of the best strains"—these phrases suggest particles of gold, "ingredients of inestimable value" for the crucible of nationality. "They were untainted by commercialism. Their pride might well have been transmuted into a mighty asset for the new race we were forming . . ." Alchemy and money again fuse into a figure of nationality. The sentence continued: "but we preferred to graft upon the sturdy stock of independence which induced our forefathers to cross the seas the sad subservience of worn-out peoples, incapable of taking the great plunge of immigration until the way had been prepared for them and made comparatively easy, fleeing to us, finally, only after they had been crushed into bent-backed humility and dull-eyed apprehension by centuries of violent oppression."[49] Worn-out peoples, subservient, bent backed, dull eyed: the very language reserved by Frederick Jackson Turner and others for Jews from the Pale.

In a passage in the 1911 draft introduction that proposes the contrast between Caucasian and Ethiopian as the measure of difference of "the American people" from all other "races," Curtis made clear that the discourse of race-based nationality played freely in his imagination. The unexpected intrusion of a figure for blackness in a discussion of "a new American race" is telling, for it showed that the absolute binary of Caucasian/Ethiopian provided a baseline for all other comparative relations. Blacks defined the lowest, whites the highest, and reds bearing the name "American" were the link, the metonym for the white nation. The old vanishing race, if recovered in its racial purity, could lend itself to the making of the new race.

The structure of this mode of nationalist thinking grounded on racial difference interestingly excluded no one but incorporates both black and red in symmetrically opposite positions of subordination. The momentous 1896 Supreme Court decision in *Plessy v. Ferguson*, which upheld segregated railroad cars in Lousiana as "separate but equal" and established the "one-drop rule" as a legitimate basis for identifying a person as white or black, loomed on the horizon of Curtis's thought and of his project. Theodore Roosevelt, who, Curtis wrote, "understood as no other person I have ever known, the great significance of my work," is reported to have regretted the absence of "a strain of Indian blood" in his system.[50] Black blood contaminated; Indian blood purified. It was essential, then, to imagine the vanished as "pure," its blood unmixed, particularly uncontaminated by black blood. "A minor factor in the disintegration of Cherokee blood," Curtis noted in Volume 19, "was the early mixture with negroes . . . A close study of these people, however, supports their claim that there was far less blending of Cherokee and negro than occurred between whites and the negro race." Meanwhile, "history indicates the Cherokee welcomed rather than discouraged intermarriage with the white race." Black blood contaminated Cherokee blood, while white blood mixed with red fostered the birth of great leaders like "quarter-bloods" John Ross and Sequoya.[51]

The imagined process of making a new race through alchemy had to negotiate this paradox. The discourse about the vanishing race insisted that "purebloods" were the true Indians, the true fountain or source of ore for revitalization of the "blended blood" that was the regrettable American fate. But unmixed Indian blood was becoming rarer and rarer, thus of greater value; that was what was meant by the "vanishing" of the Indian: depletion of the old stock. In the long run, as Roosevelt's commissioner of Indian affairs and another supporter of Curtis, Francis Leupp, put it, intermixture would be a good thing. The "pure aboriginal type" was fading, but another would "claim the name 'American' by a double title as solid as the hills on the horizon."[52] "Indian blood" contributed "keenness of observation, stoicism . . . love of freedom, a contempt for the petty things which lay so heavy a burden on our convention-bound civilization"; white blood gave "the competitive instinct, individual initiative, a constitution hardened . . . by the artificialities of modern life."[53] The process was already under way, Leupp wrote in 1910, and while he looked ahead to a perfect fusion in the future, one still counted on preserving, at least as image and idea, the purity of the Indian quotient of the new American blood.

This paradox defined Curtis's mission as an artist. Indians had been slaughtered; for the sake of the new race of Americans, they must be resurrected and commemorated, their "pure" image preserved (embalmed?) in gold. This was apotheosis by fixation. No wonder Curtis was hailed by his admirers as displaying "a fine high patriotism."[54] The opportunity for white Americans to see the savage as if for the first time must be perpetuated; "long-ago" Indians must be seen themselves fixed in the camera, surrendered to the lens as if to a howitzer. Blacks had already been incorporated as "separate but equal" citizens, and their legal equality inspired vicious hatred and disdain expressed in representations as lowly, inferior, dirty people who needed to be exorcised by fiery lynching and ritual sacrifice to assure the purity of the white nation. It was sacrifice of the base for the sake of the fine. Whites were the metaphoric gold standard on which the destiny of the nation rested.[55] Freezing the Indian image as "pure" so that it could be incorporated as an ingredient in American whiteness was a cure to both blackness and the "inferior" strains from Eastern and Southern Europe. It was sacrifice by reification.

In 1916, the Curtis studio introduced the Curt-Tone, a gold-toned image on glass. The Curt-Tone finish of his "Indian studies," he wrote, gave a "lifelike brilliancy": "We all know how beautiful are the stones and pebbles in the limpid brook of the forest where the water absorbs the blue of the sky and the green of the foliage, yet when we take the same iridescent pebbles from the water and dry them they are dull and lifeless, so it is with the orthodox photographic print, but in the Curt-Tones all the transparency is retained and they are as full of life and sparkle as an opal."[56] Gold, Curtis wrote, was "the one thing that endures." Gold preserved the look of life; it never vanished; it promised permanence. But is the look of life achieved at the expense of life? To the innocent eye, no attrition shows in Curtis's pictures, no destruction of peoples and land in the wake of successive gold rushes, as Curtis himself in his texts acknowledged had happened. "None of these pictures would admit anything which betokened civilization . . . *Historical* change is kept at bay," as Gidley has observed, while pictorialism, the soft, elegant style of which the Curt-Tone was an epitome, worked "to disguise, even deny, what was in fact and effect, a seemingly almost endless series of damaging political and economic decisions made by human individuals and agencies." By the exorcism, by the sacrifice of historical truth, the Indian was preserved as "lifelike" for the ritual of making Americans.

V

Are Curtis's pictures as still and timeless as they seem, as absent of voice and motion as he wanted them to be? Can we restore the players to the play, the actors to the act? A closer look may find less ghostliness than knowing artifice. Whatever else we say about *The North American Indian*, we have to say that its pictures record performances by many hundreds of people on the other side of the lens over some thirty years. When we think of the pictures as records of paid performances in which the performers helped to determine what got pictured and how, other ideas of these thousands of images open before us.

Curtis put his name on each picture in a copyright line; often he signed images with his familiar standard signature. As pictures they belonged to him, were his possessions. But the legal fiction and the logic of the marketplace say that the pictures were his only until exchanged by purchase, exchanged for money. "The purchase of a picture or a book already produced is but a change of ownership," Curtis noted with striking clarity about the exchange value of his work.[57] An aura of money pervaded the entire project, from the deluxe leather bindings of each volume, the lavish gravures, to the signature and copyright lines. And each picture also represented, in both the attributive and the pictorial senses of the word, the labor of the pictured people, each sitting, each staging an act, in return for cash. "They were all paid for sitting for pictures," Curtis put it bluntly; "paid Indians" was a line item in budgets submitted to Morgan.[58] They were paid for performing roles. But did they have no influence in shaping those roles, choosing their costumes, their gestures, the scenes they performed? It would be wrong to presume passive acquiescence to the directorial Curtis, to assume that the images were always conceived, scripted, and executed by Curtis alone. After all, the vast undertaking counted entirely on the willingness of the performers to hold still before the camera.

In his final volume in 1930, Curtis wrote, "it is finished," as if inscribing a tombstone. Had he lived too long with a single dream, like Fitzgerald's Gatsby? The dream of an unattainable beauty that he imagined as "the Indian" was already and always a fiction, and he must have realized this because he had to fabricate it. It was a figment of unhappy consciousness belonging to invaders and conquerors. Nowhere in his many writings did Curtis say just what he dreamed of, or explain why he so zealously gave over his creative life to chasing these particular shadows, or describe what the more than thirty years of bone-crushing labor in mountains, plains, and deserts finally meant to him, what mark it left, how he understood what he saw and felt. Late in his life he noted in a fragmentary memoir, "Now, as I look back on those years my brain is a scrambled jumble of desert sand storms, cyclone wrecked camps, exhaustion in waterless deserts, frozen feet and hands in northern blizzards, wrecked river canoes."[59] The memory is all about the difficulties of adventure and not a word about Indians or the purpose that drove him.

Edward S. Curtis, "Piegan Encampment," v. 6. *NAI*, 1911. "The picture not only presents a characteristic view of an Indian camp on an uneventful day, but also emphasizes the grand picturesqueness of the Piegan, living as they do almost under the shadow of the towering Rocky Mountains." (McCormick Library of Special Collections, Northwestern University Library)

We have one clue. "I was intensely affected," he recalled years after the event, by his initial excursion into Indian country in the summer of 1900, when he went with George Bird Grinnell to Blackfeet territory in Montana, where he witnessed a gathering of tribes for a sun dance ceremony, a life-affirming ceremony of sacrifice for the sake of strength for the individual and the good of the people. He recalled the "unforgettable" sight of the "great encampment." "Neither house nor fence marred the landscape. The broad undulating prairie stretching toward the Little Rockies, miles to the west, was carpeted with tipis."[60] That inaugural vision of another way of inhabiting space and being together, tepees swaying on the prairie, as opposed to the rigid angles and proprietary assertions of "civilized" houses and fences, suggests an enchanted world—and perhaps an unspoken motive, to reenchant a world the white Americans had stripped of charm, magic, and mystery.

For us, the task is to disenchant the images and restore them as pictures of people rather than of icons: to restore, that is, *photography*. "While primarily a photographer," Curtis remarked in Volume 1, "I do not see or think photographically; hence the story of Indian life will not be told in microscopic detail but rather will be presented as a broad and luminous picture."[61] "Broad and luminous": The terms evoke pictorialism, with its subordination of detail to broad masses of light and dark, its selective lighting and luminosity to highlight certain details as if emerging from the darkness of "long ago." Pictorialism seeks to efface photography itself, with its "microscopic detail," or, as Roosevelt put it in his Foreword to Volume 1, its "mere accuracy." "In Mr. Curtis," wrote Roosevelt, "we have both an artist and a trained observer, whose pictures are pictures, not merely photographs."[62] Picture means art, and art means stagecraft, genre scenes, allegorical titles, selective focus in portraits, a crafty use of blurs and fuzziness— devices of enchantment and ways to subdue the stubborn quiddity of the scene before the lens, transforming it into a magical mirage of the lifelike, distancing the viewer from the "mere accuracy" of the lives depicted.

Can we also free Curtis, who was indeed "primarily a photographer," from the twin myths of nationality and of art? "I made one resolve," he wrote, "that the pictures should be made according to the best of modern methods and of a size that the face might be studied as the Indian's own flesh."[63] There is another myth that hovers among his portraits, the idea that a face can reveal race, that physiognomy tells a story of racial traits. Scientific racism had fostered, in late-nineteenth-century Europe and America, photographs, chiefly head shots, of natives everywhere as examples of racial types. Curtis's close-up portraits share some of the features of pictures intended to show specimens for scientific scrutiny—tightly cropped, often with exotic wardrobe, hair style, and implements on display—or widely circulated in card-size formats, to give the pleasure of a close but safe look at exotic and picturesque colored peoples. Such pictures can be taken as analogous to the widespread (among race-minded ethnologists) collecting of bones and skulls for measurement in order to affirm the inferior mental and physical capacity of colored peoples.

But Curtis's portraits don't sit comfortably in this category. These are his best achievement, pictures through which his own best qualities shine through: his sensitivity, his respect for his subjects, his grasp of the meaning of the performances for his performers, and his willingness to let them define their roles. The captions often block our awareness of his collaborative sitters with a protective barrier of allegory or typology: for example, captions describing "the inner life" of the Apache scout as "a closed book," or telling us that "Soft, regular features are characteristic of Hopi young women" (At the Trysting Place), or offering physiognomic readings such as "The eyes speak of wariness, if not downright distrust" (A Hopi Man), or "His eyes bespeak all the curiosity, all the wonder of his primitive mind" (Son of the Desert, the title alone a veil over the face). And titles more frequently classify than name: A Young Yakima, A Piegan Dandy, The Whaler.

In 1908, the ethnologist James Mooney objected to Curtis's A Cheyenne Warrior, a portrait of a man who was not then engaged in an act of war. Curtis retorted with a brief excursus on "general principles of pictures and titles." The objection, he wrote, took a "supercritical attitude," presuming that the title meant to say 'This picture is of a chief dressed for the final conflict of battle,' while, as a fact, the

Edward S. Curtis. (*left*) "Hopi Man," v. 12, *NAI*, 1921. "In this physiognomy, we read the dominant traits of Hopi character. The eyes speak of wariness, if not downright distrust. The mouth shows great possibilities of unyielding stubbornness. Yet somewhere in this face lurks an expression of masked warmheartedness and humanity." (*right*) "Son of the Desert—Navaho," v. 1, *NAI*, 1907. "In the early morning, this boy, as if springing from the earth itself, came to the author's desert camp. Indeed, he seemed a part of the very desert. His eyes bespeak all of the curiosity, all of the wonder of his primitive mind striving to grasp the meaning of the strange things about him." (McCormick Library of Special Collections, Northwestern University Library)

Edward S. Curtis. (*top left*) "Kalispel type," v. 7, *NAI*, 1911. (*top right*) "A Cree Woman," v. 18, *NAI*, 1928. (*bottom left*) "Chaiwa—Tewa," v. 12, *NAI*, 1922. (*bottom right*) "Hidatsa Woman," v. 4, *NAI*, 1908. (McCormick Library of Special Collections, Northwestern University Library)

same title could have been used for the same man while in his lodge smoking."[64] To Mooney's nominalist conviction that universal categories correspond to no reality, Curtis replied with a defense of reified abstraction, as if "warrior" were an essence immanent in the picture.

As pictures, Curtis's images reach for universal meanings and sentiments; as photographs, they are documents of specific nameable acts. Mooney's view suggests a method for understanding these acts. Seek the player within the role, the person under the feathers and paint. Look for nuances of presence, glints in the eye, a tense muscle at the edge of the mouth, the tilt of a jaw, the record of life in a creased face, eyes seeking themselves in the eye of the lens. Barbara Davis has written of a "complicity" between photographer and sitter to stage a dream of an enchanted life, "some shared dream of pride and freedom." It can be put differently: The photograph is a visual record of a transaction across a divide, a cross-cultural dialogical event in which the depicted person is as much an agent as the photographer.

New implications for the idea of the American nation may be seen here. Contrary to Curtis's stated intention, signs of so-called civilization pervade the pictures: horses, rifles, factory-made textiles, cowboy hats, tokens of cultural exchange and improvisation, not to speak of less tangible signs such as the sitter's knowing how to pose before a camera and to take money in exchange for that service. Yet Curtis absorbed enough of native ways to capture on film a residue of the spirit if not always the letter of the cultures that enchanted him. Reawakened, these photographs tell a tortured history: of conquest and subordination, sacrifice and survival, all embodied in this very moment of sitting quietly before the white man's lens. It is a history tied to new immigrants and old myths, and also a history of reciprocity, of middle-ground transactions, the creation of mixed identities. When we imagine the breath of living people brushing the veil of stillness, Curtis's photographs offer a vision not of vanishing but of standing forth.

FIVE

Wanamaker Indians

—————

Never have I pointed my gun at an Indian that I did not do it with a feeling of regret but someone had to stand between civilization and savagery.
—William "Buffalo Bill" Cody (1913)

Because we recognize in you a great heart that realizes more than does any other man now living, the weird tragedy which the Wanamaker production of "The Song of Hiawatha" symbolizes . . .
—Joseph Kossuth Dixon, welcoming Buffalo Bill to the Wanamaker Store, May 12, 1909

Whatever poetry may be, criticism had best be comic.
—Kenneth Burke

Early in 1920, word came from Washington that the aboriginal population of the United States was on the rise. Claiming that this was due to improvements in health conditions and declining mortality rates, the Bureau of Indian Affairs pronounced that Indians were no longer a "dying race" and the "red" was no longer "vanishing." Not everyone found the news pleasing or even credible. While *The New York Times* hailed the report as good news, confirmation that "a comparatively new race has developed" according to the principles of "the survival of the fittest," the claim of a reversal in the expected pattern of decline was nevertheless "somewhat startling." A small chorus of skeptics and reformers suspected that the bureau had doctored the numbers in order to obscure the true story of disease, malnutrition, and miserable poverty among reservation Indians. But something more than accuracy was at stake. Could it really be that the Indians were no longer the "vanishing race" of time-honored belief?[1]

Joseph Kossuth Dixon, author of a book published in 1913 whose title, *The Vanishing Race*, reveals his investment in the once-steadfast image of a "dying" people, reacted as if to a blasphemy. "Can you not silence this bosh?" he scrawled in the margins of the *Times* editorial he sent to J. Walter Fewkes, head of the Bureau of American Ethnology at the Smithsonian Institution, demanding an "official statement" to "set the matter straight." After a badgering second request, Fewkes eventually obliged by passing Dixon's letter and clippings to James Mooney, the bureau ethnologist whose study of Indian population still commands respect. Mooney had statistics that satisfied Dixon. At the time of contact in 1492, the original population of Indians north of Mexico was more than a million; by 1910, the number had decreased about 65 percent. "We have now in the United States about 270,000 persons of Indian blood," Mooney concluded, "a large proportion of whom have half or more of white blood." Dixon wished that the ethnologist had said explicitly that the mixed-bloods were "mongrels," but nevertheless he trumpeted Mooney's statement in the preface to a third edition of *The Vanishing Race* in 1925: "This pronouncement . . . banishes the trivialities of inspired propaganda . . . and leaves us in the presence of THE VANISHING RACE."[2]

It's not that Dixon and others who reacted skeptically to the BIA report recognized only "purebloods" as true Indians, but many romantic admirers of Indians in these years did hold mixed "breeds" in some disdain as less than the true article. A system of gradations of blood quantum was already in place, not unlike the system by which "blackness" was identified after *Plessy v. Ferguson* by the "color" or assumed racial sign of each drop of one's blood.[3] Although Dixon did not absolutely exclude "half-breeds" from his definition of Indian, it was clearly understood that the figure who was dying out was unmistakably and necessarily a "pure" Indian. This exclusion is important to bear in mind as we focus on the process whereby out of the "vanishing race" trope there emerged another one, that of the "Indian" as the "first," the "real," the "*native* American."

The transmutation of "vanishing race" into "first American" occurred at a time when the United States was filled with alarm about the fate of the assumed Anglo-Saxon character of the nation, and voices called for restriction of non-WASP immigration and the exclusion of "aliens." Within the general problem of defining who was and who might be "American," the problem of identifying "Indian" had posed particular confusions and uncertainties. How did tribal identity figure in a more generalized Indian identity? In what sense might Indians be considered, or consider themselves, Americans? For a small group of natives educated in white boarding schools and colleges, the first decades of the twentieth century were a period of search for what the historian Hazel W. Hertzberg has called an "American Indian identity" extending beyond the limits of tribal identities. Yet controversy over who counts as "Indian" continues; blood and "race" are demonizing categories that make the counts seem essential to historical knowledge and at the same time impossible to trust.

The "vanishing race" theory made it seem simple: Indians were those born of Indians, in infinite regressions of purity, which is to say that "Indian" is something one *is*, not something that one can become by conversion or choice or petition. Yet "Indian" was also identified by behavioral traits, practices of religion, woodcraft, hunting, food preparation, and linguistic forms of prayer, poetry, and storytelling. Judging by the growing popularity among non-Indians of voluntary associations, lodges, and other organized recreational activities modeled on supposed Indian practices, many people believed that Indian traits were transferable, adaptable by others, traits of culture rather than of race: Thus, anyone could enjoy "playing Indian." Similar slippage of definition was found in the definitions of the natives' legal status in relation to the U.S. government. D'Arcy McNickle cites a U.S. Court of Claims opinion at the end of the nineteenth century as an example of the "puzzlement" regarding who, from a strictly legal point of view, were the North American Indians: "neither citizens nor aliens; they were neither persons nor slaves; they were wards of the nation, and yet . . . were little else than prisoners of war while war did not exist."[4]

The curious logic by which Indians vanish and reappear as "first Americans" appears with exceptional clarity amid the many bizarre obfuscations of a project that the same Joseph K. Dixon conceived and executed on behalf of his employer and sponsor, Rodman Wana-

maker, son and partner of John Wanamaker, founder of the famed
Wanamaker Department Stores of Philadelphia and New York. The
Rodman Wanamaker Expeditions to the North American Indians, a
project with many angles and chapters, occupied Dixon's entire working career as "educational director" of the Wanamaker Stores from
1908 (he had been hired as a publicist in 1906) until his death in 1926.
In the context of an increasingly racialized discourse of nationality, the
Wanamaker Expeditions were an extraordinary artifact, also an extraordinary "expenditure of waste," as Georges Bataille would put it,
on a project with no direct expectation of financial profit.[5] They consisted of trips to various locations in the West by a small crew of photographers led by Dixon himself that produced, in addition to
illustrated lectures, brochures, press releases, interviews, and countless ephemera, three editions of *The Vanishing Race* (1913, 1914,
1925), many thousands of still photographs, a number of motion pictures, including *The Song of Hiawatha* and *The Romance of a Vanishing Race,* edited from some fifty miles of raw footage, and an
unexecuted plan for a National American Indian Memorial in New
York harbor. This labyrinthine and gigantic enterprise was a composite text whose code remains to be deciphered: sponsored by a department store, endorsed by government authorities including two
presidents, displayed in one form or another to audiences ranging
from officials in Washington to women's clubs to immigrant schoolchildren, and inestimable numbers of Wanamaker customers. It's altogether a rather loopy story, but its bathos holds a lesson. Because so
much of it was sheer talk without depth or dimension, we can see its
bottom on its surface, its logic nakedly exposed, its motivating anxiety
everywhere apparent. In the context of the Wanamaker Expeditions
the question "Who is Indian?" translates as "Who is and who might be
American?"

I

What did a big-city department store—"one of the most important
instrumentalities in modern life for the promotion of comfort among

the people," in President William Howard Taft's words at the dedication of the new Wanamaker Store in Philadelphia in 1911—have to do with Indians, the most impoverished and allegedly backward of the diverse peoples of the United States? The question leads to another: What did Indians have to do with America itself?

The story of the "expeditions" properly begins in the store; they set out from the store and returned to the store with the "goods"— images, artifacts, recorded sounds—to display in an elaborate theatrical production staged in both the Philadelphia and New York stores, an extravaganza called "A Romance of the Vanishing Race." Why? How did this fit with the hardheaded business of buying and selling goods, putting *things* as consumable commodities into circulation?

An aura of romance clung to the Wanamaker enterprise from the beginning, a way of talking about it and giving it meaning, not just the romance of business but of the nation as well: romance as the mode of identifying business and nation as a seamless whole. "Founder" and "Originator" John Wanamaker (1839–1922), embodied the essential American romance; he "started with nothing," as his biographer wrote, "and made his way unaided to the front rank of Americans of his day."[6] He conceived of his store as the epitome of the nation and a model of its future. Through all its permutations as it evolved from a small men's shop in 1861 to a palatial emporium that opened to a presidential encomium in 1911, the store carried on its business in a glow of commercial and national romance. In Wanamaker's world, civics and piety shared a place with merchandising; he founded a religious mission in Philadelphia and served as president of the World Sunday School Convention and as postmaster general under President Benjamin Harrison from 1889 to 1893, ran unsuccessfully for governor and U.S. senator in Pennsylvania, and about the American flag wrote in 1919 that it "is bigger than any territory, more powerful than any political party, and its principles link it to a religion of duty and life broader than any creed. To live it and be for what it stands is next to the love of God." As postmaster general, Wanamaker introduced free rural delivery and parcel post, contributing to the extension of the commercial system across the country, into the rural South and the West; as a public figure, he joined the chorus that sang "civilization follows the flag," another version of "the white man's burden." Inspirational thoughts came frequently to him, and in 1923 he collected his wisdom into a book titled *Maxims of Life and Business*. In a section on "Citizenship" he observed, "The American flag in a foreign port outshines the beauty of all the scenery of sea, green cliffs and the forests growing down to water's edge."[7] Speaking before the American Academy of Political and Social Science in 1900 he described his store as if it, too, symbolized an expansive patriotism: the "First American System Store," part of "a new civilization," the model of a "new empire of retailing," an outpost in what he called the new "land of desire."[8]

With an eye quick to see opportunities for ceremony, pageantry, and ritual, Wanamaker arranged for the new building, his "New House of Business," to open its doors in the "Jubilee Year" celebrating the fiftieth anniversary of his business. Commemoration included the publication in two volumes of a *Golden Book of the Wanamaker Stores*. Ablaze in tributes to the commercial innovations and national significance of Wanamaker's career, the book recounted the history of a private enterprise that evolved and expanded in ways that echoed and mirrored the growth of the nation. When the enterprise began in the early years of the Civil War, retail trade was premodern; rather than fixed selling prices there was only "an asking price." Haggling over prices was the rule, and so was barter instead of cash wages paid "to the workpeople making clothing." At a time when home labor still provided many necessities—"Mother made Father's shirts" and "the quilting-frame took up the whole sitting room"—young merchant Wanamaker introduced the revolutionary system of a fixed price for each item, a return policy, fixed store hours, and cash paid to suppliers. "The new ideas were active quickeners of trade," the store expanded its street front, then took over an entire building, and by the early 1870s, "the Wanamaker business had already become the largest of its kind in the entire country." Wanamaker moved quickly from success to success. In the centennial year of 1876, he refurbished an old railroad depot in Philadelphia and founded a "New Kind of Store." The link to the Centennial Exhibition attracting millions to the fairgrounds in Fairmont Park made a powerful statement. "The Centennial celebrates liberty for the American colonies in 1776. The

Wanamaker Store celebrated freedom from the shackles of old, burdensome customs of business."[9]

The Grand Depot opened officially on March 12, 1877, with an expanded line of men's and ladies' furnishings and assorted dry goods, arousing ridicule and sarcasm in the local press that the *Golden Book* took delight in reprinting in 1911. Among the proofs of validity of the founder's vision, it brought forth the great socialist-utopian romance of 1887, Edward Bellamy's *Looking Backward.* "Doubtless it was this mercantile innovation of 1877 that prompted Bellamy to thus describe the ideal store of 2000 A.D.":

> I was in a vast hall full of light received not alone from the windows on all sides, but from the dome, the point of which was a hundred feet above. The walls and ceilings were frescoed in mellow tints, calculated to soften without absorbing the light that flooded the interior. Legends on the walls indicated to what classes of commodities the counters below were devoted. The business of the clerks is to wait on the people and take their orders; but it is not the interest of the clerks to dispose of a yard or a pound of anything to anybody who does not want it. Fastened to each sample was a card containing in succinct form a complete statement of the make and materials of the goods and all its qualities, as well as price, leaving absolutely no point to hang a question on.[10]

Bellamy's dream of "a single warehouse, where, without waste of time or labor, the buyer found under one roof the world's assortment in whatever line he desired," and "where the labor of distribution had been so slight as to add but a scarcely perceptible fraction to the cost of the commodity to the user," was not only prefigured by the 1877 Wanamaker but then realized as "a prophecy more than fulfilled" in the new "house of business" in 1911. The Grand Depot had counters running in concentric circles across an immense floor of two and half acres—"the largest single floor area devoted to business purposes in the world"—and 196 feet of aisles radiated from the center and other aisles, intersecting concentric counters and "strikingly" recalling, according to one Philadelphia newspaper in 1881, the Centennial Exhibition itself—and, of course, the famed panoptican of Jeremy Bentham's invention and Michel Foucault's derision. "There is the same width of display extending as far as the eye can reach, the riches of the world brought together from all lands . . . There is the same sense of spaciousness and, what is especially noticeable, the same ample illumination, the whole place being light, bright, and cheerful."[11]

The apparent simultaneity of similar modes of display at world's fairs, in department stores, in museums, and in utopian fiction (as well as in the design of prisons) suggests a representational regime centered on "goods" spreading throughout the culture. In a talk in 1921 enumerating the innovations introduced at the Grand Depot, Wanamaker remarked, "The vast area of space allotted to the many kinds of merchandise displayed made it seem more like a museum than a store"[12]—what museums, if they took a lesson from the "New Kind of Store," *should* look like. "In museums," he wrote, "most everything looks like junk even when it isn't, because there is no care or thought in the display."[13] Clothing, china, furniture, appliances, carpets, jewelry, books, and paintings in an art gallery were all on display and for sale in a building (eventually a group of adjoining buildings) illuminated by electrical power and outfitted with pneumatic tubes, elevators, a ventilation-fan system, a soda fountain, and a post office.

The store-as-nation motif wove itself inextricably into Wanamaker rhetoric and advertising. In 1904, the store published "A Short history of the United States with an Interwoven Chonology of the John Wanamaker Business," including a reprint of an article by the proprietor, "Lest We Forget."[14] The store's first location, on lower Market Street, was at the site of a house once occupied by George Washington; Independence Hall and the Liberty Bell were nearby. The store honored the centennial of the Constitution in 1887 with a display of women in Revolutionary-era costumes spinning flax amid old looms and knitting machines; in 1893, the store mounted a miniature world's fair with exhibits later transported to the Columbian Exposition in Chicago. In 1896, Wanamaker expanded to New York into the old A. T. Stewart store; by 1904, subway systems linked each store to its wider city. An exhibition space called the Egyptian Hall was added to the Philadelphia store in 1908, and in New York a two-thousand-seat auditorium where, the *Golden Book* recorded, in March 1909 "came one of the most novel undertakings ever carried to success by any business—a production, with musical accompaniment, of Longfellow's immortal 'Hiawatha' in motion pictures made from life on the various Indian reservations by a Wanamaker expedition, with the cordial co-operation of the United States Government."[15]

"Wanamaker's was no longer a store," the *Golden Book* proclaimed, "but a little city in itself—a city of countless opportunities for each of the two classes into which all men are divided,—buyers and sellers." Bunyan's Vanity Fair in the guise of the Celestial City? "Buyers and sellers" suggested that all parties profited from the store's newness, its nationlike inclusiveness and outreach. But "two classes" covertly conceded an inequality: The buyers bought goods, satisfaction of want and desire, while the seller got rich. It was precisely this disequlibrium Bellamy wished to overcome; his "buyers" exchange credits earned by labor for wanted goods, and no private profit accrues because there are no "sellers" in the Wanamaker sense.[16] Appropriating the aura of the "cooperative commonwealth" of Bellamy and other early Progressives, Wanamaker put forth the "New Kind of Store" as a model for a functioning America, a solution to the class anger and violence that had jolted America in the 1880s and continued into the 1890s. The solution was to translate "worker" into "buyer," so that the enjoyment of accessible goods (their accessibility eased by means of the charge account he was one of the first large merchants to introduce) became the fruits not of labor but of what he called "the First American System Store."[17]

In 1899, he wrote that his "new system" rested "on economic laws as immutable as the laws of gravitation," thus grounding the buyer-seller division of mankind, like the nation itself, in natural law.[18] Out of immutability, Wanamaker constructed a utopia of merchandise, a nonnarrative synchronic romance of harmony and fulfillment. Reciprocity and resonance are its inner principles, and Wanamaker's imagery carried the subliminal message of desire fulfilled. The store was a "tuning fork" that resonated with other tuning forks at the same pitch, the desires and wishes of customers; the reciprocal effects of

courtesy showed that there was "a law of rhythm in commerce";
"commerce can have no better emblem than the herb of courtesy."
Like the ardent lover of medieval romance, the "chivalrous" store
courted its customers with acts of devotion to their desires. Thus "the
gilding of a better dawn": The ascent of the sun was global; the new
system shone everywhere, "abolishing all boundaries but the ends of
the earth." Every home in the region, "every corner of the country,"
was linked to the store by the "mail and express system" that Wanamaker himself had prudently expanded during his term as postmaster
general.[19]

In the actual store, romance took several palpable forms: gratu-
itous extras such as lectures, movies, art on the walls, music in the
halls, and, in the Grand Court (one of many medievalisms), the
"largest organ in the world" offering daily concerts; these sensations
of "culture" and patriotism (flags, portraits of leaders, and commemorative plaques abounded, too), attached as free tie-ins to purchases.[20]
The store was famous for its guarantee of "Wanamaker Fidelity": All
goods were what they said they were, and that included the tie-in.
Places of both commercial transaction and display, places where
transaction took the form of display and display the character of transaction, the Wanamaker stores typified a new concept in the presentation of goods, an ostensibly new idea of "goods" themselves. Wanamaker
took the lead in making stores enchanted palaces, and temples of patriotism, and in presenting goods as magical talismans of illusory
transformation. Goods were put on sale with an aura of theatrical illusion achieved by the latest technologies of lighting, ventilation, communication, and transport. As William Leach has shown brilliantly, by
bringing together modern methods of production, marketing, financ-
ing, and credit into a new form of merchandising, department stores
across the country evolved into enclosures where the idea of the modern, the up-to-date, the advanced took tangible shape. The Wanamaker genius lay in reordering a traditional conceptual topography in
which realms of utility and culture, private and public interest, which
had seemed separate and antagonistic, now fused harmoniously. It
was nothing so crude as art prostituted to commerce but the evolution
of a new thing altogether: art fused with commerce in making a new

kind of commodity, a new "real thing" with the trademark "Wanamaker Fidelity."[21] With its tie-ins of art, music, and patriotic pageantry, the Wanamaker label promised signifying uplift. Shopping for undergarments, fountain pens, bicycles, cameras, or fake bows and arrows promised pleasure without guilt, well-being for the soul as much as the body.

Wanamaker's was not unique, only grander in scale and more explicit in its fusion of nationalist and Christian piety, its concoction of a brew of romance to make goods seem more than mere merchandise. The section on "Merchandise" in the *Golden Book* included a chapter called "Romance," which reads like an *Arabian Nights* of commodity goods:

> Out of the very merchandise itself there is woven before one's eyes a Golden Merchandising epic, such as the Golden Book of Venice never recorded.
>
> Study, for example, the exquisite beauty of yonder bit of rare Venetian lace, and here is presented to the imagination moonlit evenings on the Grand Canal.
>
> Contemplate the wondrous hues of the rare Eastern silks, and about them there still seems to cling the all-pervading sandalwood scent of the treasure-laden Orient.[22]

These "excursion[s] to the realm of fancy" began in the eye, where imagination transformed goods into magic carpets of transport. The reach was global, imperial, and orientalist, matching the high fashions then in style in American and European art and poetry. And the lesson was one of "romance": "One's eyes are the great gateways to knowledge. And in Wanamaker's every one is free to look, to see, to learn and to enjoy without feeling any obligation to buy."[23]

Not only free to look but also encouraged to do so by the design of counters, the use of color, plate-glass windows like stages where performing manikins faced the sidewalk, the display of paintings and photographs in galleries, tableaux of historical figures in wax, pantomime performances along with movies and tinted slides in the lecture hall.[24] The store obliged visitors if not to buy at least to look, to perceive. In connection with a Competitive Photographic Exhibition in 1909 (the store sponsored many of these, along with other art and music competitions), the store put on sale a camera lens ("Wanamaker-Originator") called the Prostimat and issued a remarkable advertisement showing an eye and a text: "The Wanamaker Eye is as true as the Wanamaker Lens; seeing all the lights and shades of the Wanamaker business . . . an expert eye that can see the cotton in the wool . . . the poor dye in the warp." Become a Wanamaker Eye, and if so moved, buy what you see. In a letter to his son Rodman in 1909 about plans for the new store, Wanamaker wrote, "I think that the space at the Market Street entrance should be reserved for little things that people pick up to carry way with them, such as a box of candy or Post Cards, cheap books or cheap pictures—something that people buy because it is in sight."[25]

The new store was built for seeing, with sweeping marble staircases, vistas across marble floors framed by marble arches supported by Ionic and Corinthian columns, and a seven-story tier of galleries (in a twelve-story building) overlooking the lofty domed Grand Court in the center, where two of the store's signature grand sights could be seen (and one of them heard every day at noon and on special occasions): the Great Organ and the Great Bronze Eagle, six and half feet in length and almost ten feet long, the nation's emblem of soaring power and keen eye, acquired by Wanamaker from the Louisiana Purchase Exposition in St. Louis in 1904. Designed by Daniel Burnham, who presided over the making of the "White City" at Chicago's 1893 World's Columbian Exposition, the new store was dressed in the Italian Renaissance style (the Wanamakers called it "Roman-Doric") with an exterior "of very beautiful granite." "The building as a whole," Burnham wrote, "both inside and outside, is the most monumental commercial structure ever erected anywhere in the world."[26] It was a place to look, with countless places to look from, a virtual observatory for the romantic perception of merchandise. The nation itself was also on view in this "temple of patriotism," as the store described itself; "the dedication of a house of business by the President of the United States was unprecedented," wrote Dixon in 1926, claiming credit for arranging this coup (he was master of ceremonies at the dedicatory ceremonies), and the store was arrayed with

Galleries, stairways, and Egyptian Room, Wanamaker Store, Philadelphia.
From *The Golden Book,* 1911.

bronze tablets and commemorative stones honoring "the makers and saviors of the Republic."[27]

Wanamaker was "a merchant who 'staged' his stores," wrote one of his biographers, "dramatizing them, making them living panoramas of commerce, colossal productions . . . with lavish exhibits and decorations and display rooms and auditoriums."[28] Even apart from the so-called expeditions to the Indians, the store's legend partook of legends of Indian forebears. Along with parades, military bands, choral music, and celebratory speeches, the dedicatory ceremonies included a "Grand Pageant" with "Historical Characters Impersonated": George Washington, Benjamin Franklin, Ulysses S. Grant, and, at the head of the ensemble, a nameless "North American Indian.—The first American, original owner of this soil," and "William Penn.—The Founder of Philadelphia, who said to the Indians what Mr. Wanamaker has always said to the people: 'We are met on the broad pathway of good faith and good-will, so that no advantage is to be taken on either side, but all to be openness, brotherhood and love.'"[29] The quest for origins, for firstness, was the inner desire of the Wanamaker romance. "Everyone who starts a new thing has to stand where Columbus did when he set sail," Wanamaker wrote in an advertisement in 1906. "Few had faith that he could ever reach the Land of Desire."[30]

A new thing requires the resurrection of an old thing; to call yourself founder and originator paradoxically entails following in someone else's footsteps. Wanamaker ritualized his claim to be in the same place and the recurrent time of his precursors: His first store was at the site of Washington's Philadelphia house, the first shovel-load of dirt at the groundbreaking for the new store in 1908 was on Washington's birthday, and in 1911, he claimed that Penn's famous 1682 treaty with the Indians under an elm at Shackamaxon on the Delaware River, commemorated in the famous painting by Benjamin West, had been *intended* to take place at this very site! Identifying with Penn lent the authority of local and national history to the Wanamaker enterprise: "Penn's fair dealing with the Indians, the first Americans, terminated a period of greed and graft, just as the revolutionary methods of Wanamaker dealing with latter-day Americans cleared away the bickerings and dickerings of trade."[31] Identification with Indians subliminally tapped into the magical universe of Indian belief and religious piety, the very worldview that had been dissolved and displaced by everything the department store stood for but retained as a fanciful trace for the sake of enchantment. So it was not just local pride or antiquarianism that lay behind the item included in a 1909 issue of the store newspaper called "Meaning of Local Indian Names" ("Manayunk" and "Shackamaxon"), but perhaps also an unconscious need to appropriate the charm of these autochthonous names as magical spells to further the store's primary business: selling goods at a profit.[32]

The telling point is that Wanamaker made merchandising seem the enactment of American destiny. The store imagined itself as America, which it marketed with "Wanamaker Fidelity." A palace of consumption, the store was also a machine for acculturation and Americanizing the foreign-born not yet Americans. For Wanamaker's sold not just merchandise but also a look, the appearance of belonging to America and to modernity. Goods represented means as much as functional objects. For immigrants, women especially, the "look" meant the difference between "foreign" and "American" status. As one historian puts it, "from all quarters, immigrants heard the same message—to become American women, one had to look the part." Wanamaker's set the standard: "When seventeen-year-old Eva received a cast-off garment, she wanted the world to know that the coat carried a Wanamaker's label. 'I wish I could wear the label on the front,' she said."[33] Even "just looking," window-shopping or browsing, which was encouraged by Wanamaker advertising and window tableaux, gave a boost to a new self-identification. Wanamaker's emphasis on his store as "education" spoke especially to the process of acculturation, bringing older citizens into the new scheme of things and newcomers into the mainstream look of things. At one point at the Grand Depot, the founder wrote in one of his unique advertisement editorials, "We opened our big building partially for six evenings to the new settlers in our city as a compliment and convenience to them, seeing that the mechanics were employed all day." The payoff of this pitch to the immigrant working class was to convert "new homemakers" into new customers: "by an experience in choosing fur-

niture the new customers would get a correct view of the way we conduct all of the departments in this different Kind of Store."[34]

He was more likely to see new immigrants in his store as potential
customers than as employees. The requirement for employment,
wrote Wanamaker's biographer in 1926, included coming from "homes
in which have been instilled habits of personal cleanliness and fastid-
iousness and taste in dress; they must know how to speak English, if
not without accent, at least idiomatically and with attention to grammar." Unlike factories, "where the workers do not come into personal
contact with clients," the store had to be prudent about whom it chose
to represent it. "Homogeneity was a necessity," a policy that "prevented, after the flood of the foreign-born, any serious modification in
the racial and cultural background of the store family." To be sure,
"the best class of colored people" were perfect for "certain kinds of
work, such as running elevators and restaurant service." Considering
how the "character" of the "population changed radically during his
lifetime," it was "as remarkable a feat as any of those that won him
laurels" that Wanamaker was able to keep his "vast army" of employees "dominantly of northern European stock." "The people that surrounded him were of English, Scotch, Irish, German—and to a lesser
extent Scandinavian and French—forbears [sic]. These men and
women shared his standards of truthfulness, his abhorrence of deceit,
and his contempt for the sloven and slacker."[35] Shopping at Wanamaker's gave lessons in acculturation in several registers, on both sides
of the counter as well as on it.

I I

The Outlook in July 1913, noting "the Rodman Wanamaker Expedition of Citizenship to the North American Indian" then trekking
across the country to visit each of the 169 recognized Indian "tribes,"
observed, "Our country is a melting pot for many races; the stock of all
the Old World is here assimilated and welded into useful citizenship.
There is one people, however, that has been reluctant to slough off
the attributes of its past to assume the responsibilities of our civiliza-

tion. The North American Indian yet holds a bit aloof." The many native nationalities and multitude of cultures were subsumed under a single "people," the "Indian." The expedition's "mission" was to homogenize the natives even further by enticing them into the "melting-pot" that produces "useful citizenship" by planting in "the bosoms of these original Americans a love for the flag of the country that has adopted them." The expedition, the article continued, "has the sanction of the President," and Dr. Joseph Kossuth Dixon was described as "leader of the delegation that is smoking the pipe of peace with the Indians." The impression was given of an official government mission, a familiar Wanamaker conflation of itself with the nation. "The Wanamaker party is assuring the Indian that the white man is anxious to give him a lift." The *Outlook* article predicted that Indians would "be not unappreciative of these intentions" and happily trade hatchet for melting pot.[36]

In Dixon the store had the perfect instrument for this particular brand of uplift, and its Indian program came to rest entirely in his eager hands. Dixon does not classify easily. Born in 1856 in upstate New York, he earned a degree in theology, held churches in New York State and Philadelphia, seems to have lost both church and wife in an adultery escapade, and may or may not have taken a law degree along the way. Early in the twentieth century he turned up in England as a journalist, and in 1904 as an agent for Eastman Kodak, giving lectures "offered free by the KODAK to Churches and Schools for the purpose of entertainment, instruction, and inspiration." His lectures, "The Call of the Kodak" and "The Kodak: A Moral Force," were published as a brochure titled "Just Hatched." A new age had arrived. Echoing the arguments of the economist Simon Patten[37] and others that a new regime of abundance was at hand, he let it be known: "The world is alive with new and startling messages . . . Our miracle of feeding the multitude lies close at our hands. The store house is full; every need of man may be supplied." Especially the moral need for meaning and value, which is just what Kodak would provide: "the call of the Kodak is a wooing voice to the right path; the upward hill slope extends to you, to all your fellows. Try it yourself. Photography has a moral force and from your self-attained heights there shall ripple before your eyes the shining waters of a sea of glory."[38] In 1906, he gave similar lectures at a traveling exhibition mounted by Eastman Kodak of pictorialist photographs (including work by J. Craig Annan, Edward Steichen, Alfred Stieglitz, Rudolf Eickemeyer, and Dixon himself) that toured major U.S. cities. *Photo Era* called his "always intensely interesting and instructive" lectures the main feature and described him as "an educated and refined gentleman, a man of deep learning and extensive travel."[39]

Wanamaker met Dixon late in 1906, heard one of his Kodak lectures, and read in *Photo Era* that he was a "worthy successor to John L. Stoddard, than whom America never had a more brilliant and successful lecturer." The eagle-eyed merchant would have caught too the remark in *Photo Era* that the "Eastman Kodak Company is making fresh conquests" through this "powerful combination of pictures and oratory," and that "[a]s a means of deepening the interest in photography and increasing the demand for cameras and photographic supplies," the exhibition is "an overwhelming success."[40] In January 1907, he hired Dixon "to take up work in the Photographic Departments of our New York and Philadelphia stores," deferring the starting date until the end of the Kodak tour in April, not to offend and possibly alienate George Eastman, who stood to profit in any case, Wanamaker pointed out, from the increased traffic in photographic merchandise that Dixon's golden tongue would inspire in the store.[41] Romance laced with piety: Dixon must have seemed to John Wanamaker a godsend for the store. Dixon knew the Kodak system, knew his way around cameras and darkrooms, and seemed to believe every word he uttered. Bridging late-nineteenth-century uplift oratory with the emerging style of modern publicity or public relations, Dixon represented a new hybrid type, a former preacher turned moralizing lecturer crossed with booster and huckster. The fact that he was also a maker of images—indeed, a skilled photographer—marks his modernity even further, while his personal charisma, which some dismissed as pompous verbosity, confirmed his roots in an earlier evangelical tradition.

In Dixon's mind he was taken on less strictly for photographic than for "educational" tasks. In a screed written on his own behalf in 1925 (when he complained of being mistreated by the store), he claimed that he had been hired "to carry on educational work in the Stores and to lecture on educational subjects" such as "Paris the Magnificent" and "The Land of Scott and Burns" (echoes of Stoddard), lectures that "drew great crowds." "Such was their influence in New York that during the 'panic' of 1907, when the Jews were reporting all over New York that the store was closed, I was lecturing to great crowds every afternoon, controverting the slander."[42] The reference was to rumors afloat that year that Wanamaker's was closing its doors because of overextended credit worsened by the run on New York banks; Wanamaker himself spoke of "a conspiracy of misrepresentation" and noted in his journal, "We are the target of the jews in particular, I am told, who vow they will drive us out of New York in two years. Dear me!"[43]

In any case, on October 16, during the height of the panic, Wanamaker managed to look in on one of Dixon's New York store lectures illustrated with pictures of the store itself and wrote to him that "you were very stately yourself and handsome, but your voice did not carry except when you 'thundered.'" He found the lecture "prosy," suggested Dixon use more pictures with "two or three epigrams between them," and added that he hears "on all sides congratulations over your work."[44] "I thought your speech was fine," Wanamaker wrote on another occasion, but chided him against too much flattery: "I can only get on my feet to stop you from complimenting me so greatly, lest I might become a Zeppelin and soar away. You have the habit of saying fine things, but you must not crown me so often."[45] None of these slight rebukes prevented Wanamaker from asking Dixon on occasion to stand in for him as a speaker.[46]

Dixon had found his niche, a platform for his chastened but still golden tongue, and by 1908 he had launched the project that would be his life's work, the Rodman Wanamaker Expeditions to the North American Indians. Exactly how this came about, how he persuaded the department store magnate and his partner-son that this would be a wise expenditure of the store's capital, remains a bit murky, but a letter in 1909 from John to Rodman, then in Paris, offers some clues.

Dr. Dixon calls on me this morning with large barrels of enthusiasm that overflow as he starts off for his Congress of Indian chiefs . . . I am impressed with the fact that at the present time Dixon is an Indian dictionary as big as Webster's Unabridged, and while the thing is fresh in his mind, we ought to get whatever he has got. It will not only slip away from him, but he might slip away himself, and then what has been gathered at large cost would be lost with the going out of a man. Mr. Appel [an official of the store] tells me that he has made several efforts, in vain, to get him to write out the eleven lectures that he claims to have the material for and for which he has made slides. It occurs to me that no one can influence him but yourself and that either Mr. Appel or I dabbling in it might only make him suspicious or bull-headed to keep whatever we haven't got.[47]

By now Dixon represented an investment, an asset of value; the store wanted its money's worth ("we ought to get whatever he has got," "gathered at great cost").

Dixon undertook every aspect of the expeditions—lectures, publications, contacts with the federal government, store performances— in the name of Rodman Wanamaker, "sponsor" of the project and employer of its "leader." Rodman (1863–1928) had been made a full partner in 1902 and head of the New York store in 1911; on his father's death in 1922, he became sole proprietor of all Wanamaker establishments. His major contribution to the store lay in fashioning a role for art and culture in making what his father had called the "new civilization" of merchandising. Educated at Princeton, he spent the 1880s in Paris as the firm's resident manager, became a familiar in the art world as student and collector, founded the American Art Association in 1899 and the American Art Students' Club, and made his father's store a leader in the sale of French fashions, including "fine goods in women's modes." Obituaries after his sudden death in 1928 at the age of sixty-five included praise for his philanthropic support of the arts and aviation—in 1914 he commissioned Glenn Curtis to construct the largest airplane yet built in the United States, the *America,* and gave New York City an armed air cruiser for self-defense after the United States entered World War I. He served as New York's special commissioner of police as well as chairman of the city's welcoming committee. The Indian project figured prominently in accounts of his civic achievements, including a collection of pictures donated to the government, plans for a monument, and support of a bill in 1914 to reorganize the administration of Indian affairs. Fashion, art, philanthropy, patriotism, and high society—he was friend of the British royal family—were the keynotes of his public career; in private life he was known as an ardent tennis player and yachtsman. A dapper, mustachioed man, "he was, in the grandest meaning of the expression," wrote a biographer, "a merchant prince." In 1906 he became the first person to take out a million-dollar insurance policy; at his death he carried six million dollars of protection for his family and business, making him, according to *The New York Times*, "the most heavily insured individual in the world."[48]

Dixon's relation to the Rodman Wanamaker of the project's title (the name virtually a trademark) was quite simple: He did the work; Rodman bathed in the glow of credit. Interviewed about "his Indian work" at the National Press Club in 1916, Rodman spoke of "my Indian pictures," "my expeditions," "the pictures that I have made and the fruits of my work."[49] Dixon's published pictures, books, and pamphlets all bore the name Rodman Wanamaker as holder of copyright. The contrast with Edward Curtis's relation with J. P. Morgan could not be starker. Curtis enjoyed patronage, a quasi-feudal relation between a man of wealth and power and a man of art and science. Curtis portrayed himself as romantic artist-scientist who cherished his independence and the integrity of his subjectivity. He held copyright on his own work, retained all authority as well as ownership. He worked both as a subsidized artist and free-enterprising producer of texts (including films and lectures) that took their chance in the market.

All this made for substantial differences in the character of the work the two men did, as on parallel but divergent tracks they almost simultaneously devoted a large stretch of their lives to an obsessive quest for "the North American Indian." Both staged pictures, both performed their work with skilled artifice, and both labored for particular markets. Curtis worked as a subsidized artist but reached for a popular market and a broader audience. Following fast in Curtis's footsteps, about a half step behind him, Dixon worked entirely within the marketplace as defined by the department store; his film, slides, and lectures produced for performance in the Wanamaker stores remained Wanamaker property, as did all his negatives and prints.

The imprint of Rodman Wanamaker signified not only a term of ownership under the capitalist form but also a mode of display (though this was disguised under the heading of "education") designed to bring potential customers into the store and add another facet of pleasure to Wanamaker merchandise. Dixon's "Romance of the Vanishing Race" was defined and shaped within the romance of merchandise. Dixon willingly, it seems (no doubt under the terms of his contract with his employers), abandoned credit for authorship of specific photographs; he supervised a cadre of operators of still and movie cameras (including his son Rollin Lester Dixon), didn't record who made which image (perhaps because all would be credited to Rodman Wanamaker in any case), but acknowledged his crew by name in the prefaces to his books. It was Rodman Wanamaker, not Dixon, who received the silver medal for Dixon's pictures exhibited at the Panama-Pacific International Exposition in San Francisco in 1915. The conditions of his labor help account for Dixon's virtual absence until recently from the canon of recognized American photographers.

Persuading father and son, two hardheaded if civic-minded and innovative businessmen, that talking to the Indians would be good policy for the store, good press for Rodman, and good news for the country, Dixon won for himself an extraordinary opportunity to act out composite roles and styles in the public persona of "leader" of the Rodman Wanamaker Expeditions. In the department store world, the former preacher, newspaperman, and Kodak publicist learned something about pageantry, the role of display and performance in presenting goods in their twofold aspect as things and as moral ideas. Explicit commercial motives are difficult to find among the remains of the Wanamaker Expeditions, but in the world of the "new kind of store," distinctions blur. "Mr. Wanamaker is more than a storekeeper," wrote Dixon to Commissioner of Indian Affairs Robert G. Valentine in 1909; the "beautiful halls" of the two stores "are devoted exclusively to music and educational work. The public are invited to lectures and concerts free of charge, and the educational work thus carried on is absolutely free from any allusion to commercialism." True enough, but goods for sale lay temptingly in sight on counters to and from the auditorium. Wanamaker's goal was only "to raise the standard of citizenship and patriotism, to stimulate and foster man values." The "Wanamaker Indians" belonged to the store's tie-ins, not a product put for sale in the usual sense, but part of its romance, the cultural work of the Wanamaker enterprise being to produce a new civilization of enlightened citizenship, patriotism, and "man values."[50]

Dixon seized the opportunity to act out his impulses as a romancer, not just a maker of pageant and spectacle but also a participant—indeed, perhaps modeling himself on Curtis, the leading character, the questing hero journeying through mysterious and dangerous terrain, meeting strange peoples and manners, deciphering everything inscrutable in his path, and returning with tangible proofs of victory. "On four distinct occasions," he wrote in his 1925 letter of self-defense, "while on expeditions, I barely escaped with my life."[51] The resemblance to the pattern of Curtis's self-narrative is striking, but the forms and terms of Dixon's romance were decisively different. "Expedition," for example, framed Dixon's project in an extravagant and extravagantly misleading metaphor, for it means an official dispatching of persons to set something in order or to extricate (in the root meaning of the word) something in a distant place; it has a military, diplomatic, archaeological, or treasure-hunting purpose. In 1900, John Wanamaker had already financed a Wanamaker Expedition, organized by the archaeologist and future curator Stewart Culin, to Indian sites in the West, and presented to the University of Pennsylvania's University Museum (of which he was a "manager" and vice president) items that Culin had "collected." As well as supporting archaeological digs in Italy, in 1916 Wanamaker financed a museum expedition to Alaska to study native customs and bring back "specimens of their work," another sign of emerging rapport and mutuality among department stores, museums, and ethnological collections, and displays in this era.[52]

Connotations of imperialism were inevitably attached to "expedition" in these years, linking at least by figurative association the col-

lecting of specimens and their display to more explicitly imperial
ventures. In the early 1890s, Wanamaker had introduced a kind of
military training—uniforms, marching bands with flags, the title
"cadets"—along with vocational training for the mainly "old-stock"
young employees at the store, and in 1898, when the United States
declared of war against Spain in Cuba, he volunteered to raise a regi-
ment of one thousand men from among his employees, with himself as
officer; the plan came to naught, but the patriotic intention was clear.
In an advertising circular, Wanamaker proudly disclosed that the store
was a major supplier of uniforms and other goods for U.S. troops.[53]

Dixon's expedition used the associations embedded in the word
and employed them to misrepresent what was a trip to take pictures
of Indians to display in a store. The goal was spectacle, and the misleading associations were part of the show. Not least of the misrepresentations was the explicit claim that the entire event, from picture
making to picture showing, had the sanction, endorsement, and even
sponsorship of the federal government. From start to finish it was a
private enterprise. Dixon's engineering of apparent government sanction in the staging of the first two trips in 1908 and 1909 prefigures the
charade of a national ceremony on Staten Island in 1913 to break
ground for a proposed monument, as well as—this was a key moment
in making Wanamaker's seem a *national* institution—President Taft's
appearance at the opening of the new Philadelphia store in 1911. The
publicity gained by winning government involvement was invaluable,
and Dixon's correspondence with officials in Washington shows his
persistence and dexterity, as well as the power of the Wanamaker
letterhead.

In August 1908, Commissioner of Indian Affairs Francis Leupp
granted "permission to use Indians of the Crow Reservation, Montana" and two troops of U.S. Cavalry "to reproduce on the Custer Battle field the Custer fight with the object of having motion pictures
thereof made to be used for educational purposes in the establishments of the Hon. John Wanamaker in New York and Philadelphia,"
all negatives and prints to remain Wanamaker's "exclusive property."[54]
Permission to "use" natives and U.S. soldiers as performers amounted
to tacit government subsidy readily granted by successive Indian com-

missioners. In July 1909, Dixon asked Commissioner Robert Valentine "that you allow me as his [Wanamaker's] representative, and that you give instructions to various Indian Agents" to assemble "prominent chiefs" for another spectacle, adding, "I am undertaking a task which requires a Cromwellian spirit," perhaps as a way of justifying his imperious tone. A month later he asked "that you write me a letter of introduction and authority, so far as you may (that is not a good word but you know what I mean)," addressed to the Crow agent, "stating to him that you will be pleased if he will cooperate with me heartily . . . giving me the use of his grounds for a camp." Valentine complied, leaving it up to individual agents whether to cooperate or not, letting them decide whether Dixon's needs "interfere in any way with the constructive work you are trying to enforce."

"Although I should be very glad to promote your undertaking on account of its educative value," he wrote to Dixon, "I must take into consideration the possibility that a gathering of the kind you contemplate, throwing the emphasis on the old ways of the Indians, might seriously interfere with the effort we are making on all reservations to turn the energies and thoughts of the Indians to modern economic methods, to an understanding of which they must owe such salvation as still remains for them."[55] But Dixon got his way; the agent "is quite willing to allow me to pull off almost any stunt I want."[56]

Interesting, too, that Dixon's reputation with the Wanamakers as an "Indian dictionary" depended largely on information and resources requested and received from the Bureau of American Ethnology: Indian words and names, a description of Custer's battle, remarks made by American presidents on Indians, information about "the handsomest in feature, character and beauty" of the Indian tribes, and so on. It was all grist for the mill that fashioned the Wanamaker "Romance of the Vanishing Race."[57]

When Dixon embarked on the first of what he would eventually count as eleven Wanamaker Expeditions, he bore on his body and in his demeanor overlapping associations of the term "expedition." He wore khaki leggings, high boots, and a campaign hat, the outfit of a colonel on a military mission or archaeological search for lost cities. With the good wishes of the commissioner of Indian affairs and promises of cooperation, registered in letters that lent apparent substance to the disguise, Dixon set out in 1908 for the Crow Agency in Montana "to study and photograph the Indian in his native habitat." His expeditionary force consisted of himself and three other photographers.[58] Besides making landscape pictures and shooting some of the earliest documentary footage of games and reservation life, he enlisted native performers for a film of The Song of Hiawatha, a "Wanamaker Hiawatha," which in the coming years brought tens of thousands of schoolchildren into the store's auditorium to watch the "passion play of the American Indian."

Although it was his son's name that launched the expeditions, a certain romance with Hiawatha had begun with the father Wanamaker. At the age of nineteen, swept up by the "great revival" of 1857, overtaxing himself with Sunday school classes and other church activities along with clerking in a clothing store and faithful service in a volunteer fire company, John Wanamaker's health ran down and a change of scenery was prescribed. His imagination had been fired up by Longfellow's recently published poem, so the young Wanamaker wandered westward, seeing "much to call forth admiration—much to regret." "Sailing up the great Father of Rivers," he wrote in a letter home, he "looked upon the once happy hunting grounds and homes of the Red Men of the Forest. Sad was it to witness their desolation and listen to the story of their suffering wrongs—Oh! That their history could be blotted from the page of remembrance for alas! It is a bitter reflection upon the humanity and christianity [sic] of the White Man." His reflections grew even sadder and more pitying when he contrasted this sorry history with the grandeur of "the scenery of our beloved America," the "lofty mountains" and "broad prairies" and "beautiful rivers," "the beautiful 'Laughing Waters' of the Falls of Minnehaha." "Where is the American heart that will not swell with joy and burst forth in gratitude for the blessing we enjoy?" Still, regret could not be shaken off: "it is with a sad heart I refer to the carelessness and indifference manifested in many places to those principles of vital godliness upon which I sincerely believe rests the foundation of the peace and Prosperity of the land." The revival spirit was still stirring within him, as it did during his entire career, and the experience of the nation to which Hiawatha seems to have guided him resulted in an "exhortation to the Christian people of the United States" to mend their ways, find Jesus in the Bible, the nation in the landscape, and regret for the "suffering and wrongs" of "the Red Men" in their hearts.[59] How much of the spirit of this youthful melancholic plaint Wanamaker conveyed to Dixon is impossible to know. The Hiawatha revival alone would have given motive and model enough for Dixon to put the poem on the store's agenda. An article in *The Critic* in July 1905 about the Ojibway performances described them as "almost as famous . . . as the Passion Play at Oberammergau," detailed the scenes as if describing a film script, included several photographs, and described a visitor "sinking to sleep with strange visions of the original Americans and their pagan woodland rites passing through his drowsy mind." Dreaming Hiawatha was on the rise, and in 1906 another Philadelphia store, Strawbridge & Clothier's, had given a prize to a cantata based on Longfellow's poems.[60]

At first, early in 1909, Dixon seems to have staged a reading of sections of the poem with lantern slides, music, a lecture, and a pantomime performance of scenes. An internal memo from the head of the piano department of the New York store criticized the Philadelphia production for having "little or no real Indian quality" and proposed for the New York performance music written and suggested by "Mr. Arthur Farwell, one of the highest authorities in America on Indians, their customs and music." The memo also recommended selections from "the Cantata Hiawatha" (presumably by the Anglo-African Samuel Coleridge-Taylor) "to relieve the monotony of ninety minutes of pictures." Dixon replied with a Wanamaker defense of pictures: "You will quite agree with me that the effectiveness of the pictures is a vastly important question. Too much cannot be said upon this subject and too great emphasis cannot be laid upon it. I very much want people to go from that auditorium saying that they never saw such pictures as at Wanamaker's. They will forget the music, they will forget what I say, but they will never forget what they see. The eye is a great educator." Dixon presented himself as tribune for the visual. As for the "people" he had in mind, "an engraved invitation should be sent to the best people . . . Certainly, we do not wish the

East Side [Jews?] to fill the Hall, and if we are to reach the people in New York who are to be of benefit to us, we must keep the standard up as to the manner and method of invitation . . . a good class of people."[61]

Hiawatha—The Passion Play of the American Indian must have made for quite a display. It was shown along with hand-tinted lantern slides, music, dance, pantomime, and Dixon's introductory lecture; one viewer thought it was like watching a Wagner opera. More than one schoolchild wondered whether they were "real Indians, who are on the stage." In the spring of 1909, the indomitable Dr. Dixon began taking his illustrated lectures along with the film into classrooms and school auditoriums in Philadelphia and New York (including the Lower East Side), carrying the pictures and their message to thousands of children of immigrants; in 1916, Rodman Wanamaker mentioned 311 school performances in the two cities. The film was accompanied with pedagogy; *Hiawatha: Produced in Life, A Wanamaker Primer on the North American Indians* (1909) included a section on "The Meaning of Hiawatha" and a reprise of the film with stills, drawings, and passages from the poem. "The desire was to make a Wanamaker Hiawatha that should be absolutely true to the story of poem," Dixon wrote.[62] He explained that he interviewed "over twenty one Indians" for the roles of Hiawatha and Minnehaha, ordered an "original" birch bark canoe to be shipped from Duluth, transported his crew of Indian performers up steep slopes in Wyoming to get the right scenery for this Crow and Rocky Mountain version of a poem based on Ojibway legends and set near Lake Superior, the famed shores of Gitche Gumee. It was "unremitting effort," Dixon proudly wrote, for the sake of a "true and artistic exposition." A predetermined reality effect overrode the misrepresentation of the poem, and the line between true and false was handily ignored.

With chapters on "The Indian's Yesterday," "The Indian's Today," and "The Indian's Tomorrow," the *Primer* placed Hiawatha in a kind of prehistorical period, before "any hint of the white man's foot."[63] A parallel publication, the store paper (it apparently ran for a year) called *Wanamaker-Originator*, printed weekly installments in 1909 of "The Child's Primer of Hiawatha" and retold the poem with stick-

Cover, *Wanamaker Primer*, 1909.

Joseph Kossuth Dixon, "Eli Blackhawk as Hiawatha, Angela Star Blackhawk as Minnehaha, and Wolf Lies Down as the Arrowmaker," 1908. (William Hammond Mathers Museum, Indiana University)

drawing illustrations of stereotypical "Indians," a kind of Classic Comics version of the national epic.

What Hiawatha "teaches" comes straight from the source, as it were, appropriate for a production written and copyrighted by "Wanamaker-Originator." The lessons read like a sermon on genteel culture. Poetry gives "an enriching river of inspiration and instruction . . . until the perfume mantles the mountains and the children of men gather the flowers of purified affection," and so forth. Hiawatha also teaches a love of the beautiful: "Daily bread is hallowed; daily drudgery is glorified." And then there is "the secret lore of nations," "the mystery and magic surrounding the life of the Red man" ("The unseen world ever presses down upon him"), and the truth that "the world's master passion—LOVE rules all." So Hiawatha teaches how to read this poem and derive exaltation from its romance, to learn "the deeper meaning of the Brotherhood of Man," which is "the protection and the preservation of the home, the safety and righteous guidance of the State, the upbuilding and glorification of civilization." Finally, "Hiawatha Woos the Mind of Man—To love the works of God."

This little exegesis and pedagogy may well have been Dixon's lecture preceding the film, an example of the uplift he brought to the store. In the second edition of the *Primer* in 1910, "The Meaning of Hiawatha" was replaced by an even more brazen gesture toward an originating source: "Ten Commandments From the Red Man to the White Man." They concerned Health ("Thou shall live the Natural Life"), Labor ("Thou shall do thy share of the world's work as it comes to thee"), Education, Hospitality, Kindness, Motherhood and Fatherhood, Sanctity, Frankness, Contentment, and Immortality. Teaching Sunday school lessons such as these, Hiawatha too undergoes Wanamaker acculturation.

The *Primer* gave Dixon's explanations of the purpose of the expeditions. One was to reach out to the "Red man" in the spirit of William Penn. Repeating the store legend that Penn's famed treaty (the *Primer* reproduced Benjamin West's painting, along with Penn's 1683 "Tribute to the North American Indians") was both a commercial and a political transaction, and "was first of all contemplated on the ground where now stands the great Wanamaker Store," Dixon adds that "this fact alone furnishes an enthusiastic stimulus in the study of Indian affairs."[64] Indian affairs become the ground upon which Wanamaker affairs proceed; Wanamaker history would absorb Indian history, the best side of white-Indian relations, and thus become American history, the history of Americanness itself.

A second motive was more explicitly educational; it was to make a "record" of a people, "the first American[s]," on the verge of disappearing before the superior, onward-rolling forces of Anglo-Saxon civilization. "The old Indian stands at the end of his journey," but once the public, through the good office of the Wanamaker educational department, grasped the significance of this epochal vanishing act, their sympathy would arouse support, as Dixon assured Indian Commissioner Valentine in 1909, for "your great work of housing, schooling, and home building among the various tribes of the red man." We are "absolutely together in our object," Valentine assured Dixon after going to one of his illustrated lectures in Washington, "pleased," he wrote, "with the simplicity and dignity of your program." Enjoying the imprimatur of government approval, the expeditions furthered the "new civilization" flowing from both official Washington and the Wanamaker stores.

The *Primer*, going on to tell about the "origins" of Indians, suggested that they had "Jewish blood in their veins"; whether or not in direct descent from "the lost tribes of Israel," their "chiefs and symbols and badges [are] exceedingly like those of the Mosaic institution." This echoed William Penn's speculations regarding the resemblance of Indian languages to Hebrew and the natives' small black eyes to those of Jews. "As for their original," wrote Penn in a short treatise reprinted in the *Primer*, "I am ready to believe them of the Jewish race." Dixon tacitly concurs. Quoting the head of the Smithsonian Institution, the anthropologist W. H. Holmes, Dixon suggested that Indians were all "alike": "an Indian is always an Indian," and they too were immigrants, drifters across the "Behring Strait" [sic] from Siberia and thus "allied to the Asiatic, usually referred to as the Mongolian, than to any other people."[65]

The *Primer*'s account of the "coming of the white man" suggested that the tragic defeat of "the Red man" was inevitable: "It is the law of

Nature, as mankind multiplies and spreads over the earth, that the earth must yield its treasures. To those who till the soil and dig the mines and develop the resources of a new land will that land be given. To those who will not work—who will not help Nature to produce—to them must come suffering and death."⁶⁶ And later in the text: "The Indian is by nature born to shirk tasks of toil." By their "nature" and their "race," Indians again suspiciously remind us of the fictional Jews of medieval and contemporary superstition: unproductive nonlaborers, doomed to wander and suffer unto death.

The explicit argument of the *Primer* (and of later works) concerned the skill, courage, and virility of Indians as warriors, embellished with details of diet, oratory, modes of travel, ceremonies, names and sign language, games and sports, and home life. We learn that "the Indian woman is the master [*sic*] of the house; she always carries the purse; . . . she does all the servile work, cuts the wood, builds the fire, cooks the meals and takes care of the children," while the men forage for game and stand forth in battle: a division of labor that may explain why the Indian male has such trouble adjusting to modern life, why the "fast-thinning remnant of the warrior race have set their faces toward the setting sun." They had put up a good fight, and Dixon evoked "the marvelous resources of the Red man, . . . the unconquerable virility of this type of color," which made it difficult for "progress" to "snuff out these first Americans." Still, "the day will soon dawn when the last real North American Indian will be folded in his blanket and laid amid the sighing branches of the pines."⁶⁷ The unspecified fate of the Indian woman can only be imagined.

Eventually the story in the *Primer* came to the expeditions themselves. Their educational work fulfilled Penn's promise, and so they become an event in the national history:

Because the Indian is fast moving toward his last frontier; . . . because the Indian was the first American; . . . because the platforms of the Wanamaker Auditoriums in New York and Philadelphia have for their purpose the educational uplift and stimulus of the community; and because the rising generation [read: immigrant children] needs to know more about the early history of our great country—an expedition was planned . . . to study the North American Indian on his own ground, in his own home, and in a manner that would compel a true photographic, geographic, historic and ethnic record.

And in describing the kind of records wanted by the expeditioners, Dixon explained that "in all the pictures made of Indian life, every effort was exhausted to eliminate any hint of the white man's foot—the spirit of the native environment dominated."[68] This last point, a confession in the form of a boast, offered a crucial insight into Dixon's work. He confessed to exhaustive labors to eliminate any signs of present reality, to make the staging of his "records" as "pure" as the "blood" of subjects, the "vanishing race" of "real Americans"—again the Curtis model.

Indeed, purity of "old American stock" may be what the entire enterprise was about. Among Dixon's undated lecture notes is the following:

> INTERMARRIAGE DEPRECATED—The practice of "out crossing" as it is called by breeders was, evidently, not favored by the Divine Parent of the human race as he everywhere set law and custom against it. There is not a race that has ever gained, symmetrically, by marrying beyond its blood. The pure-blooded, inbred races are those who reached and maintained a high level of excellence. The Jews, Egyptians, Greeks, Romans, Irish, might all be quoted in support of this position. The idea that a great, symmetrically formed race can ever be built up in this Continent is scouted by all history. God and history are alike against it.[69]

"I felt," Rodman Wanamaker replied to a question after the presentation of "The Romance of a Vanishing Race" to the National Press Club in 1916, "that we needed to incorporate some of his [the Indian's] splendid traits into the American manhood we are making."[70] Filed with the typescript of this interview is another typescript, undated and unascribed, that explains in language much like Roosevelt's (perhaps written by Dixon) what this means. Because "the Indian is what we once were, intimate with the soil and the sky," we shall put ourselves in his place:

Just suppose that the white race had dwindled down until a few thousands of us were left. Just suppose that you had fought, that your father's father had fought; but that the yellow race had crowded you to the wall, was tilling your ground, navigating your streams, seducing your wives and daughters, ramming down our throat its ideals, its morals, its mode of eating, of rising up, of sitting down; that, even to the manner of cutting your hair, you must live as the yellow man dictated!

This loathsome "yellow peril" fantasy was exactly what "we have done to the Indian." "Our own bigotry," however, hurt and deprived us. Because "Nature still speaks to him directly," because "he is still unafraid to face the pitiless inevitability of Nature's methods," Indian simplicity still had something of value to contribute to "our own complicated ideals of life." The point was blazingly clear. Because "Nature" is pitiless and only the strongest survive, white men must learn from the Indians how to cherish and protect themselves in a world where "one's race" means everything:

> Life on the philosophical side is to the Indian what it has long ceased to be to the white—a simple matter of facing the universe like a man, fighting to the last ditch for one's blood, then dying without a whimper. Such a simple matter, life, to the Indian's philosophy! One's own race is the best of earth's conceptions. Therefore, to keep alive one's race is the whole of man's duty.
>
>   To do this he must keep his blood untainted, must let nothing but war interfere with the propagation of his family, the unit of the tribe.[71]

"I wished to preserve by historic data and picture-record," Rodman Wanamaker told the National Press Club, "the story of this virile people for the benefit of future generations."

The Wanamaker Hiawatha and "Romance of a Vanishing Race" had all the marks of the aggressive response that was typical of America's ruling elites of the time, to what various historians have described as a crisis of morale, of masculinity, of modernity. "Race thinking" was part of this reaction to imagined threats on all sides, of embattlement in the face of immigrants, suffragists, socialists, intellectuals, and labor unions. For people of means striving to escape the constrictions of genteel culture without abandoning it altogether, the promise of revitalization held out by the "primitive" seemed brighter than ever with the results of ethnological fieldwork and collecting and displaying of artifacts. "I have refreshed myself," remarked Stewart Culin, curator of the ethnological collection at the Brooklyn Museum, about his own Wanamaker Expedition to the West, "feel myself younger and more vital. I have realized my dreams among savages in whose lives and thoughts I have had glimpses of the dawn of the world." Getting the "primitive" into goods, Culin argued, would help city people regain healthy contact with "vital elements."[72]

On the face of it, native cultures at that time hardly seemed fit sources for the revitalization project. Living under the multiple burdens of deprivation, exclusion, insult, and ambiguous legal status, they seemed to many non-Indians the ultimate image of defeat, loss, and degradation. "Total oblivion in the very near future" is how the Smithsonian anthropologist W. H. Holmes viewed the Indian future in 1910. And this lugubrious picture had its counterpart in government social policy, which held that natives should be kept in tutelage until they either learned white ways or faded away.

By the time of the Wanamaker projects, the motif of a dying or vanishing race had begun a strange metamorphosis. If attrition describes the actual social condition of most Indians, Indian life of the past began to look to many whites like a kind of "romance," something to celebrate, to emulate. "Playing Indian" reemerged in organized, institutional forms of mimesis such as civic pageants and public monuments, and in woodcraft movements like the Boy Scouts.[73] In *What the White Race May Learn from the Indian* (1908), the prolific California writer and photographer George Wharton James urged readers to imitate how Indians breathed, walked, restrained themselves, and enjoyed "the great mystery of sex." Fear of savagery gave way to celebration of its virtues, in the "beautiful simplicity and joy of naturalness."[74] Complicating the logic of his movement without disturbing its fervor was the figure carved of white marble by James Earle Fraser for the 1915 Panama-Pacific Exposition: the Indian at the "End of the Trail," stooped on his horse, his spear drooping, he and his horse at the nadir of manhood. Pathos for the vanishing race fed the pleasure of that detumescent figure's confirmation of the potency of the white conquerors and, in the same breath, pleasure in the lost "vitality" of native exoticism replaced scorn and fear. Looking at pictures replaced direct encounters, and the pictures most often exhibited showed a people frozen in the act of displaying their weird but beautiful difference, as in Curtis's "Vanishing Indian Types" in *Scribner's* in 1906 and in the Wanamaker productions.

Dixon's script for the film *Hiawatha—The Passion Play of the American Indian* set the opening scene as a "long shot of Indian standing on top of waterfalls, shading his eyes and looking and listening." The setting was a "panoramic view of mountains, prairies, forests, and waterfalls." The scene then shifted "to small white child on summit of another mountain listening as though the winds were speaking to her."[75] Yoking "Indian" and "white child" across wide spaces in open nature encapsulated a paradigm of Dixon's educational program: the infantilization of "the Indian." His illustrated school lectures, his distribution of the *Primer* in classrooms, and his invitations to schoolchilden to come to the performances of *Hiawatha* presumed a special rapport between children and the poor downtrodden but once-noble "savages."

Touching responses in letters of gratitude from youngsters, particularly from children of immigrants, testified to the success of the mission. Bessie Friedman of P.S. 36 on the Lower East Side of New York wrote, "I have learned about the Indians in my Russian school but I was not able to understand it all, until I saw your beautiful pictures. After listening to your beautiful language I have so few words strong enough to thank you but like the Indians I will let my heart speak." And Rose Tichacek: "The Indian is not to be forgotten, I hope, because Mr. Wanamaker is going to erect a statue of him. It is very thoughtful to place the statue in the New York harbor so that every foreigner could see it." One school principal could hardly contain his ecstasy: "To me, last Tuesday was an inspiration and a joy, more like the realization of a dream of my childhood that seemed to bring me

James Earle Fraser, "The End of the Trail," postcard, 1915. (Author's collection)

Joseph Kossuth Dixon, Plenty Coup and wife in car, 1909. (William Hammond
Mathers Museum, Indiana University)

into actual touch with Hiawatha, his people, the forest, the mountains, the valleys, the flowing streams and the open sky." Gertrude
Glaser wrote, "Surely the noble face and proudly perched head of the
red man, must inspire all who gaze on him with an ambition to succeed in their work, and have the same consciousness of having
accomplished something worthwhile." "From the pictures I saw at
Wanamaker's," wrote Julius Davidovitz, "I would like to live as the Indian boys used to live. All day long they were out in the woods hunting and fishing." Irma Price of the Upper West Side expressed her
gratitude in a poem for Dixon, "The Passing of the Red Man," and describes the boundlessness of her delight: "My little brother and I
bought Indian suits at Wanamaker's. We are dancing the war dance at
home. We have arrows, too, and we are shooting and playing Indians
in the little park before our house. Are they real Indians, who are on
the stage?" The question played directly into Dixon's hands: "The
multitudes who will listen to these lectures and witness these slides
and the motion pictures of Indian life and history," he promised in the
Primer, "may have every assurance that they have been executed with
Wanamaker fidelity."[76]

The "Wanamaker Hiawatha" prefigured future directions. In 1909
at the Crow Agency, Dixon staged "The Last Great Indian Council," a
centerpiece for his book on *The Vanishing Race*. This council was an
assemblage of about a hundred old chiefs under Dixon's directorial
command. He had them don full regalia, build a council lodge, light
signal fires, powwow with each other in sign language, reenact
Custer's last stand as their own last moment of glory. Dixon made no
bones of his theatrical intentions. In his letter to Commissioner
Valentine requesting permission, he described a scenario already
worked out: "As a finale to the whole program, I purpose having these
old chiefs say farewell, a last goodbye, and then ride away toward the
setting sun. This picture I intend to be a portrayal of the final dispers-
ing of all the tribes to be swallowed up in the larger civilization which
your work so effectively contemplates, but the record of such a goodbye has never been made and unless made now will never be made."[77]

Dixon's native performers played their roles well. They arrived
from their agencies by rail or automobile, costumes in hand, ready to

suit up and get into position. All the while Dixon kept at least one camera on the cameras themselves, on himself and his men working out shots and scenes. They too were performers, the cast of characters in an illustrated lecture he called "How We Photographed the Indians."[78] The lecture showed the crew making camp, clearing the ground, riding horses, sitting in tepees, taking pictures. Dixon showed himself, too, staging events and directing performances, crafting his own appearance before the camera, his dress, his posture, the angle of his head all calculating a specific theatrical effect. He apparently wanted to impress on his audiences that his pictures were indeed performances, events created for the camera, expositions whose truth lies in their artistry. The pictures showing "how we photographed the Indians" teach that the old chiefs portrayed in formal "vanishing race" images were also playing roles and performing scripts. By allowing the audience to recognize a distance between performer and role, Dixon cleverly insinuated that the *real* Indian was already moribund. The aim was to make of the already vanished people a spectacle of sunsets, empty saddles, burial sites, last arrows, a spectacle in the manner or guise of a record.

The separation of performer from role also carried a covert message that Dixon himself may not have recognized. In 1909, the old chiefs seemed to join happily in the spirit of the enterprise; many had already been photographed and filmed several times before, probably rode in Wild West shows, already mastered role playing before the camera. The cast included many already familiar names: Plenty Coup, Crow; Runs-the-Enemy, Teton Sioux; White Horse, Southern Yankton Sioux; Red Cloud, Oglala Sioux; White-Man-Runs-Him, Crow, chief of the Custer scouts; and Curly, Crow, the most famous Custer scout. The role playing put them in a position vis-à-vis the image they projected, the image of their own authenticity, represented by that part of themselves that is already vanishing (regalia and weapons and sign language), that was something like that of the white audience. It was not that role playing made them strangers to themselves, but some degree of estrangement from certain features of their past selves was presumed, since they were able (and willing) to perform themselves, to enter the picture not as who they were (the person do-

Joseph Kossuth Dixon preparing to photograph a Blackfoot man and his wife, 1913. (William Hammond Mathers Museum, Indiana University)

Joseph Kossuth Dixon, self-portrait in his tent during the filming of *The Last Great Indian Council*, 1909. (William Hammond Mathers Museum, Indiana University)

Joseph Kossuth Dixon.
(*above*) "Skirting the
Skyline," 1909, and
(*left*) "Bacon Rind—Osage."
From *The Vanishing Race*,
1913. (Author's collection)

Joseph Kossuth Dixon, "Chief Koon-Kah-Za-chy Addressing the Council in the Sign Language," 1909. From *The Vanishing Race*, 1913. (Author's collection)

ing the acting) but as who they once had been, who they might always be again in performance, on camera.

When Dixon's *The Vanishing Race* appeared in 1913, with eighty photogravures among some two hundred pages of text, Curtis called its sepia-toned illustrations "fakey imitations" of his own work. *The Nation*, calling the book "not easy to classify," neither history nor ethnology, and larded with unwarranted claims of authenticity, remarked of the pictures that, while "in their mechanical execution leave nothing to be desired," "artistically, they follow the trail first marked by Mr. Edward S. Curtis."[79] One difference was noteworthy. Unlike Curtis's consistent use of a kind of proscenium form of presentation, whereby his audience sat in its own space, spectators of the static scenes flashing by page by page, Dixon's text incorporated colloquy with the chiefs and engaged the reader in the drama of the book's making, as if it were a live performance. References to the pictures themselves appeared frequently in the speeches the chiefs gave. "I am glad at heart that this great picture is to be made of us, as we are assembled here," declared Chief Two Moons, who led the Cheyennes against Custer, "because our old chiefs are fast dying away, and our old Indian customs soon will pass out of sight, and the coming generation will not know anything about us, but this picture will cause us to live all through the years."[80] The acquiescence of the old warriors in their defeat and in the loss of their culture suggested Hiawatha's departure at the close of the poem, with advice to his people to follow where the white men lead. Dixon had the chiefs speak of their willingness to abandon traditional ways, to vanish themselves for the sake of learning the white man's superior way. The device was to have the chiefs put on their traditional garb for their photographs and then to address their old selves as something they are discarding, an ethnicity they honored in the act of abandoning it. Dixon remarked, in language that might be addressed to new immigrants in strange clothes and uttering alien speech, "There is a touch of humanness about these tall, graceful, feather-bedecked men, willingly assuming the role of children, that they may learn the better ways of the white man."[81]

Dixon described the staging of "The Last Great Council" as "the construction of a primitive council lodge along the lines of history and tradition, and again, the reproduction of primitive customs and traditions, both in paraphernalia, costume, and conduct."[82] Never mind that it was all fake; the acknowledgment of construction and reproduction and the inclusion of actors acknowledging their performance made it seem real. Working within a department-store culture of advertising, publicity, and spectacle, Dixon sought reality effects. He worked for the *"reproduction"* of vanished Indians.

Dixon introduced the performance of the chiefs with these words: "The American mind could conceive a republic but not an Indian." Whatever this might mean, it does pose the question to which the text proposed a number of answers. How might we conceive of the Indian? One method was the old familiarizing trick to call this one Roman in his physiognomy, that one displaying a "Spartan courage," another looking like an Apollo Belvedere. Another method was more complex: the incorporation of pictures of costumed chiefs along with their contemporary acknowledgment that the garb was put on for the occasion and for the sake of contemplation of the old identity. This meant that what was already "vanished" better revealed the "firstness" of the original Americans, which was now accessible as a national and nationalizing value to be memorialized, commemorated, packaged, and marketed.

In Curtis's allegory, the vanishing of the Indian "race" emptied the natural world of its governing deities, who left behind a residue of sentiment captured by the photographic artist as picturesque landscape. Landscape fulfilled a similar function for Dixon: situation shots, out-of-doors portraits placing single figures next to features of the terrain, women and children near running water, and silhouettes, whose figures seem all but absorbed by the landscape. For the loquacious Dixon, whose desires served more openly nationalist interests, the residue of the departing gods was a sentimentalized version of Indian virtue offered as a tonic to America: a tough masculinity at a time of rising American militarism, a fervent religiosity, and a disciplined loyalty to higher principles. "We cannot understand this, because the Indian chased the ethereal, the weird, the sublime, the mysterious; we chase the dollar. He heard the voice of nature; we listen to the cuckoo clock of commerce."[83]

The moving pictures of the "Romance of a Vanishing Race" inspired the equally loquacious Elbert Hubbard to write and publish at his Roycroft Press "The Indian Farewell," whose platitudes captured perfectly the relation of Indian and landscape that Dixon, like Curtis, contrived to represent. "The swinging and angular motions of the Indian's body were a poetic part of the landscape," Hubbard wrote, and the Indian "is a part of the wildness of a country untouched by the influences of civilized man."[84] The "scheme for stage setting" in the multimedia production in the Egyptian Hall, prepared by a member of Dixon's staff, emphasized the natural setting: "The curtain rises disclosing a wide vista of prairie, with mountain ranges, capped with snow and bathed in the light of a Western sunset. This vista is seen from an opening framed with pine trees and giant boulders high up the Western slope of a mountain." A figure appears with his back to the audience: "He wears a head-dress of Eagle feathers—his arms and chest are nude—from his waist down are his leggings and moccasins. His left hand is lifted to the Great Mystery, whom, alone, he fears,—across his arms rests the Ceremonial Peace Pipe with which he smokes to the four corners of the Earth. This Chief is represented by the baritone soloist."[85] To relieve the monotony of Indian music itself, another manuscript note explains that "tribal themes . . . have been set to the most modern effects of the twentieth century harmonies."[86] "And the music!" wrote Hubbard. "It was weird and wild in its beauteous monotone, primitive, majestic. There was in it the color and form of mountains, plain and stream. It was fierce. It was grand." Another fan wrote Dixon that "it was to me not a lecture, nor a concert, nor a panorama, but an Enchantment," and compared its effect to the "transport aroused by the Wagnerian Music Drama, Parsifal, at Bayreuth."[87]

The "scheme for stage setting" remarked, "In presenting 'The Last Great Indian Council—The Farewell of the Chiefs' it is a far cry from the wind swept prairies of the West, and the tragedy of the Red Man to the high-keyed rush of the average American's life. So that in presenting so grave and vital a subject, it is even more necessary than ever before, to create the proper impression or frame of mind in the audience." "Manipulate the illusion" seems more apt than "create" the proper "impression." Dixon's description of the finale of the "Last Indian Council" segment of the show, "the journey home" (the chiefs having arrived, it was said, from all corners of the land), suggested the full pathos of the desired effect.

> The finale of the pictures shows the procession of chieftains coming out of the very sky, as they ride over the crest of a hill that rises like a dome. Under the yellow rays of a setting sun, amid a rising cloud of dust and the seared grass and sagebrush of the prairie, they approach; sweeping by, they file down the historic Reno Ridge . . . Amid dust and sliding earth they face the crimson of the sunset sky . . . The purple mists of evening gathered over all the high hills and the wide, extended plain, and the chiefs were lost in the stream of time.[88]

Leslie Marmon Silko has given voice to what is expunged from this and countless similar scenarios then and since: "'Murder, murder,' sighs the wind over the rocks in a remote Arizona canyon where they betrayed Geronimo."

III

On February 22, 1913—five days after the opening of the Armory Show of new incendiary artworks and some three months before the revolutionary Paterson Strike Pageant produced at Madison Square Garden by John Reed and the I.W.W. leader Big Bill Heywood— a very different kind of ceremony took place in a cold drizzle on a rise of land at Fort Wadsworth on Staten Island, overlooking New York harbor, to "break ground" for a national monument that never materialized.[89] Appropriate to the sacral character of the day— Washington's Birthday—participants included the outgoing president of the United States, William Howard Taft, many of his cabinet, the governor of the state and the mayor of the city, officers of the army and navy, a military band, hundreds of invited guests from the highest ranks of New York society, and thirty-two men in full regalia of Plains Indians, "adorned in their barbaric finery of brilliantly colored bead work" and painted faces, identified in the accompanying brochure as "Indian Chiefs from Western Reserves," including the aged Chief Two Moons, Northern Cheyenne, who had to be carried up the hill; Chief Hollow Horn Bear, Sioux; Mountain Chief, Blackfeet; and Lone Wolf, Kiowa.

Dixon had written to the Department of the Interior, responsible for arranging the appearance of the chiefs, insisting that "they bring their War Bonnet, War shirts, Legging, Moccasins, and entire paraphernalia. I want them to dress as though they were at a ceremonial or War Dance."[90] He did not miss a trick. He asked that "some Indian bring on a thigh bone of a Buffalo, or some primitive implement used by the Indians in digging, for after the President turns the shovel full of earth I want some Indian to dig the soil so that the chief of the Nation and an Indian Chief may participate in breaking the ground. Be sure and have this done for me."[91] The power of belief (or Wanamaker influence) was such that everyone complied, from president to secretary to admirals, and the chiefs, too, in their own way. Some carried tomahawks. They smoked almost continuously, using the white man's cigars and cigarettes. Many of them were well educated and spoke English as well as white men. Some wore white men's clothes to typify their civilization. Many of those in Indian garb ordinarily wore "civilized" clothing when at home, and some confessed to feeling uncomfortable in the aboriginal costume put on for the occasion.[92]

The occasion was "the Official Inauguration of the National American Indian Memorial," and as the "founder of this monument" (echoing Washington as founder of the nation), the top-hatted Rodman Wanamaker presided. Initiated by a private citizen of great wealth, the event had the trappings of an official ritual: solemn breaking of the ground by President Taft and an Indian elder, Chief Wooden Leg, Northern Cheyenne, wielding each in turn a silver shovel and a buffalo thighbone; a military brass band filling the damp air with patriotic melodies; the performance of a "War Song" by the chiefs accompanied by drumbeats in another "national" rhythm; many speeches; the presentation of a bronze tablet commemorating the event; and, centerpiece of the day, a hoisting of the flag "by the Indian Chiefs" to the melody of "The Indian's Requiem" composed by the music director of the Wanamaker Stores. With flag aloft, the chiefs then affixed their signatures or thumbprints to a sheet of vellum inscribed with an "Indian Declaration of Allegiance."

Everything in this event, from the initial proposal (four years earlier) to the form and order of the ceremonies, was orchestrated by Dixon in his inimitable spectacle style. He declaimed the opening address, conducted the flag raising, posed for the several cameras he had placed to make a running record of the event in still and moving images. The ritual on Staten Island in 1913 was the pièce de résistance of Dixon's work as the Wanamaker emissary to the public in matters of "education" and "culture."

The story goes that in May 1909, Rodman Wanamaker hosted a banquet at the fashionable club, Sherry's, in honor of Colonel William "Buffalo Bill" Cody's birthday. In his address, the old showman confided that out of passionate concern for the fate of the "first Americans" his host had a plan: A monument to their memory should be built somewhere in New York harbor, a statue "as large as the Goddess of Liberty, with an Indian on top showing him as he was when the whites first visited America, hands extended, welcoming every one to this shore." The dinner guests, including former Indian fighters like Generals Nelson A. Miles and Leonard Wood ("the best of the brown races," Wood described the Indian), Pawnee Bill, and of course Cody himself, went wild with enthusiasm, and all this was recorded in a pamphlet that Dixon rushed into print titled "The First American," printed handsomely by Elbert Hubbard's Roycroft Press in 1909.[93] In June of that year Wanamaker wrote to President Taft (it's likely that Dixon drafted the letter) with a formal request that the president mobilize the government on behalf of the proposal, including a grant of public funds: "I would like to have your cooperation, with permission and grants from congress, in placing on Lafayette island, in New York harbor, a statue of the North American Indian—the first inhabitant and Citizen of this continent and the accepted symbol of the United States." The letter described the kind of monument Wanamaker had in mind: "This statue, heroic in size, would stand at the eastern gateway of our country, with out-stretched arms in welcome, by day or night, if it was deemed advisable to serve as a harbor light, to all those coming to this land of liberty and freedom, recognizing also the welcome which the Red Man gave to the White Man when our forefathers first came to these shores." Its symbolic beacon would supplement the message of "liberty" already stationed in the harbor with a message of welcome from a figure now recognized as the country's "first Citizen," the "first American." Another way of putting it, as Russel Lawrence Barsh has suggested, is that the monument and the "Declaration of Allegiance" would memorialize the Indian's concession of defeat and loss of land, a kind of formal though unofficial surrender.[94] The monument would signal a message of national white power especially to those masses of non-Anglo-Saxon immigrants pouring through the gates in just these years.

Taft complied by introducing a bill, which finally passed by Congress with some imaginative help from a Wanamaker lobbyist (free cigars, Christmas gifts) and was signed by him in December 1911. The act reads in part: "Be it enacted . . . That there may be erected, without expense to the United States Government, by Mr. Rodman Wanamaker, of New York City, and others, on a United States reservation, in the harbor of New York, in the State of New York, and upon a site to be selected by the Secretary of War and the Secretary of Navy, a suitable monument to the memory of the North American Indian."

Ambiguities abound. What exactly was authorized? The only demonstrable outcome of the bill was the selection of a site, responsibility for which was assigned to the secretaries of war and the navy, and by them to officers of these services. Deeper ambiguities lay in the equivocation of the phrase "may be erected, without expense to the United States Government, by Mr. Rodman Wanamaker, of New York City, and others." Presumably Congress wished merely to create conditions of possibility. What did "by Mr. Rodman Wanamaker" mean? "Without expense to the government" evidently meant that Wanamaker would pay for the monument, but what had happened to Wanamaker's initial request for a "grant"? Had he wanted enough ambiguity to convey the impression that he would take financial responsibility without actually promising to do so? Who are the unspecified "others"?

There is evidence of embarrassment on Wanamaker's part about the growing misconception that he would foot the bill. "The scheme has gone considerably beyond what Mr. R.W. originally intended," remarked one of his functionaries in a letter to Dixon in 1913, "and, having initiated it, his idea is that it should become national in the carrying of it out." The following year it was suggested that they should "get away from the statement that it was mandatory that R. W. should erect the figure entirely by himself."[95] Dixon insinuated as much in the dedicatory brochure, his equivocation disguised as eloquence: "The concept of the founder of this memorial is that he should not alone place a mammoth bronze figure of the North American Indian upon the highest hill-crest in the harbor as a witness of the passing race to all the nations of the world as they come to our shores, but his purpose is to perpetuate all that the Indian was." What did "not alone" mean but that it was up to "others" to decide whether the monument came to be or not. "It was unfortunate," wrote Dixon in a verbose memo in 1916 suggesting a variety of schemes for fund raising, "that the first general impression given to the Nation was that the Memorial . . . was to be the Rodman Wanamaker Memorial." In 1922, J. P. Morgan & Co., designated years before as treasurer of the National American Indian Memorial Association—another of Dixon's devices for lining up support for the event of 1913—informed him that $143 remained on credit and asked for further instructions. Dixon replied, with a typical defiance of reality, that this was "simply the nucleus of a larger fund which I hope will reach the amount of $1,500,000 later on." It's difficult to sort out the ratio of honest delusion to deliberate deception in Dixon's oeuvre, but of such fantasies was the National American Indian Memorial crafted.

It's hard to imagine a less substantial, more equivocal proposal for a public artwork of such proportions, without funding and, as it turned out, without a definite design, without even the pretense of a competition for a suitable design. Yet the engraved brochure for the groundbreaking displayed a sketch that made it seem that a design actually existed. The 1911 congressional act gave a commission of government officials and one private citizen, Robert C. Ogden (who happened to be a vice president of the Wanamaker stores), "full authority to select a suitable design, and to contract for and superintend the construction of the said memorial."[96] The final provision was that the design would need the approval of the Commission of Fine Arts created by act of Congress just the year before, in 1910. Daniel Burnham served as its first president from 1910 until his death in 1912, when the sculptor Daniel Chester French took over until he resigned in 1915 to take up the commission to create the Lincoln Memorial statue. As it turned out, Burnham, having declined the honor himself, suggested to Wanamaker through Dixon that French and the architect Thomas Hastings, both prominent figures in public art crusades, be commissioned without competition to produce the design. By July 1912, all parties concerned, including President Taft, had signed off on this rather chummy procedure for selecting the artists for a public work. As Dixon wrote to French, "you are booked with Mr. Hastings to design the Indian memorial . . . Doubtless you will feel the blood tingling in your right arm to model the grandest memorial on the North American Continent." French's positive reply indicated his assent. But two years later, when Dixon requested an actual model of the statue for the Wanamaker display at the Panama-Pacific Exposition, French demurred, confessed embarrassment, explained that hints of imprudence had been uttered against him on the Fine Arts Commission, and insisted that he had never meant to be the official sculptor in any case. Could it be that the lavish Lincoln Memorial commission already loomed into view and he wished not to compromise his chances for it?

The sketch reproduced in the 1913 brochure shows a standing figure with arms raised atop a pyramidal base, which in turn stands on the central section of what seems to be a classical temple with two flanking wings. A broad stairway on a landscaped hill leads up to the structure, and at the base of the stairs stands another, smaller statue of a figure on a horse. We learn from the text what the sketch does not make visible, that "this monument comprises a small museum, thirty-five feet high," to contain examples of Indian homes, weapons, costumes, domestic items, and collections of photographs and books, "the idea being that the mammoth bronze figure, which is to rise on a pedestal seventy feet high, the statue rising sixty feet, shall preside in bronze over all that represents the primeval Indian on this continent." Thus the proposal fused two prime institutions typical of those years:

monumental statuary depicting self-congratulatory patriotic allegories, and a monumental ethnographic museum with the theme of high civilization putting lower forms of life on "scientific" display. On the terrace below the templelike museum there would be an "equestrian statue of an Indian as he is known to-day." In height the monument portrayed in the sketch and described in the text would surmount the Statue of Liberty by several feet. But then, at the bottom of the page, we read: "Note.—The Indian shown in the design is tentative. It is not to be considered the work of the sculptor."

The drawing abandoned the statue to the realm of guesswork and offers only faint clues to what French's conception might actually have looked like. Dixon's words may reflect discussions with both Hastings and French, translated into the self-exalting idiom of Wanamaker events.

> As to character, it should be remembered that it is a tribute of modern civilization, and is being built by a civilized nation to a race of primitive people. No attempt has been made to establish an Indian style of architecture, but rather to incorporate the character of the people in a design which should be modern and the expression of a civilized people. The dominant feature of this design is to be an Indian in a striking and characteristic pose that will reveal the soul of the Indian himself. The bow and arrow, with the left hand hanging entirely at full length, indicates that he is through with his war weaponry; the uplifted hand, with the two fingers extended toward the open sea, is the universal peace sign of the Indian. Thus he gives, in bronze, a perpetual welcome to the nations of the world, as he gave welcome to the white man when he first came to these shores, and thus we have combined the impress of modern civilization in the base, and what the Indian thought of himself in the bronze statue.[97]

As usual, Dixon offers a hermeneutics that makes the imaginary monument into another emblem of the triumph of "civilization," the modern American commercial empire, over the "primitive," and that

Dixon's photograph of Rodman Wanamaker at the Fort Wadsworth ceremony, January 22, 1913. (William Hammond Mathers Museum, Indiana University)

Artist's rendering of the proposed Indian Memorial at Fort Wadsworth, Staten Island, 1913. (William Hammond Mathers Museum, Indiana University)

lauds the generosity of the conquerors in embracing the conquered on terms set entirely by the former.

What, finally, was this all about? It is tempting to interpret it as a parody of the very discourse to which the event subscribed. All outer show and conventional forms are in order, but the closer one looks, the more vacuous it seems. This is quite apart from the foggiest, least-coherent aspect: the conception, first, of "the North American Indian," as if there existed or had existed a unitary figure matching those words, and the very concept of a "memorial," as if it were incontrovertible that, as the brochure put it, "the North American Indian, as a race, is rapidly vanishing . . . The day is not far in the Nation's 'tomorrows' when the Indian as a type, will have passed forever from this continent—his footprints are already marking the sands of the Western ocean." The thirty living Indians in attendance gave proof by their presence, presumably, of their imminent absence. Left unsaid were the actual facts pointed out by the Denver *Republican* in an editorial titled "The Indian will Laugh": There were thousands of Indian children who had never been to school, many Shoshone, Arapahoe, and Jicarilla Apaches who were near starvation, and Apache children in Fort Sill were "born virtually in imprisonment." Indians were falsely said to have no sense of humor, but "the reservations will echo to his laughter when he hears about the honor that is being paid his race in New York."[98]

Toward the end of the ceremony, one of the speakers surprised everyone by producing a canvas bag, "and from its bulky depths," reported *The New York Times*, "drew forth a handful of shining new nickels from the mint, the first appearance of the Indian head nickel with a buffalo imprinted on the reverse side. The Indian head replaces the head of the Goddess of Liberty," observed *The Times*. "It is in profile, and the design shows the head of feathers, the coarse, half-braided hair, and the thin seamed face. It might have been a portrait of any one of the chiefs who took it into their hands yesterday, and stared at it curiously."[99] Hence the "first American" did indeed materialize (as the monument would not), and on coin of the realm, a new portrait of the old people staring back at them as a token of exchange: one identity for another. The irony could hardly have been more banal, comic, and tragic at once: the image of the old vanished Indian as an official seal, circulating in the life blood of the nation, the money economy. Signifying a past threat subdued and an old guilt expiated, the Indian coin gave assurance of stability, a symbol of the nation's reconnection with its past, its mythical origins, its authentic "firstness." Transposed into portrait, the Indian gave America legitimacy. The following year, Fraser's *End of the Trail* took the gold medal at the Panama Pacific Exposition in San Francisco.[100] A new coin and images of Indians at once mournful and celebrative circulated in the body politic. A version of *End of the Trail* in white marble is now installed at the Cowboy Hall of Fame in Oklahoma City.

Is there a text here, something the historian can bracket and identify as a subject? Was the monument ever a serious proposal? Did Wanamaker have anything else in mind than publicity and newsworthy events? Was it anything more than a publicity stunt, the staging of a rearguard symbolism? For Manfred E. Keune, who wrote a pioneering article on the proposed memorial without benefit of the Joseph K. Dixon papers, still at that time lying unexamined in the Mathers Museum, the abandonment of the project and its disappearance from public memory "remains something of a mystery."[101]

Actualization of a monument in real space may well have been less the aim of the proposal than the illusion it generated. We are witness precisely to that moment in the advent of modernity in the United States when "public" gets confused with "publicity," when image, performance, and staged event begin to displace, preempt, and presume the illusory form of the solid monumental object. The orchestrated performance, the spectacle, both displaces and becomes the monumental object. Fake monumentality was the new mode of mass experience. Indeed, the visuality and illusion in the advertising, presentation, and marketing of goods in the Wanamaker stores suggests how to understand the calculatedly ephemeral character of the proposed monument. A publicity event represented a new cultural process in which older understandings of what was private and public, native and alien, illusory and real undergo profound revision even while remaining, to all appearances, the same. The imaginary monument to an imagined "vanishing race" is a ghostly phantom of what the official culture once conceived as an appropriate memorializing gesture at the present site of the Staten Island abutment of the Verrazano Narrows Bridge.

I V

The ceremony on Staten Island launched the third and most ambitious of the Wanamaker excursions (or incursions) into Indian country, its national purpose now revised as the Rodman Wanamaker Expedition of Citizenship. The trip came off, though the monument did not. After the hoopla of the groundbreaking, the proposal vanished more precipitously than the "vanishing race" it meant to memorialize, and barely a trace survives in historical memory; at last report even the bronze tablet has disappeared. The closer we look at the event as public theater, the more blurred, elusive, ambiguous the entire story becomes, and hence significant. That in itself is a clue to the peculiar character of the "Wanamaker Indian," a performative image fabricated of Hiawathan nostalgia and department store merchandising. "Well, I see Dixon has his monument started," wrote Curtis to Hodge. "You will notice that even the Gods wept."[102]

An incessant work in progress, "A Romance of the Vanishing Race" added footage and verbiage from the Staten Island performance and the ensuing Rodman Wanamaker Expedition of Citizenship. As it did so, a polemical tone joined the elegiac music of "farewell." The version copyrighted by Rodman Wanamaker in 1916 adds a plea for reform: "Civilization has almost completely emasculated the Indian from her program. We have used him as a prey instead of a power, we have corrupted him instead of incorporating his qualities into the America we are making. He is denied all rights in the courts of the land . . . We deny him the rights and privileges of the commonest immigrant coming to these shores."[103] Jeremiad has fused with romance. Romance gives the inevitable "vanishing," while civics gives means for correcting past lapses. We've taken so much from them, let's give the poor creatures some "rights." With citizenship, with pledged allegiance to the flag, they can surrender even more of themselves to "the America we are making." They can give us "first-ness," themselves as "first Americans."

When Dixon and crew embarked on the Expedition of Citizenship, he carried with him the very flag raised on Staten Island and a Wanamaker gift of a fresh flag for each tribe he encountered. Raising the flag would signify willingness to lay down Indianness as savage enmity and take up a new Indianness as "first American." At the end of the seven-month tour across the country, the entourage returned for a culminating ceremony at Fort Wadsworth, to "close the circle." And indeed the story from 1908 to 1913 has the look of a coherent sequence: the figure of Hiawatha, mythical youth as messiah-savior, gives way to the wizened old chiefs looking back on their victory over Custer from the perspective of the "last council," which collapses into the raising of the flag and the pledge, a ritual repeated by each tribe in 1913 as final recognition that "American" is what they had always been, original warriors of a nation itself becoming increasingly warlike. The flag gives Indians a country for the first time, proclaimed Dixon. And Indians give themselves as emblems of "man values," the virility of the warrior chiefs. Before this they were divided into separate tribes, then they became prisoners of the reservation system, now there's the prospect for a new unifying identity. It's not surprising that after 1917 Dixon threw his energy, in the name of Wanamaker, into a campaign to recruit natives into separate Indian "units of the army which would show off their superior abilities in war," display their acceptance of "Americanness" as identical to their vanishing "Indianness," and at the same time remain segregated from white "Americans."[104] Citizenship would be their reward. The army rejected the proposal, but Dixon nevertheless made thousands more pictures of Indians in uniform, including pictures of wounded natives in military hosptials.

In the 1913 expedition, romance gives way to comedy, the sort of comedy that can serve, in Kenneth Burke's words, as a "corrective." A comic perspective helps to place the Wanamaker-Dixon narrative within the evolving history of nation building in the tense decades before and following World War I. We want to laugh, and yet the laughter that comes has a bitter edge. "Humor specializes in incongruities," Burke wrote, "but by its trick of 'conversion downwards,' by its stylistic ways of reassuring us in dwarfing the magnitude of obstacles or threats, it provides us relief in laughter. The grotesque is the cult of incongruity without laughter. The grotesque is not funny unless you are out of sympathy with it (whereby it serves as unintentional burlesque)."[105] How else can we take the Wanamaker narrative but in a comic mode, somewhere between pure burlesque and humorless grotesquerie? On this ground incongruities reveal their own strangely plausible logic.

In 1913, Dixon's scenario called not for prescribed role playing but for the illusion of ritual. The actors performed something more difficult to compose and indeed to control than the role of "old chiefs" played by actual old chiefs. Now the Wanamaker name was joined with those of the Pennsylvania Railroad, which donated a special railroad car decked out with a darkroom; Thomas Edison, who gave the latest phonograph with a new diamond needle; and President Woodrow Wilson, whose recorded words arose magically from the wooden console; and at the center, the sacred icon that united all these into a single focus, the national flag.

A cult of the flag had emerged in America during the Civil War and had flourished in the following decades. Naturally it was tied to the idea of the battle flag that is carried into the fray as an emblem of identity and hope; during the Indian wars of the 1870s, it represented the nation's military power against the scattered tribal foes. With the Columbian Exposition in 1893, then the wars against Spain in Cuba and the Philippines, and the prominence of the flag as a heuristic and nationalizing symbol in the Americanization of immigrants, appropriate behavior about the flag began to be codified; salute of the flag and the ritual of the Pledge of Allegiance were required in public schools in the early years of the twentieth century and were common practice by the 1920s. "Thus the pledge of allegiance was transformed from an exercise to Americanize immigrants into a ritual mandated by law," Scot M. Guenter has written. It also became a familiar icon in advertising. Department stores published guidebooks on accepted usages.[106]

The Wanamaker store in Philadelphia often displayed its collection of "flags of America." And about the time it published *Uncle Sam's Panama Canal and World History*, a semiencyclopedic volume praising the Panama Canal as "an honor to the United States," the store also issued a brochure, *My Flag*, and in 1926 on the occasion of the sesquicentennial celebrations in Philadelpia, brought out *Flags of America*. The brochure concludes with the "pledge of allegiance, issued by the Adjutant-General of the United States," and the following instructions on how to recite it: "Standing with the hand over the heart, at the words 'the Flag,' the right-hand is extended palm up, toward the flag, and this position is held until the end, when the hand, after the words 'justice for all,' drops to the side."[107] On the 1913 expedition, Dixon elaborated this stance, wrapping himself in the flag at Staten Island, kissing it, conducting churchlike rituals with bowing, touching with the lips, and praying over and to the flag.

In a novel titled *Shadow Catcher* (1991) by Charles Fergus, a man named James McLaughlin emerges as Dixon's antagonist on the 1913 excursion. The character is based on an actual figure, a longtime Indian Bureau agent who wrote a book in 1910 called *My Friend the Indian*, celebrated by his biographer in 1992 as "the man with an Indian heart." The historian Robert Utley has described McLaughlin as "the personification of the paternalistic Indian system that grew out of the reform movement of the 1880s."[108] *My Friend the Indian* is based largely on his experience as agent of the Standing Rock reservation (Sioux) at the time when the Ghost Dance religion excited Indians with the belief that their dancing would bring back the buffalo and dead warriors. McLaughlin claims pride in having been able

to guide the uncertain steps of a simple people across the threshold of civilization, and help to lead them to a realization of the domination of the white man and the impending extinction of their race as an element in the great affairs of men.

In the nature of things, it must have come about that the Indian should go to the wall before the dominating influence of the white man. When the first white placed his foot upon the shores of this continent, it was predestined that he should come into the inheritance of the Indian. And there is no use quarrelling with the processes of natural law.[109]

The book is notable for McLaughlin's palpable hatred of Sitting Bull, whose arrest he ordered in 1891, an order that led to his killing by Indian police. Just as he thought of "the Indian" as "a grown-up child," he saw Sitting Bull as a coward and a fake: "Crafty, avaricious, mendacious, and ambitious, Sitting Bull possessed all of the faults of an Indian and none of the noble attributes which have gone far to redeem some of his people from their deeds of guilt." The murder of the famous chief was a good thing because it showed that "Sitting Bull's medicine had not saved him, and the shot that killed him put a stop forever to the domination of the ancient régime among the Sioux of the Standing Rock reservation."[110]

The 1913 scenario called for a simple formula to be repeated over and again before each of the 189 tribes registered by the Indian Bureau. Each performance repeated—this was the faux ritual aspect—the raising of the Staten Island flag and the repetition of the ceremony of Indians signing or leaving thumbprints on the "Declaration of Allegiance." The fiction was that by repetition, each participating Indian across the land would become part of the promised monument, would lend his or her spirit to the imaginary bronze figure presiding over New York harbor. First Dixon in his fake uniform gave an invocation, telling the story of Wanamaker munificence and the coming memorial on Staten Island, then bowing over the Fort Wadsworth flag, held horizontally before it was raised and lowered. Then the flag bestowed on each tribe as a Wanamaker gift was raised (at times there were as many as five such gifts waving on the flagpole at once). The recorded words of President Wilson followed: "The Great White Father now calls you his 'brothers,' not his 'children,'" and the diamond needle scratched out greetings and assurance of good intentions from the secretary of the interior and the acting commissioner of Indian affairs. Next came McLaughlin in a business suit, affirming Dixon's story and giving it the stamp of Indian Bureau approval in less fanciful language, followed by the signing of the parchment "Declaration of Allegiance" by whoever was left in the audience and willing. Often there were other haranguing speeches by white and native officials and dignitaries.

It had all the look of an official government event, but it did not always go smoothly. At Isleta Pueblo, the tribal elder Pablo Abeita interrupted the script: "I wish to say a word before we sign that." He

Joseph Kossuth Dixon, with James McLaughlin standing by, Cut Finger
(Southern Arapaho) signs the Declaration of Allegiance at El Reno, Oklahoma,
June 21, 1913. (William Hammond Mathers Museum, Indiana University)

thanked Wanamaker but added, "I trust the memorial will be more of a memorial to Mr. Wanamaker than to the Indians," then explained that he could not "sign this allegiance because I feel that my people have not been treated right by the United States Government's people . . . When such men as you gentlemen come and talk friendship to us, it reminds me of the tricks that were played upon us . . . We have always been under the American flag," so why then this rigmarole? Besides, "when I consider myself and my people,—my people first, and then the flag." In the end, urged by McLaughlin, he signed: "I do trust him." But similar expressions by others were duly recorded by McLaughlin's stenographer and made part of the record.[111]

Dixon had wanted McLaughlin on the 1913 Expedition of Citizenship to shore up the illusion of official authority. His contacts with reservation agents and Indian leaders might be useful. In the novel as well as in fact, as the journey proceeded, McLaughlin grew increasingly annoyed with Dixon. The monument was a "noble idea," he thought, and the playing of President Wilson's voice was the best part of the program. What bothered him were the cameras. In his report to the bureau (which also cited numerous instances of Indian amusement, confusion, and resistance to the blandishments of Dixon's cameras), he complained "that the ceremony was held for the purpose of obtaining pictures, rather than that the pictures were taken as a record of the ceremony."[112] He feared that Dixon had commercial and self-serving ends in mind. At Isleta, Dixon concluded the ceremony with a spiel: "I would like to say another thing. These pictures are going into the monument as a record of the Pueblos. I would like to have the privilege of going through your village and take pictures. I would like to have pictures of two or three of the older people, and of some of your young people, with specimens of your beautiful pottery. These will be records; they are not to be sold, they are simply a record."[113]

Many others objected to the cameras and the role playing. At Pawhuska, Oklahoma, a rope broke during the hoisting of the flag.

During the ensuing delay many of the Indians lost interest in the proceedings, and they began to leave, and by the time the

Joseph Kossuth Dixon, playing President Woodrow Wilson's speech to the leaders of Umatilla in northern Oregon, 1913. (William Hammond Mathers Museum, Indiana University)

Joseph Kossuth Dixon conducting the flag ceremony, Wanamaker Expedition for Citizenship, 1913. (William Hammond Mathers Museum, Indiana University)

flag was finally hoisted half of them had gone. They continued
to leave, one or two at a time, throughout the ceremony, and at
the conclusion there remained but a dozen or fifteen. Fred
Lookout, who had been selected to respond on behalf of the
Indians, was among those who left before it was time for that
response, and it was therefore not given. It cannot be said that
the Osage Indians are enthusiastic over an honor that brings
them no benefits of a material sort.

"I wish to state forcibly," concluded the distressed old Indian agent in
his report, "that, in my opinion, the Expedition had no beneficial effects whatever, either on Indians or whites. That it had no evil effects
is due principally to the fact that such things are so easily forgotten."[114]

"How on earth did McLaughlin's mission turn out," asked Dixon's
son Rollin in a letter to his father in December 1915, "and what did
the old liar and fourflusher have to say? the old Catholic hypocrite!
He'd lie his head off just because you are a Protestant and feel he was
doing his Church a good turn."[115] Whatever the case, McLaughlin did
believe in an old idea of representation, that the world is more real
than pictures of the world. Even Longfellow's Hiawatha, he felt, was
a sentimental idealization. Dixon saw things differently. At the
Cheyenne and Arapaho agencies, he decided to have the Indians bow
their heads as if in reverence over the outstretched flag before raising
it while he uttered a dedication explaining the meaning of red, white,
and blue. The Kickapoos refused. "I am convinced," McLaughlin
wrote with indignation, "that this feature was added purely for the
picture it would make; and the care which was exercised in selecting
for it only Indians in costume, or old and picturesque-looking Indians,
and the way the other Indians were always asked to stand in such a
way as to form a background for the picture, made this fact so apparent as greatly to detract from the effect of the dedication."[116] "Mendacious," he cried (the same word he used against Sitting Bull). Dixon
tried "to occupy the prominent position in all pictures taken," as if the
entire project had "one great object—publicity" for this "hot-air
artist." The *Quarterly Journal* of the Society of American Indians
agreed that Dixon's speeches "reveal the astounding egoism of the
man" and gave this example: "*I took* the flag in my hands, *I ordered*

the Indians to bow their heads, *I dedicated* the Indians to the flag; *I dedicated* the flag to the Indians." The journal worried that the "fakery" would cast disrepute on Rodman Wanamker's own "worthy patriotic idea," called for a federal investigation into Dixon's behavior and character, and dubbed the whole affair "the Great Advertising Hoax" and Dixon a new P. T. Barnum, "Prince of Advertisers."[117]

Of course they were right, the journal in its scorn for the misrepresentations of citizenship and of the actual status of Indians at the time, and McLaughlin in his contempt for the movie set atmosphere that demeaned the solemnity of ceremonies he otherwise admired. Facts were less important to Dixon than effects, and the old Indian agent bristled as Dixon beat his breast over broken treaties and government treachery. McLaughlin believed that only assimilation would save the personhood of Indians, and he believed in ceremony. In 1917, he contrived the citizenship ritual that had the Indian applicant renounce his native name, shoot his last arrow, accept a plow, and attach to himself a badge that read "An American Citizen." It wasn't symbolism McLaughlin objected to but the mixing of the sacred and the profane, the patriotic and the commercial, the high purpose of citizenship with low publicity.

McLaughlin was more right than he knew. He did not understand that Dixon represented a new brand of symbol making, and he missed the point of "Wanamaker Fidelity." Out of the logic of department store culture Dixon gave priority to method over content, to art over ideology, to illusion over fact. Just as the commodity system reproduced as a way life in the department store separated use from value, Dixon separated actor from role, native performer from the performance of Indian-as-American. Reality lay in performance, in appearances "guaranteed" as faithful by the merchant's label. The "vanishing Indian" became a Wanamaker commodity whose substance lay solely in the pleasure of the consumer, the pleasure of imagining oneself descending from such proudly accommodating "first Americans."

There is another twist to the Wanamaker logic, for Dixon unwittingly stirs that troubling thought. Is "American," in the end, just the name of a role, a construct, an imaginary figure like that of the vanishing Indian itself? Like the regalia brought along by the old chiefs in 1909 as props for the "last council" performance, was the flag in 1913

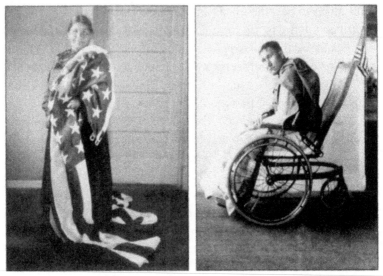

Joseph Kossuth Dixon. (*above left*) Emma, a Kickapoo, draped in an American Flag, Wanamaker Expedition of Citizenship, 1913. (*above right*) Fred Fast Horse, Sioux. Undated. (*below*) Two Blackfoot men with Kodak equipment.

simply a prop for the role of American? Dixon meant to teach Indians to see themselves as Americans under the flag. Performing the act of vanishing before the camera, Indians would join their audience in looking back upon themselves as relics of a glorious but outmoded past. But the act of vanishing plainly appeared as precisely that, an act. This logic carried to its conclusion would have the Indian performer joining with the non-Indian audience in recognizing that what they share may be no more or less than the performance space, an imagined theater where performer and audience might exchange roles and produce unexpected identities.

The half smile on the face of Emma, a Kickapoo, as she allows herself to be draped in the flag may tell it all. In the eyes of a native woman, the Wanamaker game of playing American produces riddles wrapped in enigmas, perhaps funny, perhaps not: a trickster conundrum. For the two Indians performing a parody of the arms-raised gesture of prayer staged by Dixon, as they gaze and point at themselves as negative images on a roll of film, discarded camera paraphernalia at their feet, the mockery is a pure trickster sleight-of-hand. The tripod of spears on the left challenges the camera tripod on the right. Did the performers themselves stage this event? Most likely. Meanwhile, the small drooping flag on the back of the wheelchair, a wounded veteran's similarly equivocal insignia of identity, tells another side of the same tale.

Dixon's camera was there to record and unknowingly valorize each side: the charade in which "American" stands for a potential comic freedom of impersonation and reinvention, and the camera an impotent weapon against native wit, but also the less amusing game whose rules define as American not persons but bodies surrendered to the will of the military state. At a time when Wanamaker's Uncle Sam was flexing his steel muscles in conquest of lands rich in minerals, markets, and cheap dark-skinned labor, the charade failed to hide its chilling underside of readiness to shoot in order to hold the line, in Buffalo Bill's words, between savagery and civilization.

SIX

The Great Bridge

Yes, we are mythic by conversation, conversion, and remembrance, and the pleasure is the contradiction. Natives have always been on one road of resistance or another, creating postindian myths and tricky stories in the very ruins of representation and modernity.

—Gerald Vizenor, *Postindian Conversations*

Grandfather!
A voice I am going to send,
Hear me!
All over the universe
A voice I am going to send,
Hear me.
Grandfather!
I will live!
I have said it.
—Opening prayer of the sun dance (Teton Sioux)

One morning in May 1883, Luther Standing Bear, a fifteen-year-old Lakota student at the Carlisle Industrial (Indian) School in Pennsylvania, marched at the head of the school band across a new bridge over the East River in New York City. The occasion was the opening of the Brooklyn Bridge, a festive ritual for the nation as well as the city. Told only that they were going to New York "to play before thousands of people,"[1] the Carlisle band had lined up in their uniforms on the lawn in front of the City Hall not knowing what was up; at the last minute they learned they were to lead the parade. When their bandmaster failed to appear, the school director, Captain William Henry Pratt, asked young Standing Bear, who played the cornet, to take over.

"When the parade started," Standing Bear recalled, "I gave the signal, and we struck up and kept playing all the way across the great structure." Standing Bear delighted in recollecting that heady moment and the equally delicious irony of his presence there: "So the Carlisle Indian band of brass instruments was the first *real American band* to cross the Brooklyn Bridge, and I am proud to say that I was their leader."[2]

Two years after Standing Bear told this story in *My People the Sioux*, Hart Crane, the Ohio-born poet living in New York, published another account of an ecstatic crossing of Brooklyn Bridge. "Atlantis" concludes *The Bridge* (1930), an epic poem in eight sections based on the belief that this very bridge encapsulated and fused physical and spiritual aspects of what the United States had given to the great word "America." The bridge crossing in "Atlantis" has so little similarity to Standing Bear's memory that to speak of both in the same breath may seem willfully incongruous, yet the two accounts mirror and enhance each other in unexpected ways. Standing Bear's writing is plain and straightforward (or so it seems at first), while Crane's is rhapsodic and dense with bursting metaphors of music, light, and motion.

> Through the bound cable strands, the arching path
> Upward, veering with light, the flight of strings,—
> Taut miles of shuttling moonlight syncopate
> The whispered rush, telepathy of wires,
> Up the index of night, granite and steel—
> Transparent meshes—fleckless the gleaming staves—
> Sibylline voice flicker, waveringly stream
> As if a god were issue of the strings. . . .

The walker has ears and eyes open for a message, something he wants from the bridge, as if it embodies sacral voices that might reveal what the dance through the history of the nation in the previous sections means and foretells: the bridge as "cipher-script of time," "multitudinous Verb," "pervasive Paradigm, "steeled Cognizance."[3]

In an earlier section, "Powhatan's Daughter," the poet awakens to a dream of Pocahontas. "The woman with us in the dawn" takes the poet by the hand, her smile leading him past shops and factories, "past the din and slogans of the year," into the countryside and aboriginal memory, "your blood remembering its first invasion of her secrecy, its first encounters with her kin, her chieftain, lover . . . his shade that haunts the lakes and hills." A canoe takes him deeper into the Appalachian woods, "within some boding shade" where he hears "the long moan of a dance" and joins himself with Maquokeeta burning at a stake: "Spears and assemblies: black drums thrusting on—"

> Dance, Maquokeeta! snake that lives before,
> That casts his pelt, and lives beyond! Sprout, horn!
> Speak, tooth! Medicine-man, relent. Restore—
> Lie to us,—dance us back the tribal morn!

The flaming dance restores the poet's vision promised by the smile of Pocahontas. He can now *see* Maquokeeta "kiss that destiny" and accept his perennial fate, "blent / At last with all that's consummate and free." In his identity with the aboriginal figure consumed at the stake, the modern poet tortured with history frees himself for visionary experience. This tormented dance begins the walk toward freedom from the torment of history that is to be consummated on the Brooklyn Bridge.

"The Dance" concludes with a "strong prayer" folded in the arms of the resurrected shade: "The serpent with the eagle in the boughs." The same figures are resurrected at the conclusion of "Atlantis," the terminus of the poet's crossing over. While at the end the promised transcendence seems uncertain—"Is it Cathay . . . ? / Whispers antiphonal in azure swing"—the walker experiences the crossing, like the paces through time enacted in the entire poem, as a recovery of the sacrificial Indian dance. "Through smoking pyres of love and death, / Searches the timeless laugh of mythic spears," he hears drums, feels the bridge "bearing corn," likens the sought-for experience of an "Everpresence, beyond time" to "spears ensanguined of one tolling star," and in the very end has a vision recalled from "The Dance," of rainbows ringing "the serpent with the eagle in the leaves," majestic Indian symbols for space and time fused in love.[4] It's not that Crane's crossing is an Indian experience—neither Crane nor Standing Bear, incidentally, comments on the fact that Iroquois high walkers probably helped build the structure[5]—but that the kinetic ecstasy of walking across the bridge, straining after continuity, coherence, and mystic oneness, returns him to Indian country.

Standing Bear's memory of the Brooklyn Bridge interests us not just because it is about something that once happened, but because it is something put down and thus reinvented in writing; what the author made of the recounted event matters more than the event itself. As speaker after speaker proclaimed, the ceremonies that day marked a milestone for the nation, an inauguration of America's modern era, a new world of progress, triumphant industrial and military power, and national unity from sea to sea. The Great Bridge, with its massive stone towers and spidery steel cables, epitomized the nation's leaping over rivers and hills, tunneling under mountains, stretching itself toward the immense natural wealth of the Great Plains (home of many of the Carlisle students); it bespoke a nation of diverse parts linked together in perpetuity by bands of steel, a *Pax Americana* of the national territory. How apt, then, that a *"real American band"* of pacified and transformed Indians, sons and daughters of once hostile savages now in short hair and fresh uniforms, should partake of the nation's self-congratulatory festivities. As he told the story some forty-five years later, there seemed no doubt that Standing Bear and his mates lent themselves to the event with sincere enthusiasm. If they felt any grudge against this massive symbol of their dispossession, it does not show openly in Standing Bear's text.

But what are the italicized words, *"real American band,"* if not a smile and a nod in the direction of irony? Speechmakers that day hailed the word "American" as synonym for progress, power, and triumph over space and time. Standing Bear responded by seeming to acquiesce; he "kept playing all the way across the great structure" and doubtless believed it *was* great. But what does *"real American band"* signify if not that there still remained a contest over what the word "American" meant?

Chief Standing Bear's autobiographical narrative, *My People the Sioux* (1928), was one of four books of his that were published between 1928 and 1934, when he was in his early sixties.[6] In 1905, he had been selected by tribal elders to replace his deceased father as chief of his band of Oglala Sioux, and he had worked since 1912 as a consultant and actor in Hollywood, and also as a lecturer and performer of Indian songs, dances, and stories. Repeatedly in his books, Standing Bear used figures of bridging, of crossing over and rising above. Bridging was sometimes literal, but usually rhetorical, rising above or transcending an intervening gulf.

A *"real American band"* was a uniformed brass band of, to all appearances, "reformed Indians." But as Standing Bear revealed, it was also a band in a "real American" sense: a unit of native society, a formal structure unified for a social purpose. In the Lakota lexicon, "band" is a category of indigenous social organization based on intricate kinship relations and obligations, "a scheme of life that worked" as another Lakota writer, Ella Deloria, wrote in 1944.[7] In *Land of the Spotted Eagle* (1933), Standing Bear put "band," or the Lakota word *Tiyospaye*, at the center of his discussion of Sioux "civil arrangements." The nation or people as a whole was known in Lakota as *Oyate*, he explained, which consisted of many *Tiyospaye*, many bands, themselves consisting of as many as a hundred or more, or as few as thirty, distinct families. Indeed, the word *Tiyospaye* might be understood as meaning those ties of affection and obligation typical of native families. *Tiyospaye* or "band" meant more than a unit of social organization; it meant a repository of communal values, a place or site for the preservation and reproduction of values, the customs and expectations that gave the *Oyate* its distinctive character, what might be translated into Western terms as its *national* ideals. The marching band was a *"real American band,"* Standing Bear implied, once you recognized how it evokes, by contrast and by irony, *Tioyspaye*.

> The bands were governed, as were individuals, families, and the nation, by ancient and traditional customs. And these customs which had through many years of time, become established in the minds of the people, were based upon human and individual needs. The central aim of the Lakota code was to bring ease and comfort in equal measure to all. There were no weak and no strong individuals from the standpoint of pos-

sessing human rights. It was every person's duty to see that the right of every other person to eat and be clothed was respected and there was no more question about it than there was about the free and ungoverned use of sunshine, pure air, and the rains with which they bathed their bodies. There were no groups of strength allied against groups of those weak in power.[8]

This account of how the principle of equality and solidarity pervaded a *"real American band"* seems barbed with commentary on the state of affairs in the United States, on the images of hungry children, haggard women, and homeless men that made up the Great Depression. And the presence of a *"real American band"* at the celebration in 1883 of social "progress" in the material form of the Brooklyn Bridge implied a similar demurral. The social critic Henry George had asked why a society that could erect such an inspiring structure could also fail to eliminate poverty, poverty that seemed indeed to increase in direct ratio of the accumulation of wealth.[9] Standing Bear's implicit challenge was to ask whether the civilization into which the Carlisle school inducted its charges denied *Tiyospaye*, the *"real American band."* One reviewer in 1933 remarked approvingly about Standing Bear, "The great lack he senses in modern civilization is the lack of a social conscience. And, certainly, in that respect the old-time Sioux were moral giants as compared with the white men of our day."[10]

Was Standing Bear in 1883 traveling under a false flag as a reformed savage, marching smartly and keeping his own counsel? Or was his disguise a crafted irony, a way of mocking prevailing stereotypes of "savage" and "civilized," inverting the terms and undermining the credulity of those nonnatives who took themselves to be "real" Americans? Standing Bear wore with pride his achievements in white society. He paraded his education as the real thing; or, let us say, he played it as one of the roles through which he defied and undercut the stereotypes. In *Land of the Spotted Eagle*, the question of what is truly American and how Indians stand vis-à-vis that category, of how indigenous and nonindigenous people relate respectively to what is "real" and "true" in the name *American*, is the focal center.

After the Citizenship Act of 1924, the real "first Americans" no longer had to prove "competence," only birth in the United States to win the privileges of citizenship. Of course about two-thirds of the Indian population were citizens by means of allotment or treaty or special statute, and many natives and their supporters thought the birthright act only another charade, a political maneuver to keep the real disabilities of reservation life intact, the ambiguities and anomalies of tribal membership and tribal sovereignty within the federal system unresolved. Not only did Indians remain wards of the state, but the federal state steadily expanded its domain of control over the tribes. The 1924 act only underscored how incommensurate with genuine self-determination a mere certificate of citizenship is. The act had more symbolic resonance than positive effect on the lives of natives, though Standing Bear made the best of the symbol nevertheless. Frederick Jackson Turner's vision of an original Indian identity within the term "American" had passed over into the Wanamaker spectacle of Indians raising the flag and pledging allegiance, a visual resource for Americanization.

In the same decade, other symbols arose: Indians as Americans not in the sense implied by the flag but in the sense of original inhabitants of the land. In a setting of heightened awareness of "the race problem," the hardening of lines between white and black, and alarm about immigrants and "mongrelization," a number of artists, writers, and ethnographers undertook a quest, especially in the Southwest, for "the aboriginal" as ground for a renewed national culture. The painter Marsden Hartley in his essay "The Red Man" (1921) called the ceremonial arts of dance, song, and drama in the Southwest "the only esthetic representative of our great country up to the present hour" and wrote of the "red man" as a "gift." "As Americans we should accept the one American genius we possess, with genuine alacrity. We have upon our own soil something to show the world as our own, while it lives."[11] Hartley's pronouns impose themselves as white possession of red culture, unconsciously placing natives as outside the "we" and thus "other," objects of "our" enthralled attention. It's a pronomial sleight-of-hand, D. H. Lawrence might have said, to deny the gulf between white men and red, between Europeans and the "great spirit of place" of the American continent, a too easy way of accomplishing the difficult act of freeing oneself from "the old parenthood of Europe" by identification with a half-understood culture (not to diminish Hartley's sensitivity to gesture and movement; it was genuine).

The words are from Lawrence's hypnotic hectoring of American writers for their ambivalence and evasiveness in *Studies in Classic American Literature* (1923). He gave the European perspective of an artist angry at the godless materialism of modern societies, who in New Mexico had himself fallen under the spell of the corn dance and snake dance on the dusty plazas of Indian villages. Seek "the deepest self," he advised American artists, "the dusky body of IT," and recognize the risks to the "conscious American motive" when you undertake the dark search for renewal within. Elsewhere he wrote, "There lies the real continuity, not between Europe and the new States, but between the murdered Red America and the seething White America."[12] Lawrence mixed his rapture at the corn, snake, and eagle dances he witnessed in various pueblos and Hopi villages with scorn for the hundreds of white Americans who crawled up rutted hillsides in black motor cars and squatted or stood or leaned on ancient mud-packed walls and rooftops in hot plazas, feeling entertained.[13]

One difference between Lawrence's essays on Indian dances and Hartley's—the two are often compared—is that the English writer, while advising Americans to "take up life where the Red Indian . . . left it off," was unconcerned with nationality. It wasn't the *American* genius of the dances that moved him but their animism, the mystery not so much of oneness with earth and sky and everything alive (including inanimate nature like rocks) but of ritual participation in the processes of life. "White people always, or nearly always, write sentimentality about the Indian," but between "the Indian way of consciousness" and the white way "there is no bridge, no canal of connection"; "we can understand the consciousness of the Indian only in terms of the death of our consciousness."[14]

Lawrence's insight leaves Americans seeking alternative grounds for a renewed sense of cultural nationality either with the blood hatred of Frost's miller, or at a distance respectful enough to "have a little Ghost inside you which sees both ways, or even many ways."[15] Or an American can take the native way as the ground for faulting the modern way and identifying its falsities. In "Culture Genuine and Spurious," the anthropologist Edward Sapir wrote about the same time that "the American Indian who solves the economic problem with salmon-spear and rabbit-snare" stood for a vastly superior way of life than "the telephone girl" who devoted "the greater part of the living day, to the manipulation of a technical routine . . . that answers to no spiritual need of her own."[16] Robert Flaherty's celebrated film, *Nanook of the North* (1922), underscored the point: The spearfishing Indian had more to teach us than we had to teach him.

Seeking "a source in AMERICA for everything we think or do," William Carlos Williams wrote in *In the American Grain* (1925), "I do believe the average American to be an Indian, but an Indian robbed of his world." "There *is* the Indian. We are none. Who are we? Degraded whites riding our fears to market where everything is by accident and only one thing sure: the fatter we get the duller we grow." For Williams, one man who escaped the stranglehold of puritanism was exemplary: Daniel Boone, a "great voluptuary" who "with the sense of an Indian" felt the ecstasy of "the wild beauty of the New World." "To Boone the Indian was his greatest master. Not for himself surely to be an Indian, though they eagerly sought to adopt him into their tribes, but the reverse: to be himself in a new world, Indianlike."[17] Compare this with Mary Austin, who in *The American Rhythm* (1923) said that when she heard those drums and beating feet, she "at times succeeded in being an Indian." Lawrence ridiculed her pretension.[18]

A literal fiction of "being Indian" is exactly what *American Indian Life by Several of Its Students*, edited in 1922 by the anthropologist Elsie Clews Parsons, declared as its purpose. The volume collected twenty-seven brief pieces by some of the best-known figures in American ethnography, each contribution an effort on the part of the "student" to write an account of some small aspect of the culture he or she studied as if from the perspective of an indigenous member of that culture: "A Crow Woman's Tale" by Robert Lowie, "Little-Wolf Joins the Medicine Lodge" by Alanson Skinner, "Sayach'apis, A Nootka Trader" by Edward Sapir, "An Eskimo Winter" by Franz Boas. The aim, Parsons explained, was to disregard "the white man's traditions about Indians" and write as if from inside the particular native culture and mentality, out of the "commonsense" of that culture. Quite apart from the challenge to write "popular" anthropology, the scheme had the more difficult task of being an experiment in self-abandonment. "Each author has adhered strictly to the social facts as he knew them," wrote A. L. Kroeber in his introduction. "He [sic] has merely selected those that seemed most characteristic, and woven them into a plot around an imaginary Indian hero or heroine. The method is that of the historical novel, with emphasis on the history rather than the romance." Less sanguine, Parsons remarks that "few, if any of us, succeed, in describing another culture, of ridding ourselves of our own cultural bias or habits of mind. Much of our anthropological work, to quote a letter from Spinden, 'is not so much definitive science as it is a cultural trait of ourselves.'" Not even the mantle of "science" grants immunity from the dream of "being Indian," in place of learning from natives other ways of being American.[19]

Virtually alone among writers and intellectuals, Jean Toomer challenged the very basis of defining persons by race. Author of *Cane* (1923), an intense meditation in lyrical prose and poetry on the realities of race consciousness in the rural South and in Northern cities, Toomer objected to the label "Negro writer." "Racially," he wrote in 1922, "I seem to have (who knows for sure) seven blood mixtures: French, Dutch, Welsh, Negro, German, Jewish, and Indian." He "lived equally amid the two race groups. Now white, now colored. From my own point of view I am naturally and inevitably an American." In 1925 and again in later years, he visited New Mexico, not in conscious search for that part of himself that was Indian, but among the Indians he found something there akin to his own questing spirit that did not need words to be recognized: "a penetration deep under the skin." "The Indians have developed, as far as their religious experiences and views are concerned, an effective non-violent resistance. It is a wall of silence which cannot be penetrated by outsiders. It just stops you, without hurting you, without making you angry or arousing the desire to force through it." In this silence Toomer found a deep ground for something new, a composite race, "neither white nor black nor red nor brown," the old terms that must be "discarded." He called the new race "the American race" and identified it with the human race. The new Americans will be not of America alone but "of the earth."[20]

In "Taos Night" (1935), he wrote:

> The night, the mountain, the pueblo, the silent men—all seem simply to have come into being . . . being by birth . . . created but not labored—the night from all preceding nights, the mountain from the ample earth, the pueblo from all dwellings back to the cliffs, the men from all the people of their race.
>
> It is quiet. In this silence, repose and intensity co-exist.
>
> Then comes a call, human, but like a high bark.
>
> Several robed figures emerge from the houses, pass across the plaza, and exchange greetings—"Hé-ah-ho." The voices are those of men.
>
> The men gather at a bridge over the stream.
>
> Pause. Silence.
>
> Then suddenly a Taos song. Another song and another.
>
> Then silence again . . . and life becomes existence again . . . and existence, focused for a time in a group of singing men, expands to the mountain and the close stars.

New Mexico spoke to him profoundly, not to an Indian part of him but to the part that sought to move beyond racial categories toward the universal meaning of the name American: people of all the earth in the purity of their humanity. New Mexico had a hold upon his heart, he wrote, "as home."[21]

Having lived the history cryptically inscribed in the modernist quest for origins, Luther Standing Bear at the end of the 1920s sat down in Hollywood, where he had lived and worked for almost twenty years, to reflect on his life. "I grew up leading the traditional life of my people," he wrote in *Land of the Spotted Eagle*, "learning the crafts of hunter, scout, and warrior from father, kindness to the old and feeble from mother, respect for wisdom and council from our wise men, and was trained by grandfather and older boys in the devotional rites to the Great Mystery." His book had as its subject the continuing lessons of that upbringing both for himself and for his non-Indian readers, lessons that worked steadily, he wrote, "toward humaneness instead of away from it."²² Humaneness and its cognate, humanness, were shown as defining virtues of Sioux culture, and they defined a lack in the dominating culture of Euro-America. In spelling out the message from traditional Sioux life to the United States—a translation of Sioux oral culture and communality into the middle ground of print— Standing Bear placed himself as if on a bridge between two worlds: hence the book's power as an Indian word and its complexity as an American text. It is especially American in the way it used cultural translation to braid together two worlds, two discourses, and two genres of utterance in a hybrid narrative that aimed both to elucidate its subject and to transfigure it.

Nurtured in the "ancestral life" of the Lakota Sioux in South Dakota, Standing Bear portrayed a warm, reliable, *gemeinschaftlich* world that was instilled with pedagogies of kinship, certainty of gender roles, and devotional rites. A rupture occurred at age eleven, when "Ota Kte or Plenty Kills, son of Standing Bear" (his birth name) was put on a train and transported to distant Pennsylvania, where he found himself among other bewildered and frightened native children in the inaugurating class of the Carlisle Indian School. "Soon we came to a big gate in a great high wall. The gate was locked, but after quite a long wait, it was unlocked and we marched through it. I was the first boy inside."²³ The trauma of the nightmarish journey returned, the key event of his life, an open wound to which he returned, around which he sang and danced, and out of which he fashioned a new identity as a bridge crossing antithetical worlds: as if the wound itself gave warrant of compensation or recompense, casting loss as sacrifice, marking loss as gain. "At once I was thrust into an alien world, into an environment as different from the one into which I had been born as it is possible to imagine, to remake myself, if I could, into the likeness of the invader."²⁴

Carlisle conceived of this process as a kind of resurrection: "Kill the Indian and save the man," as Pratt pithily declared the school's purpose. Once freed of their native beliefs, manners, language, and religion, and instructed to respect education, discipline, property, and Christianity, Indians were eminently redeemable, Pratt promised his philanthropic backers. Standing Bear recalled how the school went about fostering redemption. "It began with clothes," the blanket giv-

Unidentified photographer, "Chief Standing Bear the Elder Visiting His Son at Carlisle." *Land of the Spotted Eagle*, 1933.

ing way to trousers and stiff-bosomed shirts and the moccasin to stiff leather boots. Then the names went. Ota Kte became Luther when he touched with a pointer a set of characters he could not read or sound out on a blackboard, "as if I were about to touch an enemy."[25] Then came lessons in how to sit at table and eat boiled food, how to breathe and sleep in wooden barracks. Nearly half of the children from the Plains died in the first three years of the school's existence, casualties in one of the nation's earliest culture wars.

About the system of inscribing "the likeness of the invader" on bodies and minds, Standing Bear wrote:

> So we went to school to copy, to imitate; not to exchange languages and ideas, and not to develop the best traits that had come out of uncountable experiences of hundreds and thousands of years living upon this continent. Our annals, all happenings of human importance, were stored in our song and dance rituals, our history differing in that it was not stored in books, but in living memory. So, while the white people had much to teach us, we had much to teach them, and what a school could have been established upon that idea![26]

We can see Standing Bear's strategy here, to bring certain key terms into focus—school, teach, memory—in order to defamiliarize their Carlisle meanings through contrast: Lakota regard for "living memory" over training by rote and coercive discipline. The opposing Lakota system began with the senses; "half-dormant senses mean half living." "Every natural object was watched for any significance attached to its motion or appearance." In place of books, "stories were the libraries of our people." "A people enrich their minds who keep their history on the leaves of memory," he added, drawing a pun into a telling strike: "countless leaves in countless books have robbed a people of both history and memory."[27] Verbal play and indirection characterize Standing Bear's adaptation into English of Sioux methods of verbal combat; he scored his point about the Carlisle method askance, as it were, and all the more pointed.

We also hear in Standing Bear's critique a familiar American ethnic melody of lament. Why must we give up something of ourselves in order to win recognition as a qualified member of the country? Standing Bear's perception of the irony of acculturation, the real loss entailed for the sake of imagined gain, belongs to the pathos of American ethnic writing as a whole. Being Indian, his case is more extreme and more painfully ironic, for the cultural losses included losses of land, freedom of movement, and tribal autonomy and the individual rights it assured. The Carlisle discipline of imitation was experienced by those subject to it as an analog to the military violence directed at natives as a matter of course. Within this horizon, Standing Bear's contrast of "living memory" as against the "mechanical devices" of the Carlisle schooling heightened the familiar pathos of ethnic loss.

Moreover, he lamented not only the stripping away of tribal name and custom but just as keenly the missed chance for an alternative kind of school, a place of mutual instruction arising from mutual respect for cultural difference—a place, in short, of equality. His words, "while the white people had much to teach us, we had much to teach them," echo W.E.B. Du Bois's familiar words in *The Souls of Black Folk* (1903): "work, culture, liberty,—all these we need, not singly but together, not successively but together, each growing and aiding each, and all striving toward the vaster ideal that swims before the Negro people, the ideal of human brotherhood."[28] Du Bois and Standing Bear shared a vision of equality achieved by mutual teaching across the divide of cultural difference. They wanted not a separation of politics and culture but the achievement of a new realm of culture and a new heterogeneous theory of nationality.

Standing Bear's story was in the mode less of lament than of defiance, however, defiance in the style of verbal cunning. In many ways his career had been a triumphant one. At Carlisle he learned tinsmithing (which was useless when he returned to his reservation), played the cornet in the marching band, and cultivated habits of neatness and soft-spoken politeness. Chosen by Pratt for an apprenticeship at the Wanamaker Department Store in Philadelphia, he deciphered the mysteries of the retail trade and after Carlisle tried his hand at storekeeping, teaching school, preaching (he had converted to Christianity), and ranching. Like many of his fellow Sioux males, including

Black Elk, he traveled overseas with the Buffalo Bill Wild West Show and as a "show Indian" was recruited in 1912 by the Hollywood producer Thomas Ince as consultant and actor in westerns.[29]

Almost two decades later, as if reborn into yet another identity, Standing Bear emerged as a writer, with his four books aimed at correcting false views of Indian life, each an account in a different genre (memoir, ethnography, stories for youngsters) of traditional Lakota culture. Unlike his Sioux peers with boarding school experience, Charles Eastman and Gertrude Bonnin, and without benefit of further schooling, Standing Bear came to authorship late in life and by an unexpected route. His books were issued by Houghton Mifflin, the prominent Boston publishing house that counted Longfellow among its featured authors and kept *The Song of Hiawatha* perpetually in print. His Hollywood colleague and honorary Indian, William S. Hart of "cowboy-and-Indian" fame, wrote a preface to *My People the Sioux*, and it as well as the others were mentioned favorably in *The New Republic*, *The Nation*, and *The Saturday Review* by prominent critics such as Van Wyck Brooks, Mark Van Doren, and R. L. Duffus.[30] In 1931, H. L. Mencken's *American Mercury* published his article "The Tragedy of the Sioux," an angry account of the wretched conditions he found on his first visit back to his birthplace after sixteen years. He had left the reservation because "I was a bad Indian, and the agent and I never got on. I remained a hostile, even a savage, if you please. And still I am." The essay concluded with a pledge: As long as "my people . . . are not free . . . I shall never cease to be a hostile, a savage, if you please."[31]

About the craft of his books critics have only recently had much to say, beyond comments about his plain speaking and "naïve" style. His two best-known books, the autobiographical *My People the Sioux* and *Land of the Spotted Eagle* (often described misleadingly as an "ethnology"), are taken principally as sources of information about his life and views, while *My Indian Boyhood* and *Stories of the Sioux* are set aside as children's books, though their storytelling persona may be his most artful and truest, his most lucid and subtle voice, transforming the oral into the written with disarming directness. In the two major books Standing Bear acknowledged the help of collaborators. For

Unidentified photographer. Chief Standing Bear, possibly Luther Standing Bear, c. 1919. (Library of Congress)

Land of the Spotted Eagle he credited his niece as a virtual muse who gave him a second voice: "when I speak she fully understands." All his books can be described as hybrid productions, each one testing several kinds of writing, often alternating between modes in the same text, a kind of shape-shifting from narrative to exposition to polemic and exhortation, with a pull between oral and written conventions throughout. But the most important aspect of these late-blooming works was their creation of a persona, Chief Standing Bear, a figure who stepped from behind the veil to reveal hidden truths about native America to white readers. While recalling a personal and collective past, while consolidating cultural memory, Standing Bear also spoke as a go-between or translator, pointing a way across the chasm of ignorance and remembered violence.

"Outwardly," Standing Bear wrote in *My People the Sioux*, "I lived the life of the white man, yet all the while I kept in direct contact with tribal life. While I had learned all that I could of the white man's culture, I never forgot that of my people. I kept the language, tribal manners and usages, sang the songs and danced the dances."[32] Taking on "the likeness of the invader" as something outward, in his writings he remained "hostile," inwardly defiant. He was, after all, a "standing bear" or Mato Najin, who rises up when wounded, "who will stand and fight to the last."[33] And it's the verbal form of his defiance that makes Standing Bear so vitally important as a writer.

Standing Bear fell back on the verbal strength of traditional oral culture, Ruth Heflin and Penelope Kelsey have recently shown, incorporating genres of Sioux narrative and dialogue (naming stories, boasting self-narration, and pictographic sketches) to assert "living memory" over book knowledge and to show how a new "school," a middle ground of cultural exchange, might be achieved.[34] Bridging the rift between outward and inward life is the fundamental act his books perform. Hence the underlying figure of a bridge, and hence, too, the prominence of the term "American." The Indian blanket or buffalo robe appears as "a true American garment," "worn with the significance of language"; it covers beneath it "one of the bravest attempts ever made by man on this continent to rise to the heights of true humanity."

Although he left legible traces in many records—his credits in numerous films, for example, in which he played alongside the likes of Tim McCoy, Douglas Fairbanks, and William S. Hart—most of what we know of Standing Bear comes from his own pen, though he continued in the movie industry and continued lecturing on Indian life and performing. He had already crafted another role for himself and an illustrated letterhead to go along with it: a photograph of "Chief Standing Bear of the Oglala Sioux" posing in full regalia under a banner blazoned with the words "An Official Sioux Authority." The same image reappeared as a frontispiece to *Land of the Spotted Eagle*. Ever the "show Indian" in the performance of himself as warrior, hunter, or tribal chief, Standing Bear as author donned the role of a post-Indian warrior of survivance, in the Ashinaabe writer Gerald Vizenor's terms, one who encounters the enemy "with the same courage in literature as their ancestors once evinced on horses."[35] And not just courage but also skill. We need to see just how crafty Standing Bear was, with what trickster shrewdness he went about the business of authorship. It was as Chief Standing Bear that he wrote his works, though it was as Luther Standing Bear that he copyrighted them; the nexus between the two names is a story in itself. Recent editors and publishers have silently replaced Chief with Luther, the Anglo-Saxon name tagged on him at the Carlisle School. But it's important to remember that that was the original persona he chose.

I say persona, for Standing Bear seems never in fact to have performed the role of chief except rhetorically as lecturer, author, and "Official Sioux Authority," whenever he appeared in public as an authority who should be taken seriously. We can think of it as a symbolic act through which he demonstrated in writing what history had denied him the opportunity of realizing in fact: the virtues of male warrior and leader explaining his people's way of life and defending their interests. Yet behind the guise, or within it, he also remained Luther Standing Bear. In *My People the Sioux,* photographs of him performing roles such as praying, hunting, and making a speech reveal a well-honed cunning of self-imposture.

Standing Bear's account of his selection and induction as chief in Chapter 25 of *My People the Sioux*, "I am Made Chief"—the cere-

Clyde W. Champion.
(*left*) "The Hunter,"
posed by Chief Standing
Bear. (*below left*)
"Praying to the Great
Spirit Through the Pipe
of Peace," posed by
Chief Standing Bear.
(*below right*) "Chief
Standing Bear Making a
Speech." *My People the
Sioux*, 1928.

mony was elaborate, with dance and song and a giveaway before thousands of people—has several revealing features. By 1905, Sioux traditions survived in altered ways. Traditionally (here I draw on the work of the French anthropologist Pierre Clastres in his *Society Against the State*), Indian societies existed without the overarching and centralized power of a state. Chiefs were without what Western societies understand as power. In societies without writing, without metal tools and weapons, and without surpluses of food and goods—in short, without social classes—power or violence from above was precisely to be avoided and protected against. The chieftaincy was designed by the culture in such a way as to prevent the separation of power from society. Chiefs were bound in dependency (thus impotency) upon the society itself, constrained by certain immutable obligations: to be a peacemaking or moderating agency, to be generous with possessions, to speak well. The chief was known as a "master of speech . . . speech is the only power with which the chief is vested."[36] It's the obligation to speak with skill that is crucial to understanding how Standing Bear's writings—transposing speech into print—fulfill a chiefly obligation.

"A chief receives no salary," Standing Bear explains, "and at gatherings it is up to him to see that everything is done properly." He is obliged to represent the tribe in dealings with the authorities in Washington, to help his people in every way, and to share his wealth. "I was expected to give something away on this occasion," and he did, "about a thousand dollars' worth of goods." "It is a great honor to receive the title of 'Chief,'" he explained, "but there is much hard work about it also."[37]

"As the purveyor of wealth and messages," Clastres has written, "the chief conveys nothing but his dependence on the group."[38] Standing Bear expressed exactly this understanding of the office when he dedicated his books to the cause of his people's culture and welfare. He pledged to "do all in my power to help my people at all times, regardless of where I might be."[39] His books fulfill his chiefly obligation, he implied, though in a different manner of fulfillment from that of his father, who dwelled as chief among his people: His was a symbolic fulfillment of obligation without the "hard work" that dwelling with the band entailed. He acknowledged of this anomaly: "the title of 'Chief' is now right and proper for me to use, whether in California or in any other part of the United States; and my people know that as long as I live I will do what is right and proper for them."[40]

Discovering in his dealings with the resident Indian agent on his reservation that, chief or not, he was "only a helpless Indian," Standing Bear resolved to leave the reservation, to take up his allotment, and to petition for citizenship so that he could be "a free man—free to come and free to go." Freedom now was not a Sioux condition but a legal status bestowed by the national state, the same state that appointed the Indian agents to rule the reservations and that made the Indians feel unfree on their own land. Citizenship made him free in the modern American sense. Being made chief had been "a great moment; but when I got my freedom from the iron hand of Brennan, the Indian agent at my reservation, I began to feel that I had been raised higher than a chieftainship."[41]

U.S. citizenship freed him, we might say, to resume being Sioux in ways that the reservation system, enforced by the same state that granted him citizenship, denied. As Chief Standing Bear *and* U.S. citizen, no longer chief of his band in the traditional sense, he was a cultural mediator, standing between and looking and talking both ways. Standing Bear's songs and dances, along with his classes in sign language, were a featured attraction at Saturday morning powwows at the Southwest Museum in Los Angeles for "boys and girls . . . eager to hear and know more about Indians." In a 1928 issue of the museum journal, *The Masterkey*, his portrait appeared on the cover, a photograph of him in skins and feathers standing by the museum's Blackfoot tepee, a drum in hand and his long-braided niece and collaborator, Wahcaziwin, at his side. When he died in 1939 at the age of sixty-nine, the *Los Angeles Times* evoked another image of a bridge: "for more than fifty years [he had] been a sturdy link between the past and present of Indian lore and tradition."[42] His turn to authorship in the 1920s was his most heroic effort at bridge building, at standing between not just the Indian past and present but also between Indian and white worlds.

Standing Bear's assumed public literary identity as Chief Standing Bear drew on Carlisle experiences with the wider world that called itself America, experiences like leading the Carlisle band across the Brooklyn Bridge. It was after this event that Standing Bear was sent as

The Masterkey

Vol. 1   *February, 1928*   *No. 7*

Chief Standing Bear and Westewin, his niece, before the Blackfoot tipi in the Southwest Museum (Powell Press Service photo)

Powell Press Service, "Chief Standing Bear and Westewin, His Niece." *The Masterkey,* February 1928.

an apprentice to the Wanamaker store, another signal passage in his education in what his father called "the white man's way." "My boy," Pratt had told him, "you are going away from us to work for this school, in fact, for your whole race. Go, and do your best." Pratt's language echoed Horatio Alger and Booker T. Washington: "'If John Wanamaker gives you the job of blacking his shoes, see that you make them shine. Then he will give you a better job.'" Standing Bear recalled that he felt burdened by the weight of the charge, "to try and lift up a race of people before another race that had tried to hold us down . . . I was to prove to all people that the Indians could learn and work as well as the white people; to prove that Carlisle School was the best place for the Indian boy."[43]

And he succeeded. First he proved himself in the invoice department of the store, where "it was quite necessary to be quick and accurate" as he checked off goods by name and by "the cost price and the selling price"; later he was entrusted with putting price labels on jewelry, and then he was elevated to entry clerk in the bookkeeping department. This initiation into the double-entry mysteries of merchant capitalism was an enormous leap into modernity for a teenage boy who three years earlier had been riding wild on the Plains under the name of Plenty Kills. Once, Pratt brought the entire school to visit the Wanamaker store and the august John Wanamaker himself summoned Standing Bear to the stage and anointed him with praise; the merchant king told the audience that Standing Bear, who had been "promoted from one department to another, every month getting better work and more money," was the only employee he had ever promoted so rapidly, which made Captain Pratt "very proud of me," Standing Bear wrote decades later.[44]

Horatio Alger, but not quite. The young Sioux would have continued to work at Wanamaker's, but he couldn't find the right place to board in Philadelphia. Whenever a suitable place came up, "the people discovered my nationality, they would look at me in a surprised sort of way, and say that they had no place for an Indian boy." "My nationality," Standing Bear wrote interestingly, not "my race." And "Indian boy," the surprised landlords said, not Lakota or Oglala Sioux, which would have been the proper name for his nation and band. The

Wanamaker experience, which taught him how goods became commodities in the merchandising system of "the white man's way," concluded Standing Bear's Eastern education. "So I said farewell to the school life, and started back to my people, but with a better understanding of life." Like other Indians before and after who grasped the fatal danger that white civilization represented for their own traditional civilization, Standing Bear had witnessed the stark, mind-splitting differences between old and new, between the America of the *Tiyospaye* and the America of the big-city department store. "There would be no more hunting—we would have to work now for our food and clothing. It was like the Garden of Eden after the fall of man."[45] The Judeo-Christian myth of the garden was a point of reference for his reckoning with the white man's way and a way of turning his revelation of difference back upon his white readers.

Standing Bear followed the white way, not as a faux white man but as a Sioux. Was this a manageable trick? Pratt didn't think so; he often spoke against the wish of his charges to live in doubleness: "Can two mental patterns, two sets of habits, two fundamentally antagonistic attitudes exist side by side in the same individual? The attempt may only tend toward spiritual disharmony and practical futility." He worried that tragedy awaits "the half-educated, consciously inadequate in both realms," and he condemned both anthropologists and showmen like Buffalo Bill for glorifying "the old life." "The reason given out for such performances is that they [Indians] should be taught to be proud of their race! Where is the profit to them or to us in forcing Indian youth to hold on to primitive ideas? . . . Why compel them to carry two loads—to become civilized, and at the same time to remain uncivilized?" Instead of this burdensome doubleness, they should think of "the man of another race who is able to appreciate and fully accept the culture surrounding him, [and] may, and sometimes does, retain an idealized and wistful fondness for the ancestral tradition—even if he has to learn it out of books!"[46]

Though living in two (at least) cultures at once was unimaginable to Pratt, it was exactly what Standing Bear and other natives of his generation such as the Sioux writers Charles Eastman and Gertrude Bonnin (Zitkala-Ša) practiced, in the first instance by writing books in

English. Standing Bear met the challenge of making the coexistence of "civilized" and "uncivilized" imaginable, by subverting the distinction.[47] How might a Sioux walk on the path of the white man and yet remain a Sioux? Standing Bear managed the trick by deploying a rhetoric of tricks, bridging two worlds by means of irony.

In this oft-cited passage from *Land of the Spotted Eagle*, Standing Bear deployed quotation marks to bring certain common terms in the lexicon of white culture into a new perspective:

> We did not think of the great open plains, the beautiful rolling hills, and winding streams with tangled growth, as "wild." Only to the white man was nature a "wilderness" and only to him was the land "infested" with "wild" animals and "savage" people. To us it was tame. Earth was bountiful and we were surrounded with the blessings of the Great Mystery. Not until the hairy man from the east came and with brutal frenzy heaped injustices upon us and the families we loved was it "wild" for us. When the very animals of the forest began fleeing from his approach, then it was that for us the "Wild West" began.[48]

The words ring with the spirit of reverence for what was and with defiance of what is. As he explained in his preface, "In this book, I attempt to tell my readers just how we lived as Lakotas—our customs, manners, experiences, and traditions—the things that make all men what they are." In one sentence, he wrote in the present—"I attempt"—about an entire system of belief and behavior that was in the past—"how we lived." Such a sentence is the simplest link between past and present, and it is a link implying a future, the future of the act of reading, in which recollection can be realized as imaginative experience. Pastness becomes a living presence in the imagination of readers.

And it does this dialectically, in a process of opposition. For the pastness Standing Bear wrote about had been misrepresented in other texts, by which the minds of white readers had presumably been influenced. He referred to the "popular conception," the idea in "the Caucasian mind," of "the native American as a savage." And because he thought of the Indian as "savage," the word became flesh in the form of behavior: "From the Indian the white man stands off and aloof, scarcely deigning to speak or to touch his hand in human fellowship." Standing Bear intended to overcome this, to correct the representation and the behavior that flowed from it. The revisionist task was set forth explicitly: "To the white man many things done by the Indian are inexplicable, though he continues to write much of the visible and exterior life with explanations that are more often than not erroneous. The inner life of the Indian is, of course, a closed book to the white man."[49]

This book was presented, then, as the opening of a closed book, as an account of the Indians' "inner life" that is naturally ("of course") closed, to "the white man." Standing Bear's racialized portrayal of the non-Indian as "white man" becomes more complicated, however. The preface itself included a generous acknowledgment of the help of "inestimable value" given by Melvin Gilmore, curator of ethnology at the University of Michigan, who refreshed the author's memory about plant life on the Plains. "Indian life has been enriched with fine and understanding white friends," and Standing Bear commended Gilmore for "his fidelity in portraying the Sioux people in his published works." This praise foreshadowed a crucial passage in the penultimate chapter, which countered Standing Bear's Carlisle experience with a proposal for a new kind of school (it might be the nation itself): "So, while white people had much to teach us, we had much to teach them, and what a school could have been established upon that idea!" Like "Indian" and "savage" and "Caucasian" and "American," "white man" was a term under scrutiny and subject with shifts in perspective to shifts in meaning.

It is likely that Standing Bear composed the preface to *Land of the Spotted Eagle* in response to a reader's report on the manuscript, then titled *My Life as a Lakota*. The report, written by the eminent ethnologist Frederick Webb Hodge in 1931 for the publisher that was considering the work, conceded that "there is much good in what the author has to say" but firmly disapproved of the author's judgments. In the same year, Hodge had written a warmly favorable review of Standing Bear's *My Indian Boyhood*, praising its lucid exposition of Lakota folkways, games, and rituals. About the new manuscript he wrote, "In his endeavor to show that his people are God's only perfect creation," Standing Bear "takes the Caucasian race to task, and blandly satisfies himself that it never had anything to contribute to Indian progress or culture." Urging that the author "confine himself to such knowledge as he has absorbed," he suggested that Standing Bear "translate himself into a historian rather than assume the role of special pleader. His comparisons with the white race are often ridiculous." It was clear, Hodge added, that "Standing Bear knows little or nothing of what has already been done toward recording the ethnology of the Indians, or the vast body of intimate information by trained students that has been accumulated."[50]

Hodge's opinions came as no surprise to Standing Bear. He wrote to the publisher, "As ever the white man is 'authority' for he has never been nor could he ever be less. And gentleman, you could not have procured a better 'authority' if you had walked into the Indian Bureau and asked for their most expert understudy." The "prejudicial attitude" Hodge displayed was "always the stamp of those of close association with museums and universities where knowledge is dehumanized." Standing Bear defended his use of comparison as fundamental to his method. "Mr. Hodge cries that my comparisons with the white people are ridiculous. I do use comparison freely because it is one of the best (if cruelest) ways of standing off and seeing ourselves as others see us. And has not the treatment of the Indian by the white man been ridiculous and even worse?"[51]

Comparison is another way of bridging, of crossing lines, and of shifting the perspective. It entails an elementary irony, a discrepancy between word and experience. What you call wild is really, as we know it, tame. Hidden in the simple ironic effect is an intricate process of transposition, a process that Kenneth Burke called "perspective by incongruity," in which renaming, or replacing a name in a different setting, reveals previously unrecognized truths about the name and its use—a kind of "verbal 'atom cracking.' "[52] It's a corrective act, often undertaken in a comic mode. Take the word "wild," test it against your experience of the world so named (the plains, the woods, the animals, the people), and a contradiction appears. How can the places and beings we experience as tame be called wild? The contradiction or incongruity opens a gap between word and world, between name and experience, a space for questioning, for turning ideas on their head. At stake is not just the aptness of a name but the fate of a people. Names, as Burke wrote, are "shorthand designations of certain fields and methods of action." Those who come to a place with the idea of wilderness come prepared to make a wilderness. The rapaciousness and inner frenzy (for land, for riches, for power) of the "hairy man from the east" is the actual source of wildness. It comes from within, from the absence of empathy and the capacity to breathe in harmony with the world. That capacity, the prerequisite for knowing the world and oneself in the world, was exactly what Standing Bear wanted to describe and thereby to recover and preserve.

A member of the last generation to have heard "the oral stories of their tribal families before the stories were translated," and of "the first [generation] to learn how to write about their remembrance and experiences,"[53] Standing Bear sets out in *Land of the Spotted Eagle* to counter the discourse of ethnology as a body of knowledge and as the "white" way of knowing (or trying to know) Indians. An Indian answer to salvage ethnology, it alludes to the ethnological categories such as child rearing, social organization, courtship, food, dress, and religious ceremony, but it was at odds with them, defied their "objectivity" and categorization, and deployed the method of renaming, of "perspective by incongruity," to show the Lakota way. The book wished to bring back to life a culture still vibrant with possibility and of integral value to the place called America, the supreme term to which Standing Bear applied his dialectic of transposition. In the final chapter, "What the Indian Means to America," he reaped the harvest of the new perspective: "The white man does not understand the Indian for the reason that he does not understand America. He is too far removed from its formative processes. The roots of his tree of life have not yet grasped the rock and soil . . . The man from Europe is still a foreigner and an alien. And he hates the man who questioned his path across the continent." And he concluded with his most audacious gambit of trickster guile, asking, "Why should not America be cognizant of itself, aware of its identity? . . . [I]t is now time for a destructive order to be reversed, and it is well to inform other races that the aboriginal culture of America was not devoid of beauty. Furthermore, in denying the Indian his ancestral rights and heritage, the white race is robbing itself. But America can be revived, rejuvenated, by recognizing a native school of thought. The Indian can save America."[54]

This was a nice twist on Pratt and Turner and Wanamaker, by which Standing Bear would have natives and strangers imaginatively changing place with each other in order to find a place in common, an "America" where having to do with each other is exactly what makes the place what it is. In the end *Land of the Spotted Eagle* revealed the full dimensions of its inner subject: not just the life of the Sioux but also the character and meaning of America itself. A chief deprived of his estate, Standing Bear pointed a way to a postwarrior role by converting the chief's traditional obligation-based authority into that of a messenger or teacher (another kind of chieftain) to America.

The shared vision with Du Bois's *Souls of Black Folk* needs to be reiterated. The "greater ideals of the American Republic," Du Bois had declared, provided a basis for the mutual coexistence of different cultures that had so much to offer to each other and to those ideals. "We the darker ones come even now not altogether empty-handed: there are to-day no truer exponents of the pure human spirit of the Declaration of Independence than the American Negroes; there is no true American music but the wild sweet melodies of the Negro slave; the American fairy tales and folk-lore are Indian and African; and, all in all, we black men seem the sole oasis of simple faith and reverence in a dusty desert of dollars and smartness."[55] Though the aims of their pleas for recognition differed in many ways, the Negro Du Bois and the Sioux Standing Bear shared a conviction that the nation as a whole deprived itself of human gifts by scorning those it held as inferior by race and either degraded or exotic by culture. Though neither makes a special point of linking blacks and Indians as victims together of America's racial and economic order, the resonance between these two writers cannot be overlooked.

Standing Bear's message reappeared in yet another voice when in 1952 *The American Scholar* published an essay by Felix Cohen: "Americanizing the White Man." The title alone should startle the unprepared reader to attention. While working in the Solicitor's Office

of the Interior Department, Cohen had drafted the Indian Reorgani-
zation Act of 1934, which ended the allotment policy and put the revival of tribal self-government at the center of a "New Deal" for
Indians. For the Interior Department he helped compile the laws and
treaties related to Indians, which became the basis of *The Handbook
of Federal Indian Law* that appeared in 1942. While the Indians'
tribal sovereignty had been limited by treaties and legislation, he concluded, it was not a power delegated by Congress but an "inherent
power . . . which has never been extinguished."[56] Some degree of
tribal sovereignty remains an inherent right.

Cohen's pen has been described as both scalpel and sledgeham-
mer, and both are on display in "Americanizing the White Man," a
polemic, exhortation, and rhapsody of praise. Starting with the inversion in the title, like Standing Bear, Cohen cut, sliced, and hammered
away at the notion of Indian backwardness, at the ignorance and arrogance of the idea that the indigenous tribal peoples have more to gain
from Euro-America than the other way around. From agriculture to
medicine, from sports to democracy, from local government to the
homestead system based on land right as "the fruit of use and occu-
pancy," everything "distinctive about America is Indian, through and
through." Indians have been the teachers of America, teaching what
America denotes as place, as flora and fauna and habitation for human
society. And "the real epic of America is the yet unfinished story of the
Americanization of the White Man": "The more white men take on of
Indian political customs, the more important becomes the role of the
Indian as a teacher, and the more grotesque becomes the stereotype
of Indian degradation with its threadbare corollary that we who have
civilized the Indian have earned the right to take his lands, minerals,
timber and fisheries in payment."[57] To recognize what "America"
means was a matter of justice, but also of national self-knowledge.

For more than two centuries, Du Bois wrote in 1920, "America
has marched proudly in the van of human hatred." The mantra has
been, "Up white, down black." And down red. Yet Indian and black
teachers have been familiar figures in lore and legend; James Fenimore Cooper took them for granted; Longfellow portrayed them;
Turner acknowledged them as indispensable guides and models. And

Uncle Remus has been a revered figure in folklore shared by whites and blacks of wisdom and shrewd insight. In *Adventures of Huckleberry Finn*, Mark Twain created the memorable figure of a friend and teacher in the escaped slave, Jim, whose flight to freedom and kindness and generosity shape Huck's adventures (until the evasive burlesque of the final chapters). In a recent essay, the Choctow author LeAnne Howe has written of "symbiosis," the merging of separate organisms and entities into something new.[58] She has added a dimension to Cohen's exhortation and Standing Bear's message that "the Indian can save America": Natives and nonnatives have long taught each other how to become something different as a result of their symbiotic relations. Indian "intellectual capital"—knowledge of the resources of the land and skills in using them—provided the basis for European settlements and colonies, and then settlers and colonists rejected the opportunity to live in peace with native neighbors.[59] "America is a tribal creation story" in the sense that stories passed from natives to nonnatives have creatively taught lessons in coexistence and in respect and tolerance for diversity of outlook and interest. The Iroquois Covenant Chain, by which the tribes of the Iroquois Confederacy and the English colonists agreed in the seventeenth century to follow two paths with links between them, offered another vision of a bridge. It represented an agreement that differences existed but that a unifying common interest in peace did, too, which counted on mutual respect. America is a tribal creation story in that Indians taught colonists that we were the many branches of one tree: the teaching of the original Mohawk Hiawatha. Stories of the Indian "guide," the teachings of Indian chiefs and seers, grandmothers and grandfathers pervade American folklore and popular culture, alongside the restless ghosts of "the Vanishing Red."

Will the teachings outlast the ghosts, the shades that still haunt the idea and the name of America? Gerald Vizenor has written of indigenous voices: "The shadows of their words . . . are forever true on the land stolen from the tribes."[60] To lay the ghosts, to put the many shades of Hiawatha to rest, as this book proposes, is to take a significant step in recovering those shadowed words and reclaiming the vitality of ancient societies, which in turn is essential for a fundamental renovation in the name "America," let alone for the future of life on earth. Like Hart Crane and countless others in our past who were absorbed with the idea of America, Luther Standing Bear imagined a humane nation as a great bridge woven of diverse tribal stories. His challenging vision deserves to be honored in the ongoing drama of the making of Americans.

Notes

The following abbreviations are used:

AS   Henry James, *The American Scene*
AU   Mary Austin Papers
CCPM Curtis Collection, Pierpont Morgan Library
CCSM Curtis Collection, Southwest Museum
ESC   Edward S. Curtis, Special Collections
FJT   F. J. Turner Papers
FWH   F. W. Hodge Collection
HLL   Harriet Leitch Letters
HWL   Henry Wadsworth Longfellow
LC   Longfellow Collection
LM   Longfellow Materials
LP   Longfellow Papers
NAI   Edward S. Curtis, *North American Indian*
RHP: R. H. Pratt Papers
WC   Wanamaker Collection
WP   Wanamaker Papers

Preface

1. See White, *Eastern Establishment*, 31–51.
2. West, *Way to the West*, 131–32. See also Limerick, *Legacy*.
3. Trachtenberg, *Incorporation*, esp. chaps. 1, 3, and 7.
4. Though his emphasis is less on representations than on actual social and especially environmental behavior, Elliott West examines in rich detail the interac-

tion of natives and Euro-Americans in shaping life on the Great Plains in the mid-nineteenth century. See *The Contested Plains: Indians, Goldseekers, and the Rush to Colorado* (Lawrence: University Press of Kansas, 1998). My thanks to Zev Trachtenberg for calling this book to my attention.

5. Dewey, "Principle of Nationality."
6. McNickle, *Native American Tribalism*, 113–33. See also Deloria and Lytle, *Nations Within*, 1–36, and Barsh and Henderson, *Native American Tribalisms*, 113–33.
7. Jordan, *White Over Black*, 90.
8. Frederickson, *Black Image*, 246–52; Dippie, *Vanishing American*, 251–53; Malcomson, *One Drop*, 76, 79.
9. Hoxie, *Encyclopedia*, 6.
10. Gomez, *Exchanging*, 1–16.
11. Malcomson, *One Drop*, 35–38.
12. Kerber, "Abolitionist Perception," 275.
13. Malcomson, *One Drop*, 90ff.
14. Mooney, *Ghost-Dance*, 876.
15. Malcomson, *One Drop*, 53–59
16. Du Bois, "Conservation," 821.
17. Hertzberg, *American Indian Identity*, 179–212.
18. Rothenberg, *Race*, 245.
19. Malcomson, *One Drop*, 115; Kerber, "Abolitionist Perception," 292.
20. Rourke, *Roots*, 60–75.
21. Du Bois, "Souls of White Folk," 933.
22. Williams, "American Imperialism," 233–36.
23. Ibid., 237.
24. Ibid., 237–49. See also Jacobson, *Barbarian Virtues*, 51–3.
25. Du Bois, "Souls of White Folk," 937–38.
26. Mizruchi, *Science of Sacrifice*, 3–88.
27. Roosevelt, *Winning*, 61–62. See also Slotkin, *Gunfighter Nation*, 29–62.

Introduction: Dreaming Indian

1. Frost, "Vanishing Red," 136.
2. On the story of Ishi, see Kroeber, *Ishi*, 3–11, 241–48, and Vizenor, "Ishi Obscura," *Manifest Manners*, 126–37 (an earlier version appeared as "Isihi Bares his Chest" in Lippard, *Partial Recall*).
3. My thanks to John Stauffer for this suggestion.
4. Lawrence, *Mornings in Mexico*, 132.
5. Brower, *Constellations*, 122. See also Fiedler, *Return*, 26.
6. See Moffit and Sebastián, *O Brave*, 15–101.
7. Frederickson, *Black Image*, 246–55; Horsman, *Race and Manifest Destiny*, 139–58; Gossett, *Race*, 4–83; Graves, *Emperor's New Clothes*, 86–104; Gould, *Mismeasure*, 30–72.
8. Appleby, *Inheriting*, 58. See also Butler, *Becoming American*, 11–16, and Horsman, *Race and Manifest Destiny*, 98–115.

9. Deloria, *Playing Indian*, 1–37, 199–202, 181–92. See also Huhndorf, *Going Native*, 1–18.
10. Catlin, *Letters and Notes*, 1:16.
11. Ibid. On McKenney, see Horan, *The McKenney-Hall Portrait Gallery*.
12. Quoted in Dippie, *Vanishing American*, 26.
13. On Baudalaire's review of Catlin, see Anderson, "'Curious Data,'" 7. See also Cronon, "Telling Tales," 50–53, and Dippie, *Vanishing American*, 25–28.
14. Catlin, *Letters and Notes*, 1:15, 2:249–50.
15. Ibid., 1:15, 2:256.
16. Bieder, *Science Encounters*, 245. On tensions and nuances in the working relation of Morgan and Parker, see Michaelson, *Limits*, 84–106.
17. Fenton, Introduction to *League*, xv.
18. Morgan, *League*, 59, 143–49. For a different view of Morgan, see Deloria, *Playing Indian*, 71–94.
19. Engels, *Origins*, 31, 132. For more on Engels's use of Morgan, see Johansen, 121–23.
20. Morgan, *Ancient Society*, 561, 562.
21. Morgan, *League*, 312.
22. Ibid., 33, 455, 456.
23. Dewey, "Interpretation of Savage Mind," 40.
24. Kerber, "Abolitionist Perceptions," 288.
25. See White, *Eastern Establishment*.
26. Locke, *Second Treatise*, 30.
27. Ibid., 8, 30.
28. Davis, *Problem of Slavery*, 118–21; Malcomson, *One Drop*, 48–50, 525–26.
29. See Tilton, *Pocahontas*, 9–34 and *passim*, and Abrams, *Pilgrims*, 206.
30. Crèvecoeur, *Letters*, 39ff, 205–09; Douglass, "Self-Made Men."
31. See Preston, *Young Frederick Douglass*, 9–10. Douglass's 1869 remarks are quoted in Kerber, "Abolitionist Perceptions," 294. My thanks to John Stauffer and Elliott West for calling these items to my attention.
32. Quoted in Furtwangler, *Answering*, 17; Rourke, *Roots*, 72.
33. Quoted in Furtwangler, *Answering*, 67.
34. Quoted in Huizinga, *America*, 195.
35. Hartz, *Founding*, 98–99, 94.
36. McNickle, *Native American Tribalism*, 69–86.
37. Turner, *Frontier*, 4–5, 13–15.
38. See Slotkin, *Gunfighter Nation*, 1–28 and passim.
39. White, "Frederick Jackson Turner," 27.
40. Turner, "American Colonization."
41. Turner, *Frontier*, 22–25, 37–38.
42. Turner, "Stream of Immigration." For the role of the immigration restriction movement in Turner's frontier thesis, see Benson, *Turner and Beard*, 70–79.
43. See Billington, *Genesis*, 239–40, 243. My thanks to John Faragher for calling this memory of Turner's to my attention.
44. Quoted in Martin, "Neither Fish," 82. See also Hagan, "Private Property," 125–37.

45. On "Friends of the Indian," see Prucha, *Americanizing*; also Hagan, *Theodore Roosevelt*.
46. Quoted in Slotkin, *Gunfighter*, 91. See also Johnson, "Red Populism?" p. 510.
47. Quoted in Malcomson, *One Drop*, 15.
48. See Evans, "Cushing Zuni Sketchbooks."
49. Pratt, "How to Deal with the Indians," 3.
50. Pratt, *Battle Field*, 215.
51. Hertzberg, *Search*, 99, 156, and on Parker, 48–58.
52. Ibid., 93.
53. Pratt, *Battle Field*, 214.
54. Reel, Introduction to *Course of Study*.
55. Pratt, *Battle Field*, 322.
56. U.S. Congress, House Report No. 144.
57. Quoted in Baca, "Legal Status," 231 and passim.
58. Cheyfitz, "Doctrines of Discovery."
59. See Cadwalader and Deloria, *Aggression of Civiization*, 106–30.
60. Spicer, *American Indians*, 179.
61. On "competency" as "a colonial land policy," see Hoxie, *Final Promise*, chap. 5.
62. Pfaller, *James McLaughlin*, 333–38.
63. Quoted in Walker, *Indian Nation*, 213. See also Pokagon, *Queen of the Woods*, 5–33.
64. See Dippie, *Vanishing American*, 203–05.

Additional Sources

Hugh Honour's *The European Vision of America* (Kent, OH: Kent University Press, 1975) gives an outstanding account of early European images of discovery and conquest. For further discussion of European responses to America and its peoples, see Moffit and Sebastián, *O Brave New People*, and John F. Moffit, "Why Are Native Americans (Still) Called 'Indians'? The Illuminating Example of Giovanni di Paolo's *Quattrocento Mappamundi*," in *Art and the Native American*, ed. Mary Louise Krumrine and Susan Clare Scott (University Park: Pennsylvania State University Press, 2001). In "Between Science and Art: The European Representations of America, 1500–1800," Friedrich Polleross distinguishes interestingly the "overlapping phases of perception about the New World" based on "the mode of sensory perception" (in Krumrine and Scott). A fine collection of annotated early images and texts by European travelers is Stefan Lorant's *The New World: The First Pictures of America* (New York: Duell, Sloan & Pearce, 1946). For an excellent summary account of early conceptions of New World abundance, see Lears, *Fables of Abundance*, 17–39.

Roy Harvey Pearce's *Savagism and Civilization: A Study of the Indian and the American Mind* (1953; repr., Berkeley: University of California Press, 1988) is a seminal "history of ideas" approach to conceptions of "savage" in the United States. The most useful historical study, with fine attention to literature and the arts along with intellectual history, continues to be Berkhofer's *The White Man's Indian*. See also Dippie, *George Catlin and his Indian Gallery*, and on Catlin in the context of other nineteenth-century artists' depictions of Indians, see Schimmel, "Inventing the Indian," and Conn, *History's Shadow*, chapter 2, "Images of History: Indians in American Art." The section on "Conceptual Relations" in Washburn's *History of Indian-White Relations* includes valuable chapters by Berkhofer, Leslie Fiedler, Rayna D. Green, and others. Splendid analyses of the Indian as a national symbol can be found in E. McClung Fleming's "Symbols of the United States: From Indian Queen to Uncle Sam," in Browne, *Frontiers of American Culture*, and Higham, "Indian Princess and Roman Goddess." David Lubin is especially insightful on ambivalence in Indian images; see *Picturing a Nation: Art and Social Change in Nineteenth Century America* (New Haven, CT: Yale University Press, 1994), chaps. 2 and 3. In *Going Native*, Shari M. Huhndorf cogently examines the theme of going native in relation to race, imperialism, citizenship, and national identity in the late nineteenth and twentieth centuries.

On treaties, federal policy, and Indian law in general, see Baca, "Legal Status of American Indians"; Strong and Van Winkle, "Tribe and Nation"; and Robert A. Williams Jr., *The American Indian in Western Legal Thought* (New York: Oxford University Press, 1990).

Priscilla Wald's treatment of the Cherokee cases in the 1830s, in *Constituting Americans: Cultural Anxiety and Narrative Form* (Durham, NC: Duke University Press, 1995), raises provocative questions about the Supreme Court's decision that tribes were "dependent nations" and about the national identity of white citizens. The question whether, as members of tribes, Indians fell fully under U.S. jurisdiction is treated in James H. Kettner, *The Development of American Citizenship, 1608–1870* (Chapel Hill: University of North Carolina Press, 1978). In "'Congress in its Wisdom': The Course of Indian Legislation," in Cadwalader and Deloria, *The Aggression of Civilization*, Vine Deloria Jr. clarifies conundrums of Indian citizenship in the context of the history of Indian legislation. Cohen's *Handbook* is an indispensable resource. See also Haas, *The Indian & the Law*.

For additional commentary on John Locke and America, see Herman Lebovics, "The Uses of America in Locke's Second Treatise of Government," *Journal of the History of Ideas* 47, no. 4 (October–December, 1986): 567–81; Arthur J. Slavin, "The American Principle from More to Locke," in Fredi Chiapepelli, ed., *First Images of the New World* (Berkeley: University of California Press, 1976); and Marilyn Holly, "The Persons of Nature Versus the Power of Pyramid: Locke, Land, and American Indians," *International Studies in Philosophy*, 26, no. 1 (1994): 13–31. For a study of Locke's thought in general, see John Dunn's superb *The Political Thought of John Locke* (Cambridge: Cambridge University Press, 1969).

More discussion of Chief Sea'thl's speech can be found in the following works: Jerry L. Clark, "Thus Spoke Chief Seattle: The Story of an Undocumented Speech," *Prologue: Quarterly of the National Archives and Records Administration* 18, no. 1 (Spring 1985); Vi Hilbert, "When Chief Seattle (Sealth) Spoke," in Robert K. Wright, ed., *A Time of Gathering: Native Heritage in Washington State* (Seattle: University of Washington Press, 1990); Rudolph Kaiser, "'A Fifth Gospel. Almost': Chief Seattle's Speech(es) American Origins and European Reception," in Christian F. Feest, ed., *Indians and Europe* (Lincoln: University of Nebraska Press, 1999); Bruce E. Johansen, *Shapers of the Great Debate on Native Americas, Land, Spirit, and Power: A Biographical Dictionary* (Westport, CT: Greenwood Press, 2000).

On the movement to reform Indian policy and the Dawes Act, see Prucha, *Americanizing the American Indians*. Hagan's *Theodore Roosevelt* offers an illuminating study of influences on Roosevelt's role in shaping Indian policy. Smith's *Reimagining Indians* gives a sympathetic portrait of turn-of-the-century writers who viewed Indians admiringly, learned something from their encounters, and influenced the reform of government policies.

Frederick Hoxie has written several important studies of the reform era: his essential book, *A Final Promise*; "The Curious Story of Reformers and American Indians," in *Indians in Amerian History*, 205–28; and "The Reservation Period: 1880–1960," in Trigger and Washburn, *Cambridge History of the Native Peoples*, 183–258. In chapter 16 of her rich and concise *A History of the Indians of the United States*, Angie Debo discusses Indian responses to the allotment policy. See also Fey and McNickle, *Indians and Other Americans*, and Donald L. Parman, *Indians and the American West in the Twentieth Century* (Bloomington: Indiana University Press, 1994), 1–51.

1. Singing Hiawatha

1. Lockard, "Universal Hiawatha."
2. I take the biographical details from Arvin, *Longfellow*.
3. HWL to Francis Lieber, December 17, 1885, LM.
4. Miscellaneous clippings from the Boston press, LC.
5. Boston *Daily Evening Traveller*, November 13, 1855, ibid.
6. Hale, *Hiawatha*, 5, 18–19.
7. Fiske, "Mercurized Folkore."
8. Thompson, "Indian Legend."
9. Hilen, *Letters*, March 25, 1856, 3:532.
10. Ibid. For musical versions of *Hiawatha* through the 1880s, see Bordman, *American Musical Theatre*, 56–58.
11. Holmes, "Physiology of Versification," 316.
12. Frye, *Anatomy*, 186–206; Jameson, *Political Unconscious*, 103–50.
13. Folsom, *Native Representations*, 50, 58.
14. Whitman, *Complete Prose*, 315.
15. Quoted in Arvin, *Longfellow*, 322.
16. Buell, *Selected Poems*, xxix.
17. Arvin, *Longfellow*, 173.
18. Longfellow, *Life*, 2:73–74.
19. Jackson treats this paradox in her splendid essay, "Longfellow's Tradition."
20. See Carr, *Inventing the American Primitive*, 58–100.
21. Gioia, "Aftermath of Modernism," 87.
22. HWL, *Song*, 161.
23. Jackson, "Longfellow's Tradition," 473.
24. Longfellow, *Life*, 2:170. See Gould, *Mismeasure*, 42–50.
25. Longfellow, *Life*, 2:137. See Moyne, "Longfellow," 48–52.
26. Copway, *Life, Letters*, 46.
27. Hilen, *Letters*, 4:109.
28. Samuel Longfellow to Mrs. Jacobs, February 24, 1882, LC.

29. HWL, *Song*, 161.
30. I am indebted to the late David Levin and to J. C. Levenson for introducing me to Lewis's novel. For more on Schoolcraft and his first wife, see Mumford, "Mixed-Race Identity" and Michaelsen, *Limits*, 38–45.
31. Lewis, *Invasion*, 323–25.
32. On Schoolcraft's career and his place in American ethnology, see Bieder, *Science Encounters*, 146–93.
33. HWL, "Defense of Poetry," 75. See Herder, *Reflections*, 7. See also Carr, *Inventing the American Primitive*, 106–13, and Bluestein, *Voice*, 2–15.
34. Schoolcraft, *Oneota*, 246.
35. Schoolcraft, *History*, 29–30.
36. Schoolcraft, *Oneota*, 247.
37. Longfellow, *Life*, 2:267.
38. Conway, no page number. LC.
39. HWL, *Song*, xii.
40. See Cowan, "Ojibway Vocabulary," 59–67, and Vogel, "Placenames," 261–68.
41. Schoolcraft, *American Indians*, 230.
42. HWL, *Song*, 220.
43. Hymes, "In vain," 39–42. My gratitude to Professor Hymes for sharing with me his "Chant to the Fire-fly: Contexts." See also Nichols, "Chant," 113–26. Also Brotherston, *Fourth World*, 347.
44. Fletcher, "Whitman and Longfellow," 141.
45. HWL, *Song*, 48.
46. HWL, "Journal," March 23, 1855, LP.
47. Lepore, *A Is for American*, 64.
48. HWL, *Song*, 103–04.
49. Schoolcraft, *American Indians*, 293–300.
50. Schoolcraft, *Myth of Hiawatha*, xviii.
51. See Ward, "Influence of Vico," 57–63.
52. Jackson, "Longfellow's Tradition," 478.
53. Vico, *The New Science*, 74–75.
54. Schoolcraft, *Myth of Hiawatha*, xix.
55. HWL, *Song*, 83.
56. Ibid., 8.
57. HWL, "Defense of Poetry," 56–78; Ward, "Influence of Vico," 60–62.
58. Ferguson, "Longfellow's Political Fears," 181–215.
59. Lewis, *Invasion*, 325.
60. Longfellow, *Life*, 2:293.
61. HWL, *Song*, 152–53.
62. Roheim, "Culture Hero," 190; Radin, *Trickster*, xxiii.
63. Manuscript, Box 93, LP.
64. Hilen, *Letters*, 4:517.
65. Schoolcraft, *Algic Researches*, 134.
66. Longfellow, "A Visit to Hiawatha's People," v.
67. Fenton, *Great Law*, 73–76.
68. Wallace, "Return of Hiawatha," 392.

69. Bierhorst, *Four Masterworks*, 111.
70. Longfellow, *Life*, 2:265–66. For Emerson's 1855 letter to Whitman and the poet's lengthy reply, see Whitman, *Leaves of Grass*, 729–39.
71. HWL, *Song*, 154.
72. Ibid., 160.
73. Brotherston, *Fourth World*, 347.
74. DeCosta, *Hiawatha*, 5–13. Another curiosity is Woodworth's *The Godly Seer*, apparently a reprint of a 1900 work by Woodworth, "Chief Sachem" of "a bookish club," called "Sachems of the Pipe."
75. Newspaper clipping, LC.
76. Bataille, "Notion of Expenditure," 118.
77. Malmsheimer, "'Imitation White Man.'"
78. Cora M. Folsom to Mr. Dana, with "Scenes from Hiawatha," undated typescript letter, LHP. On Cora Folsom, see Lindsey, *Indians*, 211–16.
79. Baker, *Hemingway*, 5, 13, 64. See also Meredith, "They Remember Papa."
80. Eight pages of Horn's photographs also illustrate the brochure "The Indian Play 'Hiawatha.'"
81. *Song of Hiawatha: Players' Edition*, xi–xii.
82. Newspaper clippings, LC.
83. See "A Great Cantata Founded on 'Hiawatha,'" and "The Hiawatha Drama—A festival of the Ojibway Indians," 564.
84. See Glassberg, *American Historical Pageantry*, 164–99. See also Kahn, "Caliban."

Additional Sources

For further discussion of Indian figures and themes in antebellum drama and melodrama, see Sollors, *Beyond Ethnicity*, 102–48, and on the Pocahontas theme, 75–80; B. Donald Grose, "Edwin Forrest, *Metamora*, and the Indian Removal Act of 1830," *Theatre Journal* vol. 36 (May 1985): 181–91; Sally L. Jones, "The First but not Last of the 'Vanishing Indians': Edwin Forrest and Mythic Recreations of the Native Population," in S. Elizabeth Bird, ed., *Dressing in Feathers: The Construction of the Indian in American Popular Culture* (Boulder, CO: Westview Pess, 1996); Tilton, *Pocahontas*. On Black Hawk, see Milo Miton Qiaife, ed., *Life of Ma-Ka-Tai-Me-She-Kia-Kiak, or Black Hawk* (1834; repr., New York: Dover, 1994); Roger L. Nichols, *Black Hawk and the Warrior's Path* (Arlington Heights, IL: Harlan Davidson, 1992). On William Apes, see Barry O'Connell, ed., *On Our Own Ground: The Complete Writings of William Apes, A Pequot* (Amherst: University of Massachusetts Press, 1992). On George Copway (Kah-ge-ga-gah'-bowh), see Copway, *Life, Letters, and Speeches*. On the theme of the ghostliness of Indian figures in nineteenth-century American writing, see the interesting opening chapter in Renée L. Bergland, *The National Uncanny: Indian Ghosts and American Subjects* (Hanover, NH: University Press of New England, 2000), 1–24.

More discussion of Longfellow and the Mohawk Hiawatha can be found in Hale, *Hiawatha*, 5, 18–19, and "The Hiawatha Myths," in *The Iroquois Book of Rites* (Philadelphia: D. G. Brinton, 1883), 180–83. See also Morgan, *League*, 68; Arthur C. Parker, "Who was Hiawatha?" *New York Folklore* 10, no. 4 (Winter 1954): 285–91, and "The Hiawatha Tradition," in William N. Fenton, ed., *Parker on the Iroquois* (Syracuse,

NY: Syracuse University Press, 1968), 114–18; Dean R. Snow, *The Iroquois* (Cambridge, MA: Blackwell, 1994), 57–60; Anthony F. C. Wallace, "The Dekanawideh Myth Analyzed as the Record of a Revitalization Movement," *Ethnohistory* no. 1 (Winter 1958): 118–30.

Other works on Longfellow and his sources include Rose Davis, "How Indian is Hiawatha?" *Midwest Folkore* 7, no. 1 (Spring 1957): 5–25; Joseph S. Pronechen, "The Making of Hiawatha," *New York Folkore Quarterly* 2 (June 1972): 151–57, and "Hiawatha and Its Predecessors," *Philological Quarterly* 11, no. 4 (October 1932): 321–43. Leslie Fiedler has typically pithy and resonant observations to make about Longfellow in *Return of Vanishing American*.

Loren R. Graham tells the story of Schoolcraft and Shing-Wauk in his engaging history of a Lake Superior Chippewa community, *A Face in the Rock: The Tale of a Grand Island Chippewa* (Berkeley: University of California Press, 1995).

For an illuminating application of Bataille's theories to performative texts, see Joseph Roach, *Cities of the Dead: Circum-Atlantic Performance* (New York: Columbia University Press, 1996), esp. pp. 40–42, 123–25. On the Wild West shows, see Joy Kasson's excellent *Buffalo Bill's Wild West: Celebrity, Memory, and Popular History* (New York: Hill & Wang, 2000), and L. G. Moses's revealing study of the "show Indians," in *Wild West Shows and the Images of American Indians, 1883–1933* (Albuquerque: University of New Mexico Press, 1996).

On Longfellow's Hiawatha in paintings, sculpture, and music, see Cynthia Nickerson, "Interpretations of H. W. Longfellow's 'The Song of Hiawatha,' 1855–1900," *American Art Journal* 16, no. 3 (Summer 1984): 3; Rena N. Coen, "Longfellow and Some 19th Century American Painters," in *Papers Presented at the Longfellow Commemorative Conference* (Cambridge, MA: National Park Service, Longfellow National Historical Park, 1982), 69–91; Michael T. Richman, *Daniel Chester French, An American Sculptor* (New York: Metropolitan Museum of Art, 1976); *Edmonia Lewis and Henry Wadsworth Longfellow: Images and Identities*, Gallery Series no. 14 (1995); (Cambridge, MA: Fogg Art Museum); Beth Levy, "'In the Glory of the Sunset': Arthur Farwell, Charles Wakefield Cadman, and Indianism in American Music," *Repercussions* 5 (Spring–Fall 1996): 128–83; entry on Coleridge-Taylor in *New Grove Dictionary of Music and Musicians*, ed. Stanley Sadie. (London: Macmillan, 1980), 528–30.

2. Conceivable Aliens

1. Quoted in King, *Making Americans*, 127.
2. "Are We Facing an Immigration Peril?"
3. Walker, "Restriction of Immigration."
4. King, *Making Americans*, 76, 81.
5. Higham, *Send These to Me*, 4.
6. Sollors, *Beyond Ethnicity*, 76. See also Gleason, *Speaking of Diversity*, 3–31.
7. Young, "Mother of Us All."
8. Posnock, *Trial of Curiosity*, 259.
9. *AS*, xxv, xxvi.
10. Ibid., 307, xxvi.
11. Ibid., 273.

12. Auden, Introduction to *AS*, x.
13. *AS*, 273.
14. Ibid., 84.
15. Ibid., 465.
16. Posnock, *Trial of Curiosity*, 281.
17. See Higham, *Send These to Me*, 71–80.
18. Archdeacon, *Becoming American*, 113.
19. Ibid., 146.
20. "New Immigrant Station."
21. "Are We Facing an Immigration Peril?"
22. See Trachtenberg, *America & Lewis Hine*, 118–37.
23. *AS*, 85.
24. Ibid., 86.
25. Ibid., 363–64.
26. Ibid., 86.
27. Ibid., 91, 229.
28. Ibid., 87.
29. James, *The American*, 1–2.
30. Higham, *Send These to Me*, 188–89.
31. Roosevelt, "Americanism," 16, 25, 24.
32. Dewey, "Nationalizing Education," 204.
33. Roosevelt, "Duties of American Citizenship," 16.
34. Roosevelt, "True Americanism," 23–25.
35. Dewey, "Nationalizing Education."
36. Renan, "What is a Nation?" 14–15. See Hobsbawm and Ranger, *Invention of Tradition*, 1–14.
37. Kallen, *Culture and Democracy*, 67–125.
38. Du Bois Quoted in Spiller, *Universal Races*, 360–61.
39. Roosevelt, "Duties," 218–20.
40. Eastman quoted in Spiller, *Universal Races*, 375.
41. *The Red Man and Helper*, July 31, 1903.
42. Boas quoted in Spiller, *Universal Races*, 102.
43. See Ngai, "Architecture of Race."
44. *Congressional Record*, 66th Cong., 2d sess,1540–1559.
45. Quoted in "Battling for Poor Lo's Ballot"; *The Survey* 54.
46. Gleason quoted in Thernstrom, *Harvard Encyclopedia*, 32.
47. *AS*, 121, 131.
48. Ibid., 124.
49. Ibid., 126.
50. Ibid., 132.
51. Ibid., 137.
52. Ibid., 139.
53. Whitman, *Daybooks*, 732.
54. *AS*, 127, 129.
55. James, *Literary Criticism*, 663.

56. Resek, *Randolph Bourne*, 121, 130.
57. *AS*, 416.
58. Ibid., 123, 130, 139.
59. Ibid., 207, 139.
60. Ibid., 204.
61. See Jacobson, *Whiteness*, 171–200.
62. James, *Question of Our Speech*, 6, 11–12, 18, 33, 43.
63. Ibid., 42.
64. Ibid., 46.
65. Quoted in Lapore, *A Is for America*, 37, 5. See Simpson, *Politics of American English*, 63–81.
66. Compare with Gramsci on the language problems of Italy, *Cultural Writings*, 164–95.
67. James, *Question of Our Speech*, 21–22.
68. Whitman, *Daybooks*, 2, 730, 6.

Additional Sources

For typical contemporary responses to immigration, see Philip Davis, ed., *Immigration and Americanization* (Boston: Ginn, 1920); Henry Pratt Fairchild, *Immigrant Backgrounds* (New York: John Wiley, 1927). The anti-immigration argument is colorfully represented by the University of Wisconsin sociologist Edward Ross in *The Old World in the New* (New York: Century, 1914), the last chapter of which, "American Blood and Immigrant Blood," has subheadings such as "Submergence of the pioneering breed," "Primitive types among the foreign-born," "How immigration will affect good looks in this country," and "The triumph of the low-standard elements over the high-standard elements." On the movement to restrict immigration, and on the 1911 report of the congressional Dillingham Commission, see King, *Making Americans*, chap. 3. Edward George Hartman gives a careful account of the philanthropic, patriotic, and chauvinistic attitudes in the Americanization movements in *The Movement to Americanize the Immigrant* (New York: Columbia University Press, 1948). On changing meanings imputed to the Statue of Liberty, see Higham, *Send These to Me*, 71–80. On Ellis Island, a good place to begin is Virginia Yans-McLaughlin and Marjorie Lightman, *Ellis Island and the Peopling of America* (New York: New Press, 1997).

On the relation of Indians, slaves, and free blacks to birthright citizenship, see Kettner, *Development of American Citizenship*, chap. 10. Martin's "Neither Fish nor Fowl" discusses the exclusion of Indians from coverage under the Fourteenth Amendment.

On the revealing coincidence, in 1924, of the act restricting immigration according to nationality and, shortly thereafter, the act granting birthright citizenship to Indians, see Michaels, *Our America*, 29–32.

3. Yiddish Hiawatha

1. *AS*, 121–22.
2. Porte, *Emerson*, 219.

3. Harshav, *Meaning of Yiddish*, 22–28 and passim.
4. *Red Man*, March 1888. See Spack, *America's Second Tongue*, 45–78.
5. Weinreich, *Yiddish Language*, 281–84. See also Jacobson, *Whiteness*, 171–200.
6. Howe, "Pluralism in the Immigrant World," 149–55.
7. Harkavy, *Amerikanisher Briefen-Shteler*, 102.
8. Cahan, "Philologist and Lexicographer of the Ghetto," 295–97.
9. Cahan, "How Should Yiddish be Written?" 159.
10. Chametzky quoted in Shell and Sollors, *Multilingual Anthology*, 359.
11. Cahan, *Yekl*, 1. See Chametzky, *From the Ghetto*, chap. 4.
12. Goldsmith, *Architects*, 268.
13. Gilman, *Jewish Self-Hatred*, 76–81 and passim.
14. Cahan, "When I Write Yiddish," 303.
15. Rubinstein, "Becoming Modern," 13. My thanks to Rachel Rubinstein for sharing this essay with me.
16. Harshav and Harshav, *American Yiddish Poetry*, 741.
17. Ibid., 3–67.
18. Harshav, *Meaning of Yiddish*, 96.
19. Goldsmith, *Architects*, 161.
20. Ibid., 168.
21. Goldsmth, "Jewish People and the Yiddish Language," 172.
22. Goldsmith, "Zhitlovsky and American Jewry," 295. See also Cassedy, *To the Other Shore*, and Fishman, "Introducing Khayem Zhitlovski."
23. Zhitlovksy, "Vegn dem vert fun iberzetzung," viii, xviii, iv, xiii. I'm grateful to Benjamin Harshav for his translation of these passages. On Zhitlovsky, see Howe, *World of Our Fathers*, 504–07, and Weinberg, *Between Tradition and Modernity*, 83–144.
24. Goldsmith, *Architects*, 176.
25. Zhitlovksy, "Vegn dem vert fun iberzetzung," xviii–xix, xx.
26. Ibid., xxii.
27. Harshav and Harshav, *American Yiddish Poetry*, 782; on the Introspectivists, see 36–44, 773–804.
28. Lockard, "Universal Hiawatha."
29. The influence and presence of Whitman in American Yiddish poetry has been too little studied. See Prager, "Walt Whitman in Yiddish," 22–35. On Poe, see the suggestive essay by Zametkin in Cassedy, *Building the Future*, 109–15.
30. Translations from Yehoash's lyrics, including "Maid of the Mists, Niagara Waterfalls," can be found in Cooperman and Cooperman, *America in Yiddish Poetry* 8–29.
31. Howe, *World of Our Fathers*, 426.
32. In Chametzky, *Jewish American Literature*, 143.
33. In Howe and Greenberg, *Treasury of Yiddish Poetry*, 73 (translated by Marie Syrkin).
34. Zhitlovksy, "Vegn dem vert fun iberzetzung," xxii.
35. Harshav, *Meaning of Yiddish*, 91.
36. Benjamin, *Illuminations*, 69–82.

37. Zhitlovsky, "Vegn dem vert fun iberzetzung," xi–xii.
38. Ibid., xxii–xxiv.
39. Quoted in Shell and Sollors, *Multilingual Anthology*, 358–59, 367, 375.
40. "The whole character of the Indian is of course more Oriental than European": Corbin, review of Cronyn, *Path of the Rainbow*, 45–46.
41. Slobin, "From Vilna," 17–26. On Malamud's *The People*, see Ahokas, "Jewish Peddler." See also Most, "'Big Chief.'"
42. "I'm an Indian" (1920), lyrics by Blanche Merrill, music by Leo Edwards; transcribed from a 1921 recording. My thanks to Peter Antelyes for calling this to my attention and providing a copy.
43. *Poetry*, 251.
44. Translated by Meyer Shitker, cited in Rubinstein, "Becoming Modern," 22.
45. Reprinted in Ellis, *Essays of Mary Austin*, 57–58.
46. Lewisohn to Austin, March 11, 1921, AU 4391.
47. Austin, "Up Stream." To a friend she described the article as "on the Jew and his criticism of American civilization." Austin to McDougal, April 27, 1922, AU 1160. In another letter to the same correspondent a few weeks later, Austin remarked of someone she "admired . . . immensely," that he was "the only Jew I ever knew about whom the last thing I ever thought of him was that he was a Jew" (AU 1164). The notion of the "denationalised Jew" also appears in a curious essay by a Jewish writer, Florence Kiper Frank, "Jew as Jewish Artist."
48. Ibid., Introduction to Cronyn, *Path of the Rainbow*, xiii, xxviii.
49. See Castro, *Interpreting the Indian*, 3–98, on Austin's treatment of Indian poetry. For an intriguing biographical view of Austin's developing interest in Indian culture, see Smith, *Reimagining Indians*, 165–78. See also Carr, *Inventing the American Primitive*, 218–20.
50. Ibid., *American Rhythm*, 14. See Dilworth, *Imagining Indians*, 173–210.
51. Ibid., "Indian Tales for Children." In the manuscript for an essay on "Folk Literature" that was pubished in *The Saturday Review of Literature* (August 11, 1928), she wrote: "Longfellow was no Indian, not even an authentic student of them, but his Hiawatha has come so close to authentic expression that Indians themselves are disposed to accept him" (AU 171, 10). There is no sign she knew of Yehoash's translation.
52. Ibid., *American Rhythm*, 41.
53. Ibid., *Earth Horizon*, 267.
54. Ibid., undated typescript, AU 343. Africian-American music and dance, too, she believed, were sources of "local rootage." She spoke of the "chief gift of the Negro to contempoary art" as the "very ease and freshness of his resort to rhythmic sources." *The Nation* 122 (April 28, 1926): 476.
55. See Bronitsky, "Solomon Bibo," 77–86; Marks, *Jews Among the Indians*.
56. Cooperman and Cooperman, *American in Yiddish Poetry*, 65.
57. Howe, *Penguin Book of Modern Yiddish Poetry*, 138 (translated by John Hollander).
58. Ludvig, *Gezalmte Lieder*, 73 (my translation).
59. Austin, "Up Stream," 639.

Additional Sources

Irving Howe's *World of Our Fathers* may be the definitive study of Yiddish life in New York, its literature, arts, and politics. Moses Rischin's *The Promised City* is also indispensable for its social and intellectual history of the same terrain.

On the Yiddishist movement, in addition to Goldsmith, *Architects*, see Kerler, *Politics of Yiddish:* Fishman. "The Sociology of Yiddish," is rich in historical detail and bibligraphical references. On the mixing of Yiddish and Anglish, see James Loeffler, " 'Neither the King's English nor the Rebbetzin's Yiddish': Yinglish Literature in the United States," in Marc Shell, ed., *American Babel: Literatures of the United States from Abnaki to Zuni* (Cambridge, MA: Harvard University Press, 2002), 133–62. Gene Bluestein's *Anglish/Yinglish: Yiddish in American Life and Literature* (Athens: University of Georgia Press, 1989) offers a vivid account of the presence of Yiddish in American speech and writing. Also enlightening is the social worker Lillian D. Wald's essay, "New Immigrants and our Policies," in Philip Davis, ed., *Immigration and Americanization* (Boston: Ginn, 1920). On the role of institutions created by Jewish immigrants in New York, see Howe, "Pluralism in the Immigrant World."

For a provocative treatment of Abraham Cahan's uses of multilingualism in *Yekl*, see Hana Wirth-Nesher, " 'Shpeaking Plain' and Writing Foreign: Abraham Cahan's *Yekl*," *Poetics Today* 22, no. 1 (Spring 2001). See also Sabine Haenni, "Visual and Theatrical Culture, Tenement Fiction, and the Immigrant Subject in Abraham Cahan's *Yekl*," *American Literature* 71, no. 3 (September 1999).

4. Ghostlier Demarcations

1. See "Urban Indians" in Hoxie, *Encyclopedia of North American Indians*, 653–54. Also Hertzberg, *Search*, chap. 9.
2. Curtis to Leitch, March 3, 1951, "Letters to Harriet Leitch," HLL. See Davis, *Edward S. Curtis*, 19–21.
3. On the origins of the project in 1906 and the founding of North American Indian, Inc., in 1910, see Gidley, *Incorporated*, chap. 1.
4. *New York Herald*, June 16, 1907.
5. See Curtis, "Vanishing Indian Types: Southwest," "Vanishing Indian Types: Northwest Plains," "Indians of the Stone Houses," "Village Tribes of the Desert Land."
6. Untitled eight-page. typescript, 1911, CCPM, excerpted in Gidley, *Incorporated*, 129–33. The typescript contains passages that had already appeared in Curtis's "General Introduction," vol. 1, 1906.
7. Ibid., typescript, 1–2.
8. Undated two-page typescript, 1, "Writings," box 2, folder 2, ESC; apparently a fragment of a memoir, probably written late in life.
9. Typescript, 1911, 2, CCPM.
10. Ibid., 6–7.
11. Ibid., 4, 1.
12. Gidley, *Incorporated*, 8.
13. Curtis to Edward S. Meany, September 1923, "Outgoing Letters," box 1, ESC.
14. *NAI*, 3: xi.

15. Ibid., 1:50.
16. As Gidley points out, *Incorporated*, 231–33, Curtis's text for his film, *In the Land of the Head-Hunters* (1914; book version, 1915) was influenced by *The Song of Hiawatha* in its setting, several incidents, and the use of inversions of familiar diction.
17. Curtis to Hodge, June 26, 1907, FWH.
18. Julian Hawthorne, "The North American Indian: A Record of a Vanishing Race," letterpress copy, seven pages, 1, UW; Gidley, *Incorporated*, 123.
19. "Lecture 1, Indian Life—Ceremonial," one page, undated; "Misc. items," CCSM.
20. For a similar view, see Goetzman, "Arcadian Landscapes," 83–92.
21. Meany, "Hunting Indians."
22. Theodore Roosevelt, "Foreword," *NAI*, 1:x.
23. Log, 1927 trip to Alaska; quoted in Davis, *Edward S. Curtis*, 74.
24. *NAI*, 20: xvi.
25. Hawthorne, "North American Indian," 4.
26. Allan, "E. S. Curtis," quoted in Gidley, *Incorporated*, 76.
27. Quoted ibid., 55.
28. Curtis wrote to Hodge: "A thought has occurred to me that there may be several times during the summer when I see some old and interesting ruin that I would like to do a little digging in. Is there someway in which I can get permission go do a little digging? I have in the Apache country just now. I do not mean that I shall start in doing any general digging just now, but at times I might find something where it would be very unfortunate if I was not able to do a little investigation. If this can be arranged in any way will you let me know?" Curtis to Hodge, April 10, 1906, FWH.
29. *NAI*, 1: xiv; Meany, "Hunting Indians."
30. *NAI*, President's Annual Report, 1913, PML.
31. Silko, *Yellow Woman*, 27.
32. Grinnell, *Story of the Indian*, 163.
33. *NAI*, 1:xiv.
34. Ibid.
35. See Truettner, "Science and Sentiment," 17–41.
36. Jameson, *Political Unconscious*, 110–19.
37. Quoted Graybill and Boesen, *Curtis*, 13.
38. "Travelling the Route of Lewis and Clark, One Hundred Years Later," 1, box 2, folder 24, ESC.
39. He apparently conceived of the idea of this book while doing "considerable research" for Cecil B. De Mille in connection with the 1923 film, *The Ten Commandments*. He worked as a cameraman on the film and mentioned this in a letter to a Seattle librarian helping him put his papers and memories in order, adding, "The Lure of Gold—if ever published—will arouse no end of controversy, hence all facts and figures must be checked and double-checked" (letter to Harriet Leitch, May 28, 1949, HLL). In his room in his daughter's Los Angeles house he surrounded himself with hundreds of books, tacked notes on the walls, and worked obsessively, and vainly, to complete before he died his epic account of lust for gold as a motive for conquest and colonization. In August he

wrote that the book "covers more than two hundred years of American history, including Spanish America and the Conquest." On November 4, 1949, he wrote to Leitch, "The same old story. I have been so busy with the Lure of Gold that everything else is neglected." On September 22, 1950, he wrote, "I am still and yet plodding along with the Lure of Gold: the more I work on it the more I find that should be included" (SPL). He died October 21, 1952, his research notes, indexes, and manuscript pages for "The Lure of Gold" apparently lost.

40. "The Lost Mine of Dead Man's Gulch," 10, box 2, folder 10, UW. For the unhappy effects of the California gold rush on native inhabitants, see Curtis's account in *NAI*, 14:101.

41. "The Forgotten Mapmaker," 1 CCXM.

42. Cited in Davis, *Edward S. Curtis*, 22.

43. See ibid., 66–68.

44. Ibid., 42.

45. Typescript, 1911, PML.

46. November 7, 1907, PML.

47. Graybill and Boesen, *Curtis*, 54. "President's Report," 1913, CCPM.

48. Marshall, "Vanishing Red Man," 246.

49. Ibid., 253. Gidley notes a parallel between the "geographical determinism" of Curtis's view that amalgamation with native "stock" would produce a "new race," and Mary Austin's claim that, once acknowledged, Indian ancestry would regenerate American arts (*Project*, 146–47).

50. The remark was made by Leupp, quoted in Dippie, *Vanishing American*, 250.

51. *NAI*, 19:4–5. But later Curtis describes "instances of diffusion" among Southwestern Indians that include the "Stomp" dance, whose music "would seem to indicate an African origin, as the rhythm and the minor wail appear to be quite foreign to Indian musical concept" (19:216).

52. Quoted in Dippie, *Vanishing American*, 257.

53. Ibid., 250.

54. Marshall, "Vanishing Red Man," 246.

55. See Patterson, *Rituals of Blood*, chap. 2. My thanks to Curmie Price for calling this to my attention.

56. Davis, *Edward S Curtis*, 66.

57. Curtis to Hodge, December 27, 1907, FWH.

58. Curtis to Morgan, January 23, 1906, CCPM.

59. "As it Was," 5; box 1, folder 7, ESC.

60. Davis, *Edward S. Curtis*, 31.

61. *NAI*, 1:xv.

62. Ibid., x.

63. Quoted in Graybill and Boesen, *Curtis*, 13.

64. Curtis to F. W. Hodge, January 14, 1908, SWH; Davis, *Edward S. Curtis*, 55–56.

Additional Sources

On representations of Indians in the Southwest at the turn of the century, see Dilworth's trailblazing *Imagining Indians*. Truettner's "Science and Sentiment" includes a valuable discussion of photography. An indispensable study of Indian photography is Paula Richardson Fleming and Judith Lynn Luskey, *Grand Endeavors of American Indian Photography* (Washington, DC: Smithsonian Institution Press, 1993). See also Goetzmann's superb selection of images and incisive essay, *The First Americans*. Another useful volume is Alfred L. Bush and Lee Clark Mitchell, *The Photograph and the American Indian* (Princeton: Princeton University Press, 1994). On representations at the world's fairs, see Robert Rydell, *All the World's a Fair: Visions of Empire at American International Expositions, 1817–1916* (Chicago: University of Chicago Press, 1984). On cinema, a useful and provocative collection of original essays is Gretchen M. Bataille and Charles. L. P. Silet, eds., *The Pretend Indians: Images of Native Americans in the Movies* (Ames, IA: Iowa State University Press, 1980). See also Raymond William Stedman, *Shadows of the Indian: Stereotypes in American Culture* (Norman: University of Oklahoma Press, 1982), and the collection by Bird, *Dressing in Feathers*.

Additional studies of Curtis include Lyman's provocative, groundbreaking critique, *The Vanishing Race and Other Illusions*, and Faris's, *Navajo and Photography*. Mick Gidley's introduction to and presentation of selections in *Edward S. Curtis and the North American Indian Project in the Field* is another signal contribution by this eminent scholar of Curtis. See also Anne Makepeace, *Edward S. Curtis: Coming to Light*.

Critical discussion of ethnographical museum displays can be found in Karp and Lavine, *Exhibiting Cultures*, and Jenkins, "Object Lessons and Ethnographic Displays."

On views of the land in native cultures in New England, see Cronon's classsic study *Changes on the Land*. Gilmore's *Prairie Smoke* is an early sympathetic view of native conceptions of the prairies. Relevant to native views of land and place is Basso's *Wisdom Sits in Places*.

5. Wanamaker Indians

1. "The Indian is Not Disappearing,"
2. Dixon to Fewkes, March 17, 1920, April 9, 1920; Mooney to Fewkes, April 10, 1920; Fewkes to Dixon, April 12, 1920, drawer 1, WC. Dixon, *Vanishing Race*, xc–ci.
3. Thornton, *American Indian Holocaust*, 180, quotes the U.S. Census Bureau in 1915: "The results of the studies on sterility, on fecundity, and on vitality all point toward one conclusion, that the increase of the mixed-blood Indians is much greater than that of the full-blooded Indians, and that unless the tendencies now at work undergo a decided change, the full-bloods are destined to form a decreasing proportion of the total Indian population and ultimately to disappear altogether."
4. McNickle, *Native American Tribalism*, 87.
5. "Great Bankers Gather at Astor" reports that Rodman Wanamaker claimed to have spent $100,00 on the "expeditions" and $10,000 on the San Francisco exhibition. It may have been an occasion of competitive boasting among the fraternity of "great bankers." Unidentified press clipping, n.d., drawer 1, WC.
6. Gibbons, *John Wanamaker*, 2:113.
7. Wanamaker, *Maxims*, 100.
8. *Golden Book of the Wanamaker Stores*, 1:161–64. See Appel, *Business Biogra-*

phy, 95–100, Leach, *Land of Desire,* 3–12, 32–35, and Trachtenberg, *Incorporation of America,* 130–39.

9. *Golden Book,* 1:21, 28–29, 34, 43–45.
10. Bellamy, *Looking Backward,* 62–63. The quoted passage in *Golden Book,* 49–50, combines separate passages.
11. *Golden Book,* 1:45–50, 71; Foucault, *Power/Knowledge,* 146–65.
12. Quoted in Appel, *Business Biography,* 92.
13. Ibid., 81.
14. Appendix A, drawer 23, WP.
15. *Golden Book,* 1:114.
16. Bellamy, *Looking Backward,* chap. 9; Leach, *Land of Desire,* 124–25.
17. See Appel, *Business Biography,* 97–99; Leach, *Land of Desire,* 124–29.
18. "The Wanamaker System," 1899, Personal Records, box 20, WP.
19. Gibbons, *John Wanamaker,* 1:262–63.
20. Two unpublished papers that treat the pedagogical uses of paintings in the Wanamaker store are Walker, "Discovering 'Great Men,'" and Walker and Lupkin, "Sermon Pictures." Also see Tyler, "'Commerce and Poetry," and Leach, *Land of Desire,* chaps. 2 and 3.
21. See Orvell, *Real Thing,* 42–44.
22. *Golden Book,* 1:203–04.
23. Ibid., 227.
24. Tyler, "Commerce and Poetry," 86.
25. J. Wanamaker to R. Wanamaker, JW's Letterpress Books, July 21, 1909, box 13, vol. 4, WP.
26. Quoted in Hine, *Burnham,* 303.
27. *A Friendly Guide-Book to the Wanamaker Store,* 1923, 9.
28. Appel, *Business Biography,* xv–xvi.
29. *Golden Book,* 2:153.
30. Leach, *Land of Desire,* 3.
31. *Golden Book,* 1:11.
32. *Wanamaker-Orginator.* March 8, 1909, box 75, Store Publications, WP. Wanamaker, who gave financial support to these institutions, had commercial transactions as well with the Hampton Institute (selling harnesses made by black and Indian students in the store) and the Carlisle School (selling boys' and girls' clothing to the school); see Szasz and Ryan, "American Indian Education," 293. John Wanamaker to Pratt, October 14, 1879, Pratt Papers, RHP. My thanks to Joel Pfister for this information.
33. Schreier, *Becoming American Women,* 12.
34. Undated manuscript of editorial-advertisement, Store Publication, box 91b, WP.
35. Gibbons, *John Wanamaker,* 2:261, 263–65.
36. *The Outlook,* Wanamaker Expedition.
37. See Trachtenberg, *Incorporation of America,* 151–53.
38. "Just Hatched," undated brochure, HSP; J. Wanamaker to J. K. Dixon, January 5, 1907, drawer 1, WC.
39. *Photo Era,* October 1906.

40. *Photo Era*, November 1906.
41. J. Wanamaker to J. K. Dixon, February 21, 1907, J.W.'s Letterpress Book, box 13, vol. 3, WP.
42. Dixon to Wood, June 18, 1925, drawer 1, WC.
43. Journal entry, October 29, 1907, WP.
44. J. Wanamaker to Dixon, October 16, 1907, Letterpress Book, box 13, vol. 3, WP.
45. J. Wanamaker to Dixon, August 25, 1914, Letterpress Book, box 14, vol. 1, WP.
46. J. Wanamaker to Dixon, February 5, 1913, Letterpress book, Box 13, vol. 6, WP.
47. J. Wanamaker to R. Wanamaker, August 16, 1909, Letterpress Book, box 13, vol. 4, WP.
48. *The Outlook*, obituary of Rodman Wanamaker; *National Cyclopaedia of American Biography*.
49. "Rodman Wanamaker Interviewed," 1916, drawer 2, WC.
50. Dixon to Robert G. Valentine, July 7, 1909, drawer 1, WC.
51. Dixon to Wood, June 18, 1925, drawer 1, WC.
52. Culin, "A Summer Trip among the Western Indians." Gibbons, *John Wanamaker*, 1:83–84.
53. Gibbons, *John Wanamaker*, 1:35–37.
54. F. E. Leupp to Dixon, August 28, 1908, drawer 3, WC: "Subject: Request of Dr. J. K. Dixon for permission to use Crow Indians in reproduction of Custer fight for motion picture purpose."
55. Valentine to Superintendents, August 2, 1909, drawer 3, WC.
56. Dixon to R. Wanamaker, July 21, 1908, drawer 3, WC.
57. Letters, Dixon and William H. Holmes, chief of Bureau of American Ethnology, May and June 1908, drawer 2, WC.
58. It's likely that the Crow photographer Richard Throssel worked with Dixon's crew in 1908 and 1909. Earlier he was befriended by Edward Curtis, from whom he learned lessons in pictorialism; later he worked as a photographer for the Indian Service. See Albright, *Crow Indian Photographer*, 25–50.
59. Gibbons, *John Wanamaker*, 1:35–37.
60. Tyler, "'Commerce and Poetry,'" 91. Earlier in 1908 Dixon had staged "motion pictures" (this may have been a stereopticon show) of Longfellow's *Paul Revere's Ride* in the recently opened Egyptian Hall of the Philadelphia store; Hale, "Hiawatha Played by Real Indians."
61. Unsigned memo to Dixon, March 31, 1909; Dixon to Mr. M. J. Chapman, Piano Department, April 1, 1909, drawer 2, WC.
62. *Wanamaker Primer*, 45.
63. Ibid., 44.
64. Ibid., xi.
65. Ibid., 55, 5.
66. Ibid., 8.
67. Ibid., 14–37.
68. Ibid., 35, 44.
69. Undated manuscript, Misc. Notes, drawer 1, WC.
70. Rodman Wannamaker interview, drawer 2, Misc. Corr., WC.

71. Undated and unascribed manuscript, Misc. Notes, drawer 1, WC.

72. Leach, *Land of Desire*, 166–69.

73. Deloria, *Playing Indian*, chap. 9.

74. James, *What the White Race May Learn*, 181. For a fascinating portrait of the controversial and questionable James, see Smith, *Reimagining Indians*, 145–64.

75. Typescript, "Hiawatha—The Passion Play of the American Indian," Lectures and Films, drawer 1, WC.

76. *Wanamaker Primer*, 46.

77. Dixon to Valentine, July 7, 1909, 1909 Expedition, drawer 3, WC.

78. Typescript of lecture, "How We Photographed the Indians," Lectures and Films, drawer 1, WC.

79. *The Nation*, review of *Vanishing Race*. Curtis's photographs in Ryan's *Flute of the Gods* may have given Dixon some specific ideas, especially the cover image of a silhouetted figure, naked with breech cloth, standing on a cliff, arms raised in prayer against a dark sky—a compositional favorite of Dixon. Curtis's popular narrative with photographs, drawings, and texts, *Indian Days of Long Ago,* may have been a riposte to Dixon's *Vanishing Race*, though there is no exact evidence to prove this.

80. Dixon, *Vanishing Race*, 191–92.

81. Ibid., 51.

82. Ibid., 10.

83. Ibid., 7.

84. Hubbard, "The Indian Farewell," letterpress copy, Misc. Corr., drawer 2, WC.

85. "Suggestions," 2–3, Misc. Corr., Lectures and Films, drawer 2, WC.

86. Untitled memo, typescript, Misc. Corr., Wanamaker Store, drawer 2, WC.

87. E. M. Bowman to Dixon, June 3, 1912, Misc. Corr., drawer 2, WC.

88. Dixon, "Memo," 65–66, Lectures and Films, Romance of the Vanishing Race, Last Great Indian Council, drawer 1, WC.

89. On the Armory show and the Paterson Pageant, see Green, *New York*.

90. Dixon to L. H. Abbott, February 7, 1913, National American Indian Memorial, Department of Interior Corr., drawer 3, WC.

91. Dixon to Abbott, February 13, 1913, ibid.

92. Dixon, "National American Indian Memorial, Inaugural Proceedings," 14, February 22, 1913, 14, ibid.

93. "First American" pamphlet, ibid.

94. Barsh, "American Heart of Darkness," 93, 111.

95. J. F. Tams to Dixon, March 10, 1913, October 13, 1914, National American Indian Memorial, drawer 3, WC.

96. On Ogden's role in the store and his activities as a benefactor of the Hampton Institute, see Leach, *Land of Desire*, 51 and passim.

97. Program, "Ceremonies Attending the Official Inauguration of the National American Indian Memorial," National American Indian Memorial, 1913, WC.

98. Press clippings, ibid.

99. *New York Times*, February 23, 1913.

100. Truettner, "Science and Sentiment," 33.

101. Keune quotes a representative of the Department of the Interior, a Mr. Boykin, who wrote to his superior, Cato Sell, in 1915, complaining about Dixon's pretensions in his lectures and the exhibition of his photographs at the Panama-Pacific Exposition in San Francisco (where the Wanamaker exhibit won a silver medal): "Apparently the only way to stop a blatherskite like that is to kill him, but I have refrained from doing so up to this time" ("Immodest Proposal," 780).

102. Curtis to Hodge, February 24, 1913, FWH.

103. "Feature film," Lectures and Films, Romance of a Vanishing Race: Titles and Leaders, drawer 1, WC.

104. Britten, *American Indians*, 39–54.

105. Burke, *Attitudes*, 58.

106. Guenter, *American Flag*, 132, 161.

107. *Flags of America*, 32; Bishop and Peary, *Uncle Sam's Panama Canal*, 112–14, includes a section on "The Races of Man," in which we read that "the races of the black type are the least civilized," the "white races" "the most civilized, advanced, and progressive peoples of the world," comprising the Hamitic, Semitic, and Aryan groups, and "races of the yellow type" in between, ranging from the "highly civilized" Japanese and Chinese to Mongols, Malayans, Tartars, Turks, and American Indians.

108. Utley, Introduction to McLaughlin, *My Friend the Indian*, xi.

109. Ibid., 2, 260.

110. Ibid., 238, 18, 221.

111. McLaughlin, "Report," part 1, 113–17.

112. Ibid.

113. Ibid., 118–19.

114. Ibid., 12, 11.

115. Rollin Dixon to J. K. Dixon, December 14, 1915, Misc. Corr., drawer 2, WC.

116. McLaughlin, "Report," 150.

117. Keune, "Immodest Proposal," 779–78; *Quarterly Journal of the Society of American Indians*, 1913, January–March 1914. For more on the SAI's outrage against Dixon's "jingoism," see Barsh, 108.

Additional Sources

Descriptions of the Wanamaker Collection at the William Hammond Mathers Museum, Indiana University, can be found in Thomas A. Kavanagh, Introduction to *North American Indian Portraits: Photographs from the Wanamaker Expeditions* (New York: Konecky & Konecky, 1996), and Susan A. Krause, "Photographing the Vanishing Race," *Visual Anthropology* 3 (1990): 213–33. On the contributions of Wanamaker and his store to the middle-class culture of Philadelphia, see John Henry Hepp, IV, *The Middle-Class City: Transforming Space and Time in Philadelphia, 1876–1926* (Philadelphia: University of Pennsylvania Press, 2003).

On department stores as places of display, Leach's *Land of Desire* is definitive. See Schmidt, *Consumer Rites*, 159–69, for discussion of Wanamaker's Christmas displays and "the consecration of the marketplace." See also the essays collected in Bonner, *Consuming Visions.* Simon N. Patten's influential ideas about abundance and consumption can be found in his *The New Basis of Civilization* (New York: Macmillan, 1907). See Trachtenberg, *Incorporation of America*, 130–39, 151–53. On the new place of "objects" in this era, see Brown's *A Sense of Things*, especially chapter 3. Lears's *Fables of Abundance* and *No Place of Grace* are major studies of the cultural horizon within which the Wanamaker store flourished. Also relevant is Higham's important essay, "The Reorientation of American Culture."

On the belief that the American Indians descended from the "Lost Tribes" of Israel, see Elkin, "Imagining Idolatry"; Jowitt, "Radical Identities?"; and Popkin, "Rise and Fall of the Jewish Indian Theory."

Susan Applegate Krause's "Capturing the Vanishing Race: The Photographs of Dr. Joseph K. Dixon" (Master's thesis, Indiana University, 1980) is still the fullest account of the career of Dixon. On Dixon and Curtis and the image of Indians in the emerging visual culture, see Griffiths, *Wondrous Difference*, 236–52, which includes discussion of "ethnographic accuracy, filmic realism, and scientific legitimacy." See "Wanamaker Aids Indians' History," *Nickelodeon* 3, no. 9 (April 30, 1910): 224. Beth Fowkes Tobin sheds important light on the relevance of the famous West painting to the Wanamaker enterprise in "Native Land and Foreign Desire: William Penn's Treaty with the Indians." *American Indian Culture and Research Journal* 19 (1995): 87–119. Also relevant are Conn, *Museums and Intellectual Life*, and Horne, "Reservations at the Hotel Astor."

6. The Great Bridge

1. Standing Bear, *My People the Sioux*, 171.
2. Although there is no mention of the Carlisle School band in *Opening Ceremonies of the New York and Brooklyn Bridge, May 24, 1883*, there is no reason to doubt Standing Bear's account. School bands from far and wide joined the day's festivities, and it is known that the Carlisle School band was performing in Brooklyn at that time, even sharing a church platform on one occasion with the Reverend Henry Ward Beecher. Brooklyn *Eagle*, May 1, 1883. See Trachtenberg, *Brooklyn Bridge*, 115–28, and McCullough, *The Great Bridge*, 525–42.
3. Crane, *The Bridge*, 73, 75.
4. Ibid., 12, 16, 22–26, 74–76.
5. So Maurice Kenny remarks (the bridge "was built in part by Iroquois ironworkers") in his Foreword to Castro, *Interpreting the Indian*, xi. See 55–59 for Castro's discussion of Crane's poem.
6. The others were *My Indian Boyhood, Land of the Spotted Eagle*, and *Stories of the Sioux*.
7. Deloria, *Speaking of Indians*, 15–44. On Deloria's text, see Weaver, *That the People Might Live*, 110–17. On recognition in Indian law of the "band" as a unit of native society, see Haas, *The Indian and the Law*, 2, 26–28.
8. Standing Bear, *Land of the Spotted Eagle*, 123–24.
9. George, *Social Problems*, 8–9.
10. *Saturday Review of Literature.*

11. Hartley, *Adventures in the Arts*, 13, 28. See Corn, "Marsden Hartley's Native Amerika" in *The Great American Thing*, 250–56.
12. McDonald, *Phoenix*, 90.
13. Edmund Wilson's "Indian Corn Dance" fills in the details with poker-faced send-ups of some of the crowd "the Indians are up against every time they hold one of their open dances." "It's as if they felt that the Indians had some key, some integrity, some harmony with nature, which they, the white Americans, had lost" (*American Jitters*, 210–11).
14. Lawrence, *Studies*, 100, 102.
15. Ibid., 103.
16. Sapir, "Culture Genuine and Spurious." See the discussion of this essay in Stocking, "Ethnographic Sensibility of the 1920s," 288–90.
17. Williams, *American Grain*, 128, 108, 130, 137.
18. Quoted in Rudnick, *Utopian Vistas*, 99–102. Standing Bear, on the other hand, expressed a high regard for Mary Austin in correspondence with her in the early 1930s. He sent her a copy of *My People the Sioux* "to show my appreciation for the wonderful work you are doing in writing of the American Indian drama" and added that he read "your writings with more and more delight." He asked if she would exchange autographed pictures with him and invited her to visit. Standing Bear to Austin, September 8, 1930; January 10, 1931; October 28, 1933, AU.
19. Parsons, *North American Indian Life*, 13, 2. See the interesting review by Sapir, one contributor, which conceded the difficulty of thinking "oneself into the tacit assumptions of so alien a mode of life as was [sic] that of an American Indian tribe." Sapir asked whether "the conscious knowledge of the ethnologist [can] be fused with that of the intuitions of the artists" and thought the best passages of the book were those that adhere to the "letter" of "the spirit of the primitive" (*The Dial*).
20. Rusch, *Jean Toomer Reader*, 15, 252, 244, 107–10.
21. Ibid., 249, 253.
22. Standing Bear, *Land of the Spotted Eagle*, 170.
23. Standing Bear, *My People the Sioux*, 133.
24. Ibid., 230.
25. Ibid., 137.
26. Ibid., 236.
27. Ibid., 69, 75, 270.
28. Du Bois, *Souls of Black Folk*, 370.
29. Ellis, "Luther Standing Bear," 150.
30. Brooks, Review of *My People the Sioux*; Van Doren, "A Recent Eden"; Duffus, "An Indian's Story of His People."
31. Standing Bear, "The Tragedy of the Sioux."
32. Standing Bear, *Land of the Spotted Eagle*, 235.
33. Standing Bear, *My Indian Boyhood*, 53. See also Vizenor, *Postindian Conversations*, 73.
34. Heflin, "I Remain Alive." I am indebted to Penelope Kelsey for sharing with me her unpublished "Luther Standing Bear."

35. Vizenor, *Manifest Manners*, 4.
36. Clastres, *Society Against the State*, 27-48.
37. Standing Bear, *My People the Sioux*, 275, 271. See also *My Indian Boyhood*, 144-57.
38. Clastres, *Society Against the State*, 45.
39. Standing Bear, *My People the Sioux*, 27.
40. Ibid., 2.
41. Ibid., 2, 279, 282.
42. "Indian Chief's Rites Today."
43. Standing Bear, *My People the Sioux*, 178, 179.
44. Ibid., 184.
45. Ibid., 189, 190.
46. Quoted in Eastman, *Pratt*, 193-94.
47. Ellis, "Luther Standing Bear," 139-41, places Standing Bear with Eastman and Bonnin as members of the "remarkable group of Indian writers" who "gave voice to Indian attitudes and opinions that had long gone unheard." "These writers gave names to Indian authors; they cut the trails so that others might follow."
48. Standing Bear, *Land of the Spotted Eagle*, 38.
49. Ibid., xv.
50. Hodge, "Against the Wind." Hodge report on Standing Bear manuscript to Thomas Y. Crowell Company, n.d. [1931], FWH.
51. Standing Bear to Thomas Y. Crowell, June 6, 1931, FWH. Crowell either refused the book or Standing Bear preferred his old publisher, Houghton Mifflin.
52. Burke, *Attitudes Toward History*, 308-14.
53. Vizenor, *Manifest Manners*, 54-55.
54. Standing Bear, *Land of the Spotted Eagle*, 255.
55. Du Bois, *Souls of Black Folk*, 370.
56. Cohen, *Handbook*, 122.
57. Cohen, "Americanizing the White Man," 190.
58. Howe, "Story of America." See also Ball, "Stories of Origins and Constitutional Possibilities."
59. Malcomson, *One Drop*, 35.
60. Vizenor, *Manifest Manners*, 163.

Additional Sources

Studies with relevant discussions of autobiographies by native writers include Vizenor, *Manifest Manners*, Wong, *Sending My Heart Back Across the Years*, Paula Gunn Allen, *The Sacred Hoop: Recovering the Feminine in American Indian Traditions* (Boston: Beacon Press, 1986), H. David Brumble, III, *American Indian Autobiography* (Berkeley: University of California Press, 1988), Arnold Krupat, *For Those Who Come After: A Study of Native American Autobiography* (Berkeley: University of California Press, 1985), Arnold Krupat, ed., *Native American Autobiography: An Anthology* (Madison: University of Wisconsin Press, 1994).

Bibliography

Manuscript Collections

Austin, Mary, Papers. Huntington Library, San Marino, California.

Carlisle School materials. http://www.carlisleindianschool.org.

Curtis, E. S., Special Collection. University Archives, University of Washington, Seattle.

Curtis, E. S., Collection. Pierpont Morgan Library, New York.

Curtis, E. S., Collection. Southwest Museum, Los Angeles.

Curtis, E. S., materials, Seattle Public Library.

Douglass, Frederick, Papers. Library of Congress.

Hodge, F. W., Collection (MS7.NAI.1). Braun Research Library, Southwest Museum, Los Angeles.

Leach, Harriet, Letters. Seattle Public Library.

Longfellow materials. Huntington Library, San Marino, California.

Longfellow Papers. Houghton Library, Harvard University.

Longfellow, H. W., Collection. Longfellow House, National Park Service, Cambridge, Massachusetts.

McLaughlin, James, Papers. Assumption College, Richardton, North Dakota.

Pratt, R. H., Papers. Beinecke Library, Yale University.

Turner, F. J., Collection. Huntington Library, San Marino, California.

Wanamaker Collection.William Hammond Mathers Museum, Indiana University, Bloomington.

Wanamaker materials. University Museum, University of Pennsylvania.

Wanamaker Papers. Historical Society of Pennsylvania, Philadelphia.

Books and Articles

(Not all references cited in "Additional Sources" in the notes for each chapter are listed here.)

Abrams, Ann Uhry. *The Pilgrims and Pocahontas: Rival Myths of American Origin.* Boulder, CO: Westview Press, 1999.

Ahokas, Pijo. "A Jewish Peddler as an Indian Chief: The Revisionist Western and Benard Malamud's *The People.*" *Modern Jewish Studies* 9 (1994): 5–20.

Albright, Peggy. *Crow Indian Photographer: The Work of Richard Throssell.* Albuquerque: University of New Mexico Press, 1997.

Allan, Sidney [Sadakichi Hartmann]. "E. S. Curtis, Photo Historian." *Wilson's Photographic Magazine* 44 (August 1907): 361–63.

Anderson, Nancy K. "'Curious Historical Artistic Data': Art History and Western American Art." In Prown, *Discovered Lands, Invented Pasts.*

Appel, Joseph H. *The Business Biography of John Wanamaker, Founder and Builder.* New York: Macmillan, 1930.

Appleby, Joyce. *Inheriting the Revolution: The First Generation of Americans.* Cambridge, MA: Harvard University Press, 2000.

Archdeacon, Thomas J. *Becoming American: An Ethnic History.* New York: Free Press, 1983.

"Are We Facing an Immigration Peril?" *The New York Times*, January 29, 1905.

Armstrong, L. O. *Hiawatha, or Manabozho: An Ojibway Indian Play.* N.p., 1901.

Arvin, Newton, *Longfellow: His Life and Work.* Boston: Little, Brown, 1963.

Astrov, Margot, *American Indian Prose and Poetry.* New York: John Day, 1946.

Auden, W. H. Introduction to Henry James, *The American Scene.* New York: Scribner's, 1946.

Austin, Mary. *The American Rhythm: Studies and Reexpressions of Amerindian Songs.* Boston: Houghton Mifflin, 1923.

———. *Earth Horizon.* Boston: Houghton Mifflin, 1932.

———. "Indian Tales for Children." *The New Republic* (November 10, 1926): 348–49.

———. Introduction to George W. Cronyn, *The Path of the Rainbow*, xiii, xxviii.

———. "Up Stream." *The Dial* 70 (1922): 634–39.

Baca, Lawrence R. "The Legal Status of American Indians." In Washburn, *History of Indian-White Relations.*

Baker, Carlos. *Ernest Hemingway: A Life Story.* New York: Scribner's, 1976.

Ball, Milner S. "Stories of Origins and Constitutional Possibilities." *Michigan Law Review* 87 (1988–1989): 2280–2319.

Barsh, Russel Lawrence. "An American Heart of Darkness: The 1913 Expedition for American Indian Citizenship." *Great Plains Quarterly* 13 (Spring 1993): 2, 91–116.

Barsh, Russel Lawrence, and James Youngblood Henderson. *The Road: Indian Tribes and Political Liberty.* Berkeley: University of California Press, 1980.

Basso, Keith H. *Wisdom Sits in Places: Landscape and Language among the Western Apache.* Albuquerque: University of New Mexico Press, 1996.

Bataille, Georges. "The Notion of Expenditure." In *Visions of Excess: Selected Writings, 1927–1939*, edited by Allan Stoekl. Minneapolis: University of Minnesota Press, 1985.

"Battling for Poor Lo's Ballot." *Literary Digest* 99 (October 1928): 60–62.

Bellamy, Edward. *Looking Backward, 2000–1887*. 1888; repr., Boston: Houghton Mifflin, 1966.

Benjamin, Walter. *Illuminations*. New York: Harcourt, 1955.

Benson, Lee. *Turner and Beard: American Historical Writing Reconsidered*. Glencoe, IL: Free Press, 1960.

Berkhofer, Robert. *The White Man's Indian: Images of the American Indian from Columbus to the Present*. New York: Vintage Books, 1979.

Bieder, Robert E. *Science Encounters the Indian, 1820–1880: The Early Years of American Ethnology*. Norman: University of Oklahoma Press, 1986.

Bierhorst, John, ed. *Four Masterworks of American Indian Literature*. Tuscon: University of Arizona Press, 1974.

Billington, Ray Allen. *The Genesis of the Frontier Thesis*. San Marino, CA: Huntington Library, 1971.

Bishop, Joseph Bucklin, and Admiral Robert E. Peary. *Uncle Sam's Panama Canal and World History*. New York: John Wanamaker, for World Syndicate Company, 1913.

Bluestein, Gene. *The Voice of the Folk: Folklore and American Literary Theory*. Amherst: University of Massachusetts Press, 1972.

Boesen, Victor, and Florence Curtis Graybill. *Edward Sheriff Curtis: Photographer of the North American Indian*. New York: Dodd, Mead, 1977.

Bonner, Simon J., ed. *Consuming Visions: Accumulation and Display of Goods in America, 1880–1920*. New York: W. W. Norton, 1989.

Bordman, Gerald. *American Musical Theatre: A Chronicle*. New York: Oxford University Press, 2001.

Bourne, Randolph S. "Trans-national America" and "The Jew and Trans-National America." In Resek, *Randolph Bourne*, 107–33.

Boydston, Jo Ann, ed. *John Dewey: The Middle Works, 1899–1924*. Vols. 2 and 10. Carbondale: Southern Illinois University Press, 1976, 1980.

Britten, Thomas A. *American Indians in World War I: At Home and at War*. Albuquerque: University of New Mexico Press, 1997.

Bronitsky, Gordon. "Solomon Bibo: Indians and Jews at Acoma Pueblo, New Mexico." In *Jewish Assimilation, Acculturation, and Accommodation*, edited by Menachem Mor. Lanham, MD: University Press of America, 1992.

Brooks, Van Wyck. Review of Standing Bear, *My People the Sioux*. *The Independent* 120 (May 5, 1928): 436.

Brotherston, Gordon. *Book of the Fourth World: Reading the Native Americas through their Literature*. New York: Cambridge University Press, 1992.

Brower, Reuben A. *The Poetry of Robert Frost: Constellations of Intention*. New York: Oxford University Press, 1963.

Brown, Bill. *A Sense of Things: The Object Matter of American Literature*. Chicago: University of Chicago Press, 2003.

Browne, Ray B., et al. *Frontiers of American Culture*. West Lafayette, IN: Purdue University Press, 1968.

Buell, Lawrence, ed. *Henry Wadsworth Longfellow: Selected Poems*. New York: Penguin Books, 1988.

Burke, Kenneth. *Attitudes Toward History*. Boston: Beacon Press, 1959.

Butler, Jon. *Becoming American: The Revolution Before 1776*. Cambridge, MA: Harvard University Press, 2000.

Cadwalader, Sandra, and Vine Deloria Jr., eds. *The Aggression of Civilization: Federal Indian Policy since the 1880s*. Philadelphia: Temple University Press, 1984.

Cahan, Abraham. "How Should Yiddish be Written?" In Cassedy, *Building the Future*.

————. "Philologist and Lexicogapher of the Ghetto." In Rischin, *Grandma Never Lived in America*.

————. "'When I Write Yiddish, it is Pure Yiddish.'" In Rischin, *Grandma Never Lived in America*.

————. *Yekl and The Imported Bidegroom and Other Stories of the New York Ghetto*. 1896; repr., New York: Dover, 1970.

Carr, Helen. *Inventing the American Primitive*. New York: New York University Press, 1996.

Cassedy, Steven. *To the Other Shore: The Russian Jewish Intellectual Who Came to America*. Princeton: Princeton University Press, 1997.

————. ed. and trans. *Building the Future: Jewish Immigrant Intellectuals and the Making of Tsukunft*. New York: Holmes & Meier, 1999.

Castro, Michael. *Interpreting the Indian: Twentieth-Century Poets and the Native American*. Albuquerque, University of New Mexico Press, 1983.

Catlin, George. *Letters and Notes on the Manners, Customs, and Condition of the North American Indians*. 2 vols. 1841; repr., New York: Dover, 1973.

Chametzky, Jules. *From the Ghetto: The Fiction of Abraham Cahan*. Amherst: University of Massachusetts Press, 1977.

————. et al., eds. *Jewish American Literature: An Anthology*. New York: W. W. Norton, 2001.

Cheyfitz, Eric. "Doctrines of Discovery." *Common-Place* 2, no. 1 (October 2001).

Clastres, Pierre. *Society Against the State*. New York: Zone Books, 1987.

Cohen, Felix. *Handbook of Federal Indian Law*. Washington, DC.: GPO, 1941.

————. "Americanizing the White Man." *The American Scholar*, 21:2 (1952): 177–91.

Conn, Steven. *History's Shadow: Native Americans and Historical Consciousness in the Nineteenth Century*. Chicago: University of Chicago Press, 2004.

————. *Museums and Intellectual Life, 1876–1926*. Chicago: University of Chicago Press, 1998.

Conway, Moncure. "New Work." *National Intelligencer*. Washington, November 24, 1855.

Cooperman, Jehiel B., and Sarah H. Cooperman. eds. and trans. *America in Yiddish Poetry: An Anthology*. New York: Exposition Press, 1967.

Copway, George. *Life, Letters, and Speeches*, ed. A. Lavonne Brown and Donald B. Smith. Lincoln: University of Nebraska Press, 1997.

Corbin, Alice Henderson. Review of George W. Cronyn. *The Path of the Rainbow*. *Poetry* 11 (April 1919): 45–46.

Corn, Wanda. *The Great American Thing: Modern Art and National Identity, 1915–1935*. Berkeley: University of California Press, 1999.

———. "Marsden Hartley's Native Amerika." In *Marsden Hartley*, edited by Elizabeth Mankin Kornhauser, 69–94. New Haven: Yale University Press, 2002.

Cowan, William. "Ojibwa Vocabulary in Longfellow's *Hiawatha*." In *Papers of the Eighteenth Algonquian Conference*, edited by William Cowan. Ottawa: Carleton University, 1987.

Crane, Hart. *The Bridge*. New York: Liveright, 1933.

Crèvecoeur, J. Hector St. John de. *Letters from an American Farmer*. New York: E. P Dutton, 1957.

Cronon, William. *Changes on the Land*. New York: Hill & Wang, 1983.

———. "Telling Tales on Canvas: Landscapes of Frontier Change." In Prown, *Discovered Lands, Invented Pasts*.

Cronyn, George W. *The Path of the Rainbow*. New York: Boni & Liveright, 1918.

Culin, Steward. "A Summer Trip among the Western Indians (The Wanamaker Expedition)." *Bulletin of the Free Museum of Science and Art* 3 (1901): 1–22.

Curtis, Edward S. *Indian Days of Long Ago*. Illustrated with photographs by the author and drawings by F. N. Wilson. Yonkers-on-the-Hudson: World Book Company, 1914.

———. "Indians of the Stone Houses." *Scribner's Magazine* 45 (February 1909): 161–75.

———. *In the Land of the Head-Hunters*. Illustrated with photographs by the author. Yonkers-on-the-Hudson: World Book Company, 1915.

———. *The North American Indian*. 20 vols. New York: Cambridge University Press, 1907–30.

———. "Vanishing Indian Types: The Tribes of Northwest Plains." *Scribner's Magazine* 39 (June 1906): 657–71.

———. "Village Tribes of the Desert Land." *Scribner's Magazine* 45 (March 1909): 275–87.

Cutler, Charles L. *O Brave New Words! Native American Loanwords in Current English*. Norman: University of Oklahoma Press, 1994.

Davis, Barbara A. *Edward S. Curtis: The Life and Times of a Shadow Catcher*. San Francisco: Chronicle Books, 1985.

Davis, David Brion. *The Problem of Slavery in Western Culture*. Ithaca, NY: Cornell University Press, 1966.

Debo, Angie. *A History of the Indians of the United States*. Norman: University of Oklahoma Press, 1970.

DeCosta, Benjamin F. *Hiawatha: The Story of the Iroquois Sage, in Prose and Verse*. New York: Anson D. F. Randolph, 1873.

Deloria, Ella C. *Speaking of Indians*. 1944; repr., Vermillion, SD: Dakota Books, 1992.

Deloria, Philip J. *Playing Indian*. New Haven: Yale University Press, 1998.

Deloria, Vine, and Clifford M. Lytle. *The Nations Within: The Past and Future of American Indian Sovereignty*. New York: Pantheon Books, 1984.

Deloria, Vine, Jr. "'Congress in its Wisdom': The Course of Indian Legislation." In Cadwalader and Deloria, *The Aggression of Civilization*.

Dewey, John. "Interpretation of Savage Mind." In Boydston, *John Dewey*, vol. 2.

———. "Nationalizing Education." In Boydston, *John Dewey*, vol. 10.

————. "The Principle of Nationality." *Menorah Journal* 3 (1917): 203–08.

Dilworth, Leah. *Imagining Indians in the Southwest: Persisting Visions of a Primitive Past*. Washington, DC: Smithsonian Institution Press, 1996.

Dippie, Brian, et al. *George Catlin and his Indian Gallery*. New York: W. W. Norton, 2002.

————. *The Vanishing American: White Attitudes & U.S. Indian Policy*. Lawrence: University of Kansas Press, 1982.

Dixon, Joseph Kossuth. *The Vanishing Race*. 3rd and rev. ed. Philadelphia: National American Indian Memorial Association Press, 1925.

Douglass, Frederick. "Self-Made Men: Address before the Students of the Indian Industrial School at Carlisle, Pa, 1893." FDP.

Du Bois, W.E.B. "The Negro Race in the United States of America." In Spiller, *Universal Races Congress*, 360–61.

————. *The Souls of Black Folk* (1903); "The Conservation of Races" (1897); "The Souls of White Folk" (1920), in *Du Bois, Writings*. New York: Library of America, 1986.

Duffus, R. L. "An Indian's Story of His People." *The New York Times Book Review*, June 4, 1933, 4.

Eastman, Elaine Goodale. *Pratt, The Red Man's Moses*. Norman: University of Oklahoma Press, 1935.

Elkin, Judith Laikin. "'Imagining Idolotry': Missionaries, Indians, and Jews." In *Religion and the Authority of the Past*, edited by Tobin Seibers. Ann Arbor: University of Michigan Press, 1993.

Ellis, Reuben, ed. *The Selected Essays of Mary Austin*. Carbondale: Southern Illinois University Press, 1996.

Ellis, Richard. "Luther Standing Bear: 'I Would Raise Him to be an Indian.'" In Moses and Wilson, *Indian Lives*.

Engels, Frederick. *The Origin of the Family, Private Property, and the State*. 1884, repr., New York: Pathfinder, 1972.

Evans, Brad. "Cushing's Zuni Sketchbooks: Literature, Anthropology and American Notions of Culture." *American Quarterly* 49 (December 1997): 717–45.

Faris, James C. *Navajo and Photography*. Albuquerque: University of New Mexico Press, 1996.

Fenton, William N. *The Great Law and the Longhouse: A Political History of the Iroquois Confederacy*. Norman: University of Oklahoma Press, 1998.

————. Introduction to Lewis Henry Morgan, *League of the Iroquois*.

Fergus, Charles. *Shadow Catcher*. New York: Soho Press, 1991.

Ferguson, Robert A. "Longfellow's Political Fears: Civic Authority and the Role of the Artist in *Hiawatha* and *Miles Standish*." *American Literature* 50, no. 2 (May 1978): 181–215.

Fey, Harold E., and D'Arcy McNickle. *Indians and Other Americans*. New York: Harper, 1959.

Fiedler, Leslie. *Return of the Vanishing American*. New York: Stein and Day, 1968.

Fishman, Joshua A. "Introducing Khayem Zhitlovski." In *New Perspectives and Issues in Educational Language Policy*, edited by Robert L. Cooper et al., 145–54. Amsterdam: John Benjamins Publishing Co., 2001.

————. "The Sociology of Yiddish." *Never Say Die! A Thousand Years of Yiddish in Jewish Life and Letters*. The Hague: Mouton, 1981: 1–102.

Fiske, Christabel F. "Mercerized Folklore." *Poet Lore* 31 (Winter 1920): 538–75.

Flags of America. Philadelphia: The John Wanamaker Store, 1926.

Fletcher, Angus. "Whitman and Longfellow: Two Types of the American Poet." *Raritan* 10, no. 4 (1991): 141.

Folsom, Ed. *Walt Whitman's Native Representations*. New York: Cambridge University Press, 1994.

Forbes, Jack D. *Africans and Native Americans: The Language of Race and the Evolution of Red-Black Peoples*. Urbana: University of Illinois Press, 1993.

Foucault, Michel. *Power/Knowledge: Selected Interviews & Other Writings, 1972–1977*. Ed. Colin Gordon, trans. Colin Gordon et al. New York: Pantheon, 1980.

Frank, Florence Kiper. "The Jew as Jewish Artist." *Poetry* 22 (1923): 211.

Frederickson, George M. *The Black Image in the White Mind: The Debate on Afro-American Character and Destiny, 1817–1914*. New York: Harper, 1971.

Frost, Robert. *Frost: Collected Poems, Prose, & Plays*. New York: Library of America, 1995.

Frye, Northrup. *Anatomy of Criticism*. New York: Atheneum, 1957.

Furtwangler, Albert. *Answering Chief Seattle*. Seattle: University of Washington Press, 1997.

George, Henry. *Social Problems*. 1884, repr., New York: Doubleday, 1905.

Gibbons, Herbert Adams. *John Wanamaker*. 2 vols. New York: Harper, 1926.

Gidley, Mick. *Edward S. Curtis and the North American Indian Incorporated*. New York: Cambridge University Press, 1998.

————, ed. *Edward S. Curtis and the North American Indian Project in the Field*. Lincoln: University of Nebraska Press, 2003.

Gilman, Sander. *Jewish Self-Hatred: Anti-Semitism and the Hidden Language of the Jews*. Baltimore: Johns Hopkins University Press, 1986.

Gilmore, Melvin R. *Prairie Smoke*. New York: Columbia University Press, 1929.

Gioia, Dana. "Longfellow in the Aftermath of Modernism." In Parini, *Columbia History of American Poetry*.

Glassberg, David. *American Historical Pageantry: The Uses of Tradition in the Early Twentieth Century*. Chapel Hill: University of North Carolina Press, 1990.

Gleason, Philip. "American Identity and Americanization." In Thernstrom, *Harvard Encyclopedia of American Ethnic Groups*.

————. *Speaking of Diversity: Language and Ethnicity in Twentieth-Century America*. Baltimore: Johns Hopkins University Press, 1992.

Goetzmann, William H. "The Arcadian Landscapes of Edward S. Curtis." In *Perpetual Mirage: Photographic Narratives of the Desert West*. New York: Whitney Museum of American Art, 1996.

————. *The First Americans: Photographs from the Library of Congress*. Washington, DC: Starwood Publishing, 1991.

Golden Book of the Wanamaker Stores. 2 vols. Philadelphia: Wanamaker Stores, 1911.

Goldsmith, Emanuel S. *Architects of Yiddishism at the Beginning of the Twentieth Century*. Rutherford NJ: Fairleigh Dickinson University Press, 1976.

————. "The Jewish People and the Yiddish Language," in Kerler, *The Politics of Yiddish*.

————. "Zhitlovsky and American Jewery." In Fishman, *Never Say Die!*

Gomez, Michael A. *Exchanging Our Country Marks: The Transformation of African Identities in the Colonial and Antebellum South*. Chapel Hill: University of North Carolina Press, 1998.

Gossett, Thomas. *Race: the History of an Idea in America*. Dallas: Southern Methodist University Press, 1963.

Gould, Stephen Jay. *The Mismeasure of Man*. New York: W. W. Norton, 1981.

Gramsci, Antonio. *Antonio Gramsci: Selections from Cultural Writings*. Cambridge, MA: Harvard University Press, 1985.

Graves, Joseph L., Jr. *The Emperor's New Clothes: Biological Theories of Race at the Millennium*. New Brunswick, NJ: Rutgers University Press, 2001.

Graybill, Florence Curtis, and Victor Boesen. *Edward Sheriff Curtis: Visions of a Vanishing Race*. Boston: Houghton Mifflin, 1976.

"Great Cantata Founded on 'Hiawatha,' A." *Literary Digest* 20 (April 21, 1900).

Green, Martin. *New York, 1913: The Armory Show and the Paterson Strike Pageant*. New York: Macmillan, 1988.

Griffiths, Alison. *Wondrous Difference: Cinema, Anthropology, & Turn-of-the-Century Visual Culture*. New York: Columbia University Press, 2002.

Grinnell, George Bird. *The Story of the Indian*. New York: D. Appleton, 1896.

Gross, Milt. *Hiawatta: wit no odder poems*. New York: George H. Doran, 1926.

Guenter, Scot M. *The American Flag, 1777–1924: Cultural Shifts from Creation to Codification*. Rutherford, NJ: Fairleigh Dickinson University Press, 1990.

Haas, Theodore H. *The Indian & the Law—1 & 2*. Tribal Relations Pamphlets 2 and 3. Washington, DC: United States Indian Service, 1949.

Hagan, William T. "Private Property, the Indian's Door to Civilization." *Ethnohistory*. 3 (Spring 1956): 125–37.

————. *Theodore Roosevelt and Six Friends of the Indian*. Norman: University of Oklahoma Press, 1997.

Hale, Henry. "Hiawatha Played by Real Indians," *The Critic* 47 (July 1905): 41–49.

Hale, Horatio. *Hiawatha and the Iroquois Confederation, A Study in Anthropology*. Salem, MA: Salem Press, 1881.

Harkavy, Alexander. *Amerikanisher Briefen-Shteler*. Amherst, MA: National Yiddish Book Center, 1999.

Harshav, Benjamin. *The Meaning of Yiddish*. Berkeley: University of California Press, 1990.

Harshav, Benjamin, and Barbara Harshav. *American Yiddish Poetry: A Bilingual Anthology*. Berkeley: University of California Press, 1986.

Hartley, Marsden. *Adventures in the Arts*. 1921; repr., New York: Hacker Books, 1972.

Hartz, Louis. *The Founding of New Societies*. New York: Harcourt, 1964.

Heflin, Ruth J. *"I Remain Alive": The Sioux Literary Renaissance*. Syracuse: Syracuse University Press, 2000.

Herder, Johann Gottfried von. *Reflections on the Philosophy of the History of Mankind*. Abridged by Frank E. Manuel. Chicago: University of Chicago Press, 1968.

Hertzberg, Hazel W. *The Search for an American Indian Identity: Modern Pan-Indian Movements*. Syracuse: Syracuse University Press, 1971.

Higham, John. "Indian Princess and Roman Goddess: The First Female Symbols of America." *Proceedings of the American Antiquarian Society* 100, part 1 (1990): 45–79.

———. "The Reorientation of American Culture in the 1890s." In *Origins of Modern Consciousness*, edited by John Weiss, 25–48. Detroit: Wayne State University Press, 1965.

———. *Send These to Me: Immigrants in Urban America*. Baltimore: Johns Hopkins University Press, 1984.

———. *Strangers in the Land: Patterns of American Nativism, 1860–1925*. New York: Atheneum, 1963.

Hilen, Andrew, ed. *The Letters of Henry Wadsworth Longfellow*. 6 vols. Cambridge, MA: Harvard University Press, 1966–88.

Hine, Thomas S. *Burnham of Chicago: Architect and Planner*. Chicago: University of Chicago Press, 1974.

Hobsbawm, Eric, and Terence Ranger, eds. *The Invention of Tradition*. Cambridge, UK: Cambridge University Press, 1983.

Hodge, F. W. "Against the Wind." *Saturday Review of Literature*, November 14, 1931, 282.

Holmes, Oliver Wendell. "The Physiology of Versification." In *Pages from an Old Volume of Life*. Vol. 8, *The Works of Oliver Wendell Holmes*. Boston: Houghton Mifflin, 1892.

Horne, Brian A. "Reservations at the Hotel Astor: Making Room for Native Americans Under Times Square." Department of Anthropology, University of Virginia, Charlottesville, Virginia.

Horsman, Reginald. *Race and Manifest Destiny: The Origins of American Racial Anglo-Saxonsim*. Cambridge, MA: Harvard University Press, 1981.

Howe, Irving. "Pluralism in the Immigrant World." In *The Legacy of Jewish Migration: 1881 and its Impact*, edited by David Berger. Brooklyn, NY: Brooklyn College Press, 1983.

———. *World of Our Fathers: The Journey of the East European Jews to America and the Life They Found and Made*. New York: Harcourt, 1976.

———. et al., eds. *The Penguin Book of Modern Yiddish Poetry*. New York: Penguin Books, 1987.

Howe, Irving, and Eliezer Greenberg, eds. *A Treasury of Yiddish Poetry*. New York: Holt, 1969.

Howe, LeAnne, "The Story of America: A Tribalography." In Shoemaker, *Clearing a Path*, 29–50.

Hoxie, Frederick, ed. *Encyclopedia of North American Indians*. Boston: Houghton Mifflin, 1996.

———. *A Final Promise: the Campaign to Assimilate the Indians, 1880–1920*. New York: Cambridge University Press, 1984.

———, ed. *Indians in American History*. Wheeling, IL: Harlan Davidson, 1988.

Huhndorf, Shari M. *Going Native: Indians and the American Cultural Imagination*. Ithaca, NY: Cornell University Press, 2001.

Huizinga, Johan. *America*. Ed. Herbert H. Rowen. New York: Harper, 1972.

Hymes, Dell. *"In vain I tried to tell you": Essays in Native American Ethnopoetics.* Philadelphia: University of Pennsylvania Press, 1981.

"Indian Chief's Rites Today." *Los Angeles Times*, February 24, 1939, part 1, 14:1.

"Indian is Not Disappearing, The." *The New York Times*, April 12, 1920.

Irwin, John T. *American Hieroglyphics: The Symbol of the Egyptian Hieroglyphics in the American Renaissance.* New Haven: Yale University Press, 1980.

Jackson, Virginia. "Longfellow's Tradition; or, Picture-Writing a Nation," *Modern Language Quarterly* 59 (December 1998): 471–96.

Jacobson, Matthew Frye. *Barbarian Virtues: The United States Encounters Foreign Peoples at Home and Abroad, 1876–1917.* New York: Hill & Wang, 2000.

———. *Whiteness of a Different Color: European Immigrants and the Alchemy of Race.* Cambridge, MA: Harvard University Press, 1998.

James, George Wharton. *What the White Race May Learn from the Indian.* Chicago: Forbes and Company, 1908.

James, Henry. *The American.* 1877; repr., New York: Rinehart & Company, 1949.

———. *The American Scene.* 1907; repr., Bloomington: Indiana University Press, 1968.

———. *Literary Criticism.* New York: The Library of America, 1984.

———. *The Question of Our Speech: The Lesson of Balzac: Two Lectures.* Boston: Houghton Mifflin, 1905.

Jameson, Fredric. *The Political Unconscious: Narrative as a Socially Symbolic Act.* Ithaca, NY: Cornell University Press, 1981.

Jenkins, David. "Object Lessons and Ethnographic Displays: Museum Exhibitions and the Making of American Anthropology." *Comparative Studies in Society and History* 36, no. 2 (April 1994): 242–70.

Johansen, Bruce E. *Forgotten Founders: How the American Indian Helped Shape American Democracy.* Harvard and Boston: The Harvard Common Press, 1982.

Johnson, Robert. "Red Populism? T. A. Bland, Agrarian Radicalism, and the Debate over the Dawes Act." Department of History, Yale University, New Haven, Connecticut.

Jordan, Winthrop D. *White Over Black: American Attitudes Toward the Negro. 1550–1812.* Chapel Hill: University of North Carolina Press, 1968.

Jowitt, Claire. "Radical Identities? Native Americans, Jews, and the English Commonwealth." In *Cultures of Ambivalence and Contempt: Studies in Jewish-Non-Jewish Relations,* edited by Sian Jones et al., 153–80. Portland, OR: Valentine Mitchell, 1998.

Justi, Alan H. "Southern California Photographers and the Indians of the Southwest, 1888–1910." Huntington Library, San Marino, California.

Kahn, Coppelia. "Caliban at the Stadium: Shakespeare and the Making of Americans." *The Massachusetts Review* 41, no. 2 (Summer 2000): 256–84.

Kaiwar, Vasant, and Sucheta Mazumdar, eds. *Antinomies of Modernity: Essays on Race, Orient, Nation.* Durham, NC: Duke University Press, 2003.

Kallen, Horace. *Culture and Democracy in the United States.* New York: Boni and Liveright, 1924.

Karp, Ivan, and Steven D. Lavine, eds. *Exhibiting Cultures: The Poetics and Politics of Museum Display.* Washington, DC: Smithsonian Institution Press, 1991.

Kelsey, Penelope. "Luther Standing Bear." Department of Language and Literature, Rochester Institute of Technology, Rochester, New York.

Kenny, Maurice. Foreword to Michael, Castro, *Interpreting the Indian.*

Kerber, Linda K. "The Abolitionist Perception of the Indian." *Journal of American History* 62, no. 2 (September 1975): 271–95.

Kerler, Dov-Ber, ed. *The Politics of Yiddish: Studies in Language, Literature, and Society.* Walnut Creek, CA: Altamira Press, 1998.

Keune, Manfred E. "An Immodest Proposal: A Memorial to the North American Indian." *Journal of American Culture* 1, no. 4. (Winter 1978): 766–86.

King, Desmond. *Making Americans: Immigration, Race, and the Origin of the Diverse Democracy.* Cambridge, MA: Harvard University Press, 2000.

Kornhauser, Elizabeth Mankin, ed. *Marsden Hartley.* New Haven: Yale University Press, 2002.

Kroeber, Theodora. *Ishi in Two Worlds: A Biography of the Last Wild Indian in North America.* Berkeley: University of California Press, 1976.

Lawrence, D. H. *Mornings in Mexico.* New York: Knopf, 1927.

———. *Studies in Classic American Literature.* 1923; repr., New York: Viking, 1964.

Leach, William. *Land of Desire: Merchants, Power, and the Rise of a New American Culture.* New York: Pantheon, 1993.

Lears, T. J. Jackson. *Fables of Abundance: A Cultural History of Advertising in America.* New York: Basic Books, 1994.

———. *No Place of Grace: Antimodernism and the Transformation of American Culture, 1880–1920.* New York: Pantheon, 1981.

Lepore, Jill. *A Is for American: Letters and Other Characters in the Newly United States.* New York: Random House, 2002.

Lewis, Janet. *The Invasion: A Narrative of Events Concerning the Johnston Family of St. Mary's.* Chicago: Swallow Press, 1932.

Limerick, Patricia Nelson. *Legacy of Conquest: The Unbroken Past of the American West.* New York: W. W. Norton, 1987.

Lindsey, Donald F. *Indians at Hampton Institute, 1877–1923.* Urbana: University of Illinois Press, 1995.

Lockard, Joe. "The Universal Hiawatha." *American Indian Quarterly* 24, no. 1 (2000): 110–25.

Locke, John. *The Second Treatise on Government.* 1690; repr., Amherst, NY: Prometheus Books, 1986.

Longfellow, Alice. "Introductory Notes" and "A Visit to Hiawatha's People." *The Song of Hiawatha.* Boston: Houghton Mifflin, 1901.

Longfellow, Henry Wadsworth. "Defense of Poetry." *North American Review,* 34, no. 74 (January 1832).

———. *The Song of Hiawatha.* Ed. Daniel Aaron. Rutland, VT: Charles E. Tuttle, 1992.

Longfellow, Samuel, ed. *Life of Henry Wadsworth Longfellow.* 2 vols. Boston: Ticknor, 1886.

Ludvig, Reuben. *Gezalmte Lieder* [Collected Poems]. New York: Grayzell Press, 1927.

Lyman, Christopher M. *The Vanishing Race and Other Illusions: Photographs of Indians by Edward S. Curtis.* Washington, DC: Smithsonian Institution Press, 1982.

MacKaye, Percy. *Saint Louis: A Civic Pageant*. Garden City, NY: Doubleday, 1914.

Makepeace, Anne. *Edward S. Curtis: Coming to Light*. Washington, DC: National Geographic, 2001.

Malcomson, Scott. *One Drop of Blood: The American Misadventure of Race*. New York: Farrar, Straus & Giroux, 2000.

Malmsheimer, Lonna. "'Imitation White Man': Images of Transformation at the Carlisle Indian School." *Studies in Visual Communication* 11, no. 4 (Fall 1985): 54–74.

Marks, M. L. *Jews Among the Indians*. Chicago: Benison Books, 1992.

Marshall, Edward. "The Vanishing Red Man." *The Hampton Magazine* 28 (May 1912): 245–53, 308.

Martin, Jill. "'Neither Fish, Flesh, Foul, nor Good Red Herring': The Citizenship Status of American Indians, 1830–1924." *Journal of the West* 19 (July 1990).

Mathews, J. Chesley, ed. *Henry W. Longfellow Reconsidered: A Symposium*. Hartford, CT: Transcendental Books, 1970.

McCullough, David. *The Great Bridge: The Epic Story of the Building of the Brooklyn Bridge*. New York: Simon and Schuster, 1972.

McDonald, Edward D., ed. *Phoenix: The Posthumous Papers of D. H. Lawrence*. New York: Viking, 1936.

McLaughlin, James. *My Friend the Indian*. 1910; repr., Lincoln: University of Nebraska Press, 1989.

———. "Report on Tour of Indian Agencies by the Rodman Wanamaker Expedition," January 5, 1914, microfilm, roll 30, "Rodman Wanamaker Expedition of 1913," James McLaughlin Papers.

McNickle, D'Arcy. *Native American Tribalism: Indian Survivals and Renewals*. New York: Oxford University Press, 1973.

Meany, Edmund S. "Hunting Indians with a Camera." *The World's Work* 15 (March 1908): 10004–11.

Meredith, Robyn. "They Remember Papa, But Not Very Lovingly." *The New York Times*, July 26, 1999, A10.

Michaels, Walter Benn. *Our America: Nativism, Modernism, and Pluralism*. Durham, NC: Duke University Press, 1995.

Michaelsen, Scott. *The Limits of Multiculturalism: Interrogating the Origins of American Anthropology*. Minneapolis: University of Minnesota Press, 1999.

Miller, Angela. *The Empire of the Eye: Landscape Representation and American Cultural Politics, 1825–1875*. Ithaca, NY: Cornell University Press, 1993.

Mizruchi, Susan L. *The Science of Sacrifice: American Literature and Modern Social Theory*. Princeton, NJ: Princeton University Press, 1998.

Moffit, John F., and Santiago Sebastián. *O Brave New People: The European Invention of America*. Albuquerque: University of New Mexico Press, 1996.

Mooney, James. *The Ghost-Dance Religion and Wounded Knee*. 1896; repr., New York: Dover Publications, 1973.

Morgan, Lewis Henry. *Ancient Society*. Ed. Eleanor Burke Leacock. 1877; repr., New York: Meridian Books, 1963.

———. *League of the Iroquois*. 1851; repr., Secaucus, NJ: Citadel Press, 1996.

Moses, L. G., and Raymond Wilson, eds. *Indian Lives: Essays on Nineteenth- and*

Twentieth-Century Native Americans. Albuquerque: University of New Mexico Press, 1985.

Most, Andrea. "'Big Chief Izzy Horowitz': Theatricality and Jewish Identity in the Wild West." *American Jewish History* 87, no. 4 (1999): 313–41.

Moyne, Ernest J. "Longfellow and Kah-Ge-Gah-Bowh." In Mathews, *Henry W. Longfellow Reconsidered.*

Mumford, Jeremy. "Mixed-Race Identity in a Nineteenth-Century Family: The Schoolcrafts of Sault Ste. Marie, 1824–1827." *Michigan Historical Review* 25; no. 1 (Spring 1999): 1–25.

Nation, The. Review of Joseph Kossuth Dixon, *The Vanishing Race.* 98 (February 12, 1914): 162–63.

National Cyclopaedia of American Biography 21 (1931): 27–28.

"New Immigrant Station." *The New York Times,* December 3, 1900.

New York Herald, June 16, 1907.

Ngai, Mae M. "The Architecture of Race in American Immigration Law: A Reexamination of the Immigration Act of 1924." *Journal of American History* 86 (June 1999): 67–92.

Nichols, John D. "'Chant to the Fire-fly': A Philological Problem in Ojibwe." In *Linguistic Studies Presented to John L. Finlay,* edited by H. C. Wolfart. Winnipeg: Alongonquin and Iroquoian Linguistics, 1991.

Obituary of Rodman Wanamaker. *The New York Times,* March 10, 1928.

Obituary of Rodman Wanamaker. *The Outlook* 148 (March 21, 1928).

Opening Ceremonials of the New York and Brooklyn Bridge, May 24, 1883. Brooklyn: The Brooklyn Eagle, 1883.

Outlook, The. Article on Wanamaker Expedition. 133 (July 26, 1913): 642.

Orvell, Miles. *The Real Thing: Imitation and Authenticy in American Culture, 1880–1940.* Chapel Hill: University of North Carolina Press, 1989.

Parini, Jay, ed. *The Columbia History of American Poetry.* New York: Columbia University Press, 1993.

Parsons, Elsie Clews, ed. *North American Indian Life.* 1922; repr., New York: Dover, 1992 (orig. title, *American Indian Life by Several of Its Students*).

Patterson, Orlando. *Rituals of Blood: Consequences of Slavery in Two American Centuries.* Washington, DC: Counterpoint, 1998.

Pfaller, Louis L. *James McLaughlin: The Man with an Indian Heart.* Richardton, ND: Assumption Abbey Press, 1978.

Photo Era. 17 (October 1906): 271.

———. 17 (November 1906): 312.

Poetry. 9, no. 5 (February 1917): 251. Indian poetry issue.

Pokagon, Simon. *O-Gi-Maw-Kwe Mit-I-Gwaka (Queen of the Woods).* Hartford, MI: C. H. Engle, 1899.

Popkin, Richard H. "The Rise and Fall of the Jewish Indian Theory." In *Menasseh Ben Israel and His World,* edited by Yosef Kaplan, et al. New York: E. J. Brill, 1989.

Porte, Joel, ed. *Emerson in His Journals.* Cambridge, MA: Harvard University Press, 1982.

Posnock, Ross. *The Trial of Curiosity: Henry James William James, and the Challenge of Modernity.* New York: Oxford University Press, 1991.

Prager, Leonard. "Walt Whitman in Yiddish." *Walt Whitman Quarterly Review* 1, no. 3 (December 1983): 22–35.

Pratt, Richard Henry. *Battle Field and Classroom: Four Decades with the American Indian, 1867–1904.* Ed. Robert M. Utley. New Haven, CT: Yale University Press, 1964.

———. "How to Deal with the Indians: The Potency of the Environment," 1910, R. H. Pratt Papers.

Preston, Dickson J. *Young Frederick Douglass: The Maryland Years.* Baltimore: Johns Hopkins University Press, 1980.

Prown, Jules David, et al., eds. *Discovered Lands, Invented Pasts: Transforming Visions of the American West.* New Haven, CT: Yale University Press, 1992.

Prucha, Francis Paul, ed. *Americanizing the American Indians: Writings by the "Friends of the Indians" 1880–1900.* Cambridge, MA: Harvard University Press, 1973.

Quarterly Journal of the Society of American Indians 1:4 (October–December 1913): 363.

———. 2:1 (January–March 1914): 5–6.

Radin, Paul. *The Trickster: A Study in American Indian Mythology.* New York: Schocken Books, 1972.

Red Man and Helper, The. March 1888, Carlisle Indian Industrial School.

———. July 31, 1903, Carlisle Indian Industrial School.

Reel, Estelle. Introduction to *Course of Study for the Indian Schools of the United States: Industrial and Literary.* Washington, DC: GPO, 1901.

Renan, Ernst. "What is a Nation?" In *Nation and Narration*, edited by Homi K. Bhabha, 8–22. New York: Routledge, 1990.

Resek, Carl, ed. *Randolph Bourne: War and the Intellectuals: Collected Essays, 1915–1919.* New York: Harper, 1963.

Rischin, Moses. *Grandma Never Lived in America: The New Journalism of Abraham Cahan.* Bloomington: Indiana University Press, 1985.

———. *The Promised City: New York's Jews, 1870–1914.* Cambridge, MA: Harvard University Press, 1962.

Roheim, Géza. "Culture Hero and Trickster in North American Mythology." In *Indian Tribes of Aboriginal America*, edited by Sol Tax. New York: Cooper Square Publishers, 1967.

Roosevelt, Theodore, "Americanism." In *Woodrow Wilson, Franklin K. Lane, and Theodore Roosevelt on Americanism.* Pamphlet. Washington, DC. Americanization Department, Veterans of Foreign Wars of the United States, 1915.

———. "The Duties of American Citizenship" (1893). In *The Writings of Theodore Roosevelt*, edited by William H. Harbaugh. Indianapolis: Bobbs-Merrill, 1967.

———. "True Americanism." In *American Ideals and Other Essays.* New York: Putnam, 1897.

———. *The Winning of the West: The Spread of English-Speaking Peoples.* 4 vols. New York: Putnam, 1889–1896.

Rothenberg, Paula S., ed. *Race, Class, and Gender in the United States.* New York: St. Martin's Press, 1992.

Rourke, Constance. *The Roots of American Culture*. New York: Harcourt, 1942.

Rubinstein, Rachel. "Becoming Modern: *Shriftn*, Poetry, and the Beginnings of Yiddish-American Modernism." Department of English and American Literature and Language, Harvard University, Cambridge, Massachusetts.

Rudnick, Lois Palken. *Utopian Vistas: The Mabel Dodge Luhan House and the American Counterculture*. Albuquerque: University of New Mexico Press, 1996.

Rusch, Frederik L. *A Jean Toomer Reader: Selected Unpublished Writings*. New York: Oxford University Press, 1993.

Ryan, Marah Ellis. *The Flute of the Gods*. Illus. Edward S. Curtis. New York: Frederick A. Stokes, 1909.

Sapir, Edward. "Culture Genuine and Spurious." In Sapir, *Culture, Language and Personality*, 409–29. Berkeley: University of California Press, 1957. (1924)

———. Review of Elsie Clews Parsons, *North American Indian Life*. *The Dial* 73 (1922): 568–71.

Saturday Review of Literature. Review of Standing Bear, *Land of the Spotted Eagle*. 10 (August 26, 1933): 70.

Schimmel, Julie. "Inventing the Indian," in *The West as America: Reinterpreting Images of the Frontier*, edited by William H. Treuttner. Washington, DC: Smithsonian Institution Press, 1991, 149–89.

Schmidt, Leigh Eric. *Consumer Rites: The Buying and Selling of American Holidays*. Princeton, NJ: Princeton University Press, 1995.

Schoolcraft, Henry Rowe. *Algic Researches*. New York: Harper, 1839.

———. *The American Indians. Their History, Conditions and Prospects*. Buffalo, NY: George H. Derby, 1851.

———. *History of the Indian Tribes of the United States*. Philadelphia: Lippincott, 1857.

———. *The Myth of Hiawatha and Other Oral Legends*. Philadelphia: Lippincott, 1856.

———. "A Prospective American Literature Superimposed upon Indian Mythology." In *Oneota, or Characteristics of the Red Race of America, from Original Notes and Manuscripts*. New York: Wiley & Putnam, 1845.

Schreier, Barbara A. *Becoming American Women: Clothing and the Jewish Immigrant Experience, 1880–1920*. Chicago: Chicago Historical Society, 1995.

Shell, Marc, and Werner Sollors. *The Multilingual Anthology of American Literature*. New York: New York University Press, 2000.

Shoemaker, Nancy, ed., *Clearing a Path: Theorizing the Past in Native American Studies*. New York: Routledge, 2002.

Silko, Leslie Marmon. *Yellow Woman and a Beauty of the Spirit: Essays on Native American Life Today*. New York: Simon & Schuster, 1996.

Simard, Jean-Jacques. "White Ghosts, Red Shadows: The Reduction of North-American Natives." In *The Invented Indian: Cultural Fictions & Government Policies*, edited by James Clifton, 333–70. New Brunswick, NJ: Transaction Publishers, 1990.

Simpson, David. *The Politics of American English, 1776–1850*. New York: Oxford University Press, 1986.

Slobin, Mark. "From Vilna to Vaudeville: Minikes and *Among the Indians*." *The Drama Review* 24, no. 3 (September 1980): 17–26.

Slotkin, Richard. *Gunfighter Nation: The Myth of the Frontier in Twentieth-Century America.* New York: Atheneum, 1992.

———. *Regeneration Through Violence.* Middletown, CT: Wesleyan University Press, 1973.

Smith, Sherry L. *Reimagining Indians: Native Americans through Anglo Eyes, 1880–1940.* New York: Oxford University Press, 2000.

Sollors, Werner. *Beyond Ethnicity: Consent and Descent in American Culture.* New York: Oxford University Press, 1986.

Song of Hiawatha. The Players' Edition. Intro. Dr. Frank W. Gunsaulus, illus. Grace Chandler Horn. Chicago: Rand McNally, 1911.

Soule Art Company. *The Kempton Pictures,* Boston: Palmer Co., 1904.

Spack, Ruth. *America's Second Tongue: American Indian Education and the Ownership of English, 1860–1900.* Lincoln: University of Nebraska Press, 2002.

Spicer, Edward H. *The American Indians.* Cambridge, MA: Harvard University Press, 1982.

Spiller, G., ed. *Universal Races Congress: Inter-Racial Problems.* London: P. S. King, 1911.

Spofford, A. R. "American Historical Nomenclature." *Annual Report of the American Historical Association.* 1893.

Standing Bear, Luther. *Land of the Spotted Eagle.* 1933; repr., Lincoln: University of Nebraska Press, 1978.

———. *My Indian Boyhood.* 1931; repr., Lincoln: University of Nebraska Press, 1988.

———. *My People the Sioux.* 1928; repr., Lincoln: University of Nebraska Press, 1975.

———. *Stories of the Sioux.* 1934; repr., Lincoln: University of Nebraska Press, 1988.

———. "The Tragedy of the Sioux." *American Mercury* 24 (November 1931): 273–78.

Stocking, George W., Jr. "Ethnographic Sensibility of the 1920s and the Dualism of the Anthropological Tradition." In *The Ethnographer's Magic and Other Essays in the History of Anthropology.* Madison: University of Wisconsin Press, 1992.

Strong, Pauline Turner, and Barrick Van Winkle. "Tribe and Nation: American Indians and American Nationalism." *Social Analysis* 33 (September 1993): 9–26.

Survey, The. 54 (April 15, 1925): 95.

Swinton, William. *Rambles among words: their poetry, history and wisdom.* New York: Scribner, 1859.

Szasz, Margaret Connell, and Carmelita Ryan. "American Indian Education." In Washburn, *History of Indian-White Relations,* 284–300.

Takaki, Ronald T. *Iron Cages: Race and Culture in Nineteenth-Century America.* New York: Knopf, 1979.

Thernstrom, Stephan, ed. *Harvard Encyclopedia of American Ethnic Groups.* Cambridge, MA: Harvard University Press, 1980.

Thompson, Stith. "The Indian Legend of Hiawatha." *PMLA* 38 (1922): 128–43.

Thornton, Russell. *American Indian Holocaust and Survival: A Population History since 1492.* Norman: University of Oklahoma Press, 1987.

Tilton, Robert S. *Pocahontas: The Evolution of an American Narrative.* New York: Cambridge University Press, 1984.

Toomer, Jean. *Cane.* New York: Boni & Liveright, 1923.

Trachtenberg, Alan. *Brooklyn Bridge: Fact and Symbol*. New York: Oxford University Press, 1965.

———. "Ever—The Human Document." In *America & Lewis Hine Photographs 1904–1940*. Mierton, NY: Aperture, 1977.

———. *The Incorporation of America: Culture & Society in the Gilded Age*. New York: Hill & Wang, 1982.

Trigger, Bruce G., and Wilcomb E. Washburn, eds. *The Cambridge History of the Native Peoples of the Americas*. Volume 1, *North America*. New York: Cambridge University Press, 1996.

Truettner, William H. "Science and Sentiment: Indian Images at the Turn of the Century." In *Art in New Mexico, 1900–1945*, edited by Charles C. Eldredge et al., New York: Abbeville, 1986.

Turner, Frederick Jackson. "American Colonization." Paper read to Madison Literary Club, February 9, 1891, 7a. Reprinted in Ronald H. Carpenter, *The Eloquence of Frederick Jackson Turner*. San Marino, CA: The Huntington Library, 1983, 176–91.

———. *The Frontier in American History*. New York: Holt, 1947.

———. "The Stream of Immigration into the United States." *Chicago Herald Tribune*. September 25, 1901, xv.

Tyler, Linda L. "'Commerce and Poetry Hand in Hand': Music in American Department Stores, 1880–1930." *Journal of the American Musicological Society* 45 (1992): 75–120.

U.S. Congress. *Congressional Record*. 66th Cong., 2d sess., 1924.

U.S. Congress. House. Report No. 144. 66th Cong., 1st sess, 1923.

Utley, Robert M. Introduction to James McLaughlin, *My Friend the Indian*.

Van Doren, Mark. "A Recent Eden." *The Nation* 137 (July 12, 1933): 50.

Vico, Giambattista. *The New Science of Giambattista Vico*. Trans. and abridged Thomas Goddard Bergin and Max Harold Fisch. Ithaca, NY: Cornell University Press, 1970.

Vizenor, Gerald, and Robert Lee. "Ishi Bares His Chest: Tribal Simulations and Survivance." In *Partial Recall: Photographs of Native North Americans*, edited by Lucy Lippard. New York: New Press, 1992.

———. *Manifest Manners: Postindian Warriors of Survivance*. Hanover, NH: Wesleyan University Press, 1994.

———. *Postindian Conversations*. Lincoln: University of Nebraska Press, 1999.

Vogel, Virgil J. "Placenames from Longfellow's 'Song of Hiawatha.'" *Names* 39, no. 3 (September 1991): 261–68.

Walker, Andrew. "Discovering 'Great Men': John Wanamaker, *The Conquerors*, and Progressive Reform at the Turn of the Twentieth Century." Department of History, University of Pennsylvania, Philadelphia, Pennsylvania.

Walker, Andrew, with Paula Lupkin. "Sermon Pictures: Merchandising Morals in the American City." Department of History, University of Pennsylvania, Philadelphia, Pennsylvania.

Walker, Cheryl. *Indian Nation: Native American Literature and Nineteenth-Century Nationalisms*. Durham, NC: Duke University Press, 1997.

Walker, Francis A. "Restriction of Immigration." *The Atlantic Monthly* 77 (June 1986): 822–29.

Wallace, Paul A. W. "The Return of Hiawatha." *New York History.* 29, no. 4 (October 1948).

Wanamaker Primer on the North American Indian: Hiawatha. Produced in Life. Philadelphia: Wanamaker-Originator, 1909.

Wanamaker, John. *Maxims of Life and Business.* New York: Harper, 1923.

Ward, Robert Stafford. "The Influence of Vico on Longfellow." In Mathews, *Henry W. Longfellow Reconsidered.*

Washburn, Wilcomb, ed. *History of Indian-White Relations.* Vol. 4, *Handbook of North American Indians.* Washington, DC: Smithsonian Institution Press, 1986.

Weaver, Jace. *That the People Might Live.* New York: Oxford University Press, 1997.

Weinberg, David H. *Between Tradition and Modernity: Haim Zhitlovski, Simon Dubnow, Ahad Ha-Am, and the Shaping of Modern Jewish Identity.* New York: Holmes & Meier, 1996.

Weinreich, Max. *History of the Yiddish Language.* Trans. Shlomo Noble. Chicago: University of Chicago Press, 1980.

West, Elliott. *The Way to the West: Essays on the Central Plains.* Albuquerque: University of New Mexico Press, 1995.

White, G. Edward. *The Eastern Establishment and the Western Experience: The West of Frederic Remington, Theodore Roosevelt, and Owen Wister.* New Haven, CT: Yale University Press, 1990.

White, Richard. "Frederick Jackson Turner and Buffalo Bill." In *The Frontier in American Culture,* edited by James R. Grossman. Berkeley: University of California Press, 1994.

Whitman, Walt. *Daybooks and Notebooks.* Vol. 3. Ed. William White. New York: New York University Press, 1978.

———. "Emerson's Books (the Shadows of Them)," *Complete Prose Works.* Boston: Small, Maynard, 1901.

———. *Leaves of Grass: Comprehensive Reader's Edition.* Ed. Harold W. Blodgett and Sculley Bradley. New York: New York University Press, 1965.

Williams, Walter L. "American Imperialism and the Indians." In Hoxie, *Indians in American History,* 231–49.

Williams, William Carlos. *In the American Grain.* 1925; repr., New York: New Directions, 1956.

Wilson, Edmund. *American Jitters: A Year of the Slump.* New York: Scribner, 1932.

Wong, Hertha Dawn. *Sending My Heart Back Across the Years: Tradition and Innovation in Native American Autobiography.* New York: Oxford University Press, 1992.

Woodworth, Ellis. *The Godly Seer: A True Story of HI-A-WAT-HA.* 1900; repr., Syracuse, NY: Iroquois Press, 1940.

Yehoash [Solomon Bloomgarten]. *Dos Lid fun Hiavata.* New York: Yehoash Verlag, 1910.

Young, Philip. "The Mother of Us All: Pocohontas Reconsidered." *Kenyon Review* 24 (Summer 1962): 391–415.

Zhitlovsky, Chaim. "Vegn dem vert fun iberzetzung." Introduction to Yehoash, *Dos Lid fun Hiavata.*

Acknowledgments

This book has been long in the making and has incurred more debts than I can acknowledge in a brief space. I have counted on many friends and colleagues for help, advice, and inspiration. I have been long indebted to Leo Marx for his compelling example of an American Scholar at work. My particular debt here is to his help in clarifying questions of American identity relevant to this study. I am grateful to him once more for urging me to keep my eye on the larger picture, the wholeness of cultural experience. Howard Lamar's great knowledge of the subjects addressed here and his wise guidance have been invaluable resources for me. His encouragement gave me confidence as I ventured into territory new to me. Conversations with the late Martin Ridge were extremely useful. I am indebted to his kindness, reassurance, and his astute criticism.

The convergence of fields the book takes as its subject has depended on a wide assortment of sources, and I am fortunate to have had the able support of numerous scholars. Those who read and commented on the manuscript in whole or in part have helped in concrete ways. I gratefully acknowledge the generosity of time and spirit of Jean-Christophe Agnew, Jon Butler, Jules Chametzky, Mick Gidley, Benjamin Harshav, Richard Hutson, Penelope Kelsey, George Miles,

Maren Stange, John Stauffer, and Zev Trachtenberg. I am equally grateful to others who have shared knowledge with me, dropped fruitful hints, and helped light the way. They include Zachary Baker, A. L. Becker, Sacvan Bercovitch, Michele Bogart, Nancy Cott, John Faragher, John Hollander, LeAnne Howe, Dell Hymes, Bob Mezey, Charles Musser, Joel Pfister, Curmie Price, William Reese, Joe Roach, Jeffrey Stewart, Brian Swann, John Szwed, Gerald Vizenor, and Jace Weaver. Others are indicated in the notes. The untimely death of Ronald Goodman deprived the finished book of a reader whose response I would have cherished, as I do the memory of his deep knowledge, honesty, wit, and wisdom.

A fellowship in the Research Division of the Huntington Library provided an enormous boost. I am grateful to Roy Ritchie for making this possible. The book benefited not only from the extraordinary resources of the library but also from the opportunity for conversations with Tom Chaffin, William Fenton, Ed Grey, Alan Justi, Coppelia Kahn, Martin Ridge, Nancy Shoemaker, and Johann Sommerville. I thank Casey Blake for helping to arrange a short-term fellowship with the Institute for Advanced Study at Indiana University, where conversations with members of the American Studies faculty, including Casey Blake, John Bodnar, Sarah Burns, Ray DeMalle, R. David Edmunds, Kathleen Foster, Henry Glassie, and James Naremore, made for an exciting and productive period. Grants from the Griswold Fund and the Koerner Center, Yale University, contributed to sundry research and travel expenses.

Curators and staff at several collections and libraries provided generous and skilled assistance: Thomas W. Kavanaugh of the Mathers Museum, Indiana University; Jill Kogen and the staff of the Huntington Library Research Division; Kim Walters of the Southwest Museum; Linda Stanley and the staff of the Historical Society of Pennsylvania; the staff of the Beinecke Rare Book and Manuscript Library, Yale University; Barbara Landis, who replied generously to queries and provided online materials regarding the Carlisle Indian School. For their indispensable help in research I thank Andrea Becksvoort, Lisa Black, Jaime Gont, Stephen Rice, Jennifer Smythe, and especially John Stauffer.

Opportunities to send up trial balloons in the form of lectures played a key role in the unfolding of the project; I am grateful to those—too many to list here—who made these opportunities available. Earlier versions of several chapters appeared as journal articles. For permission to reclaim sections of these articles, I am thankful to the following editors: J. D. McClatchy, *Yale Review* ("Conceivable Aliens," "Wanamaker Indians," "Singing Hiawatha"); Jackson Lears, *Raritan* ("Dreaming Indian"); Murray Baumgarten, *Judaism* ("'Babe in the Yiddish Woods'"); and Roland Hagenbüchle, who included an early version of "Wanamaker Indians" in his edited volume, *Negotiations of America's National Identity* (2000).

Arthur Wang graciously supported the project when it was still wobbly. Elisabeth Sifton has guided the book to realization with grace and perfect understanding. She and her staff have my warmest appreciation. The book could not have been in better or safer hands.

Betty Trachtenberg, my wife and dearest friend, supported the project throughout and contributed immeasurably to this work, as have Zev and Tina, Lissy, and Julie. They will know for what I say thank you.

Index

9 780809 016396